# *The Concepts of Consciousness*

*Integrating an Emerging Science*

**Edited by**

**J. Scott Jordan & Dawn M. McBride**

**imprint-academic.com**

Copyright © Imprint Academic, 2007

No part of this publication may be reproduced in any form
without permission, except for the quotation of brief passages
in criticism and discussion.

Published in the UK by Imprint Academic
PO Box 200, Exeter EX5 5YX, UK

Published in the USA by Imprint Academic
Philosophy Documentation Center
PO Box 7147, Charlottesville, VA 22906-7147, USA

ISBN 9 781845 400859

A CIP catalogue record for this book is available from the
British Library and US Library of Congress

# Contents

| | |
|---|---|
| About Authors | iv |
| Editorial Introduction, *J. Scott Jordan & Dawn M. McBride* | viii |
| Consciousness and Realism, *David Leech Anderson* | 1 |
| Contextual Emergence from Physics to Cognitive Neuroscience, *Harald Atmanspacher* | 18 |
| What is Mental Representation? And How Does It Relate to Consciousness? *Timothy L. Hubbard* | 37 |
| Representation and a Science of Consciousness, *Andrew Bailey* | 62 |
| Consciousness and Intentionality, *John Barresi* | 77 |
| At the Roots of Consciousness, *Liliana Albertazzi* | 94 |
| What Needs to Emerge to Make You Conscious? *Cees van Leeuwen* | 115 |
| The Survival Value of Informed Awareness, *Robert Shaw & Jeffrey Kinsella-Shaw* | 137 |
| Consciousness and Control, *Bernhard Hommel* | 155 |
| The Role of Control in a Science of Consciousness, *J. Scott Jordan & Marcello Ghin* | 177 |
| Methods for Measuring Conscious and Automatic Memory, *Dawn M. McBride* | 198 |
| Toward a Continuity of Consciousness, *Michael Spivey and Sarah Cargill* | 216 |
| The Emergence of Self, *Natalie Sebanz* | 234 |
| Selves in Turmoil, *Sabine Maasen* | 252 |
| Index | 271 |

## ABOUT AUTHORS

***Liliana Albertazzi*** is an associate professor in philosophy and theory of languages at Trento University, Rovereto Branch. She is also Scientific Director of the Mitteleuropa Foundation at Bolzano, Italy (www.mitteleuropafoundation.it). She is author of 5 books, and more that 100 publications in Italian or foreign journals or in collected works, as well as editing 18 books (www.polaris.unitn.it). Her main fields of interest are theory of representation, subjective space and time, Gestalt psychology and cognitive semantics. She is a member of the Advisory Board of *Axiomathes*, *Brentano Studien*, *Meinong Studies* and *Polish Journal of Philosophy*.

***David Leech Anderson*** is associate professor of philosophy at Illinois State University. His primary research areas include metaphysics, epistemology, philosophy of language and philosophy of mind. He is the director of *The Mind Project* (http://www.mind.ilstu.edu), a research and curriculum project in the cognitive and learning sciences.

***Harald Atmanspacher*** studied physics in Göttingen, Zürich, and München, where he received a PhD in physics 1985. Until 1998 he worked as a research scientist in the theory division at the Max-Planck-Institute for Extraterrestrial Physics in Garching. Since 1998 he has been head of the Department for Theory and Data Analysis at the Institute for Frontier Areas of Psychology and Mental Health at Freiburg. In addition, he is a faculty member of the CG. Jung Institute Zürich and of the Parmenides Foundation Capoliveri. Since 2003 he has served as the editor of the interdisciplinary journal *Mind and Matter*, published by Imprint Academic.

***Andrew Bailey*** is an assistant professor in the department of philosophy at the University of Guelph, Ontario. He works mainly in the philosophy of mind: his main interests are the problem of naturalizing phenomenal consciousness and the embodied mind paradigm in cognitive science. He has published several articles and an introductory philosophy textbook, and is working on a monograph on arguments from illusion.

***John Barresi*** is professor of psychology at Dalhousie University with a background in social, personality, and cognitive psychology. He has special interests in the foundations of a science of persons, the history of ideas of person, self, soul and consciousness, and the evolution and development of social understanding of self and other — in particular, in the social origins of theories of mind. With Ray Martin, a philosopher of personal identity, he has co-authored *Naturalization of the Soul: Self & Personal Identity in the Eighteenth Century* (2000) and *The Rise and Fall of Soul and Self: An Intellectual History of Personal Identity* (2006). Since the publication of their target article 'Intentional relations and social understanding' in *Behavioral and Brain Sciences* in 1996, he and Chris Moore, a developmental psychologist, have continued work on what they now call Intentional Relations Theory and they are currently writing a book on the theory.

**Sarah Cargill** is a graduate student in the psychology department of Cornell University. She has a BA in psychology from Randolph-Macon College. Her research examines the reliance on the visual environment during change blindness tasks, the interaction between visual and linguistic information during sentence processing, and the role of embodied perceptual simulations during language comprehension.

**Marcello Ghin** is a research associate in philosophy at the University of Paderborn. He obtained his MA in philosophy of cognitive science from the University of Sussex in 2002 and is currently working on his doctoral thesis on agency and the relation of self- and other-awareness. His main interests have been philosophy of mind, cognitive science, AI and A-Life.

**Bernhard Hommel** studied psychology and literature at the University of Bielefeld (Germany), where he also completed his dissertation on action control. He then moved to the Max Planck Institute for Psychological Research in Munich to work on the interactions between perception, attention, and action. Since 1999 he has been a Full Professor (Chair of General Psychology) at Leiden University (the Netherlands). He has published behavioural, neurophysiological, and theoretical work on human attention and emotion, on planning and executive control of action, on the development of cognitive functions, and on the relationship between perception and action.

**Timothy L. Hubbard** is an associate professor of psychology at Texas Christian University. He received his PhD in experimental psychology from Dartmouth College. The main focus of his recent research is on dynamic properties of mental representation such as representational momentum. Other research has examined music cognition, psychophysics, aesthetics, and intersections of cognitive science with shamanism. He is the author of numerous empirical and theoretical articles, and co-edited the book *Representational Momentum: New Findings, New Directions.*

**J. Scott Jordan** is a professor in the department of psychology at Illinois State University in Normal, Illinois. He publishes empirical papers on the relationship between perception and action-planning, and philosophical papers on consciousness, volition and self-sustaining systems.

**Jeffrey Kinsella-Shaw** has a PhD in experimental psychology and a degree in physical therapy. He is assistant professor in the department of physical therapy, where he serves as the Coordinator of the Graduate Neurological Rehabilitation Curriculum. He is also a Research Fellow in the Center for the Ecological Study of Perception and Action, where he and other members have developed a Co-Laboratory across the two fields for studying the perceptual control of action, intentional dynamics, and skill acquisition after neurological insult.

**Sabine Maasen** is a professor of science studies at the university of Basel, her training being in sociology, psychology, and linguistics. She has published several articles and books in the sociology of science and knowledge including *Biology as Society, Society as Biology: Metaphors* (with E. Mendelsohn and P. Weingart, Kluwer 1994) as well as *Metaphors and the Dynamics of Knowledge* (with P. Weingart, Routledge 2000). Recently she has worked on the social construction of volition and consciousness (e.g., *Voluntary Action: On Brains, Minds, and Sociality*, with W. Prinz & G. Roth, Oxford 2002, and *On Willing Selves*, with Barbara Sutter, Palgrave 2007), with a special emphasis on the relation of self-managing selves, neurosciences, and neosocial society.

**Dawn McBride** is associate professor of psychology at Illinois State University. She has a PhD in cognitive psychology from the University of California, Irvine. Her research investigates automatic forms of memory, false memory, and forgetting.

**Natalie Sebanz** is an assistant professor in the department of psychology at Rutgers University Newark. She obtained her PhD from Ludwig Maximilian University, Munich in 2004. As a postdoctoral fellow, she worked at the Max Planck Institute for Human Cognitive and Brain Sciences, Department of Psychology, Munich, and at Rutgers University. Her research interests include perception–action links, joint action, theory of mind, and volition.

# ABOUT AUTHORS

***Robert Shaw*** is professor emeritus of psychology at the University of Connecticut, the current and founding President of the International Society for Ecology Psychology, a recipient of a NIH Career Development Award, Fellow of the Center for Advanced Study in the Behavioral Sciences, and a recent Fellow of the Japan Society for the Advancement of Science. He is also a founder (with Michael Turvey) of the Center for the Ecological Study of Perception and Action where for several decades he has been developing a theory of intentional dynamics — a method for studying the ways agents cognitively, perceptually and behaviourally interact with their environments in the service of their needs, wants, and choices.

***Michael Spivey*** is associate professor of psychology at Cornell University, and Director of its Cognitive Science Program. He has a PhD in brain and cognitive sciences from the University of Rochester. His research uses eye-tracking and computer-mouse-tracking to follow the continuous temporal dynamics of the real-time interaction between linguistic and visual processes.

***Cees van Leeuwen*** (http://pdl.brain.riken.jp/ ) is the head of the Laboratory for Perceptual Dynamics, editor of *Philosophical Psychology* and associate editor of *Cognitive Processing*. His main research interests are in perceptual organization. He has contributed well over a hundred peer-reviewed scientific articles in such fields as human visual perception, imagery, and creativity, reading and dyslexia, psychophysiology, information processing, theoretical neuroscience, neural networks, nonlinear dynamics, and adaptive control theory.

J. Scott Jordan & Dawn M. McBride

# Stable Instabilities in the Study of Consciousness
## A Potentially Integrative Prologue?

The purpose of this special issue and the conference that inspired it was to address the issue of conceptual integration in a science of consciousness. We felt this to be important, for while current efforts to scientifically investigate consciousness are taking place in an interdisciplinary context, it often seems as though the very terms being used to sustain a sense of interdisciplinary cooperation are working against it. This is because it is this very array of common concepts that generates a sense of unity among consciousness researchers, despite the fact the concepts mean different things in different disciplines. These *Concepts of Consciousness* include the following: *realism, representation, intentionality, information, control, memory* and *self*. Given this list, we believed we could best approach the issue of potential conceptual integration by addressing each concept from different perspectives and asking the following: (1) how do uses of the concept differ, (2) must these meanings be synthesized in order for there to be a unified science of consciousness, (3) is a unified conceptual scheme necessary to establish an independent science of consciousness, (4) is a unified conceptual scheme possible, (5) if it is not possible, why not, and (6) if it is possible, what might it look like? To this end we invited, for each concept, two scholars who made extensive use of the identified concept in their work. The papers entailed in this special issue constitute the outcome of this effort, and in what follows we offer a brief examination of possible forms of integration the papers seem to collectively suggest.

Instead of addressing scientific integration in terms of how the papers in the present collection can be brought together within a common empirical framework, we begin by focusing on why such a framework seems so hard to achieve. Oddly enough, the notion of *stability*, and how it is used and/or implied in empirical work regarding consciousness, seems to afford a fruitful means of divvying up the field. This is because scholars often describe consciousness in ways that express both *explicit* and *implicit* assumptions about the stability of consciousness, and these assumptions entail conceptual commitments that constrain their views on what they think consciousness is and how it relates to science.

In the *implicit*-assumption camp are those who conceptualize consciousness via terms such as *states* and *representations* (in what follows we will simply refer to this as the *state* approach). This way of conceptualizing consciousness entails *implicit* assumptions about the stability of consciousness because it focuses on conscious phenomena (e.g., memories, intentions, qualia and thoughts) that persist long enough to be considered individual conscious events entailing both *content* (i.e., the phenomenal 'feel' of a memory, intention or thought — see Bailey's contribution) and *causal efficacy* (i.e., the ability of memories, intentions and thoughts to make things happen in one's cognitive architecture). If one accepts the notion of phenomenal, causal states (and representations), it then seems appropriate to develop a science of consciousness around the idea of devising controlled experiments meant to reveal the causal role such structures play in cognition, perception and action (see van Orden & Holden, 2002, for a thorough application of this idea to the field of cognitive science in general). McBride, for example, gives a thorough description of how memory researchers devise experiments meant to reveal the causal properties of conscious and unconscious memory states. In this research participants complete memory tasks, and their responses are used as a means of revealing the nature of the cognitive architecture that makes such performance possible. Hommel describes experiments that are meant to address the role that conscious planning states (i.e., will) play in action control, and much like Wegner (2002) finds little empirical evidence for the common assumption that conscious intentions *cause* behaviours. Sebanz examines states of self-consciousness (i.e., agency), and proposes that such states emerge out of the need of individuals to engage in cooperative action with others. Barresi focuses on the development of mental states and our ability to have mental states about our own mental states, as well as those of others. Common to all of these researchers is the use of a state approach to consciousness and its implicit assumption regarding the stability of consciousness. Again, this assumption is scientifically useful because it allows researchers to address both the content and causality of conscious states and the role such states play in one's cognitive architecture.

In contrast to the implicit-assumption camp, those in the *explicit-*assumption camp approach the issue of conscious stability *directly*. That is, their research focuses on the temporal dynamics by which conscious phenomena such as memories, intentions and thoughts come to be stable. They do this because they believe there is something to be learned about consciousness by studying the 'real-time' dynamics that underlie it. Spivey and Cargill, for example, distinguish reportable and non-reportable conscious experiences in terms of continuously changing trajectory locations within an attractor landscape entailed in what they refer to as the *universal medium*. Van Leeuwen conceptualizes consciousness as an evolutionary by-product of the need to dynamically synchronize neural processes taking place in diverse brain areas. In this framework, the research focus is on the temporal dynamics by which these coherent neural synchronies come to be. Jordan and Ghin conceptualize consciousness as the embodied 'aboutness' inherent to self-sustaining systems as they work to maintain coherent relationships in *proximal-*, *distal-* and *virtual-*event space. And Albertazzi addresses consciousness in terms of its dynamic structure and the multi-scale context-dependent nature of the phenomenal structures (i.e., presentations) that emerge within it in real-time.

Both camps constitute established approaches to the science of consciousness. Yet the differences in their focus (i.e., *states* versus *dynamics*) have lead the former to look for consciousness in stable conscious states, and the latter, in stability generating dynamics. This has lead to major disagreement over *where* to look for consciousness. S*tate* theorists tend to conceptualize conscious states in terms of functional modules. As a result, they search for clearly localizable 'places' in which conscious phenomena exist (i.e., neural centres and/or information structures, depending on whether one is a neuro-reductionist or a functionalist). *Dynamics* theorists on the other hand, have moved away from the notion of modularity to some extent, because a focus on real-time dynamics often reveals that multiple 'brain-centres' (van Leeuwen), 'properties' (Albertazzi), and 'scales of reality' (i.e., scales in the universal medium — see Spivey & Cargill; scales of event-control — see Jordan & Ghin; organism-environment coordinations — see Shaw & Kinsella-Shaw) share continuous reciprocal influence, thus making it difficult to localize consciousness in any one 'brain-centre', 'property', or 'scale-of-reality.'

Given that *state* and *dynamics* theorists disagree as to where to look for consciousness, it is not clear to what extent the two can be integrated. One solution might be to assume the matter will eventually be resolved empirically in the form of an experimental methodology that clearly proves one approach correct and the other false. There are other options, however. One might, for example, utilize the notion of ontological relativity mentioned in Atmanspacher's contribution. According to this framework, one makes ontological assumptions about phenomena at a lower level of scale (i.e., one assumes the phenomena at that level truly exist as described by science), so that one can use the entities at that level to make epistemological statements (i.e., statements based on observation) about phenomena at a higher level. For example, one might make ontological assumptions about chemistry in order to make epistemological statements about biology. A similar distinction is played out in Anderson's contribution which distinguishes between realist approaches that make claims about what is metaphysically real and antirealist approaches that make claims that are relativized to a particular epistemic perspective.

An advantage of these frameworks for a science of consciousness is that they provide researchers a means of shifting the levels of ontological-epistemological comparison in ways that allow one to be ontologically flexible. One can, for example, be ontological about individual neurons, neural networks, or the brain as a whole, and use these different levels of ontology as potential mediums for consciousness. Such ontological flexibility may, in turn lead researchers to recognize the ontological assumptions inherent in their own approach to consciousness and, as a result, be more tolerant of the ontological assumptions made by others.

To be sure, there are many other possible combinations of varieties of realism and beliefs about science and reality. The point here is not to advocate one, but to simply make the case that the differences between *state* and *dynamics* theorists are not necessarily problematic. One can, for example, make ontological assumptions about the dynamics approach (i.e., believe that consciousness ultimately *is* a temporally-grounded multi-scale phenomenon) while simultaneously being epistemic about the *state* approach (i.e., statements about what consciousness *is* are restricted, when speaking scientifically, to epistemologically accessible phenomena that can be measured). Being aware of one's ontological assumptions in this manner might help to stave off arguments about a science of consciousness that emerge from one's simultaneous belief in various forms of realism. If this approach were to take hold, an integrated science of consciousness might ultimately come to be in which participants achieve an increased awareness of how their scientific assumptions play out in the varieties of realism.

Utilizing ontological-epistemological frameworks like those discussed by Atmanspacher and Anderson relies on the science of consciousness being embedded within the larger field of consciousness studies. We believe that if an integrated science comes to be, it will do so within this larger context. For it is in the larger context that the conversation shifts from the data to the relationship between the data, the concepts used to describe them, and the larger theoretical/philosophical context in which the concepts are embedded. According to Maasen's contribution, consciousness studies now constitutes a 'trading ground' in which these diverse levels of inquiry have a place to make contact and influence one another. Given that the *Journal of Consciousness Studies* is situated at the centre of this trading zone, we, the guest editors of this special issue, are delighted to have had the opportunity to contribute to its sustainment.

## References
(not in this collection)

Van Orden, G.C. & Holden, J. (2002), 'Intentional contents and self-control', *Ecological Psychology*, **14** (1–2), pp. 87–109.

Wegner, D.M. (2002), *The Illusion of Conscious Will* (London: MIT Press).

# *Acknowledgments*

We would like to extend our sincere gratitude to the persons and organizations that made possible both this special issue of the *Journal of Consciousness Studies* and the conference that inspired it. To begin, we thank the people of the Fell Trust Foundation at Illinois State University for their initial grant. We also thank Ms. Tracy Sherman from the Conference Services office for her support of our organizing efforts. From the Department of Psychology, we thank the Chair, Dr. David Barone for his continuous support, advice and encouragement, and Ms. Patricia Foltz for her patience and commitment. In addition, we thank the following graduate students for their help in tending to the details: Ms. Jennifer Coane, Ms. Kona Taylor, Ms. Jorie Colbert, Mr. Matthew Hunsinger, Mr. Berry Raulerson, Mr. Chris Wahlheim, and Mr. Eric Wesselmann. From the College of Arts and Sciences we thank Dr. Gary Olson and Dr. Sam Catanzaro for their openness to our idea and their enthusiastic commitment to its completion. And from the cognitive science community at Illinois State University, we thank our colleagues who gave of their time to participate in the conference and ensure its reflection of the field in general. We also extend a very heartfelt thanks to Mr. Joseph Dial, Executive Director of The Mind Science Foundation. His organization's enthusiastic support increased the international stature of the workshop, while simultaneously enhancing the sphere of ideas it entertained. To Teagan Nicole Jordan we cast a joyous kiss in thanks for her masterful artistic rendering of the conference's purpose. Also, we extend our sincere gratitude to the scholars who committed themselves to participating in this project. Their enthusiasm and patience inspired and sustained our efforts as we worked to bring the conference and special volume to fruition. To those scholars who reviewed papers for the special issue, we are indebted to you and hope we are able to return the favour some day. And finally, words cannot express our appreciation for the courtesy, respect and patience extended to us by the *JCS* managing editor Anthony Freeman. All throughout the process he encouraged us, praised our efforts and worked with us to make this special volume the best it could be.

*J. Scott Jordan and Dawn M. McBride*
*January 8, 2007*

# David Leech Anderson

# *Consciousness and Realism*

*Abstract: There is a long and storied history of debates over 'realism' that has touched literally every academic discipline. Yet realism-antirealism debates play a relatively minor role in the contemporary study of consciousness. In this paper four basic varieties of realism and antirealism are explored (existential, epistemological, semantic, and ontological) and their potential impact on the study of consciousness is considered. Reasons are offered to explain why there is not more debate over these issues, including a discussion of the powerful influence of externalist versions of physicalist realism. Examples are given of approaches to consciousness studies that challenge contemporary versions of physicalist realism.*

'Realism' refers to a wide range of different theories ranging from what things exist in the universe to the very nature of existence itself. The vast majority of these theories fall within a few broad categories. The purpose of this essay is to explain the essential features of each of these basic categories; first, as they can be articulated independent of any particular subject matter, and then as each one is applied to the present object of study, 'consciousness.'

There is a good deal of variation in the classification systems used to sort the myriad versions of realism. I recommend the following types of realism as drawing the most salient distinctions: existential, epistemological, semantic, and ontological.

## 1. Existential Realism

To be an *existential realist* about anything is to believe that that thing 'really exists,' that it is included within one's ontological commitments. One can be committed to the existence of a single object, a *token* (e.g., Big Ben, my wedding ring), and/or to the existence of a kind or a *type* (e.g., clocks, gold).

While it is possible to be committed to the existence of a token without thereby committing oneself to the existence of a type, we often do both. When I assert, 'I have a pain in my knee,' I seemingly commit to the existence of both a token-pain (the one in my knee) and to pain as a type. But here we must be careful. There are at least two ways in which my casual speech might belie my deepest metaphysical commitments. First, I might speak 'as if' some kind, $K$, exists when I am really committed to no such thing.

Second, even if I do include some kind, $k$, in my ontology, all this reveals is that I believe that $k$'s exist *in the same sense that* I believe more familiar things like trees and planets exist. But if it has not been specified *in what sense* that is, precious little has been expressed. Scientific disputes about the existence of theoretical entities (the aether, quarks, or pain) are almost always *local* disputes, where the rest of one's ontology is simply bracketed (for pragmatic reasons) even though all parties do *not* necessarily agree about what it means to say that something 'exists.' These *global* ontological disputes about the very nature of existence will be discussed in 'Section 4: Ontological Realism.'

'Does consciousness really exist?' is a question of local ontology. It asks us to draw a line that separates those who are *existential realists* about consciousness from those who aren't. The first cut is easy. There are eliminativists who straightforwardly argue that consciousness does not exist. Paul Churchland believes that future scientific advancements, especially in neuroscience, will force us to abandon our commitment to pre-theoretical (folk psychological) categories, including those that we would describe as 'conscious.' It may turn out that there is nothing in the universe that has the property of 'being a conscious mental state,' given current uses of that phrase. If so, then new terms, that are more neurophysiologically based, must be added to the language to successfully refer to real mental states (Churchland, 1988, p. 301).

There are some who hold a position very close to eliminativism but who are quite calculated about speaking of consciousness as if it really does exist. Daniel Dennett falls into this camp, with his commitment to the 'intentional stance.' (Dennett, 1987) He believes that we are justified for pragmatic reasons in attributing folk psychological states, including conscious mental states, to human beings (and even to artifacts) because attributing intentions (and the like) is the best, most reliable way of predicting their behaviour. This is a view variously called, pragmatism, operationalism, and instrumentalism. The latter term will be used here.

There are grounds for calling Dennett an instrumentalist, as he himself once did. For him, terms referring to mental states are convenient tools, but carry little in the way of ontological weight. Dennett, however, no longer approves of being labelled an 'instrumentalist' (1987) because he likes to think of himself as a kind of realist. Here, Dennett joins many other famous non-realists from Immanuel Kant (A369) to Hilary Putnam (1983, p. 226), who have insisted that they occupy some territory *between* realism and antirealism, a position that has all the virtues of each and is immune from the criticisms of both.[1] Such territory would be nice to occupy, if it existed, but I am not convinced that there is any such coherent place to stand. Even if I am wrong about this, however, it would be altogether misleading to label Dennett a classic realist; instrumentalism is a better fit.

Eliminativism and instrumentalism are not the only reasons to exclude 'consciousness' from one's ontological commitments. One might exclude it because one believes that conscious mental states are already listed under a different description. Those who accept the Identity Thesis are reductionists about consciousness, believing that mental states reduce, without loss, to brain states. A reductionist already includes brain states in her list of ontological commitments and it would therefore be redundant (and some believe, misleading) to add the term 'consciousness' to the list because that would imply that consciousness is something over-and-above dynamical states of the brain. So a case can be made for the view that reductionists are not *existential realists* about consciousness and thus hold precisely the same metaphysical position that eliminativists hold (Dummett, 1978, pp. 145, 156–58; Siderits, 1997).

Many people (including some reductionists) will find this last claim counter-intuitive. Some will say that there is all the difference in the

---

[1] Immanuel Kant, the grandfather of modern antirealist positions, while describing his view as a form of idealism ('transcendental idealism') nonetheless, like Dennett, claimed his position was the only reasonable, common sense kind of realism available, what he called 'empirical realism' (Kant, A369). Hilary Putnam advanced a form of antirealism in the 1980's (a kind of neo-Kantianism) that continues to influence philosophers, social scientists, and natural scientists today. Putnam too claimed that he was neither fish nor fowl with a position that he believed was best described first as 'internal realism' and then as 'pragmatic realism.' He claimed that he was charting 'a narrow path . . between the swamps of metaphysics and the quicksands of cultural relativism and historicism' (1983, p. 226). It's nice work if you can get it; but I believe Kant, Putnam, and Dennett are each important and interesting precisely because they defend sophisticated non-realist positions (Anderson, 1992).

world between Churchland's eliminative materialism and the classic Identity thesis. After all, when it was discovered that lightening is not a thunderbolt of Zeus but reduces without loss to an electrical discharge, we did not thereby discover that lightening is not real. We simply discovered what its true nature is. The appropriate thing to say is that lightening exists but its essential nature is identical to that of electricity. So on this score, we will leave it to individual reductionists (Identity theorists or others) to decide whether they consider themselves realists about consciousness, or not.

## 2. Epistemological Realism

Throughout history, it has often been the case that epistemological concerns have taken centre stage in debates over realism. One of the primary reasons for rejecting existential realism with respect to some ontological domain is the claim that there is not sufficient evidence to support belief in the existence of such entities. *Epistemological realism* is the view that some entity, *e*, not only exists but that there is sufficient evidence to support the claim that we *know* that it exists. Epistemological realism, then, entails existential realism.

The view opposing *epistemological realism* is *scepticism*. To be sceptical about *e*'s is to deny that we know whether or not they exist. Of course someone who doesn't believe that *e*'s exist will also reject epistemological realism. However, some of the most famous defenders of skepticism have admitted that they believe in the existence of the disputed entities. David Hume, for example, has given some of the most influential *sceptical* arguments against our knowledge of the 'external world,' yet he admits that given our psychological constitution we just can't help but to believe in trees and such. He simply denies that those beliefs have the evidential support requisite for knowledge.[2] Hume is an existential but not an epistemological realist.

Recently, an interesting set of arguments supporting skepticism about our own conscious mental states has been advanced. Change-blindness is a phenomenon produced when an image is gradually changed (fairly substantially) over time yet many subjects fail to detect the change because of the way the eyes naturally saccade back and forth, scanning different parts of the image at different times. Some have argued that this phenomenon, together with blindsight, demonstrate that our visual window on the world is ultimately a 'grand illusion,' threatening our knowledge of the external world

---

[2] David Hume (1740/1975), Part IV, Book 1, Section II.

(Noë, 2002a). But does this actually support a kind of Humean skepticism? Admittedly, our visual system is susceptible to certain forms of unreliability. But I must agree with Alva Noë (2002b) that this does not justify the claim that the *beliefs* generated by our visual system might profoundly misrepresent reality. The mistakes we make in change-blindness cases are *not* mistakes that result in wildly incorrect ontological commitments. Given the way that physical changes actually happen in the world and given the many checks and balances built into our belief-forming systems, there is no reason to think that our beliefs about the external world are riddled with falsehoods.

If it is not skepticism of a Humean kind, then what is at work in the 'grand illusion' phenomenon? It is not skepticism about trees, but about our tree-experiences, about our conscious mental states. When asked about the character of a visual experience, we will falsely state that we can discriminate colours on the periphery of our visual field, even though we cannot. And if we are wrong about colour, we could well be wrong about other features of our visual experience – thus raising general doubts about the character of our own experiences. Only time will tell what significance this kind of skepticism will have on our understanding of consciousness. It may prove of some importance. But since our false beliefs about our experiential states do not seem to threaten the general reliability of the beliefs about the external world, the significance may well remain modest.

## 3. Semantic Realism

In the twentieth century, analytic philosophy turned its realist attentions away from epistemology and toward language. No longer taking language for granted, philosophers plumbed its depths looking to discover its fundamental nature and its working mechanisms so as to explore the ways in which it might give up clues that could impact our ontological and epistemological commitments. Now called the 'linguistic turn,' this philosophical movement impacted virtually every sub-discipline of philosophy and its legacy remains undiminished in contemporary philosophy (Rorty, 1992; Lafont & Medina, 1999).

The linguistic turn permanently shifted the focus of the debate about realism, drawing attention to the following truths:

1. There are different ways of interpreting the claim that 'Entity, $e$, exists' which must be made explicit or fundamental disagreements about ontology will remain invisible.

2. What it means to be a realist and whether anyone is, in fact, capable of being a realist *about anything*, ultimately depends upon what our ontological utterances *mean* and in particular whether or not they succeed in making realist claims.

In the twentieth century, and especially during its second half, it became clear that the central debate about realism was not any particular, local dispute (although, those disputes continued a pace) but a *global* dispute about the very coherence of realism for *all* domains of discourse.

Early in the century, influences from sociology and anthropology (especially the Sapir-Whorf hypothesis), had already advanced the thesis that language shapes our beliefs about reality. Sapir's claim that '...the 'real world' is to a large extent unconsciously built up on the language habits of the group' (Sapir, 1929, p.) led many social scientists to hold a form of *ontological relativism*. This is the view that there is not one objective (viz. real) way that the world is, but each culture lives in its own world, constructed by the conceptual scheme unique to that culture. How you 'see' the world — whether you have a different term for blue and green or whether you have just one 'grue' term – is determined not so much by the 'real' world, but by your own interests. The activity of the conscious mind determines what is true about the 'world-of-experience' rather than the world determining the experiential and representational states of the conscious mind.

While these arguments did foster a kind of linguistic idealism among some scholars, their primary influence was on sociologists, anthropologists, and some continental philosophers. It had less impact within analytic (or Anglo-American) philosophy. Then, in the 1960's when many philosophers assumed that the debate had been settled once and for all in favour of realism,[3] a wave of new semantic arguments attacking realism were advanced.

Michael Dummett (1978) argued that no one is capable of *being* an ontological realist about 'trees' unless the 'tree'-sentences that express one's belief in trees have *realist truth-conditions*. *Realist*

---

[3] In the definitive reference work of the period, *The Encyclopedia of Philosophy*, serious challenges to realism were considered all but dead as the entry for 'realism' states: 'This battle was certainly won by the realists in that few English-speaking philosophers in the twentieth century would espouse idealism. Indeed ... in a climate of thought that respects common sense and science, realism seems so obvious a starting point that it is difficult to explain how the idealist view ever seemed plausible;' (Edwards, 1967, Volume 7, p. 78). Ironically, the *Encyclopedia* was published in 1967, four years *after* Dummett published his seminal paper, 'Realism' which ignited the antirealist movement within Analytic philosophy that continues today.

truth-conditions are contrasted with *epistemic* truth-conditions. If a statement about the external world expresses a *realist* claim, then the truth of that claim is determined solely by the conditions that obtain with respect to the intrinsic nature of mind-independent reality, independent of humans' ability to recognize those conditions. If a statement expresses an *epistemic* claim, then the truth of that claim is determined solely by conditions that can be recognized as obtaining from the perspective of some cognitive agent. [4]

One of Dummett's most influential arguments against realism is that there is no coherent theory of understanding that can explain how human language-speakers could come to grasp the meaning of statements with realist truth-conditions. For example, young children learn to say 'There is a red ball' whenever they have the subjective experience of seeing a red sphere. So initially, the only meaning that a child could attribute to the terms, 'red,' and 'ball,' are the empirical properties (i.e., how things *appear* to the speaker from her own epistemic perspective). But what the child grasps are the conditions under which the statement is *verified* rather than the conditions under which it is *realistically true*. On this account, it is inevitable that the language children begin speaking has epistemic rather than realist truth-conditions. But at what point in children's development do they come to grasp the meaning of realist truth conditions? Nothing in our use of language manifests such a knowledge. In the absence of any plausible theory of understanding, Dummett challenged the assumption than any of us have the capacity to grasp realist truth-conditions (Dummett, 1978).

Dummett's arguments greatly influenced Hilary Putnam's conversion from one of the twentieth century's most famous defenders of realism, to one of its most famous critics. To Dummett's battery of anti-realist arguments, Putnam contributed his famous 'Brains-in-a-Vat' argument (1981, pp.1–21) and his 'model-theoretic argument' (1983, pp.1–25) — which are both semantic arguments that claim to show that ontological realism cannot coherently be expressed given a sober analysis of language.

While antirealism (semantic and ontological) continues to garner respectable support within philosophy, the social sciences, and even

---

[4] Many philosophers consider the realism debate to be about the nature of truth, usually pitting a correspondence theory of truth (read: 'realist' theory of truth) against the coherence theory of truth (read: 'nonrealist' theory of truth). I believe that is a mistake, that there is only one coherent theory of truth, about which relatively little can be said. It is not a dispute about the nature of truth, but rather about the *kind of truth-conditions* that are expressed by a proposition: verificationist (non-realist) truth-conditions vs. realist truth-conditions.

among some physicists, why is it not taken more seriously within the study of consciousness? This can best be explained, I suggest, by the rise of 'global externalism', a philosophical movement that is (at least tacitly) optimistic that a wholly externalist account will eventually be forthcoming for every domain of philosophy, from epistemology to semantics to ontology, from intentionality to consciousness. The contemporary externalist movement arose in many different areas of study at basically the same time in history (the 1950's-70's). In each domain, this movement brought important new insights to their field – many elements of which are fairly uncontroversially accepted. However, the cumulative effect of these successes in a number of different areas has lead to an increasingly popular (yet, not often-enough admitted) assumption that *global externalism* ought to be the new metaphysical dogma for the twenty-first century. Consider a few areas where externalism rose to prominence.

New anthropological data about colour terms were marshalled for a direct attack on the Sapir-Whorf hypothesis and the cultural relativism that it encouraged. Using more fine-grained methods for gathering data, Brent Berlin and Paul Kay (1969) made a strong case for the position that the way humans categorize the world into colour-types is *not* determined solely by the interests of each culture. Rather, within known natural languages, there is a rather strict hierarchy of colour categories. If a language has only two colour terms (and some do), they will always be white and black. If a third colour is added, it will always be red. If there are only five colour terms the next two to be added will always be yellow and green; the sixth will be blue and the seventh brown. While the order of the final four colours (pink, orange, purple and grey) varies, the colours themselves do not. The total number of basic colour terms in a language will not exceed 11 and it will always be the *same* eleven colours just listed.[5]

Berlin and Kay defended this *universalist* account of colour in opposition to the prevailing *relativist* account, with remarkably swift success. While Berlin and Kay's views have generated recent controversy, their work has nonetheless won over a great many converts and its influence remains considerable. Many continue to believe that Berlin and Kay's research supports the position that the way mind and language conceptualizes colours is determined by objective, externalist facts about colour optics and the way that the brain processes colour.

---

[5] The phrase 'basic colour' is a technical term which Berlin and Kay (1969) were able to operationally define and which made possible the methodology they employed to gather the data just described.

At the same time that this development was changing the shape of cognitive linguistics, an even more dramatic revolution in semantics was taking place in philosophy. Up until that point, the received view about the nature of how words refer to objects in the external world could be traced all the way back to Aristotle and had its most familiar articulation in John Locke's 'way of ideas.' Locke argued that words gain their meaning by the ideas that speakers associate with them. If I think of the term, 'gold,' as being anything that is 'yellow, shiny, malleable, and dissolvable in aqua regis,' then that is precisely what the word means . . *to me*. It may mean something slightly different to you. On this account, everyone speaks a slightly different language. And the meaning (often called, the 'sense') of each term will then determine what objects in the world it refers to (its 'reference').

In the late 1960s and early 1970s, this Lockean, 'definite description' theory of reference was challenged by arguments by Saul Kripke, Hilary Putnam, Keith Donnellan, and others, who advanced a 'new theory of reference.' According to this theory many words (esp. proper names and natural kind terms) do not have a 'sense' but function more like labels that are directly hung on the objects themselves. The terms directly refer to their objects not by virtue of any thoughts floating in the heads of speakers but by virtue of the fact that the terms bear a *causal connection of the appropriate type* to either the singular object ('Aristotle') or to stuff constituting a particular kind ('gold'). Space doesn't permit a survey of the arguments advanced in defence of this theory, but their effect was dramatic. Virtually overnight the age-old view of language was dethroned and a majority of philosophers embraced the new theory — at least for natural kind terms (gold, water, tiger, etc.) and for proper names. There are many, though, who believe that causal connections can ultimately account for the semantic content of virtually all aspects of language when combined with an externalist analysis of the mental states that ground all definite descriptions (Adams *et al.*, 1992). A fully externalist account of language is the first step toward an externalist reduction of aspects of human thought and cognition.

Externalist epistemological theories have replaced internalist accounts of knowledge: The essence of knowledge no longer lies in the cognizer having epistemically accessible (viz. consciously grasped) 'reasons' for belief, rather a belief is knowledge so long as the belief is caused by a *reliable belief-forming mechanism* — whether or not the believer *knows* that it is reliable. The most popular theories of mind (e.g., behaviourism, the Identity thesis, and functionalism) analyse mental states wholly in externalist terms that can be given a third person account, making it possible to determine the content of mental states without taking any account of those (internalist) properties that characterize the subjective 'feel' of those mental states. Intentionality gains an externalist analysis by way of the externalist semantics upon which it is built. Externalism's reach has gone so far that even the technical term, 'qualia,' that was introduced to give name to the subjective *qualitative* feel of mental states, has been stripped of its internalist heritage by philosophers who have given wholly externalist reductions of the concept (e.g. externalist intentionalists).

There is not the space here to explore all the ways that the internalism–externalism debate intersects the realism–antirealism debate. Suffice it to say that while externalism need *not* lead inevitably to realism,[6] it is a matter of historical fact that the vast majority of externalists believe that it does. It is reasonable, then, to expect that if antirealism is going to be taken seriously in the study of consciousness it is likely to come from researchers not dogmatically committed to an externalist-realist perspective.

We turn now to two contributors to this volume who do not presuppose a realist ontology in their study of consciousness. One is a physicist and one is a cognitive psychologist

## 4. Ontological Realism

It is not surprising that a physicalist version of *ontological realism* seems inevitable to those who believe that *knowledge* has been reduced to reliable belief-forming mechanisms, *reference* is a causal connection of the appropriate type, and *qualia* are reduced to intentionality which has itself been reduced (again) to causal connections of the appropriate type. However, a physicist who has spent a career dealing with the Copenhagen interpretation of quantum mechanics may not feel the inevitability of ontological realism with quite the same force. Likewise, a cognitive psychologist, whose research focuses on the way that our perceptual systems go far beyond the mere 'copying' of physical phenomenon, is more likely to be open

---

[6] Putnam (1981) and Ebbs (2001) are philosophers who have embraced semantic externalism and have produced arguments intended to show that externalist commitments are incompatible with ontological realism, as traditionally conceived. Theirs is a minority view, however. Michael Devitt (1984/1991) reflects the majority view when he titles a chapter 'The Renegade Putnam' expressing his chagrin that Putnam would help launch the new theory of reference and then, inexplicably, use it to attack metaphysical realism rather than to defend it.

to the Kantian idea that our sensory and cognitive faculties make a constitutive contribution to the empirical world.

Consider first the arguments of Harald Atmanspacher and his co-authors Frederick Kronz (1999) and H. Primas (2005) who focus on realism issues as they arise in quantum theory. They appeal to two different ontological categories: (1) ontic states, and (2) epistemic states. Ontic descriptions characterize systems as they 'really are' without reference to epistemic access (viz. knowledge or ignorance). Epistemic descriptions encode knowledge by way of observation and measurement, which in turn presuppose a context of investigation. Epistemic descriptions are always local in nature, limited in scope. Ontic descriptions seek an exhaustive characterization from the proverbial 'God's eye view'. (NOTE: Echoes of this distinction are seen in the contrast drawn earlier in this paper between *existential realism* and *ontological realism*.)

This ontic–epistemic distinction reflects the apparently irreconcilable perspectives of Bohr and Einstein, with the former defending the Copenhagen interpretation of quantum mechanics with its uncompromising commitment to the empirical data and the latter striving for an account of mind-independent reality that would resolve the quantum puzzlements that defy ontic description. Within quantum mechanics, this distinction seems an unbreachable dichotomy which stands in the way of significant advances in the field. Atmanspacher and his co-authors seek to break the dichotomy by embracing both elements.

Science starts with observation and measurement, presupposing a particular epistemic context. Yet, an ontic level of analysis is also unavoidable because there is no escaping the fact that the very instruments used in measurement (i.e., epistemically) are presupposed and described as if they are robustly (i.e., ontically) real. Thus Bohr's paradigmatically epistemic perspective, itself requires both ontic and epistemic elements. The difficulty of reconciling what seem to be irreconcilable elements

> can be resolved if it is realized that the distinction ... can be applied to the entire hierarchy of (perhaps partially overlapping) domains leading from fundamental particles in basic physics to chemistry and even to living systems in biology and psychology. Ontic and epistemic descriptions are then considered as *relative to* two (successive) domains in the hierarchy (Atmanspacher & Primas, 2005, p. 59).

This approach borrows freely from two of the most influential antirealist philosophers of the twentieth century: W.V.O. Quine and Hilary Putnam. While, neither Quine, Putnam, nor Atmanspacher and friends are comfortable with the antirealist label, they share in common a commitment to *ontological relativity*, which requires ontological claims to be made relative to a particular conceptual scheme and which directly challenges traditional realism. Atmanspacher and Primas (2005, pp. 59–61) argue that in quantum mechanics, if the tension between the presuppositions of 'common sense' realism and the supposed 'absurdities' in quantum holism is ever to find resolution it will be when we are able to understand and adjudicate the ontic and epistemic levels relative to their successive domains within the hierarchy.

Atmanspacher and Kronz suggest that similar analyses might provide insights for the study of consciousness. The asymmetry of views that have consciousness emerging as a higher order property of the brain, might give way to a more fundamental symmetry which is broken when both mind and matter emerge at a higher level of description. Symmetries in quantum holism might even provide the resources necessary for discovering the deeper symmetry behind the mental and the physical (1999, p.302).

A second non-realist approach to the study of consciousness is offered by J. Scott Jordan (1998; 2000). Jordan stands firmly within the empiricist tradition, committed to the tenet that in scientific inquiry, inferences should not be allowed to extend beyond what the data justifies. Epistemology precedes ontology. Ontology only follows where the evidence and parsimony lead; it is not allowed to be the cart that goes before the horse. Parsimony is accepted by virtually everyone as one of (if not *the*) central evaluative criteria for assessing scientific theories. Current physicalist theories of the mind have beat out dualism in no small part because the latter is considered ontologically profligate, increasing metaphysical commitments 'beyond necessity.' It follows from Jordan's arguments that physicalism will suffer a similar fate if only empiricism and parsimony are allowed to have sway (Jordan 1998, pp. 66–67).

At the level of description relevant to the analysis of perception, physicalism assumes reality is populated by discrete entities with sufficiently precise boundaries to allow a Newtonian description of their interaction with one another. Perception, on this account, must be conceived in terms of one discrete entity scanning another and generating a representation of that object. Our knowledge of other objects will be measured by the accuracy of that representation. The age old epistemological dilemma, of course, is that we never 'see' reality as it is in-itself, so we can never compare our representation to the real thing to determine its reliability, which leads to sceptical worries. If perception is seen as 'representation' of an external stimulus it will always be inadequate because it will be judged as lagging behind the stimulus and incapable of capturing the totality of what is given in the stimulus (Jordan 1998, p. 66).

Jordan suggests that there is an alternative way of understanding the relationship between the knower and the world that is more rigorously empiricist, is more parsimonious, and that does not raise the same sceptical worries. Rather than reifying regularities in our experience by giving them discrete, corpuscularian properties, the relationship between knower, acts of perception, and things known should be seen instead as the dynamic workings of overlapping fields of force. On the traditional view, the organism is the passive element, bombarded by 'input' from the environment. The organism is only able to control the 'output,' its post hoc response to stimulus. Jordan wants to turn this picture on its head by considering the organism as the active element, and the environment as the passive domain which is affected by the organism-as-agent. Here perception is the dynamic process by which the organism (a field of force overlapping with the other fields comprising the environment) imposes itself on the environment, forcing a transfer of energy from the environment that allows the organism to achieve its survival-related goals.[7] The measure of success in perception is not veridicality (or 'accurate mirroring') of the proximal representations, but rather effective control of the distal environment.

Jordan and Hershberger (1994; cf. Hershberger & Jordan, 1992) conducted studies in which subjects in an otherwise dark room produce saccadic eye-movements across a fixed, rapidly blinking LED. Subjects observe a 'phantom' array of horizontal flashes in the opposite direction of the saccadic movement. Is this a failure of the perceptual system, with the subject seeing lights where there are none? Interestingly, the shifts in the perceived location of the LED's *precede* the saccade, indicating an anticipatory effect (1998, p. 74). On Jordan's account this is best understood *not* as an illusion nor the mistake of a malfunctioning system that cannot accurately 'represent' mind-independent reality, but rather as an active, anticipatory form of perception that is designed (quite appropriately by evolution) not to perform acts of 'mirroring' but to dynamically construct the perceived world in advance of direct 'input' so as to maximize the effectiveness

---

[7] This echos Kant's (1787) most famous dictum, the so-called Copernican revolution in epistemology. He insisted that the burden was not on the human knower to somehow figure out how to mirror the world, but the burden was on the world to meet the conditions necessary for the very possibility of human experience, without which it would not succeed in being a world 'for-us' (i.e., a world that we are able to experience).

of the energy transformations necessary to maintain the health of the organism.

How is Jordan's position to be described vis-à-vis the realism debate? There are distinctly Kantian themes running through his position. He also shares some commonality with the early twentieth century phenomenalist tradition by arguing that ontological commitment need not extend beyond what is given directly in experience. Jordan fits comfortably into the broader antirealist tradition that includes many of those with pragmatist leanings among the logical positivists (including the Vienna Circle) and even going back to J.S. Mill and his analysis of physical objects as 'the permanent possibility of experience.' Jordan, himself, feels more kinship with the likes of thinkers like John Dewey (Jordan, 1998) and Michael Oakeshott (1933) who don't carry quite as much philosophical baggage as do the phenomenalists. Finally, he describes himself as a 'neutral monist' — an umbrella term for a broad range of different theories that typically have in common a rejection of the mind–matter dichotomy for an ontologically 'neutral' substrate from which all things are constituted. (I leave to the reader to judge whether this description is apt.)

In briefly surveying the positions of Atmanspacher, Kronz & Primas and Jordan, we have seen how the study of consciousness shifts in interesting directions when ontological realism is not assumed to be an unimpeachable dogma.

## 5. Conclusions

The scientific method calls us to give priority to the empirical data and to hold ontological commitments tentatively, always open to revision. There is no room for dogmatism. However compelling the metaphysical perspective of a reductive-physicalist-externalist-realism, it is not methodologically appropriate to make that a presupposition immune from criticism. This is especially true when the subject of study is consciousness, that part of the universe that has thus far been so resistant to easy, uncontroversial reductive analysis. In the study of consciousness we are searching for deep insights into that puzzling relationship between the subjective, first-person perspective of the world given through immediate experience and the objective, third-person perspective of the world given through the natural sciences. In the study of realism we are also searching for deep insights into the puzzling relationship between the 'independently real' and the 'epistemically justified.' The realism debate covers territory that either overlaps with the consciousness debate or is congruent to it. A resource that could greatly benefit the study of consciousness will be lost if many centuries of critical reflection about realism are ignored.

The suggestion being offered here is *not* that antirealism necessarily holds the key to the mysteries of consciousness. The reader may be surprised to find that the author is not a committed ontological antirealist. I believe in the mind-independent existence of the middle-sized physical objects that populate a typical common sense metaphysics and I am even a scientific realist about the theoretical entities countenanced by current physical theory. I hold that human beings have the capacity to speak a language with realist truth-conditions, rejecting Kant's, Dummett's and Putnam's arguments to the contrary. I am a semantic realist, then, with respect to a broad class of statements.

I part company with most realists, though, in holding that our statements about the external world are not universally to be given a realist interpretation. A good part of our everyday discourse is properly interpreted as having antirealist truth-conditions (Anderson, 1995.) Further, I reject the triune doctrines that comprise what I have called the externalist juggernaut: semantic externalism, epistemological externalism, and externalist theories of mind. While I do not go so far as Jordan, I do believe that we will never have a satisfactory theory of consciousness without the integration of some internalist elements in all three of the domains previously mentioned and without the addition of some antirealist semantic elements in our language. As things currently stand, insights into the nature of consciousness from the broadly idealist /empiricist traditions are in short supply. The reductive power of externalist theories goes some distance to explain the popularity enjoyed by physicalist realism. However, given that it is consciousness that we are studying, it is still surprising that more attention is not paid to the constitutive role of our cognitive faculties in shaping the world of our perceptions. A much greater stock of resources is available to enrich our understanding of consciousness if only the long tradition of philosophical reflection on questions of realism and idealism is brought to the table. And if, as many people believe, the philosophical perspective of externalist-physicalist-realism does indeed prove capable of constructing a satisfactory theory of consciousness, locating and defending that theory against the backdrop of the realism-antirealism debates will help to make clear precisely how that victory was secured. It is my proposal that the doors and windows be thrown open and that the 'realism' debates be taken front and centre within the school of consciousness.

*Acknowledgements*

Many thanks to Harald Atmanspacher, Cees van Leeuwen, Scott Jordan, Mark Siderits and an anonymous reviewer for helpful comments on this paper. The remaining defects are entirely my own.

## REFERENCES

Adams, F., Stecker, R. & Fuller, G. (1992), 'The semantics of thought,' *Pacific Philosophical Quarterly*, **73**, pp. 375–89.

Anderson, D.L. (1992), 'What is realistic about Putnam's internal realism?' *Philosophical Topics*, **20** (1), pp. 49–84.

Anderson, D.L. (1993), 'What is the model-theoretic argument?' *The Journal of Philosophy*, **XC**, pp. 311–22.

Anderson, D.L. (1995), 'A dogma of metaphysical realism,' *American Philosophical Quarterly*, pp. **32**, pp. 1–11.

Anderson, D.L. (2002), 'Why God is not a semantic realist,' in *Realism and Antirealism*, ed. W.P. Alston, (Ithica, NY: Cornell University Press).

Atmanspacher, H. & Kronz, F. (1999), 'Many realisms,' in *Modeling Consciousness Across the Disciplines*, ed. J.S. Jordan (New York: University Press of America), pp. 281–306. (Originally published in *Acta Polytechnica Scandinavica*, (1998), **91**, pp. 31–43.

Atmanspacher, H. & Primas, H. (2005), 'Epistemic and ontic quantum realities,' in *Foundations of Probability and Physics* ed. A Khrennikov, American Institute of Physics, pp. 49–61. Originally published in *Time, Quantum Information*, ed. By L. Castell and O. Ischebeck, Springer, Belin, 2003, pp. 301–21.

Berlin, B. & Kay, P. (1969/1991), *Basic Color Terms: Their Universality and Growth, 2nd Ed.*. (Berkeley, CA: University of California Press).

Churchland, P. (1988). 'Reduction and the neurobiological basis of consciousness', in *Consciousness in Contemporary Science*, eds. A.J. Marcel and E. Bisiach (Oxford: Oxford University Press), pp. 273–304.

Dennett, D. (1987), *The Intentional Stance* (Cambridge, MA: The MIT Press).

Devitt, M. (1984/1991), *Realism and Truth, 2nd Edition* (Oxford: Blackwell).

Dummett, M. (1978), *Truth and Other Enigmas* (Cambridge: Cambridge University Press).

Ebbs, G. (2001), *Rule-Following and Realism* (Cambridge, MA: Harvard University Press).

Edwards, P. (1967), ed. 'Realism.' *The Encyclopedia of Philosophy, Vol. 7* (New York: The Macmillan Company & The Free Press).

Gibson, R.F. (1986), 'Translation, Physics, and the Facts of the Matter,' in *The Philosophy of W.V. Quine*, ed. L.W. Hahn & P.A. Schilpp (La Salle, IL: Open Court), pp. 139–54.

Hershberger, W.A. & Jordon, J. S. (1992), 'Visual direction constancy: Perceiving the visual direcdtion of perisaccadic flashes' in *The Role of Eye Movements in Perceptual Processes*, ed. E. Chekaluk (Amsterdam: Etsevier).

Holt, J. (2003), *Blindsight and the Nature of Consciousness* (Peterborough, Ontario: Broadview Press).

Hume, D. (1740/1975), *A Treatise of Human Nature, 2nd Ed.*, ed. L.A. Selby-Bigge, 2nd ed. revised by P.H. Nidditch (Oxford: Clarendon Press).

Jordan, J.S. (1998), 'Recasting Dewey's critique of the reflex-arc concept via a theory of anticipatory consciousness: Implications for theories of perception,' *New Ideas in Psychology*, **16** (3), pp. 165–87.

Jordan, J.S. (2000), 'The world in the organism: Living systems are knowledge,' *Psycoloquy*, **11**.
Jordan, J.S. & Hershberger, W.A. (1994), 'Timing the shift in retinal local signs that accompanies a saccadic eye movement', *Perception & Psychophysics,* **55** (6), pp. 657–66.
Kant, I. (1787/1929), *Critique of Pure Reason*, trans. N.K. Smith (New York: St. Martin's Press).
Lafont, C. & Medina, J. (1999), *The Linguistic Turn in Hermeneutic Philosophy* (Cambridge, MA: The MIT Press).
Noë, A. (ed. 2002a), *Is the Visual World a Grand Illusion, Special Issue: Journal of Consciousness Studies* (Exeter: Imprint Academic).
Noë, A. (2002b), 'Is the visual world a grand illusion?' *Journal of Consciousness Studies*, **9** (5–6), pp. 1–12.
Oakeshott, M. (1933), *Experience and Its Modes* (Cambridge: Cambridge University Press).
Primas, H. (1990), 'Mathematical and philosophical questions in the theory of open and macroscopic quantum systems,' in *Sixty-two Years of Uncertainty*, ed. A.I. Miller (New York: Plenum).
Putnam, H. (1981), *Reason, Truth, and History* (Cambridge University Press).
Putnam, H. (1983), *Realism and Reason: Philosophical Papers Vol. 3* (Cambridge University Press).
Quine, W.V. (1969), *Ontological Relativity and Other Essay.* (New York: Columbia University Press).
Quine, W.V. (1981), *Theories and Things* (Cambridge, MA: Harvard University Press).
Quine, W.V. (1986), 'Reply to Roger F. Gibson, Jr.' in *The Philosophy of W.V. Quine*, ed. L. W. Hahn & P. A. Schilpp (La Salle, IL: Open Courts), pp. 155–7.
Rorty, R. (ed. 1969/1992), *The Linguistic Turn: Essays in Philosophical Method, 2nd Ed.* (Cambridge, MA: The MIT Press).
Sapir, E. (1929), 'The status of linguistics as a science,' *Language*, **5**, pp. 207–14.
Siderits, M. (1997), 'Buddhist reductionism.' *Philosophy East and West*, **47**, pp. 455–78.

# Harald Atmanspacher

# *Contextual Emergence from Physics to Cognitive Neuroscience*

***Abstract:*** *The concept of contextual emergence has been proposed as a non-reductive, yet well-defined relation between different levels of description of physical and other systems. It is illustrated for the transition from statistical mechanics to thermodynamical properties such as temperature. Stability conditions are shown to be crucial for a rigorous implementation of contingent contexts that are required to understand temperature as an emergent property.*

*Are such stability conditions meaningful for contextual emergence beyond physics as well? An affirmative example from cognitive neuroscience addresses the relation between neurobiological and mental levels of description. For a particular class of partitions of the underlying neurobiological phase space, so-called generating partitions, the emergent mental states are stable under the dynamics. In this case, mental descriptions are (i) faithful representations of the neurodynamics and (ii) compatible with one another.*

## 1. Introduction

A basic strategy for the scientific description of any system, physical or otherwise, is to specify its state and the properties associated with that state, and then introduce their evolution in terms of dynamical laws. This strategy presupposes that the boundary of a system can be defined with respect to its environment, although such a definition is often problematic. If it can be achieved, there is usually more than one possibility for specifying states and properties. The fact that states and properties can be formally and rigorously defined in fundamental physical theories distinguishes the structure of such theories as particularly transparent. A paradigmatic example for a fundamental theory in present-day physics is quantum theory.

But how about physical theories which are not regarded as fundamental (such as thermodynamics), or how about descriptive approaches beyond physics (such as chemistry, biology or psychology)? For such situations, attempts have been made to relate descriptions of systems which are not fundamental in the sense mentioned above to descriptions which are fundamental in this sense. The usual (and often too simple) framework in which corresponding relations are typically formulated is that of a hierarchy of descriptions. In a hierarchical picture (which can be refined in terms of more complicated networks of descriptions) there are higher-level and lower-level descriptions. More fundamental theories are taken to refer to lower levels in the hierarchy.

In such a simple framework, reduction and emergence are relations between different levels of descriptions of a system, its states and properties, or the (dynamical) laws characterizing their behaviour. In the philosophical literature, the usual guiding idea behind reductionist approaches is to 'reduce' higher-level features to lower-level features. In contrast, emergentist approaches emphasize higher-level features by stressing the irreducibility of at least some of their aspects to lower levels. In this way, the emergence of features at higher levels[1] is related to the emergence of novelty.

In a recent article (Bishop and Atmanspacher, 2006), two selected examples, temperature and chirality, were used to illustrate the sophisticated way in which features at one level of description are often related to features at another level. While strict reductionists would argue that both necessary and sufficient conditions for higher-level features are already embodied at the lower level, this is false in both of these examples, and presumably false in many others as well. An alternative kind of interlevel relation, *contextual emergence*, has been proposed as a less rigid, more appropriate scheme, in which necessary but not sufficient conditions for higher-level features are provided by the lower-level description.

The scheme of contextual emergence is particularly proposed for exploring insufficiently understood interlevel relations beyond

---

[1] Emergence in the sense of an interlevel relation, as it is addressed in this paper, is always understood synchronically (i.e., as a structural relation) rather than diachronically (i.e., as a dynamical process). For details see Stephan (1999).

physics. Specifically, one may think of relations between different levels of descriptions in brain physiology, where one of the key questions is how properties of neuronal assemblies or populations are related to properties of individual neurons and synapses. However, one may also think of relations between such neurobiological levels of description and their mental correlates at cognitive or psychological levels of description. An interesting candidate for interlevel relations of the latter kind will be presented in this contribution.

We will start with a brief introduction of the idea of contextual emergence and compare it with other kinds of interlevel relations in section 2. Subsequently, in section 3, we recapitulate some details regarding the contextual emergence of temperature (and related thermodynamical properties) from a description in terms of statistical physics. The particularly important role of stability conditions as guiding principles for contextual emergence will be emphasized in section 4. Eventually, section 5 presents an example for the contextual emergence of cognitive features from their underlying neurobiological description: the emergence of compatible psychological descriptions that are consistent with the associated neural description. Section 6 summarizes the basic arguments and results.

## 2. Reduction and Emergence

Reduction and emergence are used in a variety of senses in the literature. In general terms, both concepts express ways to achieve a better understanding of some feature of a system in terms of other features which are assumed to provide such understanding. For the sake of simplicity, reduction and emergence schemes are typically organized in a hierarchical manner, such that levels of description or levels of reality are related to each other. As mentioned above, an analysis in terms of hierarchical levels often oversimplifies the picture. In general, non-hierarchical frameworks including other notions such as those of domains of description or domains of reality might be more appropriate.

As indicated by the distinction between levels of description and levels of reality, there is a difference between epistemological and ontological frameworks for reduction and emergence. Broadly speaking, descriptive terms are subjects of epistemological discourse while elements of reality are subjects of ontological discourse. Both types of discourse are used in reductionist and emergentist approaches. The concept of reference establishes a connection between descriptive terms and described elements of reality (leaving aside difficult questions about reference itself).

The distinction between epistemological discourse and ontological discourse is not sufficient to exhaust the different ways in which the notions of reduction and emergence are used. In addition, it is also important to distinguish between different types of features which are to be related to others. There are three main categories of relations: theories/laws to other theories/laws, properties to other properties, and wholes to parts. Clearly, relations between theories/laws are predominantly epistemological. The relation between wholes and parts, on the other hand, is primarily discussed ontologically insofar as it refers to elements of reality rather than their description. In the literature on property relations, both epistemological and ontological frameworks can be found. Property relations are sometimes meant ontologically (i.e., regarding properties of elements of reality) and sometimes epistemologically (i.e., regarding descriptive terms referring to properties of elements of reality).

An ontological framework of discussion is usually employed in reductive approaches, where ontic elements are restricted to a fundamental level of description, at which those properties reside to which other properties are regarded reducible and from which other properties are regarded to be exhaustively determined. An alternative idea of a 'tiered' ontology, ascribing ontic elements to all levels of description, was proposed originally by Hartmann (1935). Quine (1969) has revitalized this idea with his notion of an ontological relativity. It was adopted by Putnam (1987) when he suggested the idea of internal realism, later denoted pragmatic realism. These philosophical frameworks of thinking were for the first time fleshed out by Atmanspacher and Kronz (1999) from a scientific perspective. The key to this option is the distinction between ontic and epistemic descriptions of the behaviour of physical systems, in particular quantum systems, which goes back to Scheibe (1973) and Primas (1990).[2]

Analogous to Quine's ontological relativity, this allows us to conceive ontic elements at each level of description. In addition to Quine's notion, however, it allows us to propose formal techniques with which appropriate interlevel relations (sometimes referred to as 'bridge laws') can be designed in detail. In a nutshell, an ontic description at one level serves as the basis for an epistemic description at a higher level, where it can be 'ontologized' and then provides the

---

[2] A comprehensive recent account, which also addresses the notions of ontological versus ontic and epistemological versus epistemic, can be found in Atmanspacher and Primas (2003).

basis for proceeding to another epistemic description at yet another level. (For details see Atmanspacher and Kronz, 1999.)

If one wants to have the option of ontic elements at each level of description rather than only at one or a few fundamental levels, a straightforward and strictly reductive scheme for interlevel relations becomes impossible and must be relaxed. The way in which ontic and epistemic descriptions are related to each other motivates contextual emergence as a viable alternative.

In order to clearly distinguish between different concepts of reduction and emergence, it is desirable to have a transparent classification scheme, so that the basic characteristics of these concepts can be discussed coherently. A useful approach toward such a classification is based on the role which contingent contexts play in reduction and emergence. More precisely, the way in which necessary and sufficient conditions are assumed in the relation between different levels of description can be used to distinguish four classes of relations:

(1) The description of features of a system at a particular level of description offers *both necessary and sufficient* conditions to rigorously derive the description of features at a higher level. This is the strictest possible form of *reduction*. It was most popular under the influence of positivist thinking in the mid-twentieth century.

(2) The description of features of a system at a particular level of description offers *necessary but not sufficient* conditions to derive the description of features at a higher level. This version is called *contextual emergence*, because contingent contextual conditions are required in addition to the lower-level description for a rigorous derivation of higher-level features.

(3) The description of features of a system at a particular level of description offers *sufficient but not necessary* conditions to derive the description of features at a higher level. This version includes the idea that a lower-level description offers multiple realizations of a particular feature at a higher level, which is characteristic of *supervenience*.

(4) The description of features of a system at a particular level of description offers *neither necessary nor sufficient* conditions to derive the description of features at a higher level. This represents a form of *radical emergence* insofar as there are no relevant conditions connecting the two levels whatsoever.

For obvious reasons, class (4) is unattractive if one is interested in explanatory relations between different levels of description. Property dualism a la Davidson (1980) would be an example of radical emergence. By contrast, class (1) is extremely appealing if one is interested in simple explanations. The 'received views' of reduction — as Batterman (2002) refers to them — fall into this class (e.g., Nagel, 1961; Schaffner, 1976). They share particular features with variants of type physicalism.

From a contemporary point of view, classes (2) and (3) are viable alternative schemes for analysing relationships between different levels of description. Class (3) includes token physicalism, and some kinds of functionalism, together with supervenience relations[3] as extensively discussed on the basis of Kim's proposals (Kim, 1993). Interestingly, Kim himself has recently argued that supervenience may be inadequate for capturing relations in the sciences (Kim, 1998; 1999). This development has led to an emphasis on realization relations (e.g., Kim, 1998; 1999; Crook and Gillett, 2001; Gillett, 2002), such as the multiple realizability of higher-level states by lower-level states. For instance, Chalmers (2000) defines neural correlates of consciousness as neural systems that may realize conscious mental states in multiple ways and are minimally sufficient for the occurrence of those states.

In the remainder of this contribution we will focus our discussion on class (2), contextual emergence, which is less rigid than the strong form of reduction (1) on the one hand and provides more structure for interlevel relations than radical emergence (4) on the other. It should be mentioned that contextual emergence (2) has much in common with a notion of reduction which is different from its standard philosophical meaning and has been distinguished as a 'physicist account' of reduction (Nickles, 1973; Batterman, 2002, pp. 17-19). In addition, particular aspects of contextual emergence resemble aspects of emergent interactionism (Sperry, 1969; Stephan, 1999, Chap. 16), but there are also crucial differences between the two.

## 3. Thermodynamic Equilibrium and Temperature

This section describes a physical example of contextual emergence that is detailed enough to see how contexts can be introduced leading to emergent properties via the construction of contextual topologies.

---

[3] Some versions of supervenience require that changes in lower-level descriptions are both necessary and sufficient to bring about changes in a higher-level description. Such versions are indistinguishable from reduction (Kim, 1998) and fall into class (1).

It will be shown how necessary conditions for the emergence of novel properties are related to lower-level descriptions, whereas contingent contexts, not available at the lower-level description, serve as sufficient conditions leading to well-defined properties at higher-order levels of description.[4]

Our much discussed example is the reduction or emergence, respectively, of thermodynamic properties such as temperature to or from properties at lower-level descriptions. The lower-level descriptions in this case are statistical mechanics and point mechanics. How are these levels of description related to thermodynamics?

To start with the less controversial issue, the step from point mechanics to statistical mechanics is essentially based on the formation of an ensemble distribution. Particular properties of a many-particle system are defined in terms of a statistical ensemble description (e.g., as moments of a many-particle distribution function) which refers to the state of an ensemble rather than the states of single particles in an individual description.

An example is the mean kinetic energy of a system of $N$ particles, which can be calculated from the distribution of the momenta of all particles. The expectation value of kinetic energy is defined as the limit $N \to \infty$ of its mean value, assuming the applicability of limit theorems such as the law of large numbers. Although a *mean value* can in principle be calculated even for a small number of particles, it is illegitimate to assign an *expectation value* to a system if its number of particles is too small. An expectation value of a property whose definition is based on a statistical ensemble description presupposes (infinitely) many degrees of freedom.

The more controversial issue in discussing the reduction or emergence of temperature refers to the step from statistical mechanics to thermodynamics (cf. the discussion by Compagner, 1989), e.g. from the expectation value of a momentum distribution of a particle ensemble to the temperature of the system as a whole. In many philosophical discussions it is argued that the thermodynamic temperature of a gas *is* the mean kinetic energy of the molecules which constitute the gas. According to Nagel, this leads to a straightforward reduction of thermodynamic temperature to statistical mechanics (Nagel, 1961, pp. 341–5).

Such a rough picture, however, is a gross mischaracterization, based on a too generous treatment of some important details. First of all, as mentioned above, thermodynamic properties typically require

---

[4] See Primas (1998) for more details and for a bunch of illustrative examples.

the so-called thermodynamic limit $N \to \infty$ for their definition, as their quantification is related to an expectation value of a statistical ensemble distribution. Second, thermodynamic descriptions presume thermodynamic, or briefly thermal, equilibrium as a crucial assumption which — as will be shown next — is neither formally nor conceptually available at the level of statistical mechanics. Third, the very concept of temperature is *basically* foreign to statistical mechanics and is usually introduced phenomenologically.[5]

Thermal equilibrium is formulated by the zeroth law of thermodynamics: If two systems are both in thermal equilibrium with a third system, then they are said to be in thermal equilibrium with each other. (In this sense, the definition of temperature is relational; this does not contradict the fact that the temperature scale has an absolute zero point.) Based on this equivalence relation, the phenomenological concept of temperature can be introduced in the usual textbook way. Since thermal equilibrium is not defined at the level of statistical mechanics, temperature is not a mechanical property but, rather, emerges as a novel property at the level of thermodynamics.

Popular statements to the effect that temperature corresponds to mean molecular motion are, thus, only correct under the important condition of thermal equilibrium and in the thermodynamic limit. Without these two essential presuppositions, they are meaningless. The standard notion of temperature (and of other thermodynamical observables such as entropy) is undefined far from thermal equilibrium and for single particles.

The concept of thermal equilibrium can be recast in terms of a class of distinguished statistical states, the so-called Kubo-Martin-Schwinger (KMS) states. These states are defined by the KMS condition[6] which characterizes the (structural) stability of a KMS state against local perturbations. Hence, the KMS condition essentially implements the zeroth law of thermodynamics as a *stability criterion* at the level of statistical mechanics. The second law of thermodynamics expresses this stability in terms of a maximization of entropy for thermal equilibrium states. (Equivalently, the free energy of the system is minimal in thermal equilibrium.)

---

[5] Similarly, phenomena accounted for in geometrical optics (such as light rays or shadows) or in electric network theory (such as inductances, capacitances, resistances) are *basically* foreign to Maxwell's electrodynamics and require considering short- and long- wavelength limits, respectively.

[6] For more details concerning the significance of the KMS condition see Sewell (2002, chap. 5).

In an algebraic framework (which we cannot explain in detail here), KMS states can be used as reference states for a so-called Gel'fand-Naimark-Segal (GNS) construction. Such reference states induce a new, contextual topology in the state space of statistical mechanics, which is coarser than the original topology, and its associated algebra of observables (i.e. a set of observables obeying some basic algebraic relations). With respect to this new topology, the GNS-construction then gives rise to a new algebra of observables including thermodynamic temperature as a novel property of the system. In this spirit, Takesaki (1970) has shown that temperature emerges as a classical observable from an underlying quantum statistical description.

Because mechanical descriptions are given by a type of algebra different from the contextual algebra of thermodynamic observables, temperature cannot be an element of a mechanical description (Primas 1998). Hence, temperature is not reducible to statistical mechanics in any straightforward sense. Thermodynamic temperature is an example of a contextually emergent property, which is neither contained in nor predicted by the lower-level mechanical description alone. However, given the lower-level mechanical description and an appropriate contextual topology based on the KMS state, thermodynamic properties can be rigorously derived. The contextual topology is implied by contingent contexts given in the higher-level thermodynamic description where the notions of thermal equilibrium and thermodynamic limit are applicable.

## 4. Stability as a Guiding Principle for Contextual Emergence

After the detailed discussion of thermodynamic properties as examples for contextual emergence, it is worthwhile to step back and look at its general principles. Repeating the characterization of contextual emergence as given in section 2, the description of features of a system at a particular level of description offers *necessary but not sufficient* conditions to derive features at a higher level of description. In logical terms, the necessity of conditions at the lower level of description means that higher-level features *imply* those of the lower level of description. The converse — that lower-level features also *imply* the features at the higher level of description — does not hold in contextual emergence. This is due to the absence of sufficient conditions at the lower level of description. Contingent contexts for the transition from the lower to the higher level of description are required in order to provide such sufficient conditions.

In the example of temperature, the notion of thermal equilibrium represents such a context. Thermal equilibrium is not available at the level of description of Newtonian or statistical mechanics. Implementing thermal equilibrium in terms of the KMS condition and considering the limit $N \to \infty$ at the level of statistical mechanics, temperature can be obtained as an emergent property at the level of a thermodynamical description. It is of paramount importance for this procedure that KMS states satisfy a *stability condition* that is imported from the level of thermodynamics onto the level of statistical mechanics.

Since the Newtonian and statistical mechanical levels of description are necessary to derive the higher-level property of temperature, principles or laws at these levels of description cannot be violated by any higher-level description incorporating temperature. That the Newtonian and statistical mechanical levels of description alone are not sufficient is formally recognized by the fact that they do not give rise to an algebra of observables including temperature unless additional contingent conditions are implemented.

The significance of contextual emergence as opposed to strict reduction in this example is clear. Of course, it would be interesting to extend the general construction scheme for emergent properties to other cases. More physical examples are indicated and discussed, for example, in Primas (1998) and Batterman (2002). We propose the concept of stability, in the sense of stability against perturbations or fluctuations, as a key principle for the construction of a contextual topology and an associated algebra of contextual observables in examples even beyond physics.

One possible, and ambitious, case refers to emergent features in the framework of cognitive neuroscience. A particularly active field of research here is concerned with the emergence of new features at the level of neuronal assemblies from lower-level features of individual neurons. Particular interest in this issue derives from the fact that cognitive capabilities are usually correlated with the activity of neuronal assemblies, but detailed neurobiological knowledge refers mainly to the properties of individual neurons. Closing the gap in our understanding of the relation between neuronal assemblies and individual neurons could contribute significantly to understanding neurobiological correlates of consciousness.

As a possible framework for research in this area, the scheme of contextual emergence might be fruitfully applied as follows. Novel features at the (higher) level of neuronal assemblies would have necessary but not sufficient conditions at the (lower) level of neurons.

In order to identify contexts providing such sufficient conditions, those among the many possible assembly features which are relevant or interesting as emergent features must first be identified. Assuming that stability criteria play a role analogous to physical examples, techniques of nonlinear dynamics for modelling assemblies in terms of attractors with particular stability properties and corresponding relaxation times or escape times suggest themselves. This can be implemented easily for powerful modelling tools such as neural networks (Anderson and Rosenfeld, 1989) or coupled map lattices (Kaneko and Tsuda, 2000).

Contextual emergence might even be a viable scheme to address relations between the neurobiology of the brain at various levels on the one hand and cognitive or psychological features — in other words: to address the relation between material (brain) and mental (consciousness) features. In the following section we indicate a concrete scenario which was recently elaborated in detail by Atmanspacher and beim Graben (2006).

## 5. Contextual Emergence of Compatible Psychological Descriptions

It is an old and much discussed question to which degree psychology could become a unified science, integrating the many approaches and models that constitute its contemporary situation. It is sometimes argued that the largely fragmented appearance of psychology (and cognitive science as well) is due to the fact that psychology is still in a preparadigmatic, 'immature' state. Some have even argued that this situation is unavoidable (e.g., Koch, 1993; Gardner, 1992) and should be considered as the strength of psychology (e.g., Viney, 1989; McNally, 1992) rather than an undesirable affair.

From the perspective of the philosophy of mind, arguments against the possibility of a unified science of psychology have been presented as well. Most prominent are the accounts of Kim (1992) and Fodor (1997), both using the scheme of multiple realization in the framework of supervenience to reject unification. Shapiro (2006) has recently pointed out particular weak points in their arguments.

On the other hand, there is a growing interest in articulating visions for a unified science of psychology, and of cognitive science as well (see, e.g., Newell, 1990; Anderson, 1996). Recently, various approaches have been proposed to reach a degree of coherence comparable to established sciences as, e.g., physics with well-defined relations between its different disciplines. Examples are the 'information processing' paradigm (Lachman *et al.*, 1979; Dawson, 1998), 'psychological behaviorism' (Staats, 1996; 1999), 'unified psychology' (Sternberg and Grigorenko, 2001; Sternberg *et al.*, 2001), and the 'tree of knowledge' system (Henriques 2003). (Similar visions are currently being explored for a unified science of consciousness.) A key feature in the latter program is the *commensurability*, i.e. comparability, of competing approaches in psychology, explicated by Yanchar and Slife (1997) and Slife (2000).

This section presents a way in which the notion of commensurable models can be implemented formally. A suitable way to formulate commensurability in technical terms is given by the concept of *compatibility*. Briefly speaking, two models are considered as commensurable if they are compatible in the sense that there exist well-defined mappings between their key terms. If this is not the case, they are incompatible.[7] It turns out that the scheme of contextual emergence provides some detailed and clarifying insights on how to proceed in this regard. The two levels of description whose interlevel relations are significant for this purpose are those of neurobiology and psychology, or of neurobiology and cognitive science, respectively. Compatible and incompatible implementations of symbolic representations of cognitive states, briefly cognitive symbol systems, have recently been discussed by beim Graben (2004).

As mentioned above, a basic way in which systems at any level are described starts with the specification of their states, their observables, and their dynamics. An appropriate representation of these basic elements is usually given in terms of a state space. The state of a system at a given time is represented by a more or less refined subset of that space, the values of its associated observables are the projections of that subset onto the state space coordinates, and the dynamics is represented by the motion of the state as parametrized by time.

Let us assume a neurobiological state space $X$ with fairly fine-grained states $x$, ideally represented pointwise in $X$, and with observables $X_i$, $i = 1, ..., n$, for $n$ degrees of freedom. Typical examples for neurobiological observables are electroencephalogram (EEG) potentials at the macroscopic level, local field potentials at the mesoscopic level, or spike trains of neurons at the microscopic level of the brain. These observables are usually obtained with much higher

---

[7] Note that this notion of incompatibility is more subtle than a 'logical incompatibility' (Slife, 2000) in the sense that two models are simply negations of each other. In particular, our framework includes complementary models as maximally incompatible models. See further discussion below.

resolution than observables at a psychological level of description. We assume that the dynamics can be considered as (quasi-) continuous as a function of time.

The construction of a mental (i.e., psychological or cognitive) state space $Y$ from $X$ can be based on some coarse-graining of $X$, reflecting that a mental state is multiply realized by a variety of neural states. That is, the state space $X$ must be partitioned such that cells of finite volume in $X$ emerge, which can be used to represent mental states in $Y$. Often, such discrete states are denoted by alphabetic symbols $A$, $B$, $C$, ..., where each symbol represents an equivalence class of neurobiological states. In contrast to the dynamics of states $x$ in a continuous state space $X$, the symbolic dynamics (Lind and Marcus, 1995) in $Y$ is a discrete sequence of symbols as a function of time.

A coarse-grained partition on $X$ implies neighbourhood relations between states in $Y$ that are different from those in the original space $X$; in this sense it implies a change in topology. (For instance, neural states that are distant in $X$ can belong to the same mental state in $Y$, and neural states that are nearby in $X$ can belong to different mental states in $Y$.) Also, the definition of observables $Y_i$ for $Y$ leads to an algebra of mental observables that is different from that of neurobiological observables. Obviously, these two differences depend essentially on the choice of the partition of $X$. We will now show that a particular concept of stability is crucial for a 'proper' choice of such a partition and, thus, crucial for a 'proper' mapping from $X$ to $Y$.

First of all, it should be required that a proper partition leads to mental states in $Y$ that are empirically plausible. For instance, a plausible formation of basic equivalence classes of neurobiological states is due to the distinction between wakefulness and sleep — two evidently different psychological states.[8] However, an important second demand is that these equivalence classes be stable under the dynamics in $X$. If this cannot be guaranteed, the boundaries between cells in $X$ become blurred as time proceeds, thus rendering the concept of a mental state suboptimally defined. Although concepts or categories in psychology are typically fuzzy rather than sharp (cf., e.g., Smith and Medin, 1981), they can be less well defined than possible, even if one takes an unavoidable extent of fuzziness for granted.

In a recent contribution, Atmanspacher and beim Graben (2006) have shown in detail that a particular type of partition is needed for a

---

[8] A recent empirically based study concerning the relation between neurobiological and mental state space representations for wakefulness versus sleep and other, subtler examples (selective attention, intrinsic perceptual selection) is due to Fell (2004). For alternative state space approaches see Wackermann (1999) and Hobson *et al.* (2000).

proper definition of stable symbols in $Y$ based on cells in $X$. These partitions are called generating partitions. They exist for chaotic systems and provide the supremum of the dynamical entropy of such systems (over all possible partitions), the so-called Kolmogorov-Sinai entropy (see Atmanspacher [1997] for an annotated introduction).[9] This is equivalent with the minimization of correlations between their cells as caused by the chaotic dynamics in $X$ (cf. Cornfeld et al., 1982). This in turn minimizes the fuzziness of symbolic states in $Y$, thus providing a stable definition of such states, whose dynamics is then a faithful representation of the underlying neurodynamics. However, generating partitions are notoriously difficult to construct, and they are explicitly known for only a few examples.

It should be noted that it is possible to specify some 'optimal' partition in $X$ even in case of multiple attractors with noise at the neural level. If there are many attractors coexisting, such a partition can be approximately determined by the boundaries between the coexisting basins of attraction. Froyland (2005) and Gaveau and Schulman (2005) have recently proposed procedures how to achieve this in case of multiple fixed points.

Insofar as generating partitions are in principle defined by the dynamics in $X$, they reflect the behaviour of the system at the corresponding (lower) level of description. The reason for using them for the construction of states in $Y$ is basically that these states are multiply realized in $X$, so that an equivalence class of states in $X$ must be formed in order to define a state in $Y$. The generating partition is a tool to do this in a proper way. The contingent contexts at the level of $Y$, which are mandatory for contextual emergence, are for instance given by the choice of a 'phenomenal family' (Chalmers, 2000) to which the states of interest in $Y$ belong. The fact that contextual emergence does not work without specifying these higher-level contexts prompts us to resist the impulse, exhibited by many neuroscientists, of reducing mental states to 'nothing but' the activity of neural states.

A key result of the work by beim Graben and Atmanspacher (2006) is that a non-generating partition is incompatible with any other partition (even if this is generating) in the sense that there is no well-defined mapping between the partitions. As a consequence, models based on such partitions are incompatible as well. Since any *ad hoc* chosen partition is quite unlikely to be generating, it may be suspected that the resulting incompatibility of models based on such partitions is

---

[9] Markov partitions, a special case of generating partitions, create a Markov process for the symbolic dynamics in $Y$. Evidence for chaotic brain processes has often been reported (cf. Kaneko and Tsuda, 2000, and references therein).

the rule rather than the exception. While incompatibility may admit the possibility of 'partially coherent' models, the case of maximal incompatibility, also called complementarity, excludes any coherence between different models completely.

This represents a significant limit to the vision of a unified or integrative science of psychology. Or, turned positively, such a unification will be strongly facilitated if the approaches to be unified are based on compatible, i.e. generating, partitions providing dynamically stable, well-defined mental states. As mentioned, it is a tedious task to identify such generating partitions. Nevertheless, the necessary formal and numerical tools are available today.

If there is a good deal of empirical plausibility for a particular partition, one might hope that this implies that such a partition is generating (at least in an approximate sense) and, thus, that the corresponding mental states are stable. However, there may be cases of conflict between the empirical and the theoretical constraint on a proper partition. In such cases, one has to face the possibility that the 'empirical plausibility' of mental states may be unjustified, e.g. based on questionable prejudices. If mental states turn out to be dynamically unstable, the theoretical argument against their adequacy is very strong indeed.

Compatible partitions and, consequently, compatible psychological models show another important feature that is occasionally addressed in current literature: the topological equivalence of representations in neurobiological and mental state spaces (cf. Metzinger, 2003, p. 619, and Fell (2004) for empirically based examples). Topological equivalence ensures that the mapping between $X$ and $Y$ is faithful in the sense that the two state space representations yield equivalent information about the system. Non-generating, incompatible partitions do not provide representations in $Y$ that are topologically equivalent with the underlying representation in $X$.

As a consequence, compatible psychological (or cognitive) models that are topologically equivalent with their neurobiological basis emerge if they are constructed from generating partitions. The relevant context for this construction at the psychological level is given by the requirement of stable mental states, related to the dynamical stability of generating partitions. Without this sufficient condition for compatibility and topological equivalence, the neurobiological level of description provides only necessary conditions for psychological descriptions which will generally be incompatible.

In supervenience, the notion of sufficiency takes into account that different neural states can be correlated with the same mental state (multiple realization). Our notion of contextual emergence addresses the different question of how it can be understood that neural states are correlates of mental states. Contextual emergence tries to elucidate principles which allow us to understand the relationship between mental and neural states, even in individual instantiations, in a more profound manner. In this way, supervenience and contextual emergence complement rather than contradict each other. Applying both concepts together may, thus, provide novel insight into the nature of mind-brain relations.

## 6. Summary

The goal of reduction is to derive the description of higher-level features, e.g. properties, of a system exhaustively in terms of the description of features at a lower level. The implicit assumption in this program is that the description of all features which are not included at the lower level can be constructed or derived from this level without additional input. However, many physical examples pose serious difficulties for this program. For instance, temperature is a novel property emerging from a lower-level statistical mechanical description, but it is not derivable from this lower-level description alone.

The concept of contextual emergence addresses such situations properly. Contextual emergence is characterized by the fact that a lower-level description provides necessary, but not sufficient conditions for higher-level descriptions. The presence of necessary conditions indicates that the lower-level description provides a basis for higher-level descriptions, while the absence of sufficient conditions means that higher-level features are neither logical consequences of the lower-level description nor can they be rigorously derived from the lower-level description alone. Hence, the notion of strong reduction is inapplicable in these cases.

Sufficient conditions for a rigorous derivation of higher-level features can be introduced through specifying contexts reflecting the particular kinds of contingency in a given situation. These contexts can be implemented as a stability criterion in the lower-level description and induce a change in the topology of the corresponding state space (e.g., due to coarse-graining). There is, then, a mathematically well-defined procedure for deriving higher-level features given the lower-level description plus the contingent contextual conditions.

Contextual emergence and the associated identification of appropriate stability conditions may have applications in other domains such as biology and psychology, and, ultimately, for the relationship between the physical and the mental. The application of contextual emergence in cognitive neuroscience demonstrates its viability in this regard. Note that the scheme of contextual emergence is here understood as supplementing (rather than opposing) adequate supervenience relations.

Compatible descriptions at the psychological level, which are topologically equivalent, i.e. consistent, with the underlying neurobiological description, emerge only if the mental states defined at the psychological level are dynamically stable. If the neural dynamics is sufficiently complex, e.g. chaotic, this requires that the partition providing these states be generating. Generating partitions are defined by the dynamics of neural states and give rise to particular, dynamically stable equivalence classes of neural states that can be re-defined symbolically as mental states. A unified science of psychology, with mutually compatible domains of description, becomes problematic if those descriptions are not based on generating partitions.

*Acknowledgments*

Particular results addressed in this paper have been obtained in collaborations, quoted in the list of references, with Robert Bishop, Thomas Filk, Peter beim Graben, Hans Primas and Herbert Scheingraber. I am grateful to all of them for many fruitful discussions and helpful comments.

## References

Anderson, J.A., and Rosenfeld, E. (1989), *Neurocomputing: Foundations of Research* (Cambridge: MIT Press).

Anderson, N. (1996), *A Functional Theory of Cognition* (Mahwah, NJ: Erlbaum).

Atmanspacher, H. (1997), 'Dynamical entropy in dynamical systems', in *Time, Temporality, Now*, ed. H. Atmanspacher and E. Ruhnau (Berlin: Springer), pp. 327–46.

Atmanspacher, H. and beim Graben, P. (2006), 'Contextual emergence of mental states from neurodynamics', *Chaos and Complexity Letters*, in press.

Atmanspacher, H. and Kronz, F. (1999), 'Relative onticity', in *On Quanta, Mind and Matter: Hans Primas in Context*, ed. H. Atmanspacher, A. Amann, and U. Müller-Herold (Dordrecht: Kluwer), pp. 273–94.

Atmanspacher, H. and Primas, H. (2003), 'Epistemic and ontic quantum realities', in *Time, Quantum and Information*, ed. L. Castell and O. Ischebeck (Berlin: Springer), pp. 301–21.

Batterman, R. (2002), *The Devil in the Details* (Oxford: Oxford University Press).

beim Graben, P. (2004), 'Incompatible implementations of physical symbol systems', *Mind and Matter* **2** (2), pp. 29–51.

beim Graben, P. and Atmanspacher, H. (2006), 'Complementarity in classical dynamical systems', *Foundations of Physics*, **36**, pp. 291–306.

Bishop, R.C. and Atmanspacher, H. (2006), 'Contextual emergence in the description of properties', *Foundations of Physics*, in press.

Chalmers, D. (2000), 'What is a neural correlate of consciousness?', in *Neural Correlates of Consciousness*, ed. T. Metzinger (Cambridge, MA: MIT Press), pp. 17–39.

Compagner, A. (1989), 'Thermodynamics as the continuum limit of statistical mechanics,' *American Journal of Physics*, **57** (2), pp. 106–17.
Cornfeld, I.P., Fomin, S.V. and Sinai, Ya.G. (1982), *Ergodic Theory* (Berlin: Springer), pp. 250–2, 280–4.
Crook, S. and Gillett, C. (2001), 'Why physics alone cannot define the "physical"', *Canadian Journal of Philosophy*, **31**, pp. 333–60.
Davidson, D. (1980), *Essays on Actions and Events* (Oxford: Oxford University Press).
Dawson, M.R.W. (1998), *Understanding Cognitive Science* (Oxford: Blackwell).
Fell, J. (2004), 'Identifying neural correlates of consciousness: The state space approach', *Consciousness and Cognition*, **13**, pp. 709–29.
Fodor, J. (1997), 'Special sciences: Still autonomous after all these years', *Philosophical Perspectives*, **11**, pp. 149–63.
Froyland, G. (2005), 'Statistically optimal almost-invariant sets', *Physica D*, **200**, 205–19.
Gardner, H. (1992), 'Scientific psychology: Should we bury it or praise it?', *New Ideas in Psychology*, **10**, pp. 179–90.
Gaveau, B. and Schulman, L.S. (2005), 'Dynamical distance: Coarse grains, pattern recognition, and network analysis', *Bulletin de Sciences Mathematiques* **129**, pp. 631–42.
Gillett, C. (2002), 'The varieties of emergence: Their purposes, obligations and importance,' *Grazer Philosophische Studien*, **65**, pp. 95–121.
Hartmann, N. (1935), *Zur Grundlegung der Ontologie* (Berlin: deGruyter).
Henriques, G.R. (2003), 'The tree of knowledge system and the theoretical unification of psychology', *Review of General Psychology*, **7**, pp. 150–82.
Hobson, J.A., Pace-Schott, E.F. and Stickgold, R. (2000), 'Dreaming and the brain: Toward a cognitive neuroscience of conscious states,' *Behavioral and Brain Sciences*, **23**, pp. 793–842.
Kaneko, K. and Tsuda, I. (2000), *Complex Systems: Chaos and Beyond* (Berlin: Springer).
Kim, J. (1992), 'Multiple realization and the metaphysics of reduction', *Philosophy and Phenomenological Research*, **52**, pp. 1–26.
Kim, J. (1993), *Supervenience and Mind* (Cambridge: Cambridge University Press).
Kim, J. (1998), *Mind in a Physical World: An Essay on the Mind-Body Problem and Mental Causation* (Cambridge, MA: MIT Press).
Kim, J. (1999), 'Making sense of emergence', *Philosophical Studies*, **95**, pp. 3–36.
Koch, S. (1993), ' "Psychology" or "the psychological studies"?', *American Psychologist*, **48**, pp. 902–4.
Lachman, R., Lachman, J.L. and Butterfield, E.C. (1979), *Cognitive Psychology and Information Processing* (Hillsdale, NJ: Erlbaum).
Lind, D. and Marcus, B. (1995), *Symbolic Dynamics and Coding* (Cambridge: Cambridge University Press).
McNally, R.J. (1992), 'Disunity in psychology: Chaos or speciation?', *American Psychologist*, **47**, p. 1054.
Metzinger, T. (2003), *Being No One* (Cambridge, MA: MIT Press).
Nagel, E. (1961), *The Structure of Science* (New York: Harcourt, Brace & World).
Newell, A. (1990), *Unified Theories of Cognition* (Cambridge: Harvard University Press).
Nickles, T. (1973), 'Two concepts of intertheoretic reduction,' *Journal of Philosophy*, **70** (7), pp. 181–201.
Primas, H. (1977), 'Theory reduction and non-Boolean theories,' *Journal of Mathematical Biology*, **4**, pp. 281–301.

Primas, H. (1990), 'Mathematical and philosophical questions in the theory of open and macroscopic quantum systems,' in *Sixty-two Years of Uncertainty: Historical, Philosophical and Physics Inquiries into the Foundation of Quantum Mechanics*, ed. A.I. Miller (New York: Plenum), pp. 233–57.

Primas, H. (1998), 'Emergence in exact natural sciences,' *Acta Polytechnica Scandinavica*, **91**, pp. 83–98.

Putnam, H. (1987), *The Many Faces of Realism* (La Salle, IL: Open Court).

Quine, W.V. (1969), 'Ontological relativity', in *Ontological Relativity and Other Essays*, ed. W.V. Quine (New York: Columbia University Press), pp. 26–68.

Schaffner, K. (1976), 'Reductionism in biology: Prospects and problems,' in *PSA 1974*, ed. R.S. Cohen *et al.* (Boston: D. Reidel Publishing Co.), pp. 613–32.

Scheibe, E. (1973), *The Logical Analysis of Quantum Mechanics* (Oxford: Pergamon).

Sewell, G. (2002), *Quantum Mechanics and Its Emergent Macrophysics* (Princeton: Princeton University Press).

Shapiro, L. (2006), 'Can psychology be a unified science?' *Philosophy of Science*, in press.

Slife, B. (2000), 'Are discourse communities incommensurable in a fragmented psychology?' *Journal of Mind and Behavior*, **21**, pp. 261–71.

Smith, E.E, and Medin, D.L. (1981), *Categories and Concepts* (Cambridge: Harvard University Press).

Sperry, R.W. (1969), 'A modified concept of consciousness', *Psychological Review*, **76**, pp. 532–6.

Staats, A.W. (1996), *Behavior and Psychology: Psychological Behaviorism* (New York: Plenum).

Staats, A.W. (1999), 'Uniting psychology requires new infrastructure, theory, method, and a research agenda', *Review of General Psychology*, **3**, pp. 3–13.

Stephan, A. (1999), *Emergenz* (Dresden: Dresden Univesity Press), Chap. 16.

Sternberg, R.J. and Grigorenko, E.L. (2001), 'Unified psychology', *American Psychologist*, **56**, pp. 1069–79.

Sternberg, R.J., Grigorenko, E.L. and Kalmar, D. (2001), 'The role of theory in unified psychology', *Theoretical and Philosophical Psychology*, **21**, pp. 99–117.

Takesaki, M. (1970), 'Disjointness of the KMS states of different temperatures,' *Communications in Mathematical Physics*, **17**, pp. 33–41.

Viney, W. (1989), 'The Cyclops and the Twelve-Eyed Toad: William James and the unity–disunity problem in psychology', *American Psychologist*, **44**, pp. 1261–5.

Wackermann, J. (1999), 'Towards a quantitative characterisation of functional states of the brain: From the non-linear methodology to the global linear description', *International Journal of Psychophysiology*, **34**, pp. 65–80.

Yanchar, S.C., and Slife, B.D. (1997), 'Pursuing unity in a fragmented psychology: Problems and prospects', *Review of General Psychology*, **1**, pp. 235–55.

Timothy L. Hubbard

# What is Mental Representation? And How Does It Relate to Consciousness?

*Abstract: The relationship between mental representation and consciousness is considered. What it means to 'represent', and several types of representation (e.g., analogue, digital, spatial, linguistic, mathematical), are described. Concepts relevant to mental representation in general (e.g., multiple levels of processing, structure/process differences, mapping) and in specific domains (e.g., mental imagery, linguistic/propositional theories, production systems, connectionism, dynamics) are discussed. Similarities (e.g., using distinctions between different forms of representation to predict different forms of consciousness, parallels between digital architectures of the brain and connectionist models) and dissociations (e.g., insensitivity to gaps in subjective experience, explicit memory/implicit memory, automatic processing/controlled processing, blindsight, neglect, prediction/ explanation) of mental representation and consciousness are discussed. It is concluded that representational systems are separable from consciousness systems, and that mental representation appears necessary but not sufficient for consciousness. Considerations for future research on correspondences between representation and consciousness are suggested.*

The concept of mental representation is fundamental to studies of consciousness. In the discussion here, the idea of what it means to 'represent' in a general sense will be considered, and criteria important in defining the nature of representation are discussed. Ideas regarding representation in general are then applied to the special case of mental representation, and several hypothesized forms of mental representation are described. Possible similarities and analogies, as well as possible dissociations, of mental representation and consciousness are mentioned, and speculation on the relationship between mental representation and consciousness is offered. The presentation is selective, but broad enough to provide an introduction to issues in mental representation and how mental representation relates to consciousness.

## I: What Is Representation?

The notion of 'representation' implies at least two separate but functionally related domains or worlds: a represented world and a representing world. The representation is an element within the representing world, and it reflects, stands for, or signifies some aspect of the represented world. In understanding a representational system, it is important to specify (a) which aspects of the represented world are being represented, (b) which aspects of the representing world instantiate or otherwise encode the representation, and (c) what are the correspondences between the represented world and representing world. The answers to these questions specify a *representational system*.

### The Represented and Representing Worlds

Palmer (1978) discussed the relationship between a represented world and a representing world, and a simplified example based on his discussion is shown in Figure 1. In Panel A is the represented world, a domain consisting of just four objects. There are many types of information regarding these objects that could be represented (e.g., size, shape, colour, density, history, chemical composition, location, age, or any other quality or dimension of the objects that could be categorized or measured), and for the purpose of this example, information about the heights of objects will be represented. There are a potentially unlimited number of representing worlds or forms of representation available, and three possible worlds for representing information about the heights of objects in Panel A are illustrated in Panels B, C, and D. The representing worlds in Panels B, C, and D each differ in the content of the representing world, in which aspects of each representing world is actually doing the representing, and in the correspondence between the represented information and the representing dimension.

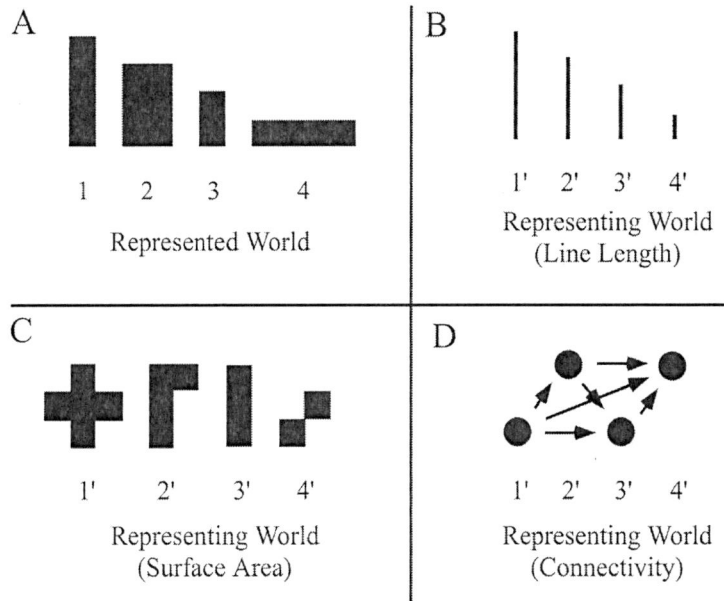

*Figure 1.* An illustration of the differences between the represented and three possible representing worlds. Panel A contains the represented world, and Panels B, C, and D illustrate three different representational systems for signifying the heights of objects in Panel A. Adapted from Palmer (1978).

In Panel B, heights of objects in the represented world are represented by line length, and greater heights in the represented world are signified by longer line lengths in the representing world. In Panel C, heights of objects in the represented world are represented by surface area, and increases in height are signified by increases in surface area. The representing objects are different shapes, but because shape is not specified in the correspondence between represented and representing worlds, shape is not relevant to the representation per se (i.e., shape is free to vary). Indeed, in many potential representing worlds, dimensions other than those involved in signifying the represented information are unconstrained or unspecified by correspondences between represented and representing worlds (i.e., are free to vary). In Panel D, heights of objects in the representing world are represented by the pattern of connectivity of the elements in the representing world, and differences in height are signified by the direction of the associations (linkages between objects point toward the shorter object).

Despite reliance on different representing dimensions and on different correspondences, Panels B, C, and D are informationally equivalent regarding heights of objects in Panel A. However, not all representations of a given type of information are equivalent in the ease of accessing or using that information (e.g., it is easier to visually retrieve height information regarding objects in Panel A from Panel B than from Panel C). Although there is no correlation between surface area (i.e., the representing dimension) and shape in Panel C, values of nonrepresenting dimensions can influence cognition of representing dimensions when significant correlations are present (e.g., Algom *et al.*, 1985; Garner, 1974; Shepard, 1991), and make a given representational system more or less easy or intuitive to use. In general, correspondences between the represented world and the representing world can be abstract and arbitrary, as long as those correspondences remain consistent within a given representational system. As a consequence, representation is not necessarily correlated with resemblance; indeed, the representations in Panels B, C, and D do not resemble the stimuli in Panel A.

## *Forms of Representation*

Several different forms of representation exist, and these different forms exhibit different properties. The form of representation most useful for a given type of information depends upon the nature of the information or the use to which that information will be put.

*Analogue Representation.* In analogue representation, there is a third potential data point between any two other data points, and the representation is relatively continuous. An example of this is a traditional clock; although the clock face is usually divided into 12 sections demarcated by the numbers 1 through 12, the space between any two points (e.g., between '1' and '2') is continuous and can be divided into an arbitrary number of smaller units. A traditional clock could in principle display an infinite number of times by dividing the continuous space of the clock face into increasingly smaller units. Older technologies of audio recording and reproduction used a form of analogue representation in which auditory information was represented by characteristics of a continuous groove cut into the surface of a vinyl album. Many measuring instruments utilize analogue representation (e.g., a thermometer in which the height of a column of mercury changes, a gauge in which weight or velocity is signified by the position of a needle on a dial).

*Digital Representation.* In digital representation, there is not necessarily a third potential data point between any two other data points, and the representation is composed of separate and discrete parts. An example of this is a digital clock, which can portray only a finite set of discrete times. Visual displays such as television screens and computer monitors are digital representations consisting of arrays of discrete pixel units. Although traditional painting involves analogue representation, pointillist painting involves digital representation. Similarly, the grain in a photographic print reflects digital representation. Newer auditory technology involving CDs and mp3s uses digital representation in which the amplitude of a continuous auditory waveform is measured at thousands of points per second, and those numerical values are electronically stored. When a recording is played, those numerical values specify the amplitude of the auditory waveform. Digital representation can be perceptually indistinguishable from analogue representation if the parts (e.g., pixels, grains, temporal intervals) are sufficiently small.

*Spatial Representation.* In spatial representation, location or orientation within an n-dimensional spatial coordinate system signifies the information being represented. An example of a spatial representation is a two-dimensional road map in which the relative positions of cities, roads, and other landmarks of a given area are the represented information. Space may be a treated as a continuous dimension as in analogue representation, but continuity is not essential for spatial representation (e.g., a grid system in which location is specified on the basis of the nearest line or intersection is a spatial representation that is non-analogue). A spatial map directly shows spatial configuration, but information regarding other quantities (e.g., the distance between any two specific locations) must be calculated by measuring map distance and adjusting for scale.

*Linguistic Representation.* In linguistic representation, information is mapped onto elements of language. Language is a useful representational form for a wide variety of information, and because connections between symbols used in language and the referents of those symbols are arbitrary, there are a potentially limitless number of written and spoken forms. However, even though language is more abstract and flexible than are many other representational systems, it is not always the optimal representational system for every purpose, as sometimes information might be more easily or efficiently encoded or retrieved using an analogue, spatial, or other form of representation (e.g., 'a picture is worth a thousand words'). Linguistic representation is similar to digital representation in that language consists of discrete units (e.g., letters, words), but language exhibits generativity that is not part of digital representation per se. Language can represent spatial information (e.g., 'the table is to the right of the chair'), but linguistic representation is always digital, whereas spatial representation can be digital or analogue.

*Mathematical Representation*. In mathematical representation, quantities are mapped onto specific (sets of) objects. An example of this is RGB color specification in which each hue is uniquely represented by a set of three numbers that reflect the percentage of red, green, or blue within that hue. Mathematical representation can involve one-to-one mapping of objects to quantities or involve many-to-one mapping of a large mass of data (information) to a single equation or set of equations. Locations along a line can be represented by the equation of that line, and in this, mathematical representation combines elements of spatial representation and digital representation. The ultimate mathematical (and digital) representation is binary coding, in which any instruction can be coded as a sequence of 0s and 1s. Indeed, a universal Turing machine capable of emulating any other computational device can in principle be programmed using only a long string of 0s and 1s. The firing of a given neuron is all-or-nothing, and so could be coded as 0 (not firing) or 1 (firing; cf. McCulloch & Pitts, 1965); thus, a given pattern of neural activity could also be coded as a long string of 0s and 1s.

## II: Mental Representation

If ideas about representation discussed in Part I are considered within the context of cognition, then the represented world is the external, perceived, lived-in physical environment, and the representing world is information regarding the represented world encoded within a cognitive system. Mental representation thus involves representation within a cognitive system. Several technical overviews of mental representation are available (e.g., Clapin, 2002; Fodor, 1985; Sigel, 1999; Stich & Warfield, 1995), and Part II provides a less technical introduction to selected issues in mental representation.

### *Critical Concepts*

Theorizing regarding mental representation has occurred within an information-processing perspective, and this perspective emphasizes the existence of multiple levels of representation, differences between structures and processing, and mapping.

*Multiple Levels of Representation.* Almost every theory and model in psychology and cognitive science posits multiple levels of representation. There are structures at each level, and properties of these structures vary from level to level. The most well-known example of a cognitive model that involves multiple levels of representation is the Atkinson-Shiffrin (1968) model of memory involving sensory memory, short term (working) memory, and long term memory. Other examples include Rosch *et al.*'s (1976) levels of subordinate, basic, and superordinate categorization, Marr's (1982) levels of primal sketch, 2½ D sketch, and 3 D representation in visual processing, and Treisman and Gelade's (1980) levels of preattentive processes and focused attention in feature integration. In each of these cases, there are different structures at each level, and representations at different levels exhibit different properties.[1]

*Structures and Processes.* 'Structures' involve parts of the representation, and 'processes' involve what is done to the information within a structure, how that information is used, and how that information is moved from structure to structure. Different levels of processing usually contain different structures and different processes, and there are different processes for moving information between different sets of structures. Earlier information-processing models drew sharp distinctions between structures and processes, but in more recent models distinctions between structures and processes are not as clear (e.g., working memory might correspond to that part of long-term memory that is most activated, Cantor & Engle, 1992). In connectionist approaches, distinctions between structure and process are blurred even more. Nonetheless, the distinction is useful, in part because different brain imaging techniques emphasize either structure (e.g., MRI, CT) or process (e.g., fMRI, PET) information.

*Mapping.* Mapping involves a connection between two structures. When information at one level of representation or in one structure is passed on to or influences information at another level of representation or in another structure, the information at the first level or structure is said to be mapped onto the information at the second level or

---

[1] A slightly different notion involves so-called 'levels of processing' or 'depth of processing' (e.g., Craik & Lockhart, 1972; Craik & Tulving, 1975), but in this case, it is not clear that so-called deeper processing actually involves changes in the structures involved, but may rather involve a different type of processing within the same structure.

structure. An example of this occurs in the visual system, in which a retinotopic map of the activation pattern in the retina is preserved in the activation patterns in the lateral geniculate nucleus and in primary visual cortex. This mapping of information from one set of structures to a second set of structures can be seen in neural network or connectionist approaches in which input units map onto internal (hidden) units which in turn map onto output units. Mapping can involve feedforward or feedback connections, and can involve one-to-one, one-to-many, or many-to-one patterns of connectivity.

*Forms of Mental Representation*

Different cognitive theories and models postulate different forms of mental representation, and correspondences between the represented external physical world and the representing cognitive domain are different in different theories and models.

*Mental Imagery.* The form of mental representation underlying the experience of mental imagery has been extensively debated. Kosslyn (1980; 1981) and Shepard and Cooper (1982) suggested properties of mental imagery reflected analogue representation, and Paivio (1986) argued for the existence of separate image-based and verbal-based forms of encoding. However, Pylyshyn (1981; 1984) suggested apparent properties of imagery reflected demand characteristics, tacit knowledge, experimenter effects, and did not reflect properties of analogue representation per se, and that there was no reason to posit a separate form of analogue representation to explain data on mental imagery. Unfortunately, this debate is muddled by 'analogue' being used in two distinct ways: in the sense mentioned earlier to suggest the presence of intermediate values (e.g., Cooper & Shepard, 1973), but more commonly, in the sense of 'analogous' to suggest that the image resembles (in a functional sense) that which it represents (e.g., Kosslyn, 1980; Shepard, 1975). The latter usage represents a strong theoretical claim, as the notion of representation does not require a representation to resemble that which it represents.

In addition to considering whether imagery involves analogue representation, investigators have considered whether mental representation involved in imagery is similar to mental representation involved in perception. Experiments that demonstrate similar patterns of responses to imaged stimuli and to perceived stimuli (e.g., Farah, 1985; Finke & Kurtzman, 1981; Finke & Schmidt, 1977; Hubbard & Stoeckig, 1988; Shepard & Podgorny, 1978), that imagery and perception within the same modality interfere with each other more than do imagery and perception in different modalities (e.g., Brooks, 1968, Segal & Fusella, 1970), and that imaged stimuli activate the same areas of the brain as do perceived stimuli (e.g., Farah, 1988; Kosslyn *et al.*, 1993; Zatorre *et al.*, 1996) are consistent with claims that mental representations underlying imagery and perception are similar. Finke (1980) suggested that mental representations underlying imagery and perception were equivalent at multiple levels of processing (see also Finke, 1989; Finke & Shepard, 1986).

*Linguistic/Propositional.* There are many theories and models in psychology and cognitive science in which linguistic or propositional representation is used. In early hierarchical models of long-term memory, information was stored locally and at the most general level possible (e.g., Collins & Quillian, 1969). In later spreading activation (e.g., Collins & Loftus, 1975) or propositional (e.g., Anderson, 1983) network models, the configuration of nodes and the lengths of the linkages reflected the association strength between concepts. In such models, semantic memory was usually the focus. The prevalence of linguistic and propositional representation within models and theories might suggest that language influences or shapes mental representation of semantic information; although a strong version of the Sapir-Whorf notion that language constrains thought overstates the case, it might be that certain distinctions are more easily perceived or remembered if appropriate verbal categories are available. Along these lines, Fodor (1975) proposed a 'language of thought' that contained the same fundamental categories as language and served as a framework or scaffolding for language.

*Production Systems.* A production system (also referred to as *procedural memory*) is similar to a linguistic or propositional representation, but is sufficiently different to be considered a distinct type of representational system. Although information within production systems might appear linguistic or propositional, the organization of such information is different from the organization typically seen in hierarchical or network models. Production systems exhibit an 'if-then' conditional structure. If information in the 'if' portion of the production system matches the current content of working memory, then information in the 'then' part of the production system is activated or executed. Production systems are typically discussed in regard to the representation of motor skills, but there is no principled reason why the range of possible actions and outputs represented by or instantiated in production systems could not be expanded. Examples of cognitive models and theories containing production systems include ACT* (Anderson, 1983) and SOAR (Newell, 1990).

*Connectionism.* Connectionist models (also referred to as *neural networks* and as *parallel distributed processing models*) describe the 'subsymbolic level' (Smolensky, 1988; 1989) and 'microstructure' of cognition (Rumelhart & McClelland, 1986). A connectionist network is made up of nodes and of linkages between those nodes. Unlike spreading activation or propositional network models in which linkages specify the type of association, in connectionist models linkages specify the strength (weight) of the association. Rather than storing information locally at a single node as in traditional symbol-manipulation models, information is instead distributed across large numbers of nodes and 'recreated' in the patterns of activation that occur in response to a stimulus (for overviews, Anderson, 1995; Bechtel & Abramson, 1991; Rumelhart & McClelland, 1986). Connectionism has been hailed by some as inaugurating a paradigm shift within psychology (e.g., Schneider, 1987), whereas others suggest connectionism involves the same functional assumptions as traditional symbol-manipulation approaches (e.g., Dawson, 1998). Regardless, such networks exhibit useful properties including spontaneous generalization, graceful degradation, and the absence of an executive.

Some theorists have suggested connectionist models are more biologically inspired or biologically consistent than are traditional symbol-manipulation models. Upon first glance, a node might seem analogous to a neuron, and a connection analogous to a synapse (e.g., Feldman & Ballard, 1982), but most investigators adopt a larger view in which a node could represent a neuron, ganglia, module, lobe, or other functional unit of any size. In this sense, both the brain and connectionist models are digital representational systems composed of numerous discrete units. Interestingly, Smolensky (1988; 1989) suggests variables (regarding the activation of a given node and the connection strength between nodes) at the subsymbolic level described by connectionism are essentially dynamic and continuous, and so connectionist approaches might embody elements of dynamic and analogue representation despite a digital architecture. However, there are also significant differences between the architecture and functioning of many connectionist models and the architecture and functioning of the brain (e.g., the brain does not exhibit connectivity consistent with major learning rules used in connectionist modelling, Crick & Asanuma, 1986; Douglas & Martin, 1991; Smolensky, 1988).

*Dynamics.* Traditional information-processing approaches considered mental representations to be relatively static entities operated upon by various processes or mapped onto various structures. A more recent view is that mental representations are dynamic entities; indeed, Giunti (1995) suggested that all cognitive systems are dynamical systems. In one sense, this is trivially true, as it has long been known that mental representation exhibits changes over time (e.g., Bartlett, 1932; Carmichael *et al.*, 1932), and although not typically characterized in such terms, high-level schemata, scripts, and frames that bias encoding, storage, and retrieval might all be thought of as reflecting dynamic aspects of mental representation (see also Kelso, 1995; Port & van Gelder, 1995; Thelen & Smith, 1995). Freyd (1987) suggested mental representation was dynamic because it exhibited spatiotemporal coherence, that is, it represented temporal information (i.e., change) intrinsically and necessarily. An example of this dynamic nature occurs in representational momentum, a bias in remembered location in which the remembered position of a target is displaced along the anticipated path of motion (for review, Hubbard, 2005). As a consequence of its dynamic nature, a mental representation is more similar to a process than to an array.

## III: Similarities of Mental Representation and Consciousness

Part I discussed relationships between a represented world and a representing world, and Part II discussed how those ideas could be applied to cognition. Part III discusses how ideas regarding relationships between a represented world and representing world can be applied to consciousness. Barring a mystical 'pure' or 'objectless' consciousness, we can reason by analogy and ask (a) which aspects of the represented world are conscious, (b) which aspects of the representing world are conscious, and (c) what is the correspondence between the represented world and what is conscious. The answers to these questions specify a *consciousness system*.

### *The Conscious World and the Representing World*

'Consciousness' has been defined or described in numerous ways (for overviews, see Blackmore, 2004; Farthing, 1992; Wallace & Fisher, 1999), but is still often treated as a relatively homogenous or monolithic phenomenon. It is possible that a consideration of distinctions within mental representation could suggest analogous distinctions within consciousness. Indeed, moving from a homogenous or monolithic conception of consciousness to distinctions of different levels of consciousness or distinctions between structures and processes within a consciousness system would parallel developments in mental representation (e.g., moving from an undifferentiated short-term memory to a more detailed working memory composed of an executive, visuo-spatial scratchpad, and articulatory rehearsal loop, Baddeley, 1986). Additionally, greater knowledge of levels, structures, or processes of consciousness, as well as greater understanding of mappings between representational systems and consciousness systems, might address subjective aspects of cognitive activity typically not addressed within theories or models in psychology and cognitive science (e.g., qualia, Hubbard, 1996).

In a representational system, it is clear that only a portion of the elements in the represented world are specified within the representation. Similarly, and barring some type of panpsychism, it seems clear that in a typical consciousness system only a portion of the elements in the represented world would be conscious. In a representational system, there are potentially many different aspects of the representing world that might be involved in instantiating the representation, and many potential correspondences between the represented and representing worlds (e.g., analogue representation might involve very different correspondences than would digital representation). However, in a consciousness system, which aspects of the representing world would be conscious, and the correspondences between the represented and representing worlds and what is conscious, is not widely agreed upon (although there have been numerous suggestions, e.g., re-entry and the dynamic core, Edelman & Tononi, 2000; temporal binding and 40 Hz oscillations, Crick & Koch, 1990; thalamocortical feedback loops, Damasio, 1999).

## Forms of Consciousness

Could consciousness correspond to a specific aspect of the representing world that was conscious or responsible for consciousness (e.g. a structural theory), or to an aspect of the correspondence between the represented and the representing world (e.g., a functional or process theory)? Panels A, B, C, and D in Figure 1 showed different correspondences between a represented world and different representing worlds. If consciousness reflects a correspondence between the represented world and the representing world, then the possibility of different correspondences suggests the possibility of different forms of consciousness. This would be consistent with the notion that consciousness is a functional property related to the processes of representation (e.g., perhaps related to the mapping of information rather than to the structure that information is mapped onto). Alternatively, consciousness might reflect some aspect of the representing world not necessarily correlated with the specific correspondence between the represented and the representing worlds. This would be consistent with the notion that consciousness is a structural aspect of the representational system (and perhaps a basic or nonreducible property, cf. Chalmers, 1996).

Just as there might be different forms of mental representation underlying different cognitive activities (e.g., analogue representation for mental imagery, propositional representations for semantic material, production systems for motor skills), so too might there be different types or levels of consciousness in different domains of cognitive activity. Indeed, if we accept a multiplicity of representational systems for different types of mental content, and if consciousness arises from (or is otherwise linked to) mental representation, then there might be a multiplicity of consciousness systems. Although it is possible that different forms of mental representation give rise to different forms of consciousness that are phenomenologically equivalent, it is possible that closer examination might reveal different forms of consciousness that are not phenomenologically equivalent. Alternatively, there might be just one type of mental representation and just one type of consciousness, but each of those types can hold a variety of contents, and thus yield the appearance of multiple types of representation and multiple types of consciousness.

## *Of Neurons and Nodes*

The structure of the brain suggests mental representation involves a digital representational system because the brain is constructed of a very large number of separate and discrete units (neurons). Furthermore, the all-or-nothing firing that characterizes normal functioning of individual neurons is a digital process, because an intermediate state between firing and not firing does not exist. However, a considerable literature within psychology and cognitive science suggests mental representation might involve other forms of representation, and so a nervous system built upon digital architecture might nonetheless be able to represent dynamic or analogue information. Similarly, a connectionist architecture is based on digital representation, but as noted earlier, might be able to represent dynamic and analogue information. The idea that a nervous system consisting of discrete neurons that are vastly interconnected, and that a connectionist network consisting of discrete nodes that are vastly interconnected, can both instantiate multiple forms of representation is suggestive. Such an architecture might offer the greatest flexibility for mental representation, and also allow the possibility of multiple forms of mental representation and conscious experience.

A consideration of parallels between the distributed architecture of the brain and the distributed architecture of a connectionist network, coupled with the absence of a clear executive in the architecture of connectionism, reveals a key point: there is no single place in the brain or in a connectionist network where 'everything comes together' and no central executive to receive the final output of that system's processing (Dennett [1991] argued that looking for a place where 'everything comes together' to be presented to consciousness reflects vestiges of Cartesian dualism, and he referred to such a place as the *Cartesian theater*). Two other properties of the distributed architecture of a connectionist network also converge with properties of the brain: spontaneous generalization (i.e., applying a response to a related stimulus) and graceful degradation (i.e., the ability to produce a correct response given degraded input). The convergence of architectures and properties suggests the existence of consciousness is consistent with a connectionist (or perhaps digital/mathematical) mental representation. Even so, the convergence is not complete (e.g., as noted earlier, there are incompatibilities of the learning rules commonly used in connectionist systems with brain architecture).

Despite the partial convergence of the architecture and properties of connectionist systems with the architecture and properties of the brain, many theories and models in psychology and cognitive science have not explicitly included or addressed consciousness. Such theories and models sometimes explicitly omit consciousness and see how much progress can be made without requiring any appeal to consciousness. Indeed, some theorists explicitly separate the 'computational mind' from the 'phenomenological mind' (e.g., Jackendoff, 1987). In one view, this amounts to leaving the 'hard problem' (i.e., why processes in the brain are accompanied by subjective experience, Chalmers, 1995, 1996) for later. Even so, many earlier theories and models implicitly included consciousness in the form of a homunculus-like executive or decision process. The hope was that further work would eventually replace a single homunculus-like executive with numerous simpler structures (i.e., would 'discharge the homunculus') until ultimately all that was left was a myriad of binary units (e.g., neurons) whose sum of activity resulted in the cognitive process in question.

## IV: Dissociations of Mental Representation and Consciousness

Part III discussed possible analogies and convergences between mental representation and consciousness, and these are consistent with the notion the representing world and conscious world were highly similar or even identical. However, the presence of mental representation does not guarantee the presence of consciousness, and there are a number of findings and considerations discussed in Part IV that suggest the representing world and conscious world are separable and can be dissociated.

### Continuous Experience, Discrete Structure

Even though the structure of our nervous system is relatively digital and discrete, our waking conscious experience seems relatively analogue and continuous. One aspect of the apparent continuity of conscious experience is an insensitivity to gaps or changes in our subjective experience of the environment. One well-known example involves the failure to notice the blind spot in the visual field that results from the lack of photoreceptors at the optic disk. Other examples include failing to notice differences between successive stimuli in change blindness (Simons, 2000; Simons & Ambinder, 2005) or inattentional blindness (e.g., Mack, 2003; Mack & Rock, 1998). In change blindness or inattentional blindness, consciousness fixes a certain portion of a scene (corresponding to the representing dimension), and other elements of the scene are left free to vary. This is consistent with the earlier observation that dimensions not specified by the correspondence between the represented and representing world were unconstrained. Also, such lack of constraint could contribute to a sense of a continuously existing self (but see Dennett, 1991) and illusory conjunctions (e.g., Treisman, 1986).

### Evidence From the Laboratory

Dissociations between mental representation and consciousness have been observed in numerous laboratory investigations. A listing of several dichotomies in which one member of a pair is accompanied by consciousness and the other member of that pair is not accompanied by consciousness is given in Table 1. Two of the more common dichotomies, explicit memory vs. implicit memory, and automatic processing vs. controlled processing, are briefly discussed.

| Associated with Consciousness | Associated with a Lack of Consciousness |
|---|---|
| Explicit Memory | Implicit Memory |
| Controlled Processing | Automatic Processing |
| Working Memory | Long-Term Memory |
| Attended Stimuli | Unattended Stimuli |
| Declarative Memory | Procedural Memory |
| Supraliminal Perception | Subliminal Perception |
| Strategic Control | Automatic Control |
| Autonoetic Memory | Noetic Memory |

*Table 1.* Pairs of Cognitive Processes in which One Process is Accompanied by Consciousness[2]

*Explicit Memory vs. Implicit Memory.* Information that a person knows, and that the person is consciously aware that he or she knows, is referred to as *explicit memory*. In other words, with explicit memory, the person has conscious awareness of possessing that information and of having been exposed to that information. A different type of memory involves information that a person has been exposed to and that influences his or her subsequent behaviour, but for which the person does not have a conscious awareness of possessing that information or of having being exposed to that information. This latter type of memory is referred to as *implicit memory* (e.g., Graf & Masson, 1993; Kirsner *et al.*, 1998; McBride, 2007).[3] An example of this occurs when observers do not explicitly remember having been previously exposed to a stimulus, but that previous exposure nonetheless results in a priming of the response to any subsequent exposure to that stimulus. Although most commonly applied to memory, the explicit/implicit distinction has also been applied to perception (e.g., Merikle & Daneman, 1998; Merikle *et al.*, 2001) and learning (e.g., Reber, 1993; Stadler & Frensch, 1997).

*Automatic Processing vs. Controlled Processing.* The presence of consciousness is often a criterion for whether a given process is considered to reflect automatic processing or controlled processing (for

---

[2] Based on Table 5.1 in Solso *et al.* (2005).

[3] There is debate whether the terms 'implicit' and 'explicit' actually refer to two types of memory or two types of tasks, but for purposes here, the resolution of that debate is not critical. What is more critical for the current purpose is that tasks characterized as explicit usually involve conscious awareness of the stimulus, whereas tasks characterized as implicit usually do not involve awareness of the stimuli.

review, Moors & De Houwer, 2006). For example, Posner and Snyder (1975) suggested an automatic process (a) occurs without conscious or deliberate intention, (b) is not open to conscious awareness and introspection, and (c) consumes few conscious resources (e.g., does not use attention). In contrast, a controlled process (a) occurs only with conscious or deliberate intention, (b) is open to conscious awareness and introspection, and (c) consumes conscious resources (e.g., uses attention). Many tasks that initially involve controlled processing can with practice come to involve automatic processing (e.g., LaBerge & Samuels, 1974; Schneider & Shiffrin, 1977; Shiffrin & Schneider, 1977). Research on learning and automatization of skills involves proceduralization of information and actions, and this suggests that production systems involve predominantly nonconscious processing. Along these lines, one possible purpose for consciousness might be to facilitate learning of a new response when an automatic procedure is not available or is no longer appropriate.

*Evidence From The Clinic*

Dissociations between conscious awareness and mental representation resulting from psychopathology have also been observed. Two of the most well-known, blindsight and neglect, are briefly discussed.

*Blindsight.* Damage to V1 in the occipital cortex can result in apparent functional blindness, even though the physical eye is intact. The blindness is for stimuli in whichever region of the visual field would have been processed by the damaged cortex. Some patients nonetheless exhibit sensitivity to visual information in the blind area, and that visual information can influence their responding even though they have no conscious awareness of that visual information. The apparent sensitivity to perceptual information, coupled with the lack of any conscious awareness of that information, is referred to as *blindsight* (for overviews, see Stoerig & Cowey, 1997; Weiskrantz, 1986; 1997). For example, if a horizontal or vertical line is presented within the area of the functional blindness, patients claim to not have visual awareness of the line. However, if patients are asked to guess the orientation of the line, some of them can 'guess' at a level significantly above chance. Other featural information such as colour, position, and shape can also be 'guessed' at an above chance level, and blindsight patients can direct their eyes to locations of objects in the blind field. The existence of blindsight suggests that at least some visual information can be processed in the absence of consciousness.

*Neglect.* Damage to the right parietal lobe results in neglect or nonresponsiveness to stimuli in the left visual field, and this has been referred to as *neglect* (for overview, see Bisiach, 1992).[4] Even though a patient might not have conscious access to information in the neglected field, such information can influence that patient's behaviour. In one example, patients were shown a drawing of two houses that were vertically aligned (Marshall & Halligan, 1988). The houses were identical, except that one was depicted with flames coming out of the left side. Patients did not seem to be aware of the depiction of flames, and they judged the houses to be the same. However, when asked which house they might prefer to live in, patients repeatedly picked the house without the flames. Patients appeared to process the presence of the flames, but they weren't consciously aware of that information. Neglect might reflect a disorder of attention (and consciousness) rather than a disorder of perception, as neglect patients bisect a line in their non-neglected visual field as if they neglected a portion of the line (Schenkenberg *et al.*, 1980) and continue to neglect a stimulus that moves from their neglected visual field into their non-neglected visual field (Behrmann & Tipper, 1994).

## *Top-Down and Bottom-Up Approaches*

A top-down method to examine potential dissociations of consciousness and mental representation would involve taking an organism that normally exhibits consciousness, removing consciousness, and then observing effects of that removal. This idea has given rise to a commonly discussed thought experiment: give blindsight patients practice in discrimination and feedback concerning the accuracy of their 'guessing'. Could such patients improve enough so that their performance would be indistinguishable from that of a normally sighted person? A person without normal conscious experience, but who could make the same behavioural responses (e.g., perceptual discriminations) as a person with normal conscious experience, has been called a *zombie* (e.g., Moody, 1994; Sutherland, 1995). The cognitive activities of a zombie could potentially be modelled using any of the forms of mental representation described earlier, and the responses of a zombie would in principle be indistinguishable (e.g., in the Turing test) from the responses of a person who possessed normal conscious experience. Such possibilities raise significant questions regarding the role and purpose of consciousness (e.g., see Holt, 1999).

---

[4] Damage to the left parietal lobe can result in neglect or nonresponsiveness to stimuli in the right visual field, but such cases are fewer and less clear (Odgen, 1987).

A bottom-up method to examine potential dissociations of consciousness and mental representation would involve adding consciousness to an organism that previously did not possess consciousness, and then observing effects of that addition. Toward this end, theorists have considered the related idea of building an artificially conscious system (i.e., constructing a device that instantiates a given representational system, and examining whether that device exhibits consciousness). Although artificially constructed devices such as conscious robots or androids have been staples of science fiction for years (e.g., Commander Data, C3PO, Robby the Robot), such devices have not yet been produced. Proponents of artificial intelligence suggest the technology is not yet sufficiently developed, but that production of such devices will eventually be possible (e.g., Kurzweil, 1999), whereas skeptics suggest such possibilities are impossible in principle regardless of how technology develops (e.g., Dreyfus, 1979; Searle, 1992). Interestingly, the computer was an important tool and metaphor in the development of cognitive science, and might become an important test case for a developing science of consciousness (e.g., see Holland & Goodman, 2003; Prinz, 2003).

*Prediction vs. Explanation*

Although knowledge of information encoded within the representation is sometimes sufficient for prediction, it is not sufficient for explanation. For example, if traffic behaviour is being predicted, it wouldn't matter if one person experienced the top light in a standard traffic light configuration as closer to magenta and another person experienced that light as closer to burgundy; both persons would stop their vehicles because they had learned to associate illumination of the upper light as a cue to stop. However, if an explanation or understanding of behaviour is the goal, then it is often necessary to appeal to subjective experience. For example, drive reduction theories refer to the internal subjective experience of the organism (e.g., hunger, thirst), and an appeal to subjective (conscious) experience is necessary in order to avoid circularity in explaining why a given stimulus can function as a reinforcer. The possibility that different subjective experiences could result in the same verbal or behavioural response, and the possibility that explanation and even some types of prediction require information regarding subjective experience, demonstrates the usefulness of a role for conscious experience in theories of mental representation (see also Hubbard, 1996).

## V: Conclusions

There has been considerable theoretical development involving the notion of representation, and it is possible that what is known about representation and systems of representation could provide insight regarding consciousness and systems of consciousness. Just as a system of representation should specify which aspects of the represented world are represented, which aspects of the representing world instantiate the representation, and the correspondences between the represented and representing worlds, so too a system of consciousness should specify which aspects of the represented world are conscious, which aspects of the representing world instantiate consciousness, and the correspondences between the represented world and consciousness. Furthermore, the success of theories of mental representation that emphasize multiple levels of representation, distinctions between structures and processes, and mapping suggest similar emphases in theories of consciousness could be very useful. Such a representational approach to consciousness could clearly further the integration of cognitive science and consciousness studies, and could provide further insight into consciousness and consciousness systems, as well as further insight into cognition.

It is likely that only a portion of the represented world is actually represented or is actually conscious. A consideration of what aspects of the representing world instantiate a representation reveals several possibilities (e.g., functional resemblances in imagery, patterns of connectivity across multiple units). Widening this to consider which aspects of the representing world are conscious is more difficult, as there is clear evidence that significant cognitive processing occurs preattentively or in the absence of consciousness. Furthermore, even when consciousness occurs, it does not necessarily reflect ongoing cognitive processing (i.e., does not accurately reflect current mental representation). As far as is known, consciousness does not occur in the absence of mental representation, although the presence of mental representation does not guarantee the presence of consciousness. Thus, mental representation of some sort appears necessary but not sufficient for consciousness. Consistent with suggestions by Baars (1988), contrastive analyses of mental representation of when one cognitive activity is accompanied by consciousness and a second cognitive activity is not accompanied by consciousness (e.g., as in Table 1) holds particular promise for increasing understanding of consciousness.

Laboratory data and clinical findings suggest mental representation is separable from consciousness. Which correspondences between the represented world and the conscious world are critical for consciousness? When correspondences between the represented world and the representing world are considered, a large number of correspondences can be observed (e.g., connection weights in network models, second-order isomorphism in imagery). An analogue or spatial representation would certainly exhibit different correspondences than would a digital or propositional representation, but how would these different correspondences impact consciousness? When correspondences between the representing world and the conscious world are considered, consciousness appears very limited, and conscious experience of only a small percentage of the elements in the represented world occurs. It isn't clear what elements of a representation result in consciousness, or even if representation must occur within an explicitly cognitive (i.e., information-processing) system in order to exhibit or achieve consciousness. If 'consciousness is a word worn smooth by a million tongues' (Miller, 1962), the road between mental representation and consciousness remains a rough and rocky trail.[5]

## References

Algom, D., Wolf, Y. & Bergman, B. (1985), 'Integration of stimulus dimensions in perception and memory: Composition rules and psychophysical relations', *Journal of Experimental Psychology: General*, **114**, pp. 451–71.

Anderson, J.A. (1995), *An Introduction to Neural Networks* (Cambridge, MA: MIT Press).

Anderson, J.R. (1983), *The Architecture of Cognition* (Cambridge, MA: Harvard University Press).

Atkinson, R.C. & Shiffrin, R.M. (1968), 'Human memory: A proposed system and its control processes', in *The Psychology of Learning and Motivation, vol. 2, Advances in Research and Theory*, ed. K.W. Spence & J.T. Spence (New York: Academic Press).

Baars, B.J. (1988), *A Cognitive Theory of Consciousness* (New York: Cambridge University Press).

Baddeley, A.D. (1986), *Working Memory* (Oxford: Clarendon Press).

Bartlett, F.C. (1932), *Remembering: A Study in Experimental and Social Psychology* (Cambridge: Cambridge University Press).

Bechtel, W. & Abramson, A. (1991), *Connectionism and the Mind: An Introduction to Parallel Processing in Networks* (Cambridge, MA: Blackwell).

Behrmann, M. & Tipper, S.P. (1994), 'Object-based attentional mechanisms: Evidence from patients with unilateral neglect', in *Attention and Performance XV: Conscious and Nonconscious Information Processing*, ed. C. Umilta & M. Moscovitch (Cambridge, MA: MIT Press).

---

[5] The author thanks Jon Courtney, Mike Czuchry, Scott Jordan, Dawn McBride, Keiko Stoeckig, and two anonymous reviewers for helpful comments on a previous draft of the manuscript.

Bisiach, E. (1992), 'Understanding consciousness: Clues form unilateral neglect and related disorders', in *The Neuropsychology of Consciousness*, ed. A.D. Milner & M.D. Rugg (London: Academic Press).

Blackmore, S. (2004), *Consciousness: An Introduction* (New York: OUP).

Brooks, L. (1968), 'Spatial and verbal components of the act of recall', *Canadian Journal of Psychology*, **22**, pp. 349–68.

Cantor, J. & Engle, R.W. (1992), 'Working memory capacity as long-term memory activation', *Journal of Experimental Psychology: Learning, Memory, and Cognition*, **19**, pp. 1101–14.

Carmichael, L.C., Hogan, H.P. & Walters, A.A. (1932), 'An experimental study of the effect of language on the reproduction of visually perceived form', *Journal of Experimental Psychology*, **15**, pp. 73–86.

Chalmers, D.J. (1995), 'Facing up to the problem of consciousness', *Journal of Consciousness Studies*, **2** (3), pp. 200–19.

Chalmers, D.J. (1996), *The Conscious Mind: In Search of a Fundamental Theory* (New York: Oxford University Press).

Clapin, H. (ed. 2002), *Philosophy of Mental Representation* (New York: OUP).

Collins, A.M. & Loftus, E.F. (1975), 'A spreading activation theory of semantic processing', *Psychological Review*, **82**, pp. 407–28.

Collins, A.M. & Quillian, M.R. (1969), 'Retrieval time from semantic memory', *Journal of Verbal Learning and Verbal Behavior*, **8**, pp. 240–7.

Cooper, L.A. & Shepard, R.N. (1973), 'Chronometric studies of the rotation of mental images', in *Visual Information Processing*, ed. W.G. Chase (New York: Academic Press).

Craik, F.I.M. & Lockhart, R.S. (1972), 'Levels of processing: A framework for memory research', *Journal of Verbal Learning and Verbal Behavior*, **11**, pp. 671–84.

Craik, F.I.M. & Tulving, E. (1975), 'Depth of processing and the retention of words in episodic memory', *Journal of Experimental Psychology: General*, **104**, pp. 268–94.

Crick, F. & Asanuma, C. (1986), 'Certain aspects of the anatomy and physiology of the cerebral cortex', in *Parallel Distributed Processing, vol. 2*, ed. J. McClelland & D. Rumelhart (Cambridge, MA: MIT Press).

Crick, F. & Koch, C. (1990), 'Towards a neurobiological theory of consciousness', *Seminars in the Neurosciences*, **2**, pp. 263–75.

Damasio, A. (1999), *The Feeling of What Happens: Body and Emotion in the Making of Consciousness* (New York: Harcourt).

Dawson, M.R.W. (1998), *Understanding Cognitive Science* (Malden, MA: Blackwell).

Dennett, D.C. (1991), *Consciousness Explained* (Boston, MA: Little, Brown).

Douglas, R.J. & Martin, K.A.C. (1991), 'Opening the grey box', *Trends in Neurosciences*, **14**, pp. 286–93.

Dreyfus, H.L. (1979), *What Computers Still Can't Do* (Cambridge, MA: MIT Press).

Edelman, G.M & Tononi, G. (2000), *Consciousness: How Matter Becomes Imagination* (New York: Basic Books).

Farah, M.J., (1985), 'Psychophysical evidence for a shared representational medium for mental image and percepts', *Journal of Experimental Psychology: General*, **114**, pp. 91–103.

Farah, M.J. (1988), 'Is visual imagery really visual? Overlooked evidence from neuropsychology', *Psychological Review*, **95**, pp. 307–17.

Farthing, G.W. (1992), *The Psychology of Consciousness* (Englewood Cliffs, NJ: Prentice-Hall).

Feldman, J.A. & Ballard, D.H. (1982), 'Connectionist models and their properties', *Cognitive Science*, **6**, pp. 205–54.

Finke, R.A. (1980), 'Levels of equivalence in imagery and perception', *Psychological Review*, **87**, pp. 113–32.
Finke, R.A. (1989), *Principles of Mental Imagery* (Cambridge, MA: MIT Press).
Finke, R.A. & Kurtzman, H.S. (1981), 'Mapping the visual field in mental imagery', *Journal of Experimental Psychology: General*, **110**, pp. 501–17.
Finke, R.A., & Schmidt, M.J. (1977), 'Orientation-specific color aftereffects following imagination', *Journal of Experimental Psychology: Human Perception and Performance*, **3**, pp. 599–606.
Finke, R.A., & Shepard, R.N. (1986), 'Visual functions of mental imagery', in *Handbook of Perception and Human Performance. Vol. 2: Cognitive processes and performance*, ed. K.R. Boff, L. Kaufman, & J.P. Thomas (New York: Wiley).
Fodor, J. (1975), *The Language of Thought* (New York: Thomas Y. Crowell).
Fodor, J. (1985), 'Fodor's guide to mental representation: The intelligent Auntie's vade-mecum', *Mind*, **94**, pp. 76–100.
Freyd, J.J. (1987), 'Dynamic mental representations', *Psychological Review*, **94**, pp. 427–38.
Garner, W.R. (1974), *The Processing of Information and Structure* (Potomac, MD: Erlbaum).
Giunti, M. (1995), 'Dynamical models of cognition', in *Mind as motion*, ed. R.F. Port & T. van Gelder (Cambridge, MA: MIT Press).
Graf, P. & Masson, M.E.J. (ed. 1993), *Implicit Memory: New Directions in Cognition. Development, and Neuropsychology* (Hillsdale, NJ: Erlbaum).
Holland, O. & Goodman, R. (2003), 'Robots with internal models: A route to machine consciousness?', *Journal of Consciousness Studies*, **10** (4–5), pp. 77–109.
Holt, J. (1999), 'Blindsight in debates about qualia', *Journal of Consciousness Studies*, **6** (5), pp. 54–71.
Hubbard, T.L. (1996), 'The importance of a consideration of qualia to imagery and cognition', *Consciousness and Cognition*, **5**, pp. 327–58.
Hubbard, T.L. (2005), 'Representational momentum and related displacements in spatial memory: A review of the findings', *Psychonomic Bulletin & Review*, **12**, pp. 822–51.
Hubbard, T.L. & Stoeckig, K. (1988), 'Musical imagery: Generation of tones and chords', *Journal of Experimental Psychology: Learning, Memory, and Cognition*, **14**, pp. 656–67.
Jackendoff, R. (1987), *Consciousness and the Computational Mind* (Cambridge, MA: MIT Press).
Kelso, J.A.S. (1995), *Dynamic Patterns: The Self-organization of Brain and Behavior* (Cambridge, MA: MIT Press).
Kirsner, K., Speelman, C. Maybery, M., O'Brien-Malone, A., Anderson, M. & MacLeod, C. (ed. 1998), *Implicit and Explicit Mental Processes* (Mahwah, NJ: Erlbaum).
Kosslyn, S.M. (1980), *Image and Mind* (Cambridge, MA: Harvard University Press).
Kosslyn, S.M. (1981), 'The medium and the message in visual imagery: A theory', *Psychological Review*, **88**, pp. 46–66.
Kosslyn, S.M., Alpert, N.M., Thompson, W.L., Maljkovic, M., Weise, S.B., Chabris, C.F., Hamilton, S.E., Rauch, S.L. & Buonanno, F.S. (1993), 'Visual mental imagery activates topographically organized visual cortex: PET investigations', *Journal of Cognitive Neuroscience*, **5**, pp. 263–87.
Kurzweil, R. (1999), *The Age of Spiritual Machines* (New York: Penguin Press).
LaBerge, D. & Samuels, S.J. (1974), 'Toward a theory of automatic information processing in reading', *Cognitive Psychology*, **6**, pp. 293–323.

Mack, A. (2003), 'Inattentional blindness: Looking without seeing', *Current Directions in Psychological Science*, **12**, pp. 180–4.

Mack, A. & Rock, I. (1998), *Inattentional Blindness* (Cambridge, MA: MIT Press).

Marr, D. (1982), *Vision* (New York: Freeman).

Marshall, J. & Halligan, P. (1988), 'Blindsight and insight in visuo-spatial neglect', *Nature*, **336**, pp. 766–77.

McBride, D.M. (2007), 'Methods for measuring conscious and automatic memory: A brief review', *Journal of Consciousness Studies*, **14** (1–2), pp. 198–215.

McCulloch, W.S., & Pitts, W.H. (1965), 'A logical calculus of the ideas immanent in nervous activity', in *Embodiments of Mind*, ed. W.S. McCulloch (Cambridge, MA: MIT Press).

Merikle, P.M. & Daneman, M. (1998), 'Psychological investigations of unconscious perception', *Journal of Consciousness Studies*, **5** (1), pp. 5–18.

Merikle, P.M., Smilek, D. & Eastwood, J.D. (2001), 'Perception without awareness: Perspectives from cognitive psychology', *Cognition*, **79**, pp. 115–34.

Miller. G. (1962), *Psychology: The Science of Mental Life* (New York: Harper & Row Publishers).

Moors, A. & De Houwer, J. (2006), 'Automaticity: A theoretical and conceptual analysis', *Psychological Bulletin*, **132**, pp. 297–326.

Moody, T. (1994), 'Conversations with zombies', *Journal of Consciousness Studies*, **1** (2), pp. 196–200.

Newell, A. (1990), *Unified Theories of Cognition* (Cambridge, MA: Harvard University Press).

Odgen, J.A. (1987), 'The "neglected" left hemisphere and its contribution to visuospatial neglect', in *Neurophysiological and Neuropsychological Aspects of Spatial Neglect*, ed. M. Jeannerod (Amsterdam: Elsevier North-Holland).

Paivio, A. (1986), *Mental Representations: A Dual Coding Approach* (New York: Oxford University Press).

Palmer, S.E. (1978), 'Fundamental aspects of cognitive representation', in *Cognition and Categorization*, ed. E. Rosch & B. B. Lloyd (Hillsdale, NJ: Erlbaum).

Port, R.F. & van Gelder, T. (ed. 1995), *Mind as Motion* (Cambridge, MA: MIT Press).

Posner, M.I. & Synder, C.R.R. (1975), 'Facilitation and inhibition in the processing of signals', in *Attention and Performance V*, ed. P.M.A. Rabbitt & S. Dornic (New York: Academic Press).

Prinz, J.J. (2003), 'Levelheaded mysterianism and artificial experience', *Journal of Consciousness Studies*, **10** (4–5), pp. 111–32.

Pylyshyn, Z.W. (1981), 'The imagery debate: Analogue media versus tacit knowledge', *Psychological Review*, **88**, pp. 16–45.

Pylyshyn, Z.W. (1984), *Computation and Cognition* (Cambridge, MA: MIT Press).

Reber, A.S. (1993), *Implicit Learning and Tacit Knowledge* (New York: Oxford University Press).

Rosch, E., Mervis, C.B., Gray, W.D., Johnson, D.M. & Boyes-Braem, P. (1976), 'Basic objects in natural categories', *Cognitive Psychology*, **8**, pp. 382–439.

Rumelhart, D.E., McClelland, J.L. (ed. 1986), *Parallel Distributed Processing, vol. 1* (Cambridge, MA: MIT Press).

Schenkenberg, T., Bradford, D.C. & Ajax, E.T. (1980), 'Line bisection and unilateral visual neglect in patients with neurologic impairment', *Neurology*, **30**, pp. 509–17.

Schneider, W. (1987), 'Connectionism: Is it a paradigm shift for psychology?', *Behavior Research Methods, Instruments, and Computers*, **19**, pp. 73–83.

Schneider, W. & Shiffrin, R. (1977), 'Controlled and automatic human information processing', *Psychological Review*, **84**, pp. 1–66.

Searle, J.R. (1992), *The Rediscovery of the Mind* (Cambridge, MA: MIT Press).

Segal, S. & Fusella, V. (1970), 'Influence of imaged pictures and sounds in detection of visual and auditory signals', *Journal of Experimental Psychology*, **83**, pp. 458–74.
Shepard, R.N. (1975), 'Form, formation, and transformation of internal representations', in *Information Processing and Cognition: The Loyola Symposium*, ed. R. Solso (Hillsdale, NJ: Erlbaum).
Shepard, R.N. (1991), 'Integrality versus separability of stimulus dimensions: From an early convergence to a proposed theoretical basis', in *The Perception of Structure*, ed. G.R. Lockhead & J.R. Pomerantz (Washington, DC: American Psychological Association).
Shepard, R.N. & Cooper, L.A. (1982), *Mental Images and their Transformations* (Cambridge, MA: MIT Press).
Shepard, R.N. & Podgorny, P. (1978), 'Cognitive processes that resemble perceptual processes', in *Handbook of Learning and Cognitive Processes* (volume 5), ed. W.K. Estes (Hillsdale, NJ: Erlbaum).
Shiffrin, R. & Schneider, W. (1977), 'Controlled and automatic human information processing: II. Perceptual learning, automatic attending, and a general theory', *Psychological Review*, **84**, pp. 127–90.
Sigel, I.E. (ed. 1999), *Development of Mental Representation: Theories and Applications* (Mahwah, NJ: Erlbaum).
Simons, D.J. (2000), 'Current approaches to change blindness', *Visual Cognition*, **7**, pp. 1–15.
Simons, D.J. & Ambinder, M. S. (2005), 'Change blindness: Theory and consequences', *Current Directions in Psychological Science*, **14**, pp. 44–8.
Solso, R.L., MacLin, M.K. & MacLin, O.H. (2005), *Cognitive Psychology*, 7th ed. (New York: Allyn & Bacon).
Smolensky, P. (1988), 'On the proper treatment of connectionism', *Behavioral and Brain Sciences*, **11**, pp. 1–23.
Smolensky, P. (1989), 'Connectionist modeling: Neural computation/mental connections', in *Neural Connections, Mental Computation*, ed. L. Nadel, L.A. Cooper, P. Culicover, & R.M. Harnish (Cambridge, MA: MIT Press).
Stadler, M.A, and P.A. Frensch (ed. 1997), *Handbook of Implicit Learning* (London: Sage Publications).
Stich, S.P., & Warfield, T.A. (ed. 1995), *Mental Representation: A Reader* (Cambridge, MA: Blackwell Publishers).
Stoerig, P. & Cowey, A. (1997), 'Blindsight in man and monkey', *Brain*, **120**, pp. 535–59.
Sutherland, K. (ed. 1995), 'Zombie earth: A symposium on Todd Moody's "conversations with zombies"', *Journal of Consciousness Studies*, **2** (4), pp. 312–72.
Thelen, E. & Smith, L. B. (1995), *A Dynamic Systems Approach to the Development of Cognition and Action* (Cambridge, MA: MIT Press).
Treisman, A.M. (1986), 'Properties, parts, and objects', in *Handbook of Perception and Human Performance. Vol. 2: Cognitive Processes and Performance*, ed. K.R. Boff, L. Kaufman, & J.P. Thomas (New York: Wiley).
Treisman, A.M. & Gelade, G. (1980), 'A feature-integration theory of attention', *Cognitive Psychology*, **12**, pp. 97–136.
Wallace, B. & Fisher, L.E. (1999), *Consciousness and Behavior*, 4th ed. (Boston: Allyn and Bacon).
Weiskrantz, L. (1986), *Blindsight: A Case Study and Implications* (New York: OUP).
Weiskrantz, L. (1997), *Consciousness Lost and Found* (New York: OUP).
Zatorre, R.J., Halpern, A.R., Perry, D.W., Meyer, E. & Evans, A.C. (1996), 'Hearing in the mind's ear: A PET investigation of musical imagery and perception', *Journal of Cognitive Neuroscience*, **8**, pp. 29–46.

Andrew Bailey

# *Representation and a Science of Consciousness*

**Abstract**: *The first part of this paper defends a 'two-factor' approach to mental representation by moving through various choice-points that map out the main peaks in the landscape of philosophical debate about representation. The choice-points considered are: (1) whether representations are conceptual or non-conceptual; (2) given that mental representation is conceptual, whether conscious perceptual representations are analog or digital; (3) given that the content of a representation is the concept it expresses, whether that content is individuated extensionally or intensionally; (4) whether intensional contents are individuated by external or internal conditions; and (5) given that conceptual content is determined externally, whether the possession conditions for concepts are external or internal. The final part of the paper examines the relationship between representation and consciousness, arguing that any account of mental representation, though necessary for a complete account of consciousness, cannot be sufficient for it.*

## 1. Introduction

Consciousness is an abiding mystery. It is especially mysterious for those — these days, most of us — of a naturalizing bent: those who seek a physicalist, empirical, scientific account of phenomenal consciousness. One philosophical response to this problem has been the attempt to understand states of consciousness as nothing more nor less than mental representations with a particular kind of content. On this approach, there need be nothing special or mysterious about the *vehicles* of conscious thought — these will be roughly the same as the vehicles for any other mental representation, which is to say brain states. Rather, what differentiates conscious from non-conscious thought (and from other species of representation) is the *content* of those representations. Insofar as mental representation, and the individuation of representations by their contents, can be naturalistically understood, this theory of consciousness — often called *representationalism*, or sometimes *intentionalism* — is a move towards a science of consciousness.[1]

The question I shall address in this paper is: *what type* of representations, if any, could *constitute* phenomenal consciousness? I hope that discussion of this question will serve both to give a 'Cook's tour' of some of the twists and turns of philosophical discussions of mental representation, as well as to lay out and briefly critique an illustrative representationalist position on consciousness.

## 2. Mental Representation

A representation is an object that can be about an object (or state of affairs). For example, a road sign is about nearby road conditions and the word *skunk* is about skunks. In virtue of this 'aboutness' or intentionality, representations will have various semantic properties: they refer, they may be true or false (i.e. have a truth value), there will be certain conditions under which they are true and others under which they are not (i.e. they have truth conditions), and they may have a content — a sense, or *intension* — that can vary independently of these other (extensional) semantic properties.

Representations are type-individuated by their content: that is, two representations with the same semantic properties are the same representation. For example, **SKUNK** and skunk are both the English word *skunk*. Thus, there may be properties of the *vehicle* of a token representation (in this case, the font in which the word is typed) that are irrelevant to the nature of the representation.

It is common for philosophers to distinguish between two classes of representation: those which have *intrinsic intentionality* and those whose intentionality — their 'aboutness' — is *derived*. A representation has derived intentionality if it is meaningful only because it is

---

[1] Some recent key proponents of this view, of slightly varying stripes, include Peter Carruthers (2000), Fred Dretske (1995), Bill Lycan (1996), Michael Thau (2002) and Michael Tye (1995; 2000). Alex Byrne (2001) defends the approach, though he thinks it needs to be supplemented before it becomes a complete theory of consciousness.

interpreted as having meaning by some consumer of that representation. For instance, a sequence of dots and dashes is a message only if it is interpretable as being, say, Morse code. Most representations in our external environment — including tokens of natural language — have merely derived intentionality. Not all meaning can be derived, however, on pain of infinite regress — the practice of interpretation itself must be grounded in antecedently meaningful thought. So, it seems, at least some of the representations involved in thinking must have their meaning *intrinsically*, independently of interpretation.

A mental representation, then, is a mental object — presumably, one whose vehicle is a brain state — that is, intrinsically, contentful, i.e. about some other object or state of affairs. The problem of mental content is the problem of understanding how certain brain states *can* be intrinsically meaningful.

Mental representations, so understood, play a key role in the main paradigm of cognitive science: the Computational-Representational (C-R) model. On this model, cognitive processes are sequences of computational operations on mental representations. C-R is thus committed to a kind of robust realism about mental representations: content-bearing objects must exist in the brain (at some level of description) and interact with each other causally in rule-governed ways. Furthermore, for most cognitive scientists, the rules governing these symbol-transformations apply in virtue of the *content* of these symbols, not merely their syntactical shape: the semantics of mental representations must necessarily be appealed to in psychological explanation.[2]

## 3. Conscious Representations

Most mental representations are not conscious. The vast majority of one's beliefs, for example, are not present to consciousness at any given time; many of the representations involved in the later stages of perceptual processing are, arguably, mental but not conscious (e.g. those representing stimuli that are perceived subliminally); the representations that — on the C-R view — guide our bodily movements (e.g. mental maps of our body and our local environment) are typically unconsciousness; and so on.

What is it, then, that is 'added' to mental representation to make it *phenomenally conscious*? What is the difference between, say, my non-occurrent belief that pain is bad and my present awareness of the badness of *this* pain when I trap my hand in the car door? It is tempting

---

[2] See Fodor (1981) and Pylyshyn (1984) for representative statements of this view.

to suppose that the difference lies in the *medium* in which those representations occur, rather than merely their *content*: unconscious perceptions are coded in 'the language of the brain,' perhaps, while conscious perceptions are 'built' of hurts and colours and shapes and smells. Indeed, one might think, a conscious and an unconscious perception could have exactly the *same* content: for example, a word flashed on a screen, seen either consciously or subliminally. Another way to put this intuition might be to say that the *vehicles* of conscious representations must have some special properties — subjective colours, sounds, tastes, tickles — that the vehicles of unconscious representations do not. Philosophers often call these putative properties *qualia*.

The worry, however, is that down this road lie grave difficulties for the naturalizer of consciousness. What kind of property could these qualia be? Could they possibly be physical properties of brains — properties that somehow 'feel' a certain way to their possessor, but look like any other physical property to, say, a neurosurgeon — or must they be metaphysical outriders: non-physical properties dangling from a physical brain? The representationalist project is to head off this prospect at the pass: to show that the difference between conscious and unconscious mental representations can be accounted for entirely[3] in terms of differences in *content* between the two classes.

*(i) Conceptual vs. non-conceptual content*

What, then, makes a content conscious? For the next few pages I shall review some of the 'choice points' between different species of content, indicating how a representationalist ought to go on each of these issues. For the sake of concreteness, we shall focus on conscious *perceptual* representations, such as colours, smells, pains and so on. By the end of this process we will have constructed a fairly focussed account of a particular type of content, and will be able to assess whether it is adequate to explain the difference between conscious and unconscious thought.

The first issue is the following: is the content of conscious representations conceptual or non-conceptual? Conceptual representations are analogous to natural language symbols: representations whose contents are specified in terms of concepts possessed by the thinker. (That is, conceptual representations are not themselves concepts but they

---

[3] Or almost entirely: the other key element for most representationalists is the way these representations are connected to the rest of the cognitive system (for example, whether they are available for immediate use in guiding behaviour). Although it is important, for the sake of clear focus I shall not emphasise this aspect of the theory here.

*express* them.) Concepts can be defined as discrete, memorable, recombinable, shareable components of thoughts and judgements, whose tokens play a role in inference. A mental state's content is non-conceptual, by contrast, if an organism can be in that state without having to possess the concepts that are canonically used to characterize that state's content. They are often thought of (at least in the visual modality) as analogous to pictures — presentations of 'regions of filled space'[4] rather than perceptions *that* some object or other is present. One way to identify the difference between the two is the following: conceptual content can be adequately captured in the form of a sentential that-clause — a statement *that p* is the case; non-conceptual content cannot be so captured.

Some representationalists, such as Tye (1995), argue that conscious perceptual representations are non-conceptual. However there are difficulties with this approach, and I suggest that representationalists may be better off emphasising the *conceptual* nature of consciousness.[5]

An initial problem is that perceptual experience is typically imbued with a robust kind of content that non-conceptual representations simply cannot provide. Since the mid-twentieth century[6] it has become a philosophical commonplace that non-conceptual representations — 'mental pictures' — cannot unambiguously refer (Is this percept a picture of a person with particular physical features, or of a brother, or of *my* brother, or of a moment of time, or of an event, or…?); cannot generalize (How can this percept caused by a red ball be generalized into a percept of redness, as opposed to of rubber, or of sphericity?); and cannot compose into more complex thoughts and perceptions (What might this percept of an aunt have as a unique common constituent with every other aunt-related perception, for example?). Unconceptualised pictures do not stand in logical relations with each other, or with practical reasons for action, and so seem unable to drive any thought or behaviour which has to do with *reasons*.[7] These considerations seem to show that conscious perception — insofar as it serves as an input to our cognitive lives — must, at the very least, be richly laden with conceptual content.

---

[4] This way of putting it is from Peacocke (1992). See Crane (1992) and Gunther (2003) for an entrée onto the debate.

[5] As with all the topics I discuss in this essay, the issues here are rich and complex and the demands of both space and overall clarity require that my treatment be extremely cursory. The point of my discussions, though, is not by any means to *settle* the questions but simply to illustrate the high-level shape that the debate takes.

[6] Two classic explorations of these sorts of problems are Wittgenstein (1953) and Sellars (1956).

[7] This is a fairly standard line, but not uncontested: see Millar (1991) and Heck (2000).

The possibility remains open that conscious perception nevertheless has a non-conceptual component, perhaps a 'foundational' or 'given' level of non-conceptual contents that might form the basis of our perceptual belief-acquisition. But phenomenologically and psychologically perception does not in fact seem to have this character. When I look around my office I seem to immediately see objects, such as desks, chairs and a computer; I do not feel as if I am conscious of coloured filled spaces which I come to believe are furniture and appliances. Psychologically, there is evidence to show that concept-acquisition alters phenomenological similarity-spaces: for example, subjects trained to make discriminations between subtly different classes of complex visual presentations — 'fergs' and 'splurgs', or 'gexes' and 'zofs' — report that they come to experience a marked phenomenological difference between the two types, even though they may have no awareness of what the distinction consists in.[8] Research on bistable percepts,[9] similarly, seems to suggest that the phenomenological difference between the two perceptions is one that is closely connected to conceptualisation — it is the difference between, for example, seeing the stimulus *as* a rabbit or *as* a duck, rather than any change in the 'regions of filled space' that are visually present.

*(ii) Digital vs. analog representations*

Let us suppose that the mental representations that putatively constitute phenomenal consciousness are conceptually laden. A second important question is whether they are digital or analog in nature. A digital representation is one which 'chunks' its target domain into discrete parts, whereas analog representations are continuous. For example, a CD records music digitally by 'sampling' a waveform, while an LP represents music along an unbroken spiral groove. In the limit case of an analog representation of some property, between any two discriminations there is a third, finer discrimination. Real world representation systems, however, may approach but never reach this limit: there is always some minimum 'grain,' such as the level of the single brain-cell.[10]

---

[8] See, for example, Goldstone (1994) and Livingstone *et al.* (1998); reference to this work is made in Carruthers (2000, p. 131).

[9] See Logothetis and Leopold (1995).

[10] This way of drawing the analog-digital distinction is similar in spirit to but differs in detail from Dretske's influential formulation: according to Dretske (1981) a representation carries the information that s is F in digital form if and only if it carries no further information about s other than that it is F, whereas whenever a representation carries the information that s is F in analogue form it always carries additional information about s.

It is fairly clear that conscious perception is more analog than digital in nature. Normal human colour vision, for example, exhibits extreme fineness of grain: between almost any two shades we can discriminate, there is a third, different, shade that we can compare and tell apart. Certainly, our ability to perceive subtly distinct colour shades (and shapes, and movements, and smells, and so on) far exceeds our ability to capture those shades in language.

It is often thought that the analog nature of perceptual representation entails that the content of such representations must be entirely non-conceptual, and thus there is a tension between the positions I recommend here and in the previous subsection.[11] However philosophers such as John McDowell (1994), Bill Brewer (1999) and Peter Carruthers (2000) argue that this is not so. Although the content of our conscious perceptual representations certainly outstrips what we might call our *linguistic* conceptual apparatus, our perception is informed by *recognitional* or *demonstrative* concepts such as the starred constituents of <that* surface is red*>. A concept is recognitional, roughly, if it is at least partially constituted by its possession conditions, and among its possession conditions is the ability to recognize at least some things that fall under the concept *as* things that fall under the concept. The idea, then, is that once these kinds of concepts are taken into account, our conceptual structure mirrors the fineness of grain of our perceptual discriminatory capacities. This kind of view is controversial,[12] but given the attractiveness of its two component positions — that perception is fundamentally conceptual but analog — I shall adopt it for the purposes of this paper.

## *(iii) Extensional vs. intensional content*

A third fundamental question about representations in general, and mental representations in particular, is whether their contents are individuated extensionally or intensionally. Content is individuated extensionally if it can be characterised exhaustively by listing the set of things which the representation denotes or of which it is true. By contrast, a representation has intensional content if it depends upon what is often called a 'mode of presentation' of the objects in its extension. For example, the phrases *ruminant* and *even-toed ungulate* have different meanings — if you like, we might say that they express different concepts — even though their extensions are identical: they are two different ways of 'presenting' that class of animals.

---

[11] See Crane (1988) and Peacocke (1992), for example.

[12] See Fodor (2000, chapters 4 and 5) for one critique.

Classical first order logic is extensional: it captures the semantics and the logical relationships that hold between symbol strings solely in virtue of their extensions. However it is clear that the contents of mental representations — including conscious perceptual representations — must be specified intensionally. The psychological roles that mental representations play are not capturable if we pay attention only to extensions: someone might believe that a cow is a ruminant but not that it is cloven-hoofed; we mentally distinguish between Santa Claus and the Easter Bunny even though the extension of those representations is the same (the empty set); we might see someone but fail to recognize them and so not perceive that *that person* is my friend, even though she is.

*(iv) External vs. internal content determination*

So far we have dodged around a central question in the field of mental representation: what is it that determines the content of representations? Assuming that conscious mental representations express concepts, the question becomes: what makes it the cases that a particular concept has the content that it does?

Traditionally, it was assumed that concepts were characterisable either by linking them to definitions (e.g. the concept of *vixen* is that of a female fox) or to sensations (*red* is that occurrent colour); in both cases, the meanings of mental representations would be knowable by their competent possessors. The prevailing philosophical tendency today, however, is to be *externalist* about the individuation of content, to such an extent that Hilary Putnam famously proclaimed 'meaning just ain't in the head' (1975). That is, the determiners of mental content substantially lie outside the knowledge and experience of the subject and have to do instead with historical causal-informational relations between the organism and its environment, plus facts about the social environment.[13] Two key reasons for this shift have been increased recognition of (a) the fact that many if not most concepts are 'fuzzy' in the sense that they have no unique necessary and sufficient conditions for their application, and hence no corresponding definition;[14] and (b) the need to account for *variations* in concepts due to variations in the environment while allowing for the *stability* of concepts through variations in individual belief.

Imagine a planet, called Twin Earth, that is indiscernible from the planet Earth except for one difference: on Twin Earth the substance

---

[13] See Dretske (1988); Fodor (1990); Millikan (1984); Papineau (1987); Putnam (1975).
[14] Consider, for example, the concept of a *game* (see Wittgenstein, 1953).

that plays the role of water — that fills its lakes and oceans, quenches the thirst of its inhabitants, condenses as clouds and falls as rain, and so on — is not $H_2O$ but some other substance, XYZ. On this planet, although all the beliefs and experiences of its inhabitants are intrinsically exactly like ours, the concept they express in Twin English as 'water' will refer, not to water, but to XYZ. Thus, the meaning of a concept is determined (at least in part) by conditions external to the individual user of that concept.

Conversely, suppose I cannot tell the difference between an elm and a beech. Indeed, suppose I have several false beliefs about these respective trees and the differences between them. Nevertheless, 'elm' and 'beech' mean the same thing in my idiolect as they do in every other English speaker's: my ignorance does not affect the concepts I express with the words; rather the concept I express is determined (at least in part) by my social context—by my language community. Concepts are shareable, public entities. Thus the meaning of a concept is invariant with respect to many of the things I idiosyncratically believe about what that concept denotes.[15]

## (v) External vs. internal possession conditions

Given that mental representations have intensional content associated with (externalistically individuated) concepts, the final choice-point we will consider in this section is: what determines the *possession conditions* for those concepts? That is, what is it to have a concept — when does someone count as having a grasp of a certain concept? Here, the pressures are in the opposite direction than those in the previous subsection: internalist rather than externalist. The dilemma is to reconcile the apparent facts that, while the representational character of mental states depends on their external relations, yet that their *psychological efficacy* — the role they play in the cognitive economy of the individual — depends on their intrinsic properties.

Human behaviour is, at least in part, causally explained by our beliefs and desires — and, moreover, our mental states seem to be causally effective because of their *content*. (We fetch a glass of water because we *want a drink* and *believe that* water will quench our thirst.) Features of the physical and social environment can affect an individual's actions only via effects on the individual's intrinsic properties (e.g. on properties of their brains): hence two intrinsically identical individuals on Earth and Twin Earth will behave in an identical

---

[15] Both these arguments originate in Putnam's seminal 1975 paper. An influential version of the second also comes from Burge (1979).

manner, despite the differences in their environment. There must therefore, after all, be an important *sameness of content* between the twins' mental representations. That is, there must be a species of 'narrow content' as well as the 'broad content' described in the previous subsection.[16]

This suggests a 'two-factor' approach to mental content. On this view, mental contents have a pair of separate, though possibly connected, components: one in the head, an internal representation playing a certain psychological role; and the other, 'some sort of co-variational law or evolutionary fact that, in a historical context, determines the reference and truth-conditions of the concept' (Rey, 1998).[17]

The adoption of narrow content is, prima facie, a mixed blessing for the representationalist about phenomenal consciousness. On the one hand, the demonstrative concepts that play a key role in the account we are developing here are difficult to accommodate with the notion of narrow content. To the contrary, thoughts of the sort <that* cat is cuddly>, for example, are often thought to have contents that are specifiable only externalistically: two individuals looking at two different cats could be in mental states that are indiscernible with respect to their intrinsic properties and yet differ in their content. On the other hand, it is crucial for the representationalist to be able to account for the intuition that phenomenal consciousness is determined by the *intrinsic* properties of the individual, and can vary independently of the relations of that individual with her environment. This is required in order to accommodate, for example, inverted spectrum-type arguments (e.g. Block, 1990): the inversion of phenomenal experience, on this view, will require changes to the subject's recognitional concepts and so changes in consciousness continue to track changes in representational content. These issues are too complex to be dealt with in a small compass, but I shall assume here that the net result will be that the representationalist finds it necessary to adopt a two-factor account of conscious representations.[18]

---

[16] See Fodor 1987. Additional arguments for narrow content include appeals to our introspective awareness of the content of our own mental states (see Loar, 1988), and arguments intended to show that individuating beliefs in terms of wide content can sometimes make a subject's beliefs appear irrational even though they are not (see Kripke, 1979).

[17] 'Two factor' views are relatively common (e.g. Block 1986, Loar 1988, McGinn 1982). However, there are defenders of both pure internalism (e.g. Bach, 1987; Crane, 1991; and Segal, 2000) and pure externalism (e.g. Burge, 1979; Stalnaker, 1999; and Wilson, 1995).

[18] Although representationalists are not always particularly explicit on this point, it seems reasonable to treat a two-factor view as being the norm rather than the exception among them. See Carruthers 2000 for a useful discussion.

## 4. Consciousness and Representation

The picture we are left with is the following. The representations that, putatively, constitute phenomenal consciousness are concrete, internal — presumably neural — objects, which are intrinsically intentional. Their content is analog but conceptually imbued, and intensional rather than extensional. This content is fixed in part externalistically, by relations between an individual and her physical and social environment; however, there must also be a key internalist component to mental content, and in particular to conscious perceptual experience.

The representationalist claims that the phenomenal character of conscious mental states is reducible, without remainder, to the intentional content of those states (plus facts about the way those states are cognitively related to the rest of the subject's cognitive system). The opposing position, sometimes called phenomenalism, denies this and holds that no accounting of the intentional properties of the mental is sufficient to explain consciousness.[19] For the phenomenalist, the painfulness of pain and the redness of red visual experience are not a matter of the intentional content of those perceptions — not captured by describing what those perceptions are *about* — but is instead, perhaps, some further intrinsic mental property of the representations themselves.

Is representationalism the correct approach to the science of consciousness? Central to representationalism is an account of the particular kind of content characteristic of conscious (as opposed to unconscious) mental representations: is the account we developed in the previous section adequate for this task? These questions will not be settled here, of course. But I think that it is, at least, not clear that representationalism is an antecedently more plausible theory of consciousness than phenomenalism: while phenomenalism runs the risk of metaphysical obscurity, representationalism faces grave difficulties of its own.[20]

---

[19] A representative sampling of phenomenalists includes Block (1996); Chalmers (1996); Evans (1982); Loar (2003); Peacocke (1983); Raffman (1995) and Shoemaker (1990).

[20] I believe that the two objections which follow go through, more or less, equally forcefully for any fully worked-out representationalist theory of consciousness, and do not trade excessively upon the particular details of the version sketched here; thus, the directions taken at the various choice-points canvassed above do not beg the question against representationalism. For example, there is nothing about two-factor versions of representationalism that make them more or less vulnerable to *these* objections (though, of course, other more detailed worries might accompany the decision to either go two-factor or not).

The first class of problems for representationalism comes from its commitment to the thesis that the properties with which we are acquainted in conscious perception — redness, tanginess, painfulness and so on — are not properties of our mental representations but of what is represented: representationalism is committed to phenomenal externalism. For example, the colours we experience are not *ways we represent* the world around us but are properties tokened by objects in that external world — the redness characteristic of certain of our visual experiences is not a property of those experiences but of the things perceived.[21] This is a view that has attractions in cases of *veridical* experience; but it is not clear that it is coherent in cases where our perception is non-veridical.

Consider the clearest-cut case: a subject who has a hallucinatory experience of something red when in fact there is nothing red in their local environment. The worry here is not that representationalists cannot give an account of misperception: clearly, they can. Rather, the worry is that the representationalist account of qualia — of, as it were, the 'redness of red' — cannot be applied to this kind of case. For the representationalist will say that the occurrent redness is not a property of the representation but of the thing represented — the redness is not 'in here' but *out there* in the world. Yet in the hallucination case, the thing represented does not exist — there *is* no red thing out there. Nevertheless, in just the sense we originally needed it explained, there is still occurrent redness: the hallucinatory visual sensation still *feels red* to its possessor. So representationalism explains nothing.

The second class of problems I shall mention here has to do with the failure of representationalism to really come to grips with the problem of consciousness. The basic idea is that representationalism is unable to account for the difference between unconscious and conscious representations *with the same content*. That non-conscious representations might have the same content as conscious ones is well supported in both science and common sense.[22] To take just one kind of example, consider cases of absent-minded perception — driving while talking and not paying attention to the road, suddenly noticing a sound that has been continuing for some time — or being woken from sleep by a sensation that only now becomes conscious. It seems plausible to say that the *content* of these states — even in some cases the role they play in guiding behaviour and so on — is identical between the conscious

---

[21] This is not something that is denied by representationalists — rather it is typically affirmed by them as a virtue of their account. It often goes by the name of the 'transparency thesis': our experience is not a picture of the world but a transparent window onto it.

[22] See Carruthers (2000, Chapter 6).

and unconscious versions; hence, the intentionality of the state is insufficient to explain its consciousness.[23]

Representationalist theories have avenues by which they can try to address this problem. The deeper issue is that these moves inevitably take us away from the intuitive heart of the position — that phenomenality reduces to intentionality — and introduce further stipulations that end up doing all the work. For example, one might move to the view that only representations which a) have a certain type of content, *and* b) are connected to the 'right sort' of high-level decision-making system are conscious. But then, the source of phenomenal consciousness seems not to be content — two states might have identical content but only one be conscious — but *extrinsic* connections between certain representations and other cognitive systems. Why moving representations into and out of these relations should render them *phenomenally conscious* remains mysterious, and appeals to content no longer do any work. Once again, it seems, representationalism explains nothing.[24]

## 5. Conclusion

Conscious mental states are contentful. It is crucial for any prospective science of consciousness to have a good account of the notion of mental representation that is relevant to phenomenal consciousness — after all, consciousness is typically if not always consciousness *of* some state of the world or our own bodies — and I have sketched here some of the main considerations for such an account. However, I have argued, a complete story about conscious mental representation will not itself be *sufficient to explain* phenomenal consciousness — representationalism, for all its attractions, is wrong-headed.

What is needed, in addition, is some account of the *medium* of consciousness: what makes certain mental contents phenomenally conscious is not (alone) the content itself but (also) that the *vehicles* of

---

[23] The scientific case for unconscious representations with the same type of content as conscious ones rests primarily on evidence from various sorts of dissociation, such as blindsight and visual form agnosia, which suggest that perceptual states with the same kind of content as normal conscious perceptions can sometimes occur undetected by their possessor.

[24] Carruthers — himself a representationalist, though a proponent of the higher-order rather than first-order version of the theory — raises a problem very much like this, and argues that his own flavour of representationalism solves it (2000). The twist he introduces, via a consumer theory of semantics, is that the extrinsic relations *change the content* of the representations. I think that this theory ultimately fails for roughly the reason given here — it fails to explain why *these* relations constitute state-consciousness — but there is no space to go into that here.

those representations have a certain character. Consistently with what has been argued here, this character might be either extrinsic, involving crucial relations with other cognitive states (as representationalists themselves often tacitly recognise and slip into their account) or intrinsic, as the phenomenalist asserts. But this is a debate which is beyond the scope of this paper.

# References

Bach, K. (1987), *Thought and Reference* (Oxford: Oxford University Press).
Block, N. (1986), 'Advertisement for a semantics for psychology,' *Midwest Studies in Philosophy*, **10**, pp. 615–78.
Block, N. (1990), 'Inverted earth,' *Philosophical Perspectives*, **4**, pp. 53–79.
Block, N. (1996), 'Mental paint and mental latex,' *Philosophical Issues*, **7**, pp. 19–49.
Brewer, B. (1999), *Perception and Reason* (Oxford: Oxford University Press).
Burge, T. (1979), 'Individualism and the mental,' *Midwest Studies in Philosophy*, **4**, pp. 73–121.
Byrne, A. (2001), 'Intentionalism defended,' *Philosophical Review*, **110**, pp. 199–240.
Carruthers, P. (2000), *Phenomenal Consciousness: A Naturalistic Theory* (Cambridge: Cambridge University Press).
Chalmers, D. (1996), *The Conscious Mind* (Oxford: Oxford University Press).
Crane, T. (1988), 'The waterfall illusion,' *Analysis*, **48**, pp. 142–7.
Crane, T. (1991), 'All the difference in the world,' *Philosophical Quarterly*, **41**, pp. 1–25.
Crane, T. (ed. 1992), *The Contents of Experience* (Cambridge: Cambridge University Press).
Dretske, F. (1981), *Knowledge and the Flow of Information* (Cambridge MA: MIT Press).
Dretske, F. (1988), *Explaining Behavior: Reasons in a World of Causes* (Cambridge, MA: MIT Press).
Dretske, F. (1995), *Naturalizing the Mind* (Cambridge, MA: MIT Press).
Evans, G. (1982), *The Varieties of Reference* (Oxford: Oxford University Press).
Fodor, J. (1981), *Representations* (Cambridge, MA: MIT Press).
Fodor, J. (1987), *Psychosemantics* (Cambridge, MA: MIT Press).
Fodor, J. (1990), *A Theory of Content and Other Essays* (Cambridge, MA: MIT Press).
Fodor, J. (2000), *In Critical Condition: Polemical Essays on Cognitive Science and the Philosophy of Mind* (Cambridge, MA: MIT Press).
Goldstone, R. (1994), 'Influences of categorization on perceptual discrimination,' *Journal of Experimental Psychology: General*, **123**, pp. 178–200.
Gunther, Y.H. (ed. 2003), *Essays on Nonconceptual Content* (Cambridge, MA: MIT Press).
Heck, R. (2000), 'Nonconceptual content and the space of reasons,' *Philosophical Review*, 109, pp. 483–523.
Kripke, S. (1979), 'A puzzle about belief,' in *Meaning and Use*, ed. A. Margalit (Dordrecht: Reidel).
Livingstone, K., Andrews, J. & Harnad, S. (1998), 'Categorical perception effects induced by category learning,' *Journal of Experimental Psychology: Learning, Memory and Cognition*, **24**, pp. 732–53.

Loar, B. (1988), 'Social content and psychological content,' in *Contents of Thought*, ed. R. Grimm and D. Merrill (Tucson: University of Arizona Press).
Loar, B. (2003), 'Transparent experience and the availability of qualia,' in *Consciousness: New Philosophical Perspectives,* ed. Q. Smith and A. Jokic (Oxford: Oxford University Press).
Logothetis, N. & Leopold, D. (1995), 'On the physiology of bistable percepts,' *MIT Artificial Intelligence Laboratory, Memo No. 1553.*
Lycan, W. (1996), *Consciousness and Experience* (Cambridge, MA: MIT Press).
McDowell, J. (1994), *Mind and World* (Cambridge, MA: Harvard University Press).
McGinn, C. (1982), 'The structure of content,' in *Thought and Object*, ed. A. Woodfield (Oxford: Oxford University Press).
Millar, A. (1991), *Reasons and Experience* (Oxford: Oxford University Press).
Millikan, R. (1984), Language, *Thought and other Biological Categories* (Cambridge, MA: MIT Press).
Papineau, D. (1987), *Reality and Representation* (Oxford: Blackwell Publishers).
Peacocke, C. (1983), *Sense and Content* (Oxford: Oxford University Press).
Peacocke, C. (1992), *A Study of Concepts* (Cambridge, MA: MIT Press).
Putnam, H. (1975), 'The meaning of "meaning"', in *Language, Mind and Knowledge*, ed. K. Gunderson (Minneapolis, MN: University of Minnesota Press).
Pylyshyn, Z. (1984), *Computation and Cognition* (Cambridge, MA: MIT Press).
Raffman, D. (1995), 'The persistence of phenomenology,' in *Conscious Experience*, ed. T. Metzinger (Paderborn: Schönigh/Exeter: Imprint Academic).
Rey, G. (1998), 'Concepts,' in *Routledge Encyclopedia of Philosophy*, ed. E. Craig (London: Routledge). Retrieved September 01, 2005, from http://www.rep.routledge.com/article/W008.
Segal, G. (2000), *A Slim Book about Narrow Content* (Cambridge, MA: MIT Press).
Sellars, W. (1956), 'Empiricism and the Philosophy of Mind,' in *Minnesota Studies in the Philosophy of Science*, vol. 1, ed. H. Feigl and M. Scriven (Minneapolis, MN: University of Minnesota Press).
Shoemaker, S. (1990), 'Qualities and Qualia: What's in the Mind?' *Philosophy and Phenomenological Research*, **50**, pp. 109–31.
Stalnaker, R. (1999), *Context and Content* (Oxford: Oxford University Press).
Thau, M. (2002), *Consciousness and Cognition* (Oxford: Oxford University Press).
Tye, M. (1995), *Ten Problems of Consciousness* (Cambridge, MA: MIT Press).
Tye, M. (2000), *Consciousness, Color and Content* (Cambridge, MA: MIT Press).
Wilson, R. A. (1995), *Cartesian Psychology and Physical Minds: Individualism and the Sciences of the Mind* (Cambridge: Cambridge University Press).
Wittgenstein, L. (1953), *Philosophical Investigations*, trans. G.E.M. Anscombe (Oxford: Blackwell Publishers).

# John Barresi

# *Consciousness and Intentionality*

*Abstract*: *My goal is to try to understand the intentionality of consciousness from a naturalistic perspective. My basic methodological assumption is that embodied agents, through their sensory-motor, affective, and cognitive activities directed at objects, engage in intentional relations with these objects. Furthermore, I assume that intentional relations can be viewed from a first- and a third-person perspective. What is called primary consciousness is the first-person perspective of the agent engaged in a current intentional relation. While primary consciousness posits an implicit 'subject' or 'self,' it is primarily oriented toward its 'object.' Acts of primary consciousness have only ephemeral existence, but when such acts are reflected upon by the agent reflexive or secondary conscious knowledge of oneself, as an embodied agent engaged in an intentional relation, is constituted. I show how these ideas relate to the understanding of intentional relations in human development and how they make possible adult understanding of philosophical notions of intentionality.*

In common sense usage intentionality occurs when an individual engages in some activity or pursues a goal with some conscious intention or purpose. On this view what is important about intentionality is that the actor is aware of the purpose or goal of his or her activity and represents the self as pursuing that goal. In philosophical usage intentionality refers to the 'aboutness' or directedness property of mental states. This is a more basic notion, and while all mental states are said to have intentionality in the philosophical sense, only some have intentionality in the manner of common sense usage. Brentano

(1874) suggested that intentionality in the philosophical sense is the essential property that distinguishes mental from physical phenomena. Unlike physical events, mental events refer to, or are about, objects or states of affairs that may or may not exist. The present article focuses on the philosophical rather than common sense understanding of intentionality, though the common sense usage will appear later on.

The particular concern of this paper is how to account for our human ability to think about mental states as intentional. How is it that we can think of our selves as organisms with minds that are distinct from the objects we think about? How is it that we can even think of our selves as purely thinking beings composed entirely of a stream of intentional mental states independent of our bodies? The answer that I will give is a naturalistic one. My goal is to explain how organisms, such as we are, develop an understanding of mental life in general, which includes an understanding of how they themselves and others have a mental life that can be distinguished from their embodied organic involvement in the world. This story will be one of beings with capacities that allow them to develop a view of themselves as beings with mental states of an intentional nature. It will also be a story of the social origins of self-understanding. But before getting into the story we must look more closely at what we mean by intentionality in the philosophical sense.

The philosophical notion of intentionality initiated by Brentano has been developed in two major approaches: the logicist or linguistic approach and the phenomenological approach. The logicist approach focuses on the representational aspect of mental states and of symbolic language, and relates the two. On this view, intentionality involves representations ('propositional attitudes') with propositional content. This approach was an outgrowth of an attempt to understand natural language and its capacity to represent truth in terms of 'true' propositions. The logicist notion was initiated in the work of Frege (1918), who tried to develop a way of converting natural language into a logical language. Subsequent theorists including Russell (1940) and Fodor (1975; 1981) have suggested that natural language, and also certain mental states, can be viewed as compositional and representational, and that there is a logical 'language of thought' wherein mental states can relate to each other in a manner similar to sentences of a language. On this view, mental states are a world of their own, separate from, yet symbolically representing, states of the world, truly or falsely, and/or defining conditions, the satisfaction of which would make them true. Fodor (1980), in an article in which he pursued this representational approach to its extreme, suggested that scientific psychologists should adopt 'methodological solipsism' when investigating mental phenomena, and avoid any attempt to develop a naturalistic psychology of embodied agents directly engaged in the world.

The parallels between language and thought developed in the logicist tradition of understanding intentionality have been productive in developing computational models of mind (mainly serial computational models). However, a problem arose in how to connect these representational states of mind to the world - what has been called the symbol-grounding problem (Harnad, 1990). This has led in recent years to increased interest in embodied approaches to mind (e.g., Clark, 1997; Gallagher, 2001; Lakoff & Johnson, 1999; Varela *et al.*, 1991). Concurrent with this developed interest in embodiment has been an interest in consciousness and phenomenological approaches. As a result, the second philosophical tradition in the analysis of intentionality, initiated by Husserl's phenomenology (e.g., Husserl, 1960), has received increasing attention. Works by Gurwitsch (1966), Sartre (1936–7; 1964) and Merleau-Ponty (1962; 1964) are within this tradition. More recently some analytical philosophers, like Galen Strawson (2003), have also found inspiration in the phenomenological approach to intentionality. The goal of the phenomenological approach is to focus more directly on how conscious mental phenomena link persons to each other and to their worlds. It tries to analyse the complex structure of consciousness, and the processes by which conscious states become linked together in abstract and reflexive ways that ultimately constitute both subjects and objects. It is this latter approach, which most directly relates to the developmental account of intentionality as a natural phenomenon taken in this article. By speculating on the development of self-consciousness, I hope to show how we can come to understand the mind as representational in a logicist/linguistic sense out of our early and developed conscious engagement with each other and the world.

## Primary Consciousness and Intentionality

Building upon the phenomenological tradition, but moving it toward a naturalized account of intentionality, we can define primary consciousness as the first-person perspective of the agent engaged in a current intentional relation - a relation that connects a subject of consciousness to an object of consciousness through a particular mode of experience, e.g., perception, thought, wish, etc. Primary consciousness is the form of consciousness that is usually understood to be the basis of intentionality. Acts of primary consciousness have only ephemeral existence but they can be linked together through various processes (see, e.g., Gurwitsch, 1966; Strawson, 2003). Primary consciousness posits an implicit 'intentional subject' (Martin & Barresi, 2003; Barresi, 2004b) or 'self,' but is primarily oriented toward its 'intentional object.' In each act of primary consciousness or experience, there is both an implied subject pole and object pole, but neither of these has more than an immediate existence. A self or ego, and an object must be constituted through linking ephemeral acts, primarily through intentional relations that constitute the self (ego) and/or objects as the same through those acts. For instance, if an infant engages in a continued interaction with an object, through attention to it and an attempt to reach for it, the unity of the experiences directed at the object serve to constitute a self pole and object pole of a series of intentional relations that are interconnected through their common integrated activity.

While Husserl focused on how consciousness can constitute objects of experience through intentional relations, his views varied throughout his career on the status of the subject. In some of his work he posited the ego as a pure transcendental subject, the centre or pole that is the source of all intentional acts, but is not itself constituted in any of those acts. In opposition to this notion of a pure ego, Gurwitsch (1966), a later phenomenologist influenced by Gestalt psychology, wrote that the ego, like the object, is also constituted, but through a process of reflection on acts of consciousness:

> [The ego] derives its unity and its coherence from the . . . acts that . . . constitute it; and it is nothing other than the organized totality of these acts. Hence when the subject, reflecting upon the act he experiences, ascertains that this act is his, this only means that the act in question . . . has its place within this united and organized whole. In this theory there is obviously no place for a center or a pole of conscious life from which the acts might issue or emerge. (Gurwitsch, 1966, p. 288)

In Gurwitsch's view there is no self or ego prior to the acts that constitute it. Nor is the self constituted by acts of primary consciousness in the absence of reflection. Rather, when the subject reflects on these acts and ascribes them to a self, the person constitutes an objective self by bringing together the particular acts which it integrates into an organized whole that it attributes to the self:

> When a grasped act appears as connected with the ego, the latter presents itself as exceeding this act . . . .. It offers itself as a permanent entity,

as continuing to exist, beyond the grasped act.... The ego thus appears *through* rather than *in* the grasped act. (Gurwitsch, 1966, p.295)

This process of reflection on one's acts as one's own, involves another level of consciousness beyond primary consciousness, sometimes called secondary consciousness. Secondary consciousness reflects on first-order intentional relations involving primary consciousness, but shifts attention toward the agent of the acts and the intentional relation in which the agent is engaged, thus making explicit the self or ego's involvement in an intentional relation. Whereas in primary consciousness the ego is implicit, and constituted in part through connected ephemeral acts involving integrated intentional relations, secondary consciousness involves an objective awareness of those acts as integrated and belonging to the subject.

Unlike primary consciousness, knowledge of an ego and its intentional relations is not limited to private knowledge of the acting agent; the ego is also available for public knowledge, it can be known by others. Gurwitsch considers two examples, hate from a first-person perspective, and love from a third-person perspective. In discussing the latter he states:

> When I talk with my friend about his love, both of us have identically the same object in view — namely, a constituted psychic unity as distinct from multiple conscious acts through which it appears. This object, his love, is for him no less open to uncertainty and doubt than it is for me. (Gurwitsch, 1966, pg. 297)

While we may come to know the love of self and other in different ways, the intentional content of our knowledge is the same, the agent's love. Gurwitsch concludes:

> My ego and my psychic facts, in contradistinction to the conscious acts, are then no longer my exclusive property, for they are accessible to other people, whereas my consciousness is not so; it is and remains closed and impenetrable for everyone except myself. The problem of the comprehension of other persons' minds is thus simplified and must be raised in quite new terms. The condition, however, of this simplification is the non-egological conception of consciousness (Gurwitsch, 1966, p. 297).

The implication here is that self knowledge, gained through secondary consciousness of self, is no different from knowledge of another agent gained through primary consciousness of the other, because the self and its acts treated as objects of knowledge are accessible to both self and other, whereas the first-person perspective of engaging in those acts, or primary consciousness, is not. But how are we to understand this process by which private experiences and activities become capable of public knowledge? I believe that Intentional Relations Theory (IRT; Barresi, 2001; 2004a; Barresi & Moore, 1996; Moore, 1999) can provide such a perspective, as well as provide a basis for the development of our understanding of intentionality.

## Intentional Relations Theory

Intentional Relations Theory (IRT) differs from traditional phenomenological approaches to the intentionality of consciousness in one major respect. Whereas, phenomenology begins with an analysis of consciousness, and, in effect, constructs the world, including self and other out of this analysis, IRT's starting position is that of positing a material embodied agent, whose states of consciousness are based in brain activity that relates the agent directly to the world and to comparable activities of other agents. From this starting point an attempt is made to provide a naturalistic account of intentional relations and the developmental emergence of knowledge of those relations and of the intentional properties of consciousness. Thus, rather than beginning with phenomenological analysis, IRT provides a naturalistic account of the possibility of phenomenological analysis. Without the developmental process through which we can come to know of consciousness as consciousness with its intentional properties, we would be unable to enter into any analysis of it. IRT provides that account by explaining how an embodied agent comes to view its activities as involving mental states with intentional content. As we shall see, that account implies a necessary social foundation to understanding individual minds.

According to IRT, an intentional relation (IR) connects an embodied agent to an object through a relation existing in virtue of an agent's sensorimotor, emotional/motivational and cognitive capacities. In most cases the relationship is direct, not mediated through concepts or representations, except insofar as states of the brain that mediate these processes are defined as, or can be inferred to use, representations.

Intentional relations are thus taken here to be, primarily, objective or external relations that exist between agents and objects, real and counterfactual, rather than internal relations between a mental state and its intentional content. IRs can be taxonomically categorized into three basic types: Actions: 'Jamie chases the cat'; Affective/motivational: 'Mackenzie fears the dog'; and Epistemic: 'Columbus sees land.' Each IR takes the form of an agent or subject of activity, a form of activity, and an object or goal of the activity. Furthermore, each of the activities are ones in which an animate agent or person performs a conscious act directed at some object, event or state of affairs, and does not simply describe a causal process involving two physical objects. However, it should be noted that IRs can also involve collective agents: 'The carpenters built the house,' where each particular agent may be said to be individually conscious of a shared common activity or goal, and where each agent engages in specific acts that take into account past and anticipated future acts of other agents. If there were two carpenters, this would be a case of triadic interaction involved in a shared intentional relation toward a common object - the house to be built. But there are more complexities in this kind of example that we will shortly consider.

So far we have considered only first order IRs. Second order IRs take first order intentional relations as their object. Typically, second order IRs involve agents with affective or epistemic relations to the first order activities of an agent, where the latter agent can be self or another person. For instance: 'Fiona knows that she is in love with Ian' and 'Fiona knows that Mary is in love with Ian,' are two second order intentional relations where Fiona is an agent of the second order epistemic state of 'knowing' and 'x loves Ian' is the first order intentional relation of that epistemic state, where x is self in one case and Mary in the other. In IRT, second order IRs of this sort are the basis upon which we understand self and other as embodied agents of the same kind and to which the same intentional states can be attributed. The fact that people are capable of acquiring such second order intentional understanding that applies uniformly to self and other is the key to understanding how mental states can be intentional. But how is this possible?

Viewed from the perspective of IRT, there are three fundamentally different basic answers to this question in the psychological literature. All fall under the notion of a 'Theory of Mind (ToM).' According to what is called the 'Theory' Theory of Mind (TT) humans have innately or acquire a ToM or ToM mechanisms that can be applied uniformly to self and other based purely on inference from behaviour (e.g., Gopnik & Meltzoff, 1997; Leslie, 1987). Uniformity of inference in this account is based on the fact that one can interpret one's own behaviour in the same way that one can interpret the behaviour of others. Hence, in the case of Fiona, it could be said that, since love is a public concept, whose criteria of application is based on behaviour (though perhaps also requiring innate ideas or mechanisms by which we understand love as involving mental properties), she can know when she or Mary is in love by noticing the same kinds of behaviour of

Mary and herself vis-à-vis Ian. Simulation theorists (ST) take a different view of how Fiona knows about her own love versus Mary's love (e.g., Goldman, 1992; Gordon, 1986; Humphrey, 1984; Harris, 1989). On their view, love may have some behavioural consequences that can be used to identify it in another person, but that it is fundamentally a subjective mental state, and without a personal appreciation of the feeling state that usually goes with the overt behaviour, we cannot truly understand love as a psychological state. On this view, we understand love directly in our own case, but only indirectly and by simulation in the case of another person. We can understand what someone else feels only by placing ourselves imaginatively in their situation, when we observe their behaviour in context (e.g., Mary around Ian). Only by placing our mind in their body in this way can we understand the psychological, intentional, and subjective meaning of their behaviour. By contrast, in our own case, our behaviour is only a consequence of this subjective state, not the state itself, so no inference is necessary from our own behaviour to the mental state that we are in.

A third kind of theory invokes the notion of matching or mirroring between self and other. Ingredients of matching theory can be found in Hobson (1991; 1998) and elsewhere (see, Moore & Corkum, 1994; also Gallese *et al.*, 2004), but IRT (Barresi & Moore, 1996; Barresi, 2001; 2004a; Moore, 1999) may provide the most elaborated version of this approach. It will be developed further in the present account. The key notion in matching theories, particularly in IRT, is that the first-person information that we have about our own IRs (e.g., Fiona's feeling for Ian) is distinctly different from the third-person information that we have about the IRs of others (e.g., Mary's behaviour toward Ian), and that in order to develop uniform second order concepts or representations of IRs that can be applied equally to self and other, we need to match these two types of information in a single concept or form of knowledge that contains both types of information. In Barresi and Moore (1996) we posited an 'intentional schema' to integrate this multimodal information from self and other. On this view, being in love should not be thought of primarily as a private, subjective experience, as in the ST view, nor as a mental intentional state that can be inferred from behaviour, as in the TT view, but as an embodied IR between the agent and object that, in the case of love, involves both feelings and concomitant behavioural expressions. Moreover, in learning the concept of love or any other IR, it is supposed that we must learn both the first-person, 'inner' aspect, of the IR, as well as the third-person, 'outer' aspect; otherwise, we fail to have the concept. For instance, one can be in love, say for the first time, without knowing it, because all one knows about love is the outer aspect, and one does not recognize this outer aspect in one's feelings for another until it is pointed out to one. Of course, love in our culture is primarily a social concept, and learned to a large extent through language. But other more basic IRs, like chasing, fearing, or seeing, are more fundamental, and may be understood to some extent by an organism without the mediation of language.

To be more explicit, and to relate it to our prior discussion of consciousness, IRT proposes that first-person information about our own IRs is contained in primary consciousness as we are engaged in the IR, that it is directed outward to the object, which is experienced in terms of the relation, and that the self as agent, is implicit in this information, but not explicitly represented. Thus when the child fears the dog, her whole attention is on the dog and her emotional reaction is projected onto the dog as a fearful object. She has no explicit awareness of herself as an agent in the state of fear. By contrast, the observer of her reaction to the dog, has third-person information of her reactions and expressions, and tends to attribute these reactions of fear to the child, not to intrinsic properties of the dog, though aware that the dog is the cause of the reactions. In order for the child herself to become aware of her state of fear, she has to take her own first level intentional relation as an object of a second level epistemic intentional relation, secondary consciousness in our previous discussion. In order to do so, she must have the concept of self as agent and fear as an intentional relation with two sides, an inner first-person side and outer third-person side, which are united in the concept of that kind of IR. In the same way, an external observer may see her fear, in primary consciousness of the other, but, unless that observer also has the concept of the first-order intentional relation, all that is seen is the behavioural expression of the agent, and not the IR, with its inner and outer aspect. However, in this case, this second level is not secondary consciousness, but remains primary consciousness of the other. Only if the observer becomes aware of being aware of the other's IR, does secondary consciousness appear in the observer.

In our first account of IRT (Barresi & Moore, 1996), the intentional schema was hypothesized to account for the integration of the first- and third-person aspects of the IR. The intentional schema was described as an intermodal perceptual and conceptual structure that linked the two sources of information into a concept under conditions in which matched information of the two types are attended to at the same time. There are a variety of possible conditions of matching that were considered, but the focus was on imitation and triadic interaction, where two individuals, usually an infant and an adult, are engaged in a shared IR directed at some object or situation, and the infant becomes aware of their shared activity and its first- and third-person aspects, the first-person of self and the third-person of other. In our developmental account, such triadic activity of share IRs laid the conceptual foundation for later attribution of IRs to self and other as independent agents. However, without the prior sharing of common IRs, no concept of the IR could be developed that integrated first- and third-person properties of the IR. In the present account I wish to go somewhat further in analysing the developmental process, in part to deal better with recent developments in the neuroscience of social understanding (cf. Barresi, 2004c).

## Four Developmental Steps in the Consciousness of Intentional Relations

In our original account of IRT (Barresi & Moore, 1996), we described a four level model of the development of social understanding of intentional relations. This account was applied phylogenetically and, in the case of humans, ontogenetically. In the present account the same four levels will be used but modified to some extent to deal with more recent findings. Level one of the model presupposed that organisms develop distinct representations of their own and other individuals' intentional relations. In the case of self, only first-person information entered into representations of one's own IRs. Such representations would not explicitly represent the self in a manner that combined first- with third-person information of self as a unitary agent of IRs. In the case of others, representations would be based on third-person information, but not include any first-person information. Hence there would be no way to match self to other, and understand self and other within the same representational system. It was hypothesized that most organisms had representations of self and other of this sort, and that young infants also represented the IRs of self and other in this manner. Representations that integrated first- and third-person information of IRs first appeared at level two of the model, when two individuals engaged in triadic interaction where they shared IRs with some common object. This was thought rarely to occur in organisms other than higher primates and humans, but was described only in the case of adult-infant triadic interaction, beginning around 9 months in the infant's social interactions.

In light of recent developments, it seems worthwhile to make some finer distinctions that allow for earlier phases of social understanding that lie between levels 1 and 2. The focus originally was on understanding IRs in the full sense of agent-relation-object. But, partial common understanding of self and other can occur at a subagent level. For instance, research on monkey 'mirror neurons,' seems to show that monkeys can understand the goal-directed actions of another organism in the same manner as they understand their own actions (Gallese *et. al.*, 1996). These pre-motor neurons fire in the planning of one's own actions, but also in perceiving comparable goal directed actions in another animate being. It is not clear yet the extent to which experience comes to play in the development of such neurons. But, one hypothesized means of making the generalization from self to other (e.g., Keysers & Parrett, 2004) is that one first connects one's first-person internal information of intentional action to the perceptual feedback that one receives, through vision or audition, of one's own action. Then vision or audition mediates the connection to the action of others. Vision and audition here serve as modalities through which one acquires third-person information not only of others but also of self. Thus, strictly first-person information (of goal-directedness, kinesthetics, and proprioception) of purposive goal-directed action, where self is implicit, can be linked to self as object in vision and audition, and to another person as a comparable object engaged in a similar activity. That a developmental account of this type might work in humans is indicated by research that shows self-recognition of body parts through vision develops in 4–6 month infants (Bahrick & Watson, 1985), and that infants around 6 months are able to recognize goal-directed actions of others involving particular objects (Woodward, 1998). Even further, teaching an infant to grasp an object at an earlier age is correlated with understanding similar grasping actions of another person (Sommerville *et al.*, 2005). Thus, at least for simple actions, it seems that learning to succeed at an action, which involves coordination of first-person (e.g., proprioceptive) and typically third-person (e.g., visual) information of one's own action, may be correlated with understanding the integrated first- and third-person aspects of another's actions. However, such action understanding can be viewed as sub-personal. Other research (Woodward & Guajardo, 2002) suggests that the infant's understanding of 'pointing,' which can be regarded as an agent-level attempt at shared triadic interaction involving an epistemic IR of attention, is not understood until the end of the first year in humans, and not understood at all, under natural conditions, in any other primate. It is also important to note that here again, acquiring the ability to point, and acquiring the ability to appreciate the pointing intention of another person, are correlated developmentally, though not necessarily involving unidirectional understanding from self to other, as the reverse direction of apparent understanding also occurs, at least as indicated by temporal order of achievement. In all these cases we have evidence that a correlated matching between first- and third-person information about actions is essential for understanding the goal-directed nature of action, whether it be of self or other. However, the understanding here is not yet an understanding of self and other as intentional agents.

The second year of life is a period of major transition in an infant's understanding of the embodied intentionality of self and other. Prior to that period the infant has no objective sense of self or other, certainly not one that treats self and other as agents of the same kind, and having intentional properties that can apply separately to each of them. The understanding of shared intentionality that we have been describing at Level 2 of IRT, while sensitive to shared concurrent activity, does not yet objectify that activity in a second order intentional relation involving 'we' as the agent of the activity. It is a situational understanding of the second order relation, not requiring a conceptual understanding. During the first half of the second year this begins to change as the infant becomes increasingly aware of differences between self and other in their orientations to the world. The infant becomes more flexible in his or her involvement in the activity of the other. As Braten (1998) puts it, the infant can co-enact at a sub-personal first-person level the activity of the other as the other engages in the activity, but it can increasingly distinguish this co-enactment of the other's intentional relation from its own separate first- and third-person point of view. As a result, the infant is in a position to triangulate an objective situation or world to which two separate agents, self and other, have different embodied subjective intentional relations (cf., Hobson, 1998). In IRT, this third level of social understanding requires the development of a memory based, but generic, form of imagination, which can be used to match appropriate first-person information to perceived third-person information of the activity of the other, and to match appropriate third-person information to current first-person information of one's own activity. Thus second-order representations of IRs of self and other can be constructed, which differ from each other. The infant's developing capacity to understand the 'common sense' intentionality or intentions of others, separately from overt actions, and their ability to empathize with the other's specific desires and to help them achieve them, separate from their own desires, are examples of how imagining the first-person information about other's intentional relations is used.

Their acquired capacity for self-recognition with mirrors and their developing self-consciousness are signs of their ability to imagine information of self from a third-person point of view. Because of the role that imagination plays in differentiating between IRs of self and other, it is at this level that phenomena typically associated with simulation theory (ST) begin to emerge. Imagination of how the other might feel, even if it conflicts with our own feelings, can be imagined from a first-person perspective. However, whereas ST focuses entirely on how we can make use of our own minds (or first-person information) to interpret the third-person information that we have directly of the other, IRT posits that we also use imagined third-person information in order to have a better appreciation of how our own agency appears to others. One consequence of this is that the 2-year-old begins to exhibit self-reflective emotions like embarrassment.

The achievement of Level 3 forms of understanding of IRs in the 2-year-old provides the infant with the capacity for reflective or secondary consciousness of his or her own first-order IRs, as well as the capacity of using primary consciousness for understanding first-order IRs of others. In both cases it involves understanding that individual embodied agents have distinct intentional orientations toward the world. But the IRs that can be understood at this level are limited to current embodied IRs, such as emotional expression directed at a current object, or intention directed at an immediate goal. The infant is not yet able to deal with IRs involving imagined or counterfactual objects or states of affairs, or goals at greater distance in space and time. In order to understand these more complex IRs the child must acquire what has been called a representational theory of mind (Perner, 1991). At about the age of 4, the child becomes able to deal with a variety of these more complex IRs, including the understanding of false belief in self and other, differences between own and other's representation of a current object, differences between one's past, present, and future self in beliefs and desires, and the ability to think of one's self as a changing mental self, extended in time (see Moore & Lemmon, 2001). All these capacities require distinguishing between a current IR and some imagined or counterfactual IR in some way related to the current IR, but different from it. Barresi and Moore (1996) suggested that a developmentally acquired ability for double imagination provides the necessary ingredient for this achievement. With double imagination it is possible to represent an imagined IR, with an imagined first- as well as an imagined third-person component, and not just one imagined component as in Level 3. So, now the child can think of the object of an IR, not only as a real object, but also as a counterfactual, 'inexistent,' or intentional, object. It is at this point that the child can be said to have acquired the necessary ingredients in order to understand later, as an adult, intentionality in the philosophical sense, as the child of this age already has practical use of a notion of this sort in understanding of self and other. To state it simply, and perhaps provocatively, where philosophers — particularly of the logicist/representational sort — begin in their analysis of the intentionality of consciousness is just at this point where the present naturalized account of intentionality ends. This is the point where a child is able to distinguish its own private representational perspective from those of other persons.

## Conclusion

Understanding intentionality in a philosophical sense requires being able to view one's own present conscious mental states, as well as other mental states, in self and other, as representational, having content that may be true or false. Taking this stance on one's point-of-view of reality requires disembedding one's self mentally from embodied engagement in the world, and conceptualizing, at an abstract level, this engagement. The fact that human beings as adults have the capacity to develop such a point-of-view, with the necessary abstraction, is a social-cognitive achievement, not an intrinsic capacity of the human mind to reflect upon itself. So, I have argued in the present paper. I have provided a developmental account of how the ingredients necessary for this achievement emerge during the first 4 years of human life. Predominant among the ingredients that are necessary is the ability to view self and other on the same plane as animate agents in the world engaged in intentional relations with the world and each other. In developing the ability to reflect on one's own as well as another person's intentional relations, it is necessary to integrate the first- and third-person aspects of IRs, in order to see them as having an 'inner' and 'outer' aspect, and having this same form whether it be one's own or another's IRs. It is through shared IRs, and dialogical communication with others, that we come to be able to form this integrated perspective of IRs, and, also eventually to distinguish self from other as having potentially different IRs. Early understanding of IRs is of current embodied relations with the world. However, to achieve an understanding of intentionality as having content that merely represents rather than directly relates to the world, the concept of different 'mental' perspectives, and the understanding of the possibility of misrepresentation are required. This is an achievement added onto an understanding of current embodied IRs that develops in the fourth year of life, and it provides not only an understanding of the possible purely mental nature of intentionality, but also provides the ground for a notion of a purely mental self, distinct from its body and world, and conscious of both. But this detached abstract view of self in the world has its naturalistic origins in a more fully embodied and adapted engagement in our social and biological worlds.

*Acknowledgement*

In addition to thanking Scott Jordan for organizing the Concepts of Consciousness workshop, where an early version of this paper was first presented, I would also like to thank the SSHRC of Canada and the RDF of Dalhousie University for research support, which resulted in this article. Requests for reprints should be sent to the author at jbarresi@dal.ca.

## References

Bahrick, L. & Watson, J. (1985), 'Detection of intermodal proprioceptive-visual contingency as a potential basis of self-perception in infancy', *Developmental Psychology*, 21, pp. 963–73.

Barresi, J. (2001), 'Extending self-consciousness into the future', in *The Self in Time: Developmental Perspectives*, ed. C. Moore & K. Lemmon (Hillsdale, NJ: Erlbaum).

Barresi, J. (2004a) 'Intentional relations and divergent perspectives in social understanding', in *Ipseity and Alterity: Interdisciplinary Approaches to Intersubjectivity*, ed. S. Gallagher & S. Watson (Rouen: Presses Universitaires de Rouen).

Barresi, J. (2004b) 'Intentionality, consciousness and intentional relations: From constitutive phenomenology to cognitive science', in *Gurwitsch's Relevancy for Cognitive Science*, ed. L. Embree (Dordrecht: Kluwer Academic Publishers).

Barresi, J. (2004c) 'The neuroscience of theory of mind', presented at *The Eight Annual Conference of the Association for the Scientific Study of Consciousness*, Antwerp, Belgium, June 28.

Barresi, J., & Moore, C. (1996), 'Intentional relations and social understanding', *Behavioral and Brain Sciences*, 19, pp. 107–54.

Braten, S. (1998), 'Infant learning by altercentric participation: The reverse of egocentric observation in autism', in *Intersubjective Communication and Emotion in Early Ontogeny*, ed. S. Braten (Cambridge: Cambridge University Press).

Brentano, F. (1874/1973), *Psychology from an Empirical Standpoint* (London: Routledge and Kegan Paul).

Clark, A. (1997), *Being There* (Boston, MA: MIT Press).

Frege, G. (1918/1967), 'The thought: A logical inquiry', in *Philosophical Logic*, ed. P.F. Strawson (Oxford: Oxford University Press).

Fodor, J.A. (1975), *The Language of Thought* (Cambridge, MA: Harvard University Press).

Fodor, J. (1980), 'Methodological solipsism considered as a research strategy in cognitive science', *Behavioral and Brain Sciences*, **3**, pp. 63–109.
Fodor, J.A. (1981), *Representations* (Cambridge, MA: The MIT Press).
Gallagher, S. (2001), 'The practice of mind: Theory, simulation, or interaction?', *Journal of Consciousness Studies*, **8** (5–7), pp. 83–107.
Gallese, V., Keysers, C. & Rizzolatti, G. (2004), 'A unifying view of the basis of social cognition', *Trends in Cognitive Science*, **8**, pp. 396–403.
Gallese, V., Fadiga, L., Fogassi, L. & Rizzolatti, G. (1996), 'Action recognition in the premotor cortex', *Brain*, **119**, pp. 593–609.
Goldman, A. (1992), 'In defense of the simulation theory', *Mind & Language*, **7**, pp. 104–19.
Gopnik, A. & Meltzoff, A. (1997), *Words, Thoughts, and Theories* (Cambridge, MA: MIT Press).
Gordon, R. (1986), 'Folk psychology as simulation', *Mind & Language*, **1**, pp. 158–71.
Gurwitsch, A. (1966), *Studies in Phenomenology and Psychology* (Evanston, IL: Northwestern University Press).
Harnad, S. (1990), 'The symbol grounding problem', *Physica D*, **42**, pp. 335–46.
Harris, P. (1989), *Children and Emotion* (Oxford: Basil Blackwell).
Hobson R.P. (1991), 'Against the theory of "theory of mind"', *British Journal of Developmental Psychology*, **9**, pp. 33–51.
Hobson, R.P. (1998), 'The intersubjective foundations of thought', in *Intersubjective Communication and Emotion in Early Ontogony*, ed. S. Braten (Cambridge: Cambridge University Press).
Humphrey, N. (1984), *Consciousness Regained* (Oxford: Oxford University Press).
Husserl, E. (1960), *Cartesian Meditations: An Introduction to Phenomenology*, trans. D. Cairns (The Hague: Martinus Nijhoff).
Keysers, C. & Perrett, D.I. (2004), 'The neural correlates of social perception: a Hebbian network perspective', *Trends in Cognitive Sciences*, **8**, pp. 501–7.
Lakoff, G. & Johnson, M. (1999), *Philosophy in the Flesh. The Embodied Mind and its Challenge to Western Thought* (New York: Basic Books).
Leslie, A. (1987), 'Pretense and representation: The origins of 'theory of mind'", *Psychological Review*, **94**, pp. 412–26.
Martin, R. & Barresi, J. (2003), 'Personal identity & what matters in survival: An historical overview', in *Personal Identity*, ed. R. Martin & J. Barresi (Oxford: Blackwell Pub.)
Merleau-Ponty, M. (1945/1962), *Phenomenology of Perception*, trans. C. Smith (London: Routledge).
Merleau-Ponty M. (1964), *The Primacy of Perception*, trans. W. Cobb (Evanston: Northwestern University Press).
Moore, C. & Corkum, V. (1994) 'Social understanding at the end of the first year of life', *Developmental Review*, **14**, pp. 349–72.
Moore, C. (1999), 'Intentional relations and triadic interaction', in *Developing Theories of Intention*, ed. P.D. Zelazo, J. W. Astington & D.R. Olson (Hillsdale, NJ: Erlbaum).
Moore C. & Lemmon, K., ed. (2001), *The Self in Time: Developmental Perspectives* (Hillsdale, NJ: Erlbaum).
Perner, J. (1991), *Understanding the Representational Mind* (Cambridge, MA: MIT Press).
Russell, B. (1940), *An Inquiry into Meaning and Truth* (London: Allen and Unwin).

Sartre, J.-P. (1936-7/1957), *Transcendence of the Ego: An Existentialist Theory of Consciousness*, trans. F. Williams & R. Kirkpatrick (New York: Noonday Press).
Sartre, J.-P. (1964), *Being and Nothingness*, trans. H.E. Barnes (New York: Citadel Press).
Sommerville J.A., Woodward, A.L. & Needham, A. (2005), 'Action experience alters 3-month-old infants' perception of others' actions', *Cognition,* May, B1–B11.
Strawson, G. (2003), 'What is the relation between an experience, the subject of the experience, and the content of the experience?' *Philosophical Issues*, **13**, pp. 279–315.
Varela, F.J., Thompson, E. & Rosch, E. (1991), *The Embodied Mind. Cognitive Science and Human Experience* (Boston, MA: MIT Press).
Woodward, A. (1998), 'Infants selectively encode the goal object of an actor's reach', *Cognition*, **69**, pp. 1–34.
Woodward, A. & Guajardo, J. (2002), 'Infants' understanding of the point gesture as an object-directed action', *Cognitive Development*, **17**, pp. 1061–84.

Liliana Albertazzi

# *At the Roots of Consciousness*
## *Intentional Presentations*

***Abstract**: The Author argues for a <u>non-semantic theory of intentionality</u>, i.e. a theory of intentional reference rooted in the perceptive world. Specifically, the paper concerns two aspects of the original theory of intentionality: the structure of intentional objects as <u>appearance</u> (an unfolding spatio-temporal structure endowed with a direction), and the cognitive processes involved in a psychic act at the <u>primary level</u> of cognition. Examples are given from the experimental psychology of vision, with a particular emphasis on the relation between phenomenal space and colour appearances.*

In the cognitive sciences and in classic journals such as *Behavioural and Brain Sciences, Perception, Perception and Cognition, Perception and Psychophysics, Cognition, Mind and Machines* or *Nature*, regular use is made of such apparently taken-for-granted terms as *perception, awareness, consciousness, intentionality,* and in correlation with them, terms such as *mental image, picture, shape, form, contour, content* and *object*. The ill-considered use of these terms often reveals that the ability has been lost to distinguish among different disciplinary *ambits* (brain sciences, psychophysics, philosophy of mind, artificial intelligence, linguistics, or robotics), as well as aspects of cognitive processes which substantially differ (consider, for instance, the difference between *visual consciousness* and *visual awareness*).

The present paper addresses some of these conceptual problems as they pertain to *intentionality* in general, and *intentional presentations*, specifically. It does so by contrasting contemporary approaches to representation and intentionality with phenomenological theories that emphasize the notion of intentional presentations.

## Representations and Presentations

Many terms assume different connotations not only in different disciplinary ambits but also according to the author: Fodor, Edelman, Chalmers, Kubovy or Shepard, to cite only some examples, mean very different things by the term 'internal image'.

For several years there has been broad consensus on the *inner* character of representation, although once again this character has variously been considered to be a neuronal or perceptive property, or representational property in the strict sense. Representational states, for example, have been conceived in very different ways: as *propositional symbols* (Fodor), as *coherent oscillations* able to unite diverse percepts (Singer), as *quantum processes* in the microtubules of the neurons (Penrose), as caused by *reentrant signalling* among cortical maps (Edelman), or as *neuronal correlates* of consciousness (Chalmers).

Consequently, 'representation' has been used in the cognitive sciences synonymously with 'symbolic representation', 'perception' (mainly in the sense of the visual perception of space), or 'underlying neuronal mechanism' as a detailed representation in the brain of a stable and equally detailed surrounding reality which we are able to internalize with great precision. In this regard, a dominant position has recently been assumed by the notion that *cortical maps* — where visual information seems to be organized retinotopically — constitute the sites of perception.

Externalist theories have also been put forward in recent years. One of them proposes a sensory motor account of vision, in opposition to the idea that, in seeing, the *brain* produces an inner representation of the world which generates the experience of seeing itself.[1] The new externalist theory essentially states that *seeing is a form of action, a way of exploring the environment*. In short, the experience of seeing thus arises at the moment when the organism is able to override the laws of sensorimotor contingency. Cited *inter alia* as evidence in favour of the theory are phenomena relative to change-blindness, or the stability of vision despite eye-movements, although these are phenomena that occur at different levels of information organization and processing.

---

[1] O'Regan & Noë (2001). Externalist conceptions are, for example, Putnam (1975); Burge (1985); Davidson (2001); Clark (1991); Chalmers & Clark (1999).

This externalist theory concerns only vision, and has not yet been applied to hearing, touch, smell or synaesthesia. But in these cases, too, the essential shortcoming of the theory is that it does not give an account of the *ontological* levels of reality. That is, despite recurrent references to phenomenology, the theory fails to realize that the phenomenal level of visual experience is emergent on the neurological level and has different laws of organization, which are of qualitative (Gestalt) type. Finally, ongoing sensorimotor exploration comprises action but not qualia, image or representational content. Reducing the specific spatio-temporal structure of the actual presentation to a sensorimotor action does not explain how the representational level of consciousness comes into being. Still unanswered, therefore, is the question of how a shared and objectified representational content is formed.

Moreover, whether from an externalist or internalist position, the proposals put forward leave a number of crucial issues unresolved:

(1) Definition of what constitutes a *stimulus*, and — because the process of perceptive organization is not contained within the stimuli themselves– how the primary process of phenomenal organization *goes beyond the information given* (understood as a stimulus).

(2) The emergence of qualitative differences, for example among colours, or among sensory modules. Conceiving neuronal activity as an arbitrary code does not explain the nature of the perceptive experiences associated with the elements of the code.

(3) The *format* of the representation (which may be varyingly determined), the *place of its emergence*, its intrinsic *structure*, and above all the fact that the properties of the perceptive object are experiences in the *moment-now*; so that it is not a matter of re-presentation of the world in the strict sense, as in the case of the phenomena of memory, but of an actual *presentation* which has specific rules of formation (Albertazzi, 2001b,c).

*Presentation*, as it is used here, corresponds to the kind of information flow that takes place in a very short time, say around 700 ms (specious present). The information which occurs in the spatio-temporal structure of the presentation consists in a correlation between the state of the environment and a modification of the cognitive system state, resulting in what Koffka (1935) called 'manifest' or 'non-silent organization'.[2] From this point of view this primary information partially corresponds to Gibson's notion of affordance, however attention is to be put on the following:

(1) The specific nature of *space* and *time* which rules the information flow, and which do not correspond to metrical version of space–time (Albertazzi, 2002a, b).

(2) The nature and the behaviour of the *subjective* components as well.[3]

There will be more to say about *presentations* at a later point in the paper. As regards the challenges facing internalist and externalist theories of representation however, there is a problem neither addressed nor noticed underlying the debate: the problem of *reductionism*. Many of the linguistic and conceptual misunderstandings that surround the concepts of 'mental image', 'representation', 'consciousness' or intentionality derive from the tendency of researchers to absolutize the results of inquiries conducted within a particular disciplinary ambit and/or with methods and formalizations specific to that ambit.

Philosophically, according to the still dominant position of analytic philosophy, which informs many of the epistemological assumptions of different disciplines (for example, the theory of perception as inference), there exists *a single reality*, devoid of emergent categorial novelties, which is *described differently* by the different sciences. A position of this kind — which impoverishes reality into a depressing Flatland — is an effective impediment against the advancement of science because it impedes recognition of the *emergence of ontologically different levels of reality*, which require a *differentiated categorial apparatus* because of their categorially diverse nature. Examples are the phenomena of biology, which cannot be analysed with the methodological tools of physics because they involve distinct phenomena of *anticipation* (Rosen 1985) and *dynamic structure*.

## Intentionality

In addition to representation, among the most widely abused words in terms of synonymy is *intentionality*. In modern philosophy it is inextricably bound up with phenomenology, and today a philosophy of

---

[2] On the role of presentation see also below, in the Conclusions.

[3] The original Gestalt theory on the *Afforderungscharakter* of the tertiary qualities implied a specific analysis of subjective processing (*Spannung*, for example). See Metzger (1963, chap. 2).

intentionality comprises an area of analytic philosophy close to a philosophy of mind and restricted to the field of beliefs and/or of speech acts.

Analytical philosophy examines intentionality starting from linguistic propositions, on the assumption that language *represents* the various ways in which we are intentionally directed towards the objects of our experience. A philosophy of intentionality is therefore widely viewed as an analysis of the propositions and/or sentences that remand to and report on mental *states*.

Today, then, the theory of intentionality is oversimplified in a semantic theory whose representative scholars are considered to be Searle (1992), Dreyfus (1984), Dennett (1987; 1991) and Davidson (1980). Some of these authors have played a significant role in the revival of phenomenology in AI research (Winograd, 1972; Dreyfus & Haugeland, 1978). However, they have almost nothing to do with the original conception of Brentanian descriptive psychology. This claim will become clear in the discussion that follows.

Generally speaking, nowadays a state is intended to be intentional if it is directed toward or makes reference to something, i.e. if it is *about* something. Shortly, intentionality is viewed as the *property of aboutness* possessed by certain *states*, which however not necessarily has to be about an object or an individual particular in modern parlance (Bealer 1982). From this point of view aboutness is conceived not in psychological but in *logical* terms, and analysed consequently. An example of the theory of intentionality in analytic terms is given by Chisholm (1957), who gave logical criteria for intentional *language*, trying to define basic logical notions in terms of intentional ones.

Positions, however, are not always univocal. According to Searle (1983), for example, it is not possible to give a logical analysis of the intentionality of the mental; vice versa, any explanation of intentionality should refer to the realm of intentional concepts.

In general, in the analytic framework the philosophy of intentionality brackets off a constitutive part of its original theory — which was eminently psychological — if not denying it, nevertheless delegating some parts of it to other scientific fields, in particular psychology or the broader area of the cognitive sciences. I refer to the nature of psychic *acts* (i.e. *not states*), their spatial, temporal and qualitative *structure*, as well as to their *modes of representation* of objects. Nowadays, in fact, these aspects are usually addressed not by philosophers but, as said, by scientists, for example in the analysis of perception or of imagery processes.

By contrast, the term 'intentionality', in its original sense, embraces a theory much broader than the one now current in philosophy. The Latin etymon denoted both the directing of a psychic *act* towards an object *and* the *object* towards which the act is directed. One of the controversial aspects of this definition therefore lies in defining what constitutes *an objective intention*, whether this is a seeing, hearing, imagining, etc. of an object of some kind.

A second difficulty arises from the fact that the Latin term *actus* translates to both the Aristotelian terms *energheia* and *entelecheia*, which denote respectively *coming-into-being* and the enduring being that results, i.e. *accomplished being* as such or one of its effective, actual or present properties. The expression '*actus mentis*' then has a metaphysical connotation and as such constituted the basis of Franz Brentano's theory of *intentional reference*, which became the standard source for subsequent and even contemporary citations on intentionality.[4]

Historically speaking, Franz Brentano was an exponent of European neo-Aristotelianism. Although his theories arose within a classical framework (in particular Aristotelianism and scholastic philosophy), from the beginning they took the form of an attempt to found philosophy as an *exact science*, in the manner of the natural sciences. For Brentano, experimental psychology, mathematics, geometry, and presumably physiology and biology — given his interest, for example, in the theories of Johannes Müller and Purkinje — were *sciences akin* to philosophy. It was from these that it drew its method, and it was their results that were to be considered when constructing a metaphysics or an ontology, or even when undertaking a reform of traditional logic. Brentano therefore did not forgo construction of a metaphysics, but what he wanted was, so to speak, an empirical, experiment-based metaphysics on the science of psychology.

In Brentano, the term 'intentional' simply denotes a *characteristic of the psychic act*: that is, it is directed towards an object of some kind. This concept of intentionality does not have 'mentalist' overtones, to use a contemporary expression, because Brentano's structures of intentional reference are firmly grounded in *actual perceptive experience*, here and now (the perceptive gist). Perception, however, in this conceptual framework, does not coincide with *brain activity* as such, as is nowadays frequently assumed in cognitive science, but *lies at an emergent level of the organization of information*.

---

[4] Brentano (1995). On Brentano see Albertazzi (2005).

For Brentano, in fact, that which *exists in the proper sense*— i.e in metaphysical terms — is only the *psychic act* of the *concrete presentation* in the actual present: there exist only *things* (individual particulars) in the sense of *temporal-spatial-qualitative actual structures*. The presentation of 'seeing a colour', 'hearing a sound' (i.e. the psychic phenomena in Brentano's terms), occurs at pre-categorial, pre-semantic access to reality. Consequently, it is the *event* itself (seeing, etc. as an *act*, not as a state) which firmly grounds our ontic, primary access to reality, i.e. the phenomenal organization of information.

Information at this level is to be understood neither in terms of the mathematical theory of Weaver and Shannon nor in terms of probabilistic Bayesian terms, which would see perception as theory of inference (Weaver & Shannon, 1947; Dretske, 1981). Classical statistical theories of communication are technologically oriented, and concern technological communication (in Shannon, how to separate noise from information carrying signals), so that they are not immediately suitable for being applied to cognitive phenomena. In this respect, two strong constraints of that theory are the following:

(1) The model implies *a one-way process*.

(2) The *meaning* is assumed to be contained within the physical flow.

Vice versa, the phenomenal organization of information is grounded on the foundational role of psychology (i.e. not of classical physics) in metaphysics and ontology, and this explains the often successful attempts by Brentano and his pupils to create psychology laboratories in which theorizing could be flanked by experimental research. The two branches of Gestalt psychology — those of Berlin and Graz — can, in fact, be traced back to Brentano's theories in various respects (Albertazzi, 2001a; Albertazzi *et al.*, 2001). It is this feature that links the Brentanists with contemporary researchers (psychologists, philosophers, logicians, information technologists, neurophysiologists) in the cognitive sciences. Indeed, the experimental psychology laboratories of the end of the last century performed that same role for theoretical research as do the laboratories of cognitive sciences and artificial intelligence today.

In my opinion, therefore, the need for a Brentanian programme is felt not only in philosophical inquiry but also in *various areas of psychophysical research*. The point to stress is that the areas of research just mentioned often explicitly call for a *non-semantic theory of intentionality*, or in other words a theory of intentional reference rooted in the perceptive world. Paradoxically, this restores wholeness to Brentano's overall project, which was not *mentalist*, nor *linguistic*, nor even *hermeneutic* in its unfortunate Heideggerian developments.

Brentano, moreover, despite the widely held belief to the contrary, did not develop a thoroughgoing theory of intentionality; but rather one in only embryonic form, and especially in his unpublished writings. A thoroughgoing theory of intentionality should fulfil a number of conditions, namely:

(1) The moment-now of the intentional presentation must extend through a continuing set of durations which comprise *fringes* of the past and of the future contents (in experimental terms, the dynamics of the time of presentness),[5] i.e. in its anticipatory structure.

(2) Distinctions must be made among the various *ways* in which the psychic act is directed towards an object (presenting, judging, loving, etc., and their modalizations).

(3) The relation between psychic act, object and content must be reconstructed, with a precise distinction being drawn between the distinctive *parts* of the whole phenomenon.

A modern version of a theory of intentionality of this type, which focuses on the relationship between act, object and content, has been developed by Husserl with some modifications which accentuated the feature of temporal dynamicity.[6]

In my opinion, however, a thoroughgoing development of the Brentano-Husserl conception is to be found in the Gestalt analyses, which distinguish between 'physical' objects as internal to the perceptive field (the objects of seeing, hearing, touching, imagining, loving, etc.), which are directly given, and 'transcendent' objects (stimuli) as externally and indirectly given. On the basis of the above considerations, the argument that I wish to develop below is the following:

(1) Reference to a theory of intentionality is much more complex than the currently canonical versions employed by analytic philosophy.

---

[5] The first outline of a theory of intentionality, in fact, is to be found in an essay written by Husserl in 1894, *Intentionale Gegenstände,* in reply to a question raised by Twardowski in §§ 13 and 14 of his 1894 book (*Zur Lehre vom Inhalt und Gegenstand der Vorstellungen*) on the content and object of presentations.

[6] From a philosophical point of view see Husserl (1966a,b); from an experimental point of view see Benussi (1913). On the topic see Albertazzi (1999).

(2) It can serve the purposes of cognitive science in the development of an empirical-experimental theory of cognitive space, specifically as it pertains to perception (see Albertazzi, 2002b).

My concerns here are two aspects of the original theory of intentionality:

(1) The structure of intentional 'object' as *appearance*, i.e. as un *unfolding spatio-temporal structure endowed with a direction*.

(2) The subjective processes involved in a psychic act at *primary cognitive and ontological level* as well.

An appearance, moreover, should not to be confused with a kind of unreality (*Schein*). An appearance is a *form which manifests itself* (*Erscheinung*), and in which information is directly and qualitatively given.

Here I shall present, on experimental bases, examples of 'phenomenal colour' (appearances) as a non-independent component of phenomenal space.

## Phenomenal Visual Space

A critical issue in the analysis of visual space is the difference among *optical space*, generally identified with the space of physics, and *phenomenal space*, i.e. the anisotropic space of figural and chromatic appearances (see Albertazzi, 2006). The difference is not always thematized in science, for reasons ranging from provenance and disciplinary pigeon-holing to the tools used for analysis and modelling, and more generally the lack of a systematic categorial scheme of the architecture of spaces.

Numerous areas of contemporary science are still dominated by the Galilean conception of science with its general tendency toward reductionism.[7] In other words, the *primary qualities* of observed objects still predominate over their *foundational qualities*, so that, for example, the metric qualities of optical space are taken to be the epistemological (and ontological) foundation of every other type of visual quality.

By 'phenomenal space', instead, is meant the space embedded in the various perception modes. It is the space in which we see, hear, locate, manipulate and evaluate objects, and in which we move. This space possesses not only physical but also ecological and expressive

---

[7] On non-Galilean science see Rosen (1985); Ulanowicz (1997).

properties to which design, for example, pays particular attention. In the cognitive sciences, the physics of this space are often termed 'naïve physics' in order to emphasize that its properties do not always coincide with those of classical physics (Hayes, 1985a,b). In any case, the objects of phenomenal visual space present a *necessary relation of form and colour* (appearances).

In developing my argument, I shall describe in particular a number of experiments on the *microgenesis*[8] *of this phenomenal visual space in actual perception*. The experiments have been conducted as part of experimental inquiry in the area of Gestalt phenomenology. In this research, colour — which has physical, chemical, qualitative and expressive properties — is a paradigmatic example of phenomenal visual space in the same way as phenomena of apparent movement, with which it shares certain features.

The forerunners of this experimental approach to the colour of phenomenal space were Helmholtz and Hering. In fact, for what concerns the psychophysics, both Helmholtz and Hering posed the question of how to achieve the transition from an empirical geometry of the intuitive phenomenal space to its intrinsic realization and idealization in Euclidean form, and thereafter their elaboration in Riemannian, Cantorian, or other terms (Albertazzi, 2002a,b).

For what concerns the aspect of colour, i.e. the way of appearing of perceptive forms, Hering (1964) propounded a sort of 'natural colour system' and maintained that for a systematic grouping of colours the only thing that matters is *colour itself*. From this point of view, therefore, neither frequency nor amplitude, i.e. the physical properties of the radiations, are relevant. As regards the psychophysical measurement of colour, after distinguishing certain reference colours (the *unique* colours: white, black, yellow, blue, red, green), Hering argued that it is possible to quantify a colour by expressing numerically the extent to which it resembles one of these reference colours. However, the concept of similarity does not depend on that of the *mixture of quantitative parts*. Hence one can obtain a plain yellow by mixing radiations which individually appear to be red and green but which, as yellow, do not at all resemble either red or green. A plain yellow (one, that is, which has neither green nor red tints) has zero similarity to red while it has 100% similarity to 'yellow'. An orange may have 40% similarity to red and 40% similarity to yellow, but this does not mean that this orange consists of 40 parts of red and 60 of yellow. Other characteristics of perceived colour are the fact that the parts of colour

---

[8] The term explicitly refers to the approach of the *Ganzheitspsychologie*. See Sander (1930).

perceptions obey, not psychophysical laws but those of figural organization (Benary, 1924), and that a coloured surface is not the sum of the coloured zones into which it can be decomposed by, for example, reduction screens. In fact, the more or less blurred outlines of two surfaces of identical colour change the perception of that colour (Kanizsa, 1960).

The phenomenological point of view on colour has been summed up by Wertheimer, who writes:

> I stand at the window and see a house, trees, sky. Theoretically I might say there were 327 brightness and nuances of colour. Do I have 327? No. I have sky, house, and trees. It is impossible to achieve '327' as such. And yet even though such droll calculation were possible – and implied, say, for the house 120, the trees 90, the sky 117 – I should at least have this arrangement and division of the whole, and not, say, 127 and 100 and 100; or 150 and 177 (Wertheimer, 1938, p. 71).

Both Hering and Wertheimer therefore stress that the structure of visual space, and specifically of colour 'as it appears', has a complexity that cannot be reduced to physical, psychophysical or neurophysiologic properties, despite the presence and reciprocal dependence of these (and other) levels in the organization of the visual field.[9]

## The Physicalistic Trap

To use an expression from Mausfeld, the contemporary theory of perception, in its various versions, constantly risks falling into a 'physicalist trap' (Mausfeld, 2002; 2003a). Put in very rough terms, contemporary epistemological theories of perception are essentially psychophysical and connect with the empiricist/commonsense view of the mind. From this point of view, the perceptual system informs us about elementary physical quantities of whatever type, intended as energy of sounds, intensity and wavelength of light. In short, these theories take identification of the *phenomenal object* with the *physical* (i.e. transphenomenic) *object* for granted and do not consider it at all problematic.[10]

The position has been taken up and strengthened by a functionalist and computational theory which views perception as the *recovery of physical world structure* from sensory structure by means of input-based computational processes (Poggio, 1990), so that, for example, in inverse optics we go from image to the true 3D layout of physical

---

[9] For a theory of levels see Poli (2001; 2007). For what concerns the psychic level see Albertazzi (2001b,c).
[10] See also Gibson (1979).

objects in a scene through distinct scenes and primitives. Added to this position are particular forms of abstractions derived from the technology-shaped refinement of commonsense taxonomies — as happens, for example, with the colour terms in the analysis of colour.[11] This general psychophysical framework is based on specific assumptions:

(1) The ontological and epistemological *priority* of the stimuli over the percept.

(2) The distinction between *stimulus* and *sensation*.

(3) The concept of *transformation* of stimuli.

(4) The *direction* of the stimulus arrow pointing from the external physical world to the interior of the psychic representation. In other words, primary components are solely the stimuli, and perception is somehow parasitic on them.

This psychophysical framework is often applied to colorimetry and neurophysiology, which are the main trends in colour analysis: from this point of view, in fact, the goal of colour vision is to recover the invariant spectral reflectance of objects, i.e., surfaces. These theories, however, are entirely unable to explain other relevant properties of 'phenomenal surfaces', like colour, mode of appearance, stability, tenacity, ruggedness, orientation, etc., i.e. affordances which have a structural *subjective* determination as well (Mausfeld, 2003b). Consider, for example, the different appearance of a square angled at 45° (diamond) and the new properties that it acquires, such as less stability, the sharper outline of the corners, and less compactness.

## The Phenomenological Stance

Köhler was the first to raise serious doubts about classical psychophysics, and the model was subsequently challenged by Gestalt psychology, with its view of a *functional* correspondence between the *spatio-temporal structure* of events and their *modes of behaviour* in the field.

The phenomenological approach to the theory of perception, in fact, starts from an assumption profoundly different from that of classical psychophysics. Aside from individual positions, which may differ markedly (consider the differences within Gestalt theory between the positions of Benussi and Koffka, or of Köhler or Brunswick), a

---

[11] On colour terms analysis see Kay *et al.* (1997).

phenomenological approach to the theory of perception highlights the existence of a *subjective aspect* which is constitutive of the construction of empirical reality and which is due to the constraints of the dynamic structure of presentation.

As Michotte (1950) writes, it is through *events* — which must be understood in a very broad sense as sensory, intellectual, affective, etc. — that we come to know not only objects, processes or group of objects or processes, but also complex spatial-temporal situations. These events are the basis of *all* the knowledge that we acquire about the physical world. In other words, in this framework the directional 'arrow' of inquiry goes in the opposite direction, from the perceptual events (of qualitative nature) to stimuli (of quantitative nature), and consequently perception is *not* viewed as the *mere* transformation of a stimulus into something else.

The 'objects' of intentional presentations, however, strictly speaking are not even *re-presentations of the external stimulus*. 'Seeing a colour' does not simply concern the wavelength, in the sense of the recovery of physical qualities. Vice versa, presentations *exhibit their own structures*, which are governed by internal constraints (objects in Brentano's terms). Phenomenal objects, then, have a complex structure: for example, there is almost always a 'double representation' in the phenomenal field consisting of the figure/ground articulation. More generally, phenomenal objects are characterized by multistability, occlusion, anomalous contour, stereokinesis, masking, and transparency. Consequently, more than 'objects' identifiable according to well-defined classes of properties, there are *appearances* in the perceptual field with strong dynamic and contextual connotation.

The 'stuff' these appearances are made of is not reducible to purely physical dimensions. Consider the brightness and the whiteness of Kanizsa's amodal triangle, which is entirely non-existent from the point of view of stimuli, the 'incorporeal' appearance of shadows, or conversely the corporeality of stereokinetic objects, the transparency of certain surfaces, the continuous transformation of colour on a surface, and colour 'illusions' (Da Pos, 1991; 1997; Harnkil, 1996).

An excellent example of this type of complexity, with particular reference to colour, is provided by Bidwell's Ghost (see Figure 1). The configuration consists of a disc whose surface is half white, half black, with a slit through which a red lamp flashes. When the disc is spinning, you see a bluish green surface of the disc illuminated by an incandescent lamp. Bidwell's Ghost is a clear example of the difference between *veridicality* and *coherence* of structure in the theory of perception and, more generally, of intentional objects. The question is

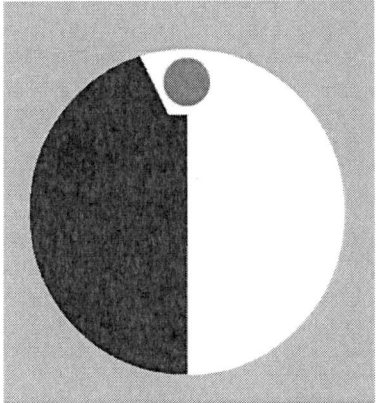

*Figure 1.* Bidwell's Ghost
The grey circle represents the flashing red lamp

the following: Is it correct to talk of the non-veridicality of the appearances of colour if they do not conform with the stimuli? Veridicality, in fact, is classically defined as 'correspondence with a fact or truth', or as the extent to which 'a knowledge structure reflects the *information environment* it *represents*'. Consequently, the question of veridicality is meaningful if:

(1) The primary *ontological* level of reference is assumed to be the physical level.

(2) Information is assumed to be totally *contained in the physical message* transmitted by the stimuli.

(3) *Representation* is a *reflection* of information environment, i.e. it is parasitic on the physical flow.

However, assuming these premises, if one considers the intrinsic difficulty in understanding the *relationship* between information environments and knowledge structures, veridicality becomes a very weak criterion (Walsh *et al.*, 1988).

The Gestalt approach, vice versa, underlines that most visual objects are objects operating on the *presentational structures* of vision, or as field objects, i.e. they have another primary ontological level of reference, the phenomenal level of appearances. They are, indeed, as Brentano maintained, *intentional* objects (Brentano, 1955; Koenderink & van Doorn, 2003), and not mere *re*-presentations of stimuli. From this point of view, even the primary process of thinking has its own value, which consists in the coherence of the presentational structure, so-called visual illusions included.[12]

## Microgenesis of Appearances

The fact that the 'objects' of the phenomenal field are appearances and cannot be reduced to the physical level of reality is particularly evident if one analyses their *dynamic onset in actual perception* here and now (the time of presentness). What one sees, in fact, is not so much well-defined objects as *unfolding patterns*, with environmental, qualitative, salient features, ruled by internal constraints given by the spatio-temporal duration. In these situations, even movement does not have the characteristics of physical movement, but rather that of a *qualitative change* (Husserl 1977; Rensink 2002).

In particular, the microgenesis of the objects of vision highlights the intrinsic connection between movement and colour in visual space.

In demonstration of this point, I shall now describe some experiments of varying complexity — some classic, some recent, and some pertaining to Gestalt inquiry.

*Benham's Top*. The configuration, in black and white, consists of a disc with concentric semi-arcs drawn on it. If you spin the disc counter clockwise, the innermost arcs form dark violet rings, the next arcs pale blue rings, the next green, and the outermost red. If you spin the disc clockwise, the sequence of colours reverses, from dark violet at the outermost to red at the innermost.

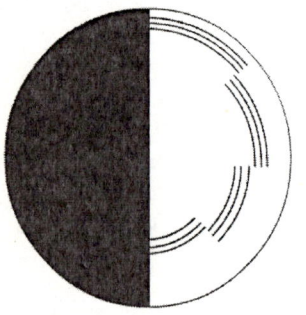
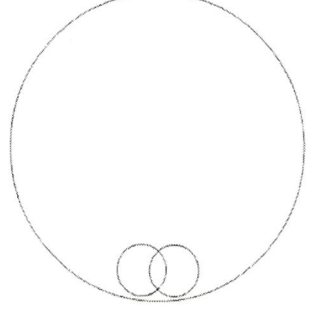

*Figure 2.* Benham's Top          *Figure 3.* Benussi's Circles

[12] On the distinction between primary process thinking and objective secondary process thinking see Piaget (1923); Harris (2001).

*Benussi's Circles.* The configuration, in white and black, consists of a disc with two partly overlapping circles near its lower edge. When the disc is not in motion, what you see are two complete circles. However, when slightly revolving the disc around its axis, you see two circles in eccentric rotational movement sliding over each other (which is a case of figure/ground reversal in movement).

If the same configuration is coloured, it furnishes further information on the nature and quality of visual space. If one removes the outlines of the figures and colours one region red, the other yellow, and their zone of intersection orange, what one sees are *two rotating discs*, of which one is transparent and uniform in colour. What one sees, in fact, is a hollow cylinder rotating and swaying in space. The cylinder is blue on the outside, red on the inside, and it has a yellow base, which we perceptively complete as perfectly circular. The most surprising aspect is its *stable 3D configuration* in visual space (i.e. an intentional object in the strict sense!).

In these phenomena the gestalt law of common fate governs:

(1) The continuous ongoing transformation in successive phases in the time of presentness.
(2) The role performed by the parts unfolding as the whole is constituted.
(3) The non-independence of the parts from the whole.

These features produce the *visual quality* of the three-dimensional corporeality of the stereokinetic whole (the hollow cylinder), and they show that different formats, i.e. *different internal primitives*, must be available (Albertazzi, 2003; 2004).

*Hoffman's Dots.* In this experiment there are 900 red random dots uniformly distributed on a display, and the same number on another display, but some are coloured green. The dots do not move in both displays. If the two frames are presented in succession with brief ISIs, one sees the appearance of a green disc, like a spotlight or a green filter moving over the field of red dots. The green disc has a ghostly glow, and a well-defined subjective border surrounding it.

Other experiments have been conducted using the same display. The subjects have to fix their gaze on the centre of the display. As the speed of the display increases, so does the perception of apparent motion and colour spreading on the disc. Which means that the *construction of motion and the construction of colour go hand in hand.*

Then, in a static display, green appears *at a different depth* slightly in front of the red. With motion, they appear on a single plane. Also, the green dots cease to appear as green and they are perceived as red, like the others. The green of the green dots is detached and reattached in modified form to the newly created disc, and *the entire field of dots is then of uniform depth and colour.*

The diameter of the disc matters, in that the ratings of colour spreading were stronger for disks having a diameter of 1.2°. This also depends on the number and placement of dots within this region.

*Cortese and Anderson.* Cortese and Anderson have conducted a variant on the previous experiment using a black display with a few hundred scattered white dots which never move (Cortese & Anderson, 1991). Some of them, however, turn off and on, simulating the rotation of a rigid ellipsoid floating in front of the field of the white dots. Any dots that are occluded by the ellipsoid are turned off, the rest are turned on. As the ellipsoid rotates from frame to frame, some dots switch off and some switch on, all near the boundary of the simulated ellipsoid. One sees an ellipsoid in 3D whose surface appears to be blacker than the background. The ellipsoid is bounded by a clear 'illusory' contour.

As Hoffman (2003) observes, these experiments conducted on the microgranularity of ongoing perception demonstrate that phenomenal objects are *achievements*. In fact, from a few dots that change colour but do not move:

1. We coordinate the quality of the surfaces we construct with the depth at which we place them.
2. We construct movement, even if all dots remain static.
3. We construct an object and give it a shape, in 2 or 3D.
4. We often endow the object with a border, with somehow smooth and sometimes sharp corners.
5. We place the object in space, in front of a white sheet or behind it.
6. We move that object in space, rotating it or translating it, or both.

According to these experiments, *phenomenal visual space* is configured, to use Husserl's expression, as a dynamically unfolding 'room for movement'.[13] These experiments also shed light on the intentional objects of phenomenal space, on the persistence of their identity, and on the continuity of their existence in the time of presentness, that is,

---

[13] The expression is in Husserl (1997).

during the visual event. They also show that *reality* is a *dimension of our visual experience* closely linked with the *potential for being manipulated* (Michotte, 1991).

As specifically regards colour, the experiments confirm the phenomenological theory of colour, namely that:

1. Colour is not a natural kind.
2. Colour appearance does not pertain to the physical nature of objects.
3. Colour is not an autonomous attribute but a non–independent part of a phenomenal whole.
4. Colour plays different roles in different presentational primitives.
5. Colour exists *in the way it appears*, i.e., it has essentially a qualitative nature (Katz, 1935; Kanizsa, 1960; Sivik, 1997; Mausfeld, 2003a,b).

## Conclusions

On the basis of the previous observations and experiments, intentional objects, i.e., prima facie, *appearances*, appear to be rooted in actual presentations and subjectively (however, non totally) constructed. The perceiver, in fact, is a real part of the 'object', which means that he/she does not have the role of the ideal observer of contemporary epistemology.

The experiments show the presence of an *emergent level of organization* which lies *at the roots of consciousness*: the level of intentional presentations, which are the underlying structures of phenomenal events or, in other words, what effectively *rules* the events.

Presentations are sort of anticipatory structures, i.e. a *processualistic unfolding* (as stereokinesis shows), not merely a passage from state to state as it is generally intended by contemporary theories of dynamics (Port & van Gelder, 1995). These structures are endowed with a direction, so that they can be defined structures of an *oriented dynamics*. However, the structure of presentation refers only to the initial level of awareness of consciousness, i.e. to the act dimension. To develop a complete theory of intentionality, in fact, we should be able to find the inner relations between the continuity of diverse acts of presentation at microgranular level, realizing the Husserlian programme. For this purpose, the first step is constructing a thoroughgoing theory of space, time, and qualitative continua of appearances (and of its abstractions at higher level of conceptualization) (Arnheim, 1969), which are the foundations of our representational experience (Albertazzi, 2002a.).

## References

Albertazzi, L. (1999), 'The time of presentness: A chapter in positivistic and descriptive psychology', *Axiomathes,* **X**, pp. 49–73.
Albertazzi, L. (2001a), 'Back to the origins', in *The Dawn of Cognitive Science. Early European Contributors,* ed. L. Albertazzi (Dordrecht: Kluwer).
Albertazzi, L. (2001b), 'Presentational primitives. Parts, wholes and psychophysics', in *The Dawn of Cognitive Science. Early European Contributors,* ed. L. Albertazzi (Dordrecht: Kluwer).
Albertazzi, L. (2001c), 'The roots of ontics', *Axiomathes,* **XII**, pp. 299–315.
Albertazzi, L. (2002a), 'Continua', in *Unfolding Perceptual Continua,* ed. L. Albertazzi (Amsterdam: Benjamins Publishing Company).
Albertazzi, L. (2002b), 'Towards a neo-Aristotelian theory of continua: Elements of an empirical geometry', in *Unfolding Perceptual Continua,* ed. L. Albertazzi (Amsterdam: Benjamins Publishing Company),
Albertazzi, L. (2003), 'From Kanizsa *back* to Benussi: Varieties of intentional reference', *Axiomathes,* **XIII**, pp. 239–59.
Albertazzi, L. (2004), 'Stereokinetic shapes and their shadows', *Perception* **XXXIII**, pp. 1437–52.
Albertazzi, L. (2005), *Immanent Realism. Introduction to Franz Brentano* (Berlin and New York: Springer).
Albertazzi, L. (ed. 2006), *Visual Thought. The Depictive Space of the Mind* (Amsterdam: Benjamins Publishing Company).
Albertazzi, L., Jacquette, D. & Poli, R. (ed. 2001), *The School of Alexius Meinong* (Aldershot: Ashgate).
Arnheim, R. (1969), *Visual Thinking* (Los Angeles: University of California Press).
Bealer, G. (1982), *Quality and Concept* (Oxford: Oxford University Press).
Benary, W. (1924), 'Beobachtungen zu einer Experiment über Helligkeitskontrast', *Psychologische Forschung,* **V**, pp. 131 ff.
Benussi, V. (1913), *Psychologie der Zeitauffassung* (Wien: Hölder).
Brentano, F. (1995), *Psychology from an Empirical Standpoint,* ed. L. McAlister *et al.* (London: Routledge)
Burge, T. (1985), 'Cartesian error and the objectivity of perception', in *Contents of Thoughts,* ed. R.H. Grimm & D.D. Merrill (USA: University of Arizona Press).
Chalmers, D. & Clark, A. (1999), 'The extended mind', *Analysis,* **58** (1), pp. 10–23.
Chisholm, R.M. (1957), *Perceiving: A Philosophical Study* (Ithaca: Cornell U.P.).
Clark, A. (1991), *Being There: Putting Brain, Body and World Together* (Cambridge, MA: MIT Press).
Cortese, J.M. & Andersen, J. (1991), 'Recovery of 3-D shape from deforming contours', *Perception and Psychophysics,* **XXXXIX**, pp. 315–27.
Da Pos, O. (1991), *Trasparenze* (Milan: Icone).
Da Pos, O. (1997), '*Color Illusions*', in *AIC Color 97* (The Color Science Association of Japan, Kyoto).
Davidson, D. (1980), *Essays on Actions and Events* (Oxford: Clarendon Press).
Davidson, D. (2001), *Epistemology Externalized* (Oxford: Clarendon Press).
Dennett, D. (1987), *The Intentional Stance* (Cambridge, MA: MIT Press).
Dretske, F. (1981), *Knowledge and the Flow of Information* (Cambridge, MA: MIT Press).
Dreyfus, H. (1984), 'Beyond Hermeneutics: Interpretation in late Heidegger and recent Foucault', in *Hermeneutidcs: Questions and Proposals,* ed. G. Shapiro & A. Sica (Amherst MA: University of Massachusetts Press).

Dreyfus, H. & Haugeland, J.(1978), 'Husserl and Heidegger: Philosophy's last stand', in *Heidegger and Modern Philosophy*, ed. M. Murray (New Haven: Yale University Press).
Gibson, J.J. (1979), *The Ecological Approach to Visual Perception* (Boston, MA: Houghton Mifflin).
Harnkil, H. (ed. 1996), *Aspects of Colour* (The University of Art and Design, Helsinki).
Harris, P.L. (2001), 'The veridicality assumption', *Mind and Language,* **16** (3), pp. 247–62.
Hayes, P. (1985a), 'The naive physics manifesto', in *Expert Systems in the Microelectronic Age,* ed. D. Mitchie (Edinburgh: Edinburgh University Press).
Hayes, P. (1985b), 'Naive physics: Ontology for liquids', in *Formal Theories of the Common-Sense World,* ed. J. Hobbs & R. Moore (Norwood, NJ: Ablex Publishing Corp.).
Hering, E. (1964), *Outlines of a Theory of Light Sense* (Cambridge, MA: Harvard).
Hoffman, D.D. (2003), 'The interaction of colour and motion', in *Colour Perception. Mind and the Physical World,* ed. R. Mausfed & D. Heyer, (Oxford: Oxford University Press)..
Husserl, E. (1966a), *Zur Phänomenologie des Inneren Zeitbewusstseins,* ed. R. Boehm, Husserliana X (Den Haag: Nijhoff).
Husserl, E. (1966b), *Analysen zur Passiven Syntesis,* ed. M. Fleischer, Husserliana XI (Den Haag: Nijhoff).
Husserl, E. (1997), *Thing and Space* (Dordrecht: Kluwer).
Kanizsa, G. (1960), 'Randform und Erscheinungsweise von Oberflächen', *Psychologische Beiträge,* **V**, pp.93–101.
Katz, D. (1935), *The World of Colour* (London: Kegan Paul, Trench, Trubnov and Co.)
Kay, P., Berlin, B., Maffi, L. & Merrifield, W. (1997), 'Color naming across languages', in *Color Categories in Thought and Language,* ed. C.L. Hardin & L. Maffi (Cambridge: Cambridge University Press).
Koenderink, J. J., van Doorn, A. (2003), 'Pictorial space', in *Looking into Pictures,* ed. H. Hecht, R. Schwartz & M. Atherthon (Boston, MA: MIT Press).
Koffka, K. (1935), *Principles of Gestalt Psychology* (London: Lund Humphries).
Mausfeld, R. (2002), 'The physicalistic trap in perception theory', in *Perception and the Physical World,* ed. D. Heyer & R. Mausfeld (Chichester: John Wiley & Sons).
Mausfeld, R. (2003a), 'Conjoint representations and the mental capacity for multiple simultaneous perspectives', in *Looking into Pictures,* ed. H. Hecht & R. Mausfeld (Cambridge, MA: MIT Press).
Mausfeld, R. (2003b), '"Colour" as part of the format of different perceptual primitives: The dual coding of colour', in *Perception. Mind and the Physical World,* ed. R. Mausfed & D. Heyer (Oxford: Oxford University Press).
Metzger, W. (1963), *Psychologie: die Entwicklung ihrer Grundannahmen seit der Einführung des Experiments* (Dresden: Steinkopf).
Michotte, A. (1950), 'A propos de la permanence phénoménale: Faits et théories', *Acta Psychologica,* **VII**, pp. 298seq.
Michotte, A. (1991), 'On phenomenal permanence. Facts and theories', in *Michotte's Experimental Phenomenology of Perception,* ed. G. Thinès *et al.* (Hillsdale, NJ: Erlbaum).
O'Regan, K. & Noë, A. (2001), 'A sensory motor account of vision and visual consciousness', *Behavioural and Brain Sciences,* **XXIV**, pp. 939–1031.
Piaget, J. (1923), 'La pensée symbolique et la pensée de l'enfant', **18** (72), pp. 275–304.

Poggio, T. (1990), 'Vision: The other face of AI', in *Modelling the Mind,* ed. K.A. Mohyeldin Said *et al.* (Oxford: Clarendon Press).

Poli, R. (2001), 'The basic problem of the theory of levels of reality', *Axiomathes,* **XII** (3-4), pp. 261–83.

Poli, R. (2007), 'First steps in experimental phenomenology', in *Artificial Cognition Systems* ed. A. Loula, R. Gudwin, & J. Queiroz (Hershey: Idea Group Publishing).

Port, R. & van Gelder, T.J. (1995), *Mind as Motion*: *Dynamics, Behaviour and Cognition* (Cambridge, MA: MIT Press).

Putnam, H. (1975), *Realism and Reason* (Cambridge: Cambridge University Press).

Rensink, R.A. (2002), 'Change detection', *Ann. Rev. Psychol.* **53**, pp. 245–77.

Rosen, R. (1985), *Anticipatory Systems. Philosophical, Mathematical and Methodological Foundations* (New York: Pergamon Press).

Sander, F. (1930), 'Structures, totality of experience and gestalt', in *Psychologies of 1930,* ed. C. Murchison (Worcester, MA: Clark University Press).

Searle, J. (1983), *Intentionality* (Cambridge: Cambridge University Press).

Searle, J. (1992), *The Rediscovery of the Mind* (Cambridge MA: MIT Press).

Shannon, C.E. &, Weaver, W. (1947), *Mathematical Theory of Communication* (Urbana & Chicago, IL: University of Illinois Press).

Sivik, L. (1997), 'Color system for cognitive research', in *Color Categories in Thought and Language* ed. C.L. Hardin & L. Maffi (Cambridge: Cambridge University Press).

Ulanowicz, R. (1997), *Ecology. The Ascendent Perspective* (New York: Columbia University Press).

Walsh, J.P., Henderson, C.M. & Deighton, J. (1988), 'Negotiated belief structures and decision performance: An empirical investigation', *Organizational Behaviour and Human Decision Processes,* **42**, pp. 194–216.

Wertheimer, M. (1938), 'Laws of organization in perceptual forms', in *A Source Book of Gestalt Psychology* ed. W.E. Ellis (London: Routledge).

Winograd, T. (1972), *Understanding Natural Language* (New York: Academic Press).

Cees van Leeuwen

# *What Needs to Emerge to Make You Conscious?*

*Abstract: Perceptual experience can be explained by contextualized brain dynamics. An <u>inner loop</u> of ongoing activity within the brain produces dynamic patterns of synchronization and de-synchronization that are necessary, but not sufficient, for visual experience. This inner loop is controlled by evolution, development, socialization, learning, task and perception-action contingencies, which constitute an outer loop. This outer loop is sufficient, but not necessary, for visual experience. Jointly, the inner and outer loop may offer sufficient and necessary conditions for the emergence of visual experience. This hypothesis has methodological, empirical, theoretical, and philosophical implications.*

## 1. Basic concepts:
### Necessary and sufficient conditions for visual experience

Perceptual theorists have made phenomenal experience the basis for understanding brain mechanisms; let us start, however, from mechanisms in an effort to approach phenomenology. It is generally understood that neurons located early in the visual processing stream, for instance, the lateral geniculate nuclei or the primary visual cortex, respond to relatively simple local features. Later neurons, e.g. in the infero-temporal cortex, respond to a variety of often strikingly complex features (e.g. Tsunoda *et al.*, 2001). When the visual system is stimulated, within a few hundreds of milliseconds all these neurons become engaged in a pattern of activity. I shall refer to the mechanisms that give rise to this pattern as the *inner loop*. Its dynamics will explain the *intensity* with which certain collective patterns of features are experienced.

One way to connect these activity patterns to phenomenology is by an identity postulate (Macauley & Bechtel, 2001). O'Brien and Opie (1999) presented a theory in which the inner loop was treated as constituting the vehicle of consciousness. By this they mean that the patterns of activity within this system are both necessary and sufficient for experience. This is unsatisfactory because it leaves unanswered the important question of what accounts for salience or *attensity*, the likelihood that something is attended to. For designed machines, as well as for evolved biological systems, we may expect the system to respond strongly to the presence of certain objects — e.g. a tiger emerging from the bushes, or a stone to throw at it and make it go away. Such predispositions make neurons sensitive to salient object features — the eyes of the tiger staring at you.

Attensity is essentially context-sensitive. Predispositions to respond to objects such as tigers need be explained in terms of their past or present status in the world outside the brain. This means the inner loop is necessary, but not sufficient for experience. A similar view, which was called contextual emergence, has been discussed in depth by Jordan and Ghin (2006). External factors contribute on a huge variety of time scales: evolution, development, socialization, learning, task and both indirect (Hommel *et al.*, 2001; Ziessler, Nattkemper & Frensch, 2004) and instantaneous (Gibson, 1979; Lee & Reddish, 1981) perception/action contingencies. Let us call the totality of all these interactions the *outer loop*. Naturalist explanations consider the outer loop as necessary and sufficient for experience. 'Brain-in-a-vat' and 'Swampman thought experiments may readily convince us however, that it is not the case (Davidson, 2001; Putnam, 1981; Steinitz, 1994). Contrary to what externalists would like us to believe, environments quite different from ours, including those in which a brain is kept alive and stimulated artificially in a vat, permit experience. Swampman, a molecular replica of a human but without having ever participated in an outer loop, could have consciousness just the same. I, therefore, propose that the outer loop is sufficient, but not necessary for the emergence of consciousness.

## 1.1. Brain dynamics and evolution

We can hope to obtain sufficient and necessary conditions only by studying the interplay of both the inner and outer loop; of brain activity and the mechanisms that tune it to the world. According to Fodor

(1983), through learning and evolution, the outer loop optimizes the inner loop for information processing, so we can quickly throw the stone at the tiger. Evolution made certain processes local, or informationally encapsulated, in order to prevent processing from becoming an exhaustive search. On account of salience, brains became modular.

Fodorean modularity however, may be insufficiently flexible for perception — without the tiger you wouldn't be so desperate for that stone. Salient objects are usually characterized by rather disparate collections of features; for bush fires the heat, the smell, and the glow. For these reasons evolutionary pre-tuning can only be achieved by non-local communications between neurons; evolution needs to optimize global as well as local communication. Fodor (1983) believed that both could not be done within the same system. His solution was to divide the system into lower and higher level functions and have the lower ones optimized for local and the higher ones for global communication. For these, he postulated isotropy, meaning, among other things, that anything could, in principle, be connected to anything.

Criticizing Fodor is easier than showing that alternative possibilities exist within the given assumptions. For Fodor, absence of isotropy is part of the definition of modularity. However, Carruthers (2003; 2005ab) and Barrett (2005; Barrett & Kurzban, 2006) argue that encapsulation is not actually a necessary or even relevant requirement for a multi-modular (or massively modular) cognitive architecture. Fodor's idea that evolution optimizes the attensity of information processing could therefore be realized in a way that combines modularity and isotropy into one single system. To demonstrate this possibility, let us first formalize the notions a bit to allow their application to neural network connectivity. Modules have many internal and few external connections, so the connectivity is characterized by a large proportion of 'triangles'. This property is expressed in the clustering coefficient of a network. This is the average proportion that, given a unit A is connected to units B and C, there is also a connection between B and C. Isotropy, on the other hand, implies a low number of intermediate nodes that need to be visited, on average, to travel between two arbitrary nodes A and B. This measure is called the network's *characteristic path length*. In regular network structures, both the path length and clustering coefficient are high and in random ones, both are low. What we are looking for are networks with high clustering coefficients in combination with low characteristic path lengths. These do, indeed, exist and are called 'small-world' networks (Watts & Strogatz, 1998).

Small world networks, with their combination of high clustering coefficient and short characteristic path length, offer the best of both worlds. In exchange of information, they are both globally and locally efficient (Latora & Marchiori, 2001). From an evolutionary perspective, it is therefore plausible that this design is found throughout the brain. The prominence of small-world network connectivity is increasingly being recognized in the neurosciences; small-world structure has been detected on the large scale using magnetoencephalography in the functional connectivity of brain areas (Stam, 2004), as well as on the small scale, in the anatomy of the visual cortex (Mountcastle, 1997)[1] and the connectivity arising in cultured neuronal networks (Shefi et al., 2002).

Small-world connectivity may be a desirable property, but how could evolution ever have selected it, given that it is unlikely all details of brain connectivity are represented in the human genome? We propose that evolution has predisposed the system to develop this connectivity in adaptation to spontaneous activity. In other words, the inner loop comes to the help of the outer loop: the intrinsic dynamics of network activity has a constructive role in making network connectivity optimal for information processing.

To realize this idea, we proposed to apply the Hebbian principle of 'what fires together wires together' to spontaneous network activity (Gong & van Leeuwen, 2003; 2004; Kwok et al., in press; van den Berg & van Leeuwen, 2004). In these studies, networks are rewired according to a rule that connects pairs of neurons that spontaneously fire in synchrony, and disconnects ones that fail to synchronize. Kwok et al. (in press) showed that a network of Hindmarsh-Rose model neurons, starting from random connection distributions, rewires itself into a small-world network. The gist of these studies is that spontaneous, intrinsic brain activity helps establish optimal brain structure.

In mammals prior to or briefly after birth, spontaneous activity clearly differs from that in the developed brain. It resembles that of adults in deep (slow wave) sleep: recurrent bursts, leading to massive synchronization (Feller, 1999; van Pelt et al. 2004). In the retina, for instance, such activity takes the form of travelling waves, which are essential for the organization of connectivity in the lateral geniculate nuclei prior to birth (Penn et al., 1998). I propose that this kind of

---

[1] Although this author did not make explicit claims that the structures they observed were small worlds, the combination of modules (micro columns) and a limited number of long-range connections was observed that, according to Watts and Strogatz (1998), is characteristic of small world networks.

activity itself is not necessary for consciousness, but is a necessary precursor that contributes to its formation.

Bursts of activity in the brain are traditionally associated with pathological conditions involving epilepsy. However, the developing circuits show spontaneous bursts of a different kind. Whereas in epileptic activity, there is evidence of a low-dimensional chaotic signal at the level of EEG (Babloyantz & Destexhe 1986; Breakspear *et al.*, 2006), bursts of synchronized activity in immature rat hippocampal slice preparations that lead to depolarizing potentials are locally generated from different initiation sites (Menendez de la Prida & Sanchez-Andres, 2000). Nakatani *et al.* (2003) analysed these signals and concluded that they possess deterministic, dynamical structure. Maeda *et al.* (1998) found that bursts of synchronized spikes led to long-term potentiation (LTP) of synapses in neurons cultured in vitro. Postsynaptic bursting was found to be associated with Hebbian induction of long term potentiation (Otsu *et al.*, 1995; Pike *et al.*, 1999). Thus the dynamics of spontaneous activity appears to play a constructive role in the development of an evolutionary optimal architecture. With this we may conclude that the interplay of inner and outer loop, depicted as self-sustained growth and development of a well-connected brain, is logically coherent and empirically plausible.

## 2. Methodological Perspective: Perceptual experience reliably observed

Consciousness' 'hard' problems (Chalmers, 1995) are referred to as such, not because they are hard for zombies, but because we may question whether it is possible to get a handle on conscious experience. Philosophers have admonished us that our experience is shaped by the concepts we are using to describe it (Hanson, 1958). According to Churchland (1985), this is unavoidable because each perception implies a judgement that something is the case. There must, therefore be a naïve theory implied in this talk, even in the most mundane utterances, such as: 'I prefer this food-processor because of its colour'. As all naïve theories are likely to be false, so is this one. This would render our own everyday consciousness talk just as fake as that of zombies.

Should philosophical qualms concerning zombies and other false consciousness phenomena concern us? Whereas in machines, conscious experiences would at best be epiphenomenal and at worst a legal liability (i.e., issues regarding computer rights), questions about our own conscious experience have always been our sciences' raison d'être. Perhaps, therefore, we should be concerned. Fortunately, we need not deny the cognitive element in perception to disagree with Churchland's view. Theory-ladenness does not always stand in the way of treating our experiences as real: Competing theories may have access to the truth (Putnam, 1987) and some phenomena are likely to survive changes in our theoretical beliefs.

Often overlooked in the philosophical debate, Gestalt phenomena of perceptual organization are particularly resilient against our beliefs. Many of them have been known throughout the history of psychology; some of them have only drawn attention recently. For about a century, they have been studied using experimental techniques. Some of these have not stood the test of time, or better, that of the theory-ladenness of observation; others have proven useful to address the 'hard' problem. These typically rely on low-level 'easy problem' capabilities such as discrimination or detection, rather than on the capacity to report directly what we see. Even though these procedures do not involve experience directly, they can only be understood in reference to experience.

Consider, for example, the Kanizsa triangle: on a light background of uniform illumination, three pac-man figures are facing towards an equidistant centre. Between them, a slightly brighter illusory triangle is experienced, while none is actually drawn. We could measure the strength of the illusion quantitatively by adjusting the illumination of the surface of the triangle until it can no longer be detected. We can correct our measurement for response biases by asking participants to rate the confidence in what they report. None of this makes sense without the assumption that the participants in these experiments are actually experiencing the triangle.

Phenomena we cannot eliminate and that follow observational laws make an excellent basis for a theory. And while at first glance, Gestalt phenomena might appear to constitute isolated phenomena, there are many that are quite pervasive. One example is organization by proximity. Here, Kubovy et al. (1998) were the first to propose quantitative laws. Another pervasive Gestalt phenomenon is symmetry. Object symmetry is hard to ignore and is pervasive in art and design, as well as nature. As a pioneer in studying the laws of symmetry, we may consider Garner (1962), whose laws of symmetry fit the data with surprising accuracy (Garner & Clement, 1963).

Gestalt phenomena have repeatedly been used as tools to uncover brain mechanisms. See Ehrenstein et al. (2003) for a recent overview. As a result, we can explain certain illusions of achromatic contrast from properties of the receptive fields of individual neurons in brain area V1 (Baumgartner, von der Heydt & Peterhans, 1984). Kanizsa's triangle could be explained by spreading of brightness from edges (Paradiso & Nakayama, 1991). Churchland (2005) recently proposed a similar approach to the perception of colour. Note that all these studies use an identity postulate, in which functional brain architecture is considered sufficient and necessary for the occurrence of a phenomenon.

The phenomena discussed so far seem to be predominantly static. This raises two issues. First: is our visual experience more than a succession of intrinsically static snapshots (Neisser, 1967)? Second: if considered dynamically, is it more appropriately described as autonomous or as controlled by outer-loop variables such as task, experience, expectation? The latter may be palpable in cases with direct perception-action couplings. Some have argued that this pertains to all perception (Gibson, 1979; O'Regan & Noë, 2001). How strongly, therefore, does the outer loop control typical inner loop phenomena? The next two sections deal with these issues and what Gestalt phenomena have to say about them.

## 2.1. Experiences are dynamical

Gepshtein and Kubovy (2000) showed how the snapshot metaphor fails in perception of motion. They used a dynamical stimulus in which they could control independently the perceptual organization within each frame (spatial grouping) and the process that links the successive spatial structures toward the experience of apparent motion (temporal grouping). The study showed that the experience of apparent motion cannot be explained as a sequence of independent processes encapsulated in separate time slices. Rather, spatial grouping constantly interacts with temporal grouping such that outcomes of the spatial process within each frame depend on temporal grouping. Under some special circumstances, temporal grouping can be weakened to the degree that the experienced direction of apparent motion (e.g., the perceived direction of motion) depends entirely on the outcomes of spatial grouping. Yet, as Gepshtein and Kubovy (2000) demonstrated, this is only a special case of a quantitative law in which an interaction of spatial and temporal processes determines the visual awareness of motion.

The dynamics of perception is revealed also when the stimulus is static. Fixate on Figure 1a. While the figure remains present you will repeatedly experience spontaneous changes in intensity of different groupings of its components. This phenomenon has traditionally been called perceptual *multistability* (even though, strictly speaking, no stability is involved). Special cases are the widely-known bi-stable or ambiguous figures, such as the Necker cube (Figure 1b), in which perception switches back and forth between two approximately equally preferred orientations.

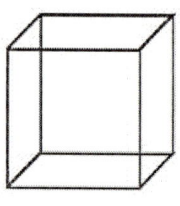

Figure 1a
Multi-stable figures

Figure 1b
Bistable figure: the Necker cube

Dwell times, the durations between two switches, seem to follow a Gamma distribution (Borsellino *et al.*, 1972; Murata *et al.*, 2003) although also other right-skewed and fat-tailed distributions have been proposed. It might, therefore, seem that switching is a purely stochastic process. However, deterministic dynamic processes can produce such distributions as well (van Leeuwen *et al.*, 1997). In fact, certain properties can be observed in the dwell times, such as inertia and memory, that are characteristic of dynamic rather than stochastic systems (Gao *et al.*, 2006; Hock *et al.*, 1993). Perceptual multistability therefore, is best characterized by dynamics.

## 2.2. The dynamics of experience is non-autonomous

Perceptual dynamics explains why we actively maintain the continued presence of a percept, even though less than 100 ms is enough to extract enough visual information for identification purposes. This is because there is an infinity of structural information to be discovered. The 'inner loop' dynamics is particularly powerful and useful. It will allow a perceiver to make discoveries, such as a camouflaged animal not observed at first sight. While enjoying the beauty of a Japanese garden, you may discover after a while that the tops of the trees that you see, and originally believed to be lining the garden actually belong to the hills much further away. Looking longer at a work of abstract, geometrical art, you will always discover new ways in which the same display can be organized, which will contribute to your appreciation of it. Discovering the hidden structure in a visual display plays a role in the creative process of designers (Verstijnen *et al.*, 1998a,b) and artists (van Leeuwen *et al.*, 1999).

The power of inner loop dynamics might alone be considered sufficient for experience, and best described as spontaneous, autonomous, or intrinsic. However, with ambiguous figures, the ability to switch between different interpretations depends on learned, culturally mediated knowledge (Rock et al., 1994). It could still be maintained that, once learned, switching occurs independently of what we believe, so that external context operates at a time scale sufficiently different from the experiential dynamics to argue that the latter is autonomous. We may counter that perceivers can, to some extent, control perceptual switching. Instruction or intention can bias one interpretation over another (Peterson & Hochberg 1983). But still this could be said to happen at a different time scale, as perceivers do not control individual reversals but rather their overall rate (Struber & Stadler, 1999; Toppino, 2003).

I propose that the separation in time scales is based on an illusion. We experience perceptual switching as instantaneous. But in fact the processes in the visual system that produce it typically require approx 0.5 s (Ito *et al.*, 2003; Nakatani & van Leeuwen, 2005; 2006). This is, by all means, a noticeable duration. Why, then, do we have the illusion that it is instantaneous? In a wider context, why do people often report that creative solutions to problems occur to them instantaneously? We may expect theoretical answers to these questions in the next section. For now, what matters is that the proposed distinction between levels breaks down. The inner loop, therefore, cannot be sufficient to explain experience even in key phenomena such as perceptual switching.

## 3. Theoretical implications:
## Ongoing Dynamics, Synchrony, Chaotic Itinerancy

After we have reached a conclusion of what is to be modelled, let us think about what type of model to choose. When we think of models in cognitive science, we distinguish between symbolic (Baars, 1993) and dynamic ones. As we are interested in evolution through time, we shall only consider the latter ones. These describe the evolution of a set of features. Each feature may be considered as a value on a different dimension; accordingly we have a space, in which there are as many dimensions as there are features to the system. This space is the state space of the system. A dynamical system is a system of which the future state depends deterministically on the present one, according to a law that governs its evolution through time. This is called its trajectory. There are linear systems and nonlinear ones. In linear systems small changes have small effects on the trajectory and large changes big effects. By allowing consciousness to have, for instance, a threshold, we consider nonlinear systems only. We further distinguish low-dimensional and high-dimensional dynamical systems, depending on the number of features used to describe the current system states. Because the vehicles of consciousness were conceived as distributed patterns, we will consider high-dimensional systems only.

The high-dimensional, nonlinear dynamical systems most widely used within psychology are connectionist models. These are neural networks used to model a psychological function. In these models, activation values characterize the state of a set of units (typically, but not necessarily, thought of as neurons). These values change over time as a function of the other units with which they are connected. The influence of each connection is determined by a strength, or weight. The weights determine the movements of activity within the network. With these dynamics, it is theoretically possible to build computers equivalent to Turing machines, the most powerful machinery of symbolic computation (Siegelmann & Sontag, 1991, van der Velde, 1993).[2] To enable computation, some units receive external input while others receive input from other units, with the values of certain units being read off as output. Starting from the input, activation spreads until it reaches the output units. When the network has loops, there is no such obvious ending. Spreading activation loops back, in principle, indefinitely. However, the process is likely to lead the network into certain subsets of states. These are called attracting sets. Trajectories within such a set are called *attractors* (Amit, 1986; Freeman *et al.*, 2001; Hirsh, 1989; Parisi, 1986; Skarda & Freeman, 1987; Yao & Freeman, 1990). Computation in such systems means coming sufficiently close to an attractor state. At that time, the values of the output units constitute the outcome of the computation.

In most models, this means that all changes come to a halt. That is, the system has become *static*. Alternatively, the activation values keep oscillating within a certain range and the system loops through a sequence of patterns that, as a whole, is stable (von der Malsburg & Schneider, 1986). Note that this loop could be infinite (technically: a strange attractor). In a static attractor model, the outcome of a

---

[2] Neural networks may, in fact, yield computational power that is even greater than symbolic computation on account of continuous valuation. See Costa and Mycka (2005) for a recent overview and Siegelmann (1999) for an extensive treatise.

computation can only be a single pattern at a time; with oscillations, these can be multiple patterns, which we may distinguish by their *phase*; features belonging to the same pattern are synchronized. Oscillatory systems can distinguish multiple visual objects from each other and from the ground (von der Malsburg & Schneider, 1986), store them in working memory (Raffone & Wolters, 2001), or learn associations between multiple objects simultaneously (Raffone & van Leeuwen 2001).

Nevertheless, these kinds of dynamics do not lead to multi-stability. In perceptual switching the system does not loop through a predictable sequence of states (Borsellino et al., 1972). Since by definition, spontaneous changes are excluded in the case of stable attractors, perhaps we should consider transient states of synchronized oscillation. This view has gained enormous ground in neuroscience since seminal work in the 80s and 90s (Engel & Singer, 2001). Singer and his colleagues proposed that brain tissue involved in processing certain information reaches a brief, transient state of synchronization. How these temporal patterns could be used to encode visual information has recently been suggested by Hopfield and Herz (1995). Synchronizations that are transient in time, however, cannot account for the extendedness in time of a visual experience (Gepshtein & Kubovy, 2000). That is, regardless of multi-stability or ambiguity, there is always an experienced duration in which experience does not change. Let us call this the *psychological present* (Stroud, 1967).

If neither stable attractors nor transients can account for the psychological present, we might seem to have run out of alternatives. But in fact, connectionist models, mathematically speaking, belong to the family of complex systems, many of which have dynamics known as *chaotic itinerancy* (Kaneko, 1985; Kaneko & Tsuda, 2001; Tsuda, 2001). These systems are characterized by fragile attractors corrupted by noise. Regions where such attractors used to be are still preferably visited, as the system is attracted to them. The system will dwell in such regions for some time, and subsequently escape to another part of its state space. The time periods during which a system dwells near a corrupted attractor are referred to as *laminar periods*. We may envisage models in which the system that dwells in a laminar period shows a pattern of synchronized activity that persists for a while, without being stable. This system will spontaneously trade one pattern for another from time to time.

Our preferred models should have synchronization, fragile attractors, and noise. Synchronization is a natural characteristic of physical oscillators; fragile attractors are predominant in complex systems

(Kaneko, 2002), and finally, (thermodynamical) noise is always given in physical systems. Thus we are not dealing with a freak phenomenon, but one we may expect to be widespread in nature. The utility of this dynamics for information processing has been argued extensively in Tsuda (2001). Models based on these principles have been used in neuroscience, most notably the model of the olfactory bulb proposed by Basu and Liljenstrøm (2001) and Skarda and Freeman (1987). We used these principles to model certain visual illusions (van Leeuwen et al., 2000) as well as switching in ambiguous figures (van Leeuwen et al., 1997). These models illustrate that chaotic itinerancy qualifies as a plausible candidate mechanism for the inner loop.

## 4. Conceptual Implications: hologenesis and coherence interval

The dynamics of chaotic itinerancy offers patterns of synchrony that appear during the laminar periods. These are the basis for the unity of experience which, therefore, need not be illusory at all. Laminar intervals have a certain duration; the phenomenal counterpart of which is the psychological present (Stroud, 1967). The laminar intervals are, thus conceived, the vehicles of consciousness. In multi-stability, they are co-existent in time with the persistence of a certain percept. Recall the puzzle that perceptual switching appears instantaneous whereas the switching processes lasts at least 0.5 s (Ito et al, 2003). During the switching, the system is on a transient between two laminar intervals, so there is no persistent synchrony and no duration.[3]

Being the vehicles of consciousness is probably not the reason why these laminar intervals exist. In line with what was said in Section 1, I proposed that they have been selected for their information processing function (van Leeuwen, 1998; van Leeuwen & Bakker, 1995). Information processing is taking place in a distributed fashion within neural groups, or clusters. At the level of the dynamics of their collective signal, this is manifested as irregular activity that is noise to the rest of the brain. As time proceeds, the smaller units connect into larger ones to form temporary cooperative clusters. This is manifested in the activity growing more regular; certain units synchronize their activity and the system enters a laminar period. In order to communicate information computed in a certain region of the brain to the rest of the brain, it is essential that the information not change during this

---

[3] From this explanation the interesting hypothesis follows that time intervals with perceptual switching are perceived to last shorter than ones without. Incidentially, I tested this hypothesis in my masters thesis (van Leeuwen & Leeuwenberg, 1984).

interval. This is why laminar intervals are functional for distributed computation. Laminar periods with this function are called *coherence intervals*. The length of functional coherence intervals depends on how long it takes for other parts of the brain to receive this information. Information takes variable time to travel from one region to another and as a result, the coherence interval will vary in duration.

This leads to the prediction that the duration of synchronized activity is correlated with information processing demands — the more complex the information, the longer the duration. The prediction follows simply from the distributed character of information processing. The more complex the information, the larger the number of different circuits, or clusters, involved. The larger this number, the longer the interval will have to be for information transmission to be effective. Information will arrive from different clusters at different rates. The total transmission time is determined by the slowest transmission rate. The maximum transmission rate from a random sample of almost any distribution will increase with sample size. This principle, when applied to coherence intervals, is called *hologenesis*.

To understand the concept of hologenesis, consider that when a coherence interval is short, all communication beyond a certain level is cut off. Thus information of a certain complexity can never be reached. As a result, the shorter the interval, the more restricted is the range of interaction, and the less complex the information communicated. The resulting direct relationship between complexity and response latencies has been fundamental to mental chronometry since Donders (1969). The difference with Donders' approach is that response latencies do not measure processing times but 'waiting' times needed for neural communication. The limited duration of the coherence interval prevents feature integration from reaching a level of full saturation –in the sense that information is prevented from becoming available everywhere in the system. This prevents the percept from becoming an undifferentiated global whole, but enables it to be more than a set of pair-wise connections (Hommel & Colzato, 2004). Note: I use 'global' and 'local' exclusively as functional notions, referring to the complexity of the information. So these notions are unrelated to spatial extent of a stimulus. However, because many parts of the brain have a topological organization, functionally and spatially local or global are sometimes correlated. According to our current concepts, processing starts from local features and proceeds in time towards an increasingly encompassing range of integration automatically (van Leeuwen & Bakker, 1995). But this does not necessarily mean that small comes before big. See Love *et al.* (1999)

for one of the rare empirical studies in which these important distinctions were carefully made.

Some tasks require more complex information than others. For instance, detecting symmetry in the plane can be done through detecting pair-wise correspondences between points; for detecting symmetry in three dimensions, four-tuples of points are needed (Wagemans, 1993). To enable the same system to calculate information of different complexity in minimal time, we consider the length of coherence intervals to be controlled via the outer loop. Longer coherence intervals automatically imply the availability of a wider range of contextual information. In experiments, this will enhance priming and interference effects. Context-dependence is itself context-dependent. This explains the way in which perceptual priming (Stins & van Leeuwen, 1993), shape detection (Hogeboom & van Leeuwen, 1997), and interference (van Leeuwen & Lachmann, 2004) depend on task.

## 4.1. Hologenesis and coherence interval in brain dynamics

If coherence intervals are a fundamental property of brain activity, they should be observable in the EEG of the resting brain. This activity shows dynamic patterns of synchrony that last for sufficient time to count as coherence intervals. They qualify as deterministic in nature, indicating that they originate from a dynamic rather than a stochastic process (Gong *et al.*, 2003; Ito *et al.*, 2005, in press).

When the brain is processing information, its dynamics are irregular but once a perceptual state has been reached, a period of synchronous activity can be observed (Nakatani & van Leeuwen, 2005, 2006). Such periods also occur prior to the presentation of stimuli that are being being anticipated (Nakatani *et al.*, 2005). We measured the length of coherence intervals in single trials of event-related EEG and obtained preliminary evidence that the length depends on task (Nikolaev *et al.*, 2005). A display was presented in which a hidden triangle had to be detected and its orientation reported. Coherence intervals starting 200 ms after stimulus presentation were longer in this condition than in a control condition, where participants merely viewed the triangle displays and responded by pressing an arbitrary button. We are currently investigating whether coherence intervals are adjusted in accordance with the complexity of information processed.

In perception, adaptive control is efficient, subtle, and therefore difficult to observe. We may, therefore, consider cases where regulation fails. These have been discussed, most eloquently, by Susan Greenfield in her book *Journey to the Centres of the Mind* (1995) reviewed for this journal by Campbell (1999). Like I do, Greenfield considers consciousness at the physiological level as the dynamic cooperation of groups of neurons. These form temporary associations that last for varying durations called neuronal Gestalts. Greenfield applies these notions, extending them into the realm of pathology. Failure to make neuronal Gestalts larger than a certain size might result in experiences characteristic of schizophrenics. Failure to make ones that are small will result in a few becoming dominant, leading to experiences characteristic of depression.

## 5. Conclusion & Discussion

In the present paper, I have proposed that the necessary conditions for conscious experience are to be found in the ongoing dynamic activity of brain — what I refer to as the inner loop. Of central importance are the concepts of hologenesis and coherence interval. These intervals are the vehicles for the moments of our conscious experience. Brain dynamics are the only dynamics we know of that produce experience. We do not know how, but an accurate description would help us progress. Here I proposed a description along the lines of chaotic itinerancy. As we have suggested elsewhere (Gong et al., 2003), different principles, such as self-organized criticality (Bak, 1996), might also be considered.

Evolution did not have experience in mind when it produced the conditions sufficient for its emergence. It may have been optimizing the conditions for information processing. Chaotic itinerancy has clear information processing utility. It allows systems to avoid getting stuck in attractors, and enables rapid transitions and exploration (Tsuda, 2001). These features are achieved with maximal autonomy and minimal external control. Still, without external control these systems would not be able to function. I discussed some of the control mechanisms that are nested within the outer loop. I propose that coherence intervals are optimized in length with respect to task-specific information processing demands. Context-dependency of information processing thereby becomes context-dependent itself: groups of neurons may or may not interact depending on the task, which automatically implies that the receptive fields of individual neurons are task-dependent.

I proposed that our brains are also optimized for information processing demands by mechanisms that work on the scale of development. The mechanism to optimally configure the network structure prior to experience is based on the intrinsic dynamics of the brain itself. Whereas the activity helps shape this architecture, the architecture, once established, supports these patterns of activity and makes them more robust (Gong & van Leeuwen, 2004). Activity and structure, therefore, constitute a symbiotic pair. I predict that we will encounter them frequently in the brain. The view that brain activity and architecture are symbiotic is consistent with a perspective on which personality traits, mental disorders etc. are neither exclusively a product of brain nor environment, nor a meaningful additive mixture of both.

Besides task demands and development, I briefly discussed the role of the outer loop at the scale of perception-action contingencies. Ultimately, all these time scales are contained within the 'outermost' loop: evolution. It is possible that this is the source from which they derive their constraints. However, within the present framework there is also room for independent sources of non-local constraints. How should we theoretically describe the mechanisms by which brain dynamics is adaptively controlled? I cannot offer an answer. Mathematically speaking, the adaptive control of unstable dynamical systems constitutes an entirely new field, in which important work is to be done (Tyukin & van Leeuwen, 2006).

That evolution may have selected brain dynamics for the sake of information processing rather than experience may be a downer; it is naïve, however, to believe that just because evolution produced conscious experience, it must have been selected. If it had been, evolution would probably have done a better job. More likely therefore, experience is an exaptation; an incidental by-product of information processing constraints.

A by-product of evolution is not an epiphenomenon in the sense of dualism. If we construe experience in opposition to brain mechanisms ('easy versus hard problems'), we may be condemning ourselves to an epiphenomenalist view. Instead, the current proposal yields a contextual embedding to consciousness in the mechanisms of inner and outer loops. This is not a reduction from one level to another; inner loop brain dynamics and outer loop control are both characterized at many different levels (Machamer & Sullivan, 2001). Whereas the inner loop gave necessary conditions, sufficient conditions were provided by the outer loop. Necessary but not sufficient conditions alone would allow us to conclude that when consciousness emerges, a whole new ontological category comes into being. I proposed a weaker form of emergence for which sufficient conditions may be found within the encompassing context of evolution, development, learning, and perception/action contingency; conditions only an appropriately contextualized brain can satisfy.[4]

## References

Amit, D.J. (1986), 'Neural networks - achievements, prospects, difficulties', Paper presented at the *International Symposium on The Physics of Structure Formation*, Tuebingen.
Baars, B.J. (1993), *A Cognitive Theory of Consciousness* (Cambridge, UK: Cambridge University Press).
Babloyantz A, Destexhe, A (1986), 'Low-dimensional chaos in an instance of epilepsy', *Proceedings of the National Academy of Science of the U S A*, **83**, pp. 3513–17.
Bak P. (1996), *How Nature Works: The Science of Self-Organized Criticality* (New York: Springer Verlag).
Barrett, H.C. (2005), 'Enzymatic computation and cognitive modularity', *Mind and Language*, **20**, pp. 259–87.
Barrett, H.C. & Kurzban, R. (2006), 'Modularity in cognition: Framing the debate', *Psychological Review*, **113**, pp. 628–47
Basu, S. & Liljenstrøm, H. (2001), 'Spontaneously active cells induce state transitions in a model of olfactory cortex', *Biosystems*, **63**, pp. 57–69.
Baumgartner, G.R., von der Heydt, R. & Peterhans, E (1984), 'Anomalous contours: a tool in studying the neurophysiology of vision', *Experimental Brain Research, Suppl.* **9**, pp. 413–19.
Borsellino, A., De Marco, A., Allazetta, A., Rinesi, S. & Bartolini, B. (1972), 'Reversal time distribution in the perception of visual ambiguous stimuli', *Kybernetik*, **10**, pp. 139–44.
Breakspear M., Roberts, J.A., Terry, J.R., Rodrigues, S., Mahant N. & Robinson, P.A. (2006), 'A unifying explanation of primary generalized seizures through nonlinear brain modeling and bifurcation analysis', *Cerebral Cortex*, **16**, pp. 1296–313.
Campbell, A. (1999), 'Book review of: Greenfield, S.A.', in *Journal of Consciousness Studies*.
http://www.accampbell.uklinux.net/bookreviews/r/greenfield.html
Carruthers, P. (2003),'Is the mind a system of modules shaped by natural selection?', in *Contemporary Debates in the Philosophy of Science*, ed. C. Hitchcock, (Oxford: Blackwell).
Carruthers, P. (2005), 'The case for massively modular models of mind', in *Contemporary Debates in Cognitive Science*, ed. R.Stainton (Oxford: Blackwell).
Carruthers, P. (2005),'Distinctively human thinking: modular precursors and components', in The Innate Mind: Structure and Content, ed. P. Carruthers, S.Laurence & S.Stich (Oxford University Press).
Chalmers, D.J. (1995), 'Facing up to the problem of consciousness', *Journal of Consciousness Studies*, **2** (3), pp. 200–19.
Churchland, P. (1985), 'Reduction, qualia, and the direct introspection of brain states', *Journal of Philosophy*, **82**, pp. 8–28.
Churchland, P. (2005), 'Chimerical colors: some phenomenological predictions from cognitive neuroscience', *Philosophical Psychology*, **18**, pp. 527–60.

---

[4] The author would like to thank Gary Brase, Sergei Gepshtein, Scott Jordan, Michael Kubovy, and two anonymous reviewers for useful suggestions.

Costa, J.F. & Mycka, J. (2005). 'What lies beyond the mountains, computational systems beyond the Turing limit', *Bulletin of the European Association for Theoretical Computer Science*, 85, 181-189.
Davidson, D. (2001), '*Subjective, Intersubjective, Objective*', (Oxford: Clarendon Press).
Dennett, D.C. & Kinsbourne, M. (1992), 'Time and the observer', *Behavioral and Brain Sciences*, **15**, pp.183–247.
Donders, F.C. (1969), 'On the speed of mental processes', *Acta Psychologica*, **30**, pp. 412–31.
Ehrenstein, W.H., Spillmann, L. & Sarris, V. (2003), 'Gestalt issues in modern neuroscience', *Axiomathes*, **13**, pp. 433–58.
Engel, A.K. & Singer, W. (2001), 'Temporal binding and the neural correlates of sensory awareness', *Trends in Cognitive Science*, **5**, pp. 16–25.
Feller, M.B. (1999), 'Spontaneous correlated activity in developing neural circuits', *Neuron*, **22**, pp. 653–6.
Fodor, J.A. (1983), *The Modularity of Mind* (Cambridge, MA: MIT Press).
Freeman, W.J., Kozma R. & Werbos, P.J. (2001), 'Biocomplexity: adaptive behavior in complex stochastic dynamical systems', *Biosystems*, **59**, pp. 109–23.
Gao, J.B., Billock, V.A., Merk, I., Tung, W.W., White, K.D., Harris, J.G. & Roychowdhury, V.P. (2006), 'Inertia and memory in ambiguous visual perception', *Cognitive Processing*, **7**, pp. 105–12.
Garner, W.R. (1962), *Uncertainty and Structure as Psychological Concepts* (New York: Wiley).
Garner, W.R. & Clement, D.E. (1963), 'Goodness of pattern and pattern uncertainty', *Journal of Verbal Learning and Verbal Behavior*, **2**, pp. 446–52.
Gepshtein, S. & Kubovy, M. (2000), 'The emergence of visual objects in space-time', *Proceedings of the National Academy of Sciences*, USA, **97**, pp. 8186–91.
Gibson, J.J. (1979), *The Ecological Approach to Perception* (Boston, MA: Houghton Mifflin).
Gong, P. & van Leeuwen, C. (2003), 'Emergence of scale-free network with chaotic units', *Physica A, Statistical Mechanics and its Applications*, **321**, pp. 679–88.
Gong, P. & van Leeuwen, C. (2004), 'Evolution to a small-world network with chaotic units', *Europhysics Letters*, **67**, pp. 328–33.
Gong, P., Nikolaev, A.R. & van Leeuwen, C. (2003), 'Scale-invariant fluctuations of the dynamical synchronization in human brain electrical activity', *Neuroscience Letters*, **336**, pp. 33–6.
Greenfield, S.A. (1995). *Journey to the Centres of the Mind. Towards a Science of Consciousness* (New York: WH Freeman).
Hanson, N.R. (1958), *Patterns of Discovery: An inquiry into the Conceptual Foundations of Science* (Cambridge, UK: Cambridge University Press).
Hirsh, M.W. (1989), 'Convergent activation dynamics in continuous time networks', *Neural Networks*, **2**, pp. 331–49.
Hock, H.S., Kelso, J.A.S., Schöner, G. (1993), 'Bistability and hysteresis in the perceptual organization of apparent motion', *Journal of Experimental Psychology: Human Perception and Performance*, **19**, pp. 63–80.
Hogeboom, M. & van Leeuwen, C. (1997), 'Visual search strategy and perceptual organization covary with individual preference and structural complexity', *Acta Psychologica*, **95**, pp. 141–64.
Hommel, B., Müsseler, J., Aschersleben, G. & Prinz, W. (2001), 'The theory of event coding (TEC): A framework for perception and action planning', *Behavioral and Brain Sciences,* **24**, pp. 849–937.

Hommel, B. & Colzato, L.S. (2004), 'Visual attention and the temporal dynamics of feature integration', *Visual Cognition*, **11**, pp. 483–521.

Hopfield, J.J. & Herz, A.V.M. (1995), 'Rapid local synchronization of action potentials:Toward computation with coupled integrate-and-fire neurons', *Proceedings of the National Academy of Science USA*, **92**, pp. 6655–66.

Ito, J., Nikolaev, A.R., Luman, M., Aukes, M.F., Nakatani, C. & van Leeuwen, C. (2003), 'Perceptual switching, eye-movements, and the bus-paradox', *Perception*, **32**, pp. 681–98.

Ito, J, Nikolaev, A.R. & van Leeuwen, C. (2005), 'Spatial and temporal structure of phase synchronization of spontaneous EEG alpha activity', *Biological Cybernetics*, **92**, pp. 54–60.

Ito, J., Nikolaev, A.R. & van Leeuwen, C. (in press). 'Dynamical rule in the spontaneous transitions between brain states', *Human Brain Mapping*.

Jordan, J.S. & Ghin, M. (2006), '(Proto-) Consciousness as a contextually-emergent property of self-sustaining systems', *Mind & Matter*, **4**, pp. 45–68.

Kaneko, K. (1985), 'Spatiotemporal intermittency in coupled map lattices', *Progress of Theoretical Physics*, **74**, pp. 1033–44.

Kaneko, K. (2002), 'Dominance of Milnor attractors in globally coupled dynamical systems with more than 7 +/− 2 degrees of freedom', *Physical Review E*, **66**, art. No. 055201.

Kaneko, K. & Tsuda, I. (2001), *Complex Systems: Chaos and Beyond* (Berlin: Springer Verlag).

Kubovy, M., Holcombe, A.O. & Wagemans, J. (1998), 'On the lawfulness of grouping by proximity', *Cognitive Psychology*, **35**, pp. 71–98.

Kwok, H.F., Jurica, P., Raffone, A. & van Leeuwen, C. (in press), 'Small-world structure evolves with a Burst', *Cognitive Neurodynamics*, DOI : 10.1007/s11571-006-9006-5.

Latora, V. & Marchiori, M. (2001), 'Efficient behavior of small-world networks', *Physical Review Letters*, 87198701.

Lawson, R. & Jolicoeur, P. (1999), 'The effect of prior experience on recognition thresholds for plane-disoriented pictures of familiar objects', *Memory & Cognition*, **27**, pp. 751–8.

Lee, D.N. & Reddish, P.E. (1981), 'Plummeting gannets: A paradigm of ecological optics', *Nature*, **293**, pp. 293–4.

Love, B.C., Rouder, J.N. & Wisniewski, E.J. (1999), 'A structural account of global and local processing', *Cognitive Psychology*, **38**, pp. 291–316.

Machamer, P. & Sullivan, J. (2001), 'Leveling Reduction', http://philsciarchive.pitt.edu/archive/00000400/

Maeda, E., Kuroda, Y., Robinson, H.P.C. & Kawana, A. (1998), 'Modification of parallel activity elicited by propagating bursts in developing networks of rat cortical neurons', *European Journal of Neuroscience*, **10**, pp. 488–96.

Menendez de la Prida, L. & Sanchez-Andres, J.V. ( 2000), 'Heterogeneous populations of cells mediate spontaneous synchronous bursting in the developing hippocampus through a frequency-dependent mechanism', *Neuroscience*, **97**, pp. 227–41.

McCauley, R. N. and Bechtel, W. (2001), 'Explanatory pluralism and the heuristic identity theory', *Theory and Psychology*, **11**, pp. 736–60.

Mountcastle, V.B. (1997), 'The columnar organization of the neocortex', *Brain*, **120**, pp. 701–22.

Murata, T., Matsui, N., Miyauchi, S., Kakita, Y. & Yanagida, T. (2003), 'Discrete stochastic process underlying perceptual rivalry', *Neuroreport*, **14**, pp. 1347–52.

Nakatani, C., Ito, J., Nikolaev, A.R., Gong, P. & van Leeuwen, C. (2005), 'Phase synchronization analysis of EEG during attentional blink', *Journal of Cognitive Neuroscience*, **17**, pp. 343–54.

Nakatani, H., Khalilov, I., Gong, P. & van Leeuwen (2003), 'Nonlinearity in giant depolarizing potentials', *Physics Letters A*, **319**, pp.167–72.

Nakatani, H. & van Leeuwen, C. (2005), 'Perceptual switching rates-dependent theta and alpha band activity in occipital and frontal areas', *Biological Cybernetics*, **93**, pp. 343–54.

Nakatani, H. & van Leeuwen, C. (2006), 'Transient synchrony of distant brain areas and perceptual switching', *Biological Cybernetics*, **94**, pp. 445–57.

Neisser, U. (1967), *Cognitive Psychology* (New York: Appleton Century Crofts).

Nikolaev A.R., Gong P. & van Leeuwen, C. (2005), 'Evoked phase synchronization between adjacent high-density electrodes in human scalp EEG: Duration and time course related to behavior', *Clinical Neurophysiolology*, **116**, pp. 2403–19.

O'Brien, G. & Opie, J. (1999), 'A connectionist theory of phenomenal experience', *Behavioral and Brain Sciences*, **22**, pp. 127–96.

O'Regan, J.K. & Noë, A. (2001), 'A sensorimotor account of vision and visual consciousness', *Behavioral and Brain Sciences*, **24**, pp. 939–1011.

Otsu Y, Kimura F, Tsumoto T. (1995), 'Hebbian induction of LTP in visual cortex: perforated patch-clamp study in cultured neurons', *Journal of Neurophysiology*, **746**, pp. 2437–44.

Paradiso, M.K. & Nakayama, K. (1991), 'Brightness perception and filling-in', *Vision Research*, **31**, pp. 1221–36.

Parisi, G. (1986), 'Asymmetric neural networks and the process of learning', *Journal of physics A: Mathematical General*, **19**, pp. L675–L680.

Penn, A. A., Riquelme, P. A., Feller, M. B., Shatz, C. J. (1998), 'Competition in retinogeniculate patterning generated by spontaneous activity' *Science*, **279**, pp. 2108–12.

Peterson, M.A. & Hochberg, J. (1983), 'Opposed-set measurement procedure: a quantitative analysis of the role of local cues and intention in form perception', *Journal of Experimental Psychology: Human Perception and Performance*, **9**, pp. 183–193.

Pike, F. G., Meredith, R. M., Olding, A. W. A. & Paulsen, O. (1999), 'Postsynaptic bursting is essential for 'Hebbian' induction of associative long-term potentiation at excitatory synapses in rat hippocampus', *The Journal of Physiology*, **518**, pp. 571–6.

Putnam, H. (1981), *Reason, Truth, and History* (Cambridge: Cambridge University Press), pp.1–21.

Putnam, H. (1987), *The Many Faces of Realism* (La Salle, Ill, Open Court),

Raffone, A. & van Leeuwen, C. (2001), 'Activation and coherence in memory processes: Revisiting the parallel distributed processing approach to retrieval', *Connection Science*, **13**, pp. 349–82.

Raffone, A. & Wolters, G. (2001), 'A cortical mechanism for binding in visual working memory', *Journal of Cognitive Neuroscience*, **13**, pp. 766–85.

Rock, I., Hall, S. & Davis, J. (1994), 'Why do ambiguous figures reverse?', *Acta Psychologica*, **87**, pp. 33–59.

Siegelmann, H.T. (1999). 'Stochastic Analog Networks and Computational Complexity', *Journal of Complexity*, **15**, pp. 451–75.

Siegelmann, H.T. & Sontag E.D. (1991). 'Turing computability with neural nets'. *Applied Mathematics Letters*, **4**, 77–80.

Shefi, O., Golding, I., Segev, R., Ben-Jacob, E. & Ayali, A. (2002), 'Morphological characterization of in vitro neuronal networks', *Physical Review E*, **66**, pp.1–5.

Skarda, C. A. & Freeman, W.J. (1987), 'How brains make chaos in order to make sense of the world', *Behavioral and Brain Sciences*, **10**, pp.161–95.

Stam, C.J. (2004), 'Functional connectivity patterns of human magnetoencephalographic recordings: a 'small-world' network?' *Neuroscience Letters*, **355**, pp. 25–8.

Steinitz, Y. (1994), 'Brains in a Vat: Different perspectives', *Philosophical Quarterly*, **44**, pp. 213–22.

Stins, J. & van Leeuwen, C. (1993), 'Context influence on the perception of figures as conditional upon perceptual organization strategies', *Perception & Psychophysics*, **53**, pp. 34–42.

Stroud, J.M. (1967), 'The fine structure of psychological time', *Annals of the New York Academy of Science*, **238**, pp. 623–31.

Struber, D. & Stadler, M. (1999), 'Differences in top-down influences on the reversal rate of different categories of reversible figures', *Perception*, **28**, pp.1185–96.

Toppino, T.C. (2003), 'Reversible-figure perception: Mechanisms of intentional control', *Perception & Psychophysics*, **65**, pp.1285–95.

Tsuda, I. (2001), 'Towards an interpretation of dynamic neural activity in terms of chaotic dynamical systems', *Behavioral and Brain Sciences,* **24**, pp. 793–847.

Tsunoda, K., Yamane, Y., Nishizaki, M. & Tanifuji, M. (2001), 'Complex objects are represented in macaque inferotemporal cortex by the combination of feature columns', *Nature Neuroscience*, **4**, pp. 832–8.

Tyukin, I. & van Leeuwen, C. (2006), 'Decentralized adaptation in interconnected uncertain systems with nonlinear parametrization', *Lecture notes in Control and Information Sciences*, **336**, pp. 251–70.

van der Velde, F. (1993), 'Is the brain an effective Turing machine or a finite-state machine?', *Psychological Research*, **55**, pp. 71–9.

van Leeuwen, C. (1998), 'Visual perception at the edge of chaos', in *Systems Theories and Apriori Aspects of Perception*, ed. J.S. Jordan (Amsterdam, NL: Elsevier), pp. 289–314.

van Leeuwen, C. & Bakker, L. (1995), 'Stroop can occur without Garner interference: Strategic and mandatory influences in multidimensional stimuli', *Perception & Psychophysics*, **57**, pp. 379–92.

van Leeuwen, C. & Lachmann, Th. (2004), 'Letters and shapes have opposite congruence characteristics'. *Perception & Psychophysics*, **66**, pp. 908–25.

van Leeuwen, C. & Leeuwenberg, E. (1984). 'Duration as a function of perceptual code revisions' *Perception*, **13**, pp. A35–A36.

van Leeuwen, C., Steyvers, M. & Nooter, M. (1997), 'Stability and intermittency in large-scale coupled oscillator models for perceptual segmentation', *Journal of Mathematical Psychology*, **41**, pp. 319–44.

van Leeuwen, C., Verstijnen, I.M. & Hekkert, P. (1999), 'Common unconscious dynamics underly uncommon conscious effect: A case study in the iterative nature of perception and creation' in *Modeling Consciousness Across the Disciplines*, ed. J.S. Jordan (Lanham, MD: University Press of America), pp. 179–218.

van Leeuwen, C., Verver, S. & Brinkers, M. (2000), 'Visual illusions and outline-invariance in non-stationary activity patterns', *Connection Science*, **12**, pp. 279–98.

van Pelt, J., Corner, M.A., Wolters, P.S., Rutten, W.L.C. & Ramakers, G.J.A. (2004), 'Long term stability and developmental changes in spontaneous network burst firing patterns in dissociated rat cerebral cortex cell cultures on multielectrode arrays', *Neuroscience Letters*, **361**, pp. 86–9.

Verstijnen, I.M., van Leeuwen, C., Goldschmidt, G., Hamel, R. & Hennessey, J.M. (1998a), 'Sketching and Creative Discovery', *Design Studies*, **19**, pp. 519–46.

Von der Malsburg, C. & Schneider, W. (1986), 'A neural cocktail-party processor', *Biological Cybernetics*, **54**, pp. 29–40.

Wagemans, J. (1993). 'Skewed symmetry: a nonaccidental property used to perceive visual forms', *Journal of Experimental Psychology: Human Perception and Performance*, **19**, pp. 364–80.

Watts, D.J. & Strogatz, S.H. (1998), 'Collective dynamics of 'small-world' networks', *Nature*, **393**, pp. 440–2.

Yao, Y. & Freeman, W.J. (1990), 'Model of biological pattern recognition with spatially chaotic dynamics', *Neural Networks*, **3**, pp. 153–70.

Ziessler, M., Nattkemper, D. & Frensch, P.A. (2004). 'The role of anticipation and intention for the learning of effects on self-performed actions', *Psychological Research/Psychologische Forschung*, **68**, pp. 163–75.

# Robert Shaw and Jeffrey Kinsella-Shaw

# *The Survival Value of Informed Awareness*

*Abstract*: *Various hypotheses about the importance of psycho-neural concomitants are reviewed and their implications discussed for the 'easy' and 'hard' problems of consciousness — especially, as viewed by cognitive and ecological psychology. In Ecological Psychology, where the subjective–objective dichotomy is repudiated, these concepts are without foundation, and are replaced by informed awareness, which is argued to play an important, perhaps, indispensable role in goal-directed actions and thus to have survival value. The significance of informed awareness is illustrated in several real-world goal-directed tasks.*

## Introduction

> Perhaps no aspect of mind is more familiar or more puzzling than consciousness and our conscious experience of self and world' (Van Gulick, 2004, p. 1).

This pessimistic appraisal is not overstated; for philosophers have argued for centuries about the nature of consciousness without reaching a consensus — disagreeing whether consciousness entails mind–body dualism, physical reductionism, or epiphenomenalism. More recently, materialists and radical behaviorists have argued that consciousness does not exist, while logical positivists, seeing its verification so problematic, banished it to the limbo of meaningless concepts. In the current climate, however, consciousness is treated with more deference, being recognized as a problem uniting psychology, neurophysiology, cognitive science, and, perhaps, even physics.

This revival of interest owes much to the seminal work done in Europe more than a century ago by Wilhelm Wundt, the father of experimental psychology, and by his brilliant English student, Edward Titchener, who imported these interests into America. Other hypotheses about consciousness are also discussed that help set the stage for the hypothesis eventually introduced.

The so-called 'easy' and 'hard' problem distinction tie together many of the historical threads — from Wundt and Titchener to Chalmers and Gibson. We follow these threads and knit them together to form the fabric of our own thesis that consciousness construed as *informed awareness* has survival value. Where traditional approaches emphasize the phenomenology of consciousness, its contents, referents and neurophysiological support, our emphasis is different. Instead, we focus on the putative pragmatic value of consciousness that allows agents to notice the information needed to remain adaptive in a complex and challenging environment. In brief, we argue that where determining the nature of consciousness has proven difficult — even intractable, studying its ecological significance (at least in many cases) seems straightforward. Examples are discussed that support this idea.

The paper is in three parts: Part I introduces historical analogs of the easy and hard problems of consciousness and discusses implications for contemporary approaches. Part II discusses the pragmatic and evolutionary implications of information and consciousness when construed by ecological psychology as 'informed awareness.' Finally, Part III presents our thesis and evaluates its implication for consciousness studies.

## I: Consciousness: Approaches and Problems

Wilhelm Wundt (1832–1920) resisted the lure of scientific materialism spawned by the success of classical mechanics, and in 1879 founded the first experimental psychology laboratory in Leipzig. Because of its scientific pretensions, his laboratory soon became the Mecca for scientists who wished to study mind. Wundt made a succinct and incisive argument opposing reductionism thusly: 'Materialism is contradicted by the fact of consciousness!' He then initiated a monumental experimental program called *voluntarism* (sometimes wrongly identified with later 'structuralism') with two main goals: first, to discover all simple constituents of experience and, second, to formulate laws for combining those constituents into complex ideas — a process called *creative synthesis*, or, alternatively, *psychic resultants*.

Creative synthesis included the combining of simple passive ideas by association and an active process of apperception. This process was similar to John Stuart Mills 'mental' chemistry where something new emerges from combining parts into a whole. This active process is a person's volition to focus thinking in a logical and meaningful direction. Because voluntary purposive thinking was central to his concern, Wundt called his approach *voluntarism*; and defined psychology as the study of consciousness of all things — eschewing the distinction between inner and outer experiences as being artificial. In this one way, Wundt anticipated James J. Gibson's repudiation of the subjective-objective dichotomy — a move that undercuts the mind-body dualism of traditional cognitive psychology.

Wundt provided guidelines by which participants could give precise reports of their immediate experiences. Unfortunately, this method failed to replicate over laboratories, or even over expertly trained experimenters within the same laboratory. Thus in spite of its worldwide appeal, voluntarism was eventually rejected as a failed attempt to elevate the study of consciousness to being a science. Nevertheless, despite its ultimate failure, Wundt's program had a lasting influence on the new field's attitude toward the study of mind — if not on its methods.

In 1892 E.B. Titchener, Wundt's brilliant English student, transported the voluntarist program from Leipzig to Cornell University in America, where he added a plank to its platform and renamed it *Structuralism*. Unlike Wundt, he insisted that the introspective search for simple mental aspects and their laws of composition should be supplemented by a search for their neural correlates — an adumbration of contemporary concerns for finding brain correlates for mental functions. Titchener also rejected Wundt's notion of creative synthesis of mental contents as being a mistake that made consciousness study unscientific.

To counter creative synthesis, Titchener introduced the concept of the 'stimulus error.' The *stimulus error* is committed whenever mental experiences are described by meaningful conventional labels, such as, 'the smell of roses,' 'the taste of honey,' a person of tall stature,' 'the sound of a waterfall,' etc. Instead, one should describe experiences solely in terms of their simplest attributes: colour, texture, potency, etc. Wundt retaliated against Titchener's exclusion of psychic resultants by claiming this made psychology sterile, eliminating its most fundamental character and significance. In this regard, Wundt's attitude was quite modern.

Voluntarism and Structuralism were gradually diluted by the eclecticism of functionalism, which allowed introspection, behavioural methods, or any other method deemed useful. Their demise was virtually complete by the time Behaviourism prospered. Still, fascination with consciousness did not disappear from scientific psychology any more than it did from folk psychology. In fact, over the ensuing years, interest has waxed more than waned, no doubt because scientists and nonscientists alike find that introspection is as natural as it is unavoidable. Where the cognitive revolution of the 1960s reclaimed consciousness studies, current cognitive neuroscience has successfully promoted it. However this is not to say the issue of its scientific legitimacy has been completely settled or its character well understood. Efforts continue.

*The Easy and Hard Problems*

Chalmers (1996) has identified two problems faced by serious students of consciousness — the 'easy' problem and the 'hard' problem. For Chalmers these are primarily problems of general philosophical concern (e.g., panpsychism and dualism) and are not to be identified solely with the concerns of neuro-cognitive scientists — although, for a science of consciousness, they might be, as Chalmers himself suggests in a published interview (Chalmers, 2002):

> I said that by 'consciousness' I always mean the first-person data. But a science of consciousness will be all about connections and correlations between consciousness and processes in the brain, aspects of behavior, and so on. The latter are the third person data, e.g., the search for the neural correlates of consciousness is a currently very active project, and an extremely important one on my view. This is all about connecting physical processes (third person) with consciousness (first person).

This sentiment is echoed by others who find Chalmers' easy-hard problem distinction useful. For instance, Van Gulick (2004) (in the *Stanford Encyclopedia of Philosophy*) asserts:

> Progress may seem likely on some of the so-called 'easy problems' of consciousness, such as explaining the dynamics of access consciousness in terms of the functional or computational organization of the brain (a view with which Baars, 1988, concurs). Others may seem less tractable, especially the so-called 'hard problems' (Chalmers, 1995) which is more or less that of giving an intelligible account that lets us see in an intuitively satisfying way how phenomenal or 'what it's like' consciousness might arise from physical processes in the brain.

The beauty of this distinction is that it portrays the conflicted concerns of Wundt and Titchener in a new light and channels renewed interest in solving these two perennial problems. Solution to the easy problem involves discovering the alignment between experiences and their concomitant neurological events, an effort with which Titchener would have strongly concurred. By contrast, solving the 'hard' problem assumes solution to the 'easy' problem but goes beyond mere correspondence to show how the character of experience necessarily derives from the character of physiological events (Figure 1).

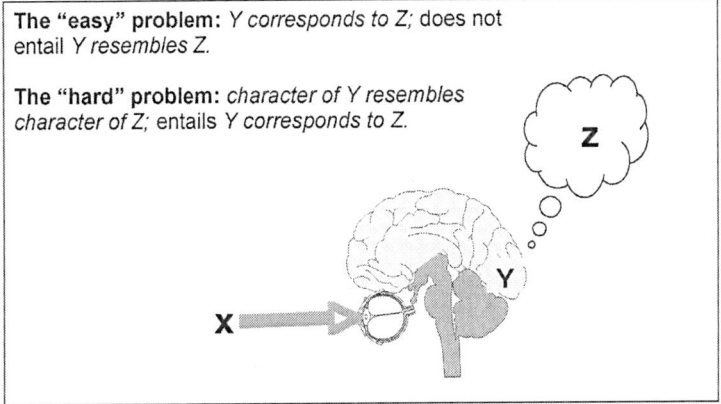

Figure 1: The 'Easy' and Hard' Problems Illustrated

Although Wundt did not seek neurological foundations for experience, he should have liked the hard problem. For its existence seems to vindicate the need for a process of creative synthesis — but one capable of extracting a super-resultant from superposing inner psychical resultants and outer neurological resultants. Still, though Wundt might eventually have come to appreciate the hard problem, so Titchener would have continued to disdain it for encouraging the stimulus error and thus, in his mind, posing a thwart to achieving a science of consciousness.

The functionalists, immediately following William James' lead (e.g., E.B. Holt), continued to reject the inner-outer experience distinction in favour of his so-called 'pure' experience which construed experience as 'neutral' in the sense of being neither subjective nor objective. This ploy of collapsing inner and outer, subjective and objective, and even mind and body was inherited by latter day functionalists, like James J. Gibson, but without allegiance to the trappings of James' 'pure' experience philosophy (radical empiricism) and its accompanying metaphysical doctrine of neutral monism. One might see in this ignoring of radical empiricism the vestiges of behaviourism's stern anti-metaphysical attitude.

Ironically, by broadening of this process, Wundt would simply have re-discovered the Gestaltist's principle of Psycho-neural Isomorphism. This principle says the character of '... molar events in experience are structurally identical to the corresponding molar physiological events in the brain' (Henle, 1978, p. 25). This is of course a neurological interpretation of the Fechner-Spinoza Concomitancy Hypothesis which hypothesizes an in principle basis for solving the 'hard' problem but fails, as do all known concomitancy hypotheses, to offer any practical guidelines for actually identifying the concomitants.

A deeper problem is the likelihood that localization of concomitants is a faulty concept. For if the concomitants are functionally distributed over many locations, or worse, vary over time, then finding them might not be feasible. The Gestaltist's dynamical field concept seems more promising but has its own limitations (Kadar and Shaw, 2000; Lehar, 2003).

The Fechner-Spinoza Concomitancy Hypothesis, like James' Neutral Monism suffers from the same defect. They postulate a metaphysical solution to the problem rather than finding a scientific one. Gustav Fechner, like Spinoza, postulated the existence of a psychophysical correspondence — a restatement of the 'easy' problem rather than a scientifically earned solution. It asserts, *for every physical event there is a concomitant mental event, and for every mental event there is a concomitant physical event* (Bain, 1873). At best, it assumes license for a neuropsychological fishing expedition to find valid inner and outer event pairings and avoids the issue of how experience arises, where its content comes from, and only addresses those aspects of the physiological processes to which an experience corresponds.

The English philosopher, Bertrand Russell (1927), offered a variant on William James' Neutral Monism. Russell's view is admirable for its clarity and brevity: *The brain is the mind looked at from the outside and the mind is the brain looked at from the inside*. This is a kind of perspectival 'realism' — instead of mind-body dualism where there are two incommensurate *kinds* (of fundamental 'stuff'), there is a single 'kind' viewed from two different perspectives. This view is consistent with Wundt's claim that there is really no difference between 'inner' and 'outer' experiences with respect to 'kinds' but goes beyond Wundt in claiming there is a significant difference between perspectives that most philosophers take as different 'kinds'. Again, this is not a solution to the easy problem but a way of explaining away any need for a solution. Since the perspectives are assumed to share the same neutral referent, they cannot help but be coordinated.

Unfortunately, this view either exacerbates the hard problem or trivializes it. It exacerbates it by treating the perspectives as so different the mind-body problem is unavoidable; or trivializes it by emphasizing that since the two perspectives derive from the same neutral object, their characters do not differ in kind. Hence this hypothesis hardly seems helpful.

A facile solution to both the easy and hard problems, respectively, would be to somehow combine the concomitancy hypothesis with the perspectival realism hypothesis and thereby cover our bases. For this strategy to work, the 'somehow' would have to be principled; *the character of the correspondence would have to guarantee the correspondence of the characters*. To do so, the meaning of the experience would have to pick-out the corresponding neurological event and the character of the neurological event would have to pick-out the corresponding meaning. Unfortunately, nothing in either hypothesis tells us how this might be done. Let's examine this criticism more closely.

Concomitancy, or correspondence, entails nothing more than correlation between two series and says nothing about the character of the items correlated — whether the pairing is mental-physical, mental-mental, physical-physical, or even a meaningless abstract-abstract pairing. Perspectival realism fairs no better; for there must be something which coordinates contrasting perspectives by anchoring them to something that is not itself a perspective. A perspective of a perspective makes no sense; every perspective must have an object which it relates to an observer. No observer, no perspective and no object, no perspective. Perspective-taking requires the observer taking the perspective, the object on which the perspective is taken, as well as of course the perspective itself. The ecological scale embodies this requirement.

In the next section we ask how well the easy and hard problems fare at the ecological scale. The answer will be, 'Not so well.'

## II: Informed Awareness

The fact that creatures (e.g., humans, others?) experience conscious awareness is still somewhat an evolutionary mystery, although many reasonable hypotheses have been offered. One hypothesis about the 'why' of consciousness is that it helps integrate global information and allows focusing in on specific information that remains on call but pre-conscious. A prominent consciousness theorist observes that the information conveyed by conscious mental states may also be available for use by diverse mental subsystems and thereby get involved in a wide range of potential situations and actions (Baars, 1988).

Another possible function it serves is making control more flexible and sophisticated, hence more adaptive. Also, it is believed that unconscious automatic processes may be more efficient and rapid than conscious processes; they also seem more rigid and predetermined. Typical accounts of skill learning or its tuning by monitoring subtleties to be exploited or avoided give conscious awareness a central, even necessary role to play (Schneider & Schiffrin, 1977). Thus consciousness may be the most important ingredient in dealing with the unpredictable, novel, or unexpected — those unplanned for occurrences (Armstrong, 1981; Penfield, 1975).

Ecological psychology would agree generally that conscious awareness facilitates the detection and use of information; in principle, it can improve its integration, specification, interpretation, application, and generalization, as well as making control more flexible and coordinated over a wider range of situations and tasks. Including all these, ecological psychology places special emphasis on the adaptive value of being aware of ones needs, wants, intentions, preferences, values, priorities, and goals with respect to actual or potential situations. A deliberate decision is made to move from consciousness as an intransitive state to awareness of something — a transitive relation, where the greater the ecological significance of this something, the more likely it will be attended to. Gibson (1979) explains it this way:

> Perceiving is an achievement of the individual, not an appearance in the theater of his consciousness. It is a keeping-in-touch with the world, an experiencing of things rather than a having of experiences. It involves awareness-of instead of just awareness. *It may be awareness of something in the environment or something in the observer or both at once*, but there is no content of awareness independent of that of which one is aware (Gibson, 1979, p.239; emphasis added).

If one accepts this 'transitive' relation as necessary to perception (as we do), then Chalmers' 'hard' problem *does not even arise*. This was Gibson's 'radical idea' that he often referred to (Shaw, 2002), and one that bore a striking resemblance to the idea that consciousness (and mind) was a physical relation put forward by one of his teachers, E.B. Holt (Reed, 1988): Holt thought mind-matter dualism was mistaken.

Instead he favoured a physicalism in which the mental and material had equal status. If so, then consciousness must be capable of physical characterization as well. To help make this idea clear, Holt offered an analogy between the ephemeral character of a rainbow and the insubstantial character of consciousness.

A rainbow seems almost preternatural in its ghostly luminosity, intangibility, and impermanence — appearing to some observers but not others, disappearing when weather conditions change or as one changes perspective. In short, it seems hardly physical at all, but of course it is. A rainbow is a complex physical phenomenon comprising a cloud of prismatic water droplets, the rays of the sun falling upon these droplets so as to liberate a spectrum of colours, and an observer with a proper perspective. If any of these physical conditions are violated, the rainbow fails to form or, if present, disappears. Here is the key point:

For the rainbow to appear, the aforementioned complex of physical relations must remain indissoluble. Similarly, for awareness to appear, a complex of physical relations must also be indissoluble. If one is physical, then the other must be as well. Holt (1915) observes: 'If organism and environment are sundered, the cognitive relation is dissolved and merely matter remains; precisely as only water remains when a rainbow is pulled apart. Mind is a relation' (p. 99). Likewise subtract consciousness from a human, and only biological stuff remains; subtract life from the biological stuff, and only matter remains. Life is a relation.

Gibson agreed with Holt's functionalism, as inherited from William James, but replaced the notion of physics at arbitrary scales with the notion of physics at the ecological scale — the scale of an animal's eco-niche, or more briefly, *eco-physics*. Let's examine the implications of this notion of a physics of the world in which animals' perceptions and actions are properly situated.

Cognitive theories typically construe information as the correspondence between objective facts in the world and subjective mental constructs. The basis of this view is the subjective-objective-dichotomy, a thinly disguised version of mind-body dualism. Chalmers' 'hard' problem clearly assumes the reality of this dichotomy. Ecological psychology repudiates this dichotomy and thus the 'hard' correspondence problem it engenders. It replaces belief in the reality of the underlying troublesome dichotomy with a belief in the reality of the logical reciprocity of animals with their environments.

Given its importance, it is worth reiterating that the environment in which an animal is situated is not the environment of the physicists but is that portion of the physical environment which is ecologically scaled, that is, the functionally defined portion which affords suitable agents opportunities for perceiving and acting. In this properly defined environment appropriately attuned agents, from microbes and insects to animals and humans, can directly perceive their situation and themselves in that situation without benefit of a consciousness-copy of it. [Although a cognitive 'map' may be developed by perceiving and acting in that situation, it need not be for perception and action to depend on situated (informed) awareness]. Gibson introduced the principle of animal–environment reciprocity in this way:

> But they [self-experiences] should not be thought of as a different realm of existence or a different kind of reality than the ecological, nor are they 'mental' as against 'physical'.... Awareness of the persisting and changing environment (perception) is concurrent with the complementary awareness of the persisting and changing self ... (Gibson, 1978, cited in Reed & Jones, 1982, p. 418)

If what things mean is given part and parcel with their perception, then there is no need for cognitive contributions. Gibson states this thesis most elegantly:

> What a thing is and what it means are not separate, the former being physical and the latter mental, as we are accustomed to believe. ... The perception of what a thing is and the perception of what it means are not separate, either (Gibson, 1971. Cited in Reed & Jones, 1982, p. 408).

Information specifies affordances, those real properties of the environment whose perceived meaning is the actions they both allow and invite an agent to perform. The affordance concept is pivotal for ecological psychology, for affordances provide the bi-directional coupling between an agent and its environment — a coupling that usurps the role traditionally played by the subjective–objective dichotomy. Gibson explains:

> An important fact about affordances of the environment is that they are in a sense objective, real, and physical, unlike values and meanings, which are often supposed to be subjective, phenomenal, and mental. But, actually, an affordance is neither an objective nor a subjective property; or it is both if you like. An affordance cuts across the dichotomy of subjective-objective and helps us to understand its inadequacy. It is both physical and psychical, yet neither. An affordance points both ways, to the environment and to the observer (Gibson, 1979/1986, p. 129).

In sum: Ecological psychology is the science of agents — individuals whose actions are successful if they maintain appropriate contact with a potentially changing reality where threats and opportunities abound. On the spot, opportunistic awareness of what is changing and what is persisting is demanded for doing so. *Direct* perception is evolution's way of allowing agents to maintain 'situational awareness' so that its actions are appropriately grounded by the detection of the relevant invariant information. In short, grounded situational awareness is the agent's direct perception of what surrounds it, what is changing, and what is emerging (Shaw, 2003).

The general sense of the ecological approach — its assumptions, aims, and problems — can be obtained by taking a moment to ponder the quote with special attention being paid to the terms emphasized. Roughly, if in the previous paragraph, one replaces the phrase 'direct perception' with 'noticing' little meaning is lost. An agent must notice environmental 'objects' with their parameters — i.e., what it is, where and when it is, what actions it affords, etc. defined relative to the agent and its parameters — i.e., body dimensions, needs, wants, etc. Of course, *to notice* is synonymous with *to be aware of*. Noticing object parameters is to be aware of information, or, more briefly, to exhibit informed awareness.

If evolution produces agents with the capabilities for survival, then there must have been functional and anatomical properties selected for. To the critic who wrongly surmises that ecological psychology has nothing to say about the brain and other physiological processes, know that Gibson wrote a whole book on the subject to clarify his position (Gibson, 1966). Here is a good summary statement:

> What might be a physiological or functional equivalent of the external information, if it cannot be anatomical? How could invariants get into the nervous system? (Gibson, 1966, p.4).

He offers this answer:

> Instead of looking to the brain alone for an explanation of constant perception. It should be sought in the neural loops of an active perceptual system that includes the adjustments of the perceptual organ. Instead of supposing that the brain constructs or computes the objective information from a kaleidoscopic inflow of sensations, we may suppose that the orienting of the organs of perception is governed by the brain so that the whole system of input and output resonates to the external information. ... The function of the brain is not even to organize the sensory input or to process the data, in modern terminology. The perceptual systems, including the nerve centers at the various levels up to the brain, are ways of seeking and extracting information about the environment from the flowing array of ambient energy (Gibson, 1966, p. 5).

Informed awareness is not just information about the environment, but of course information about oneself in relation to that surrounding environment as well. Figure 2 illustrates how information, awareness, and control interrelate to make an agent.

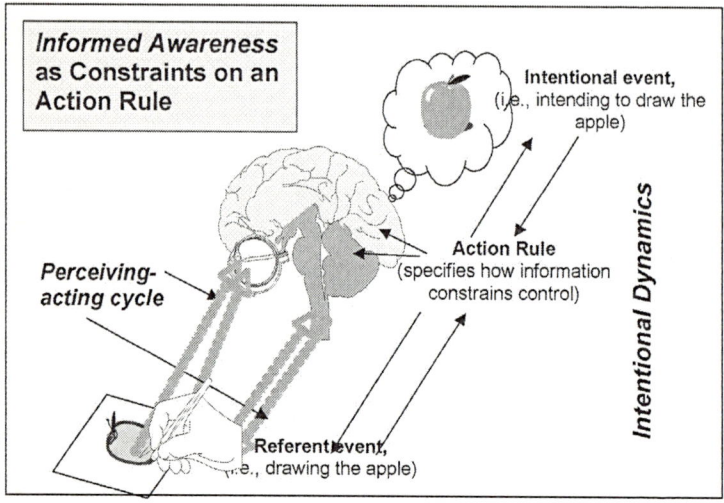

Figure 2: Shows how an Action Rule is embedded in the ecological system with respect to information and control, intention and goal, and neurophysiological support.

In Figure 2 the Action Rule refers to the perceiving-acting cycle (note the closed 'cycle' of arrows) and denotes the mutual interactive support of perception and action. Here the cartoon balloon represents information about an apple currently perceived or previously perceived. Our contention is that 'to situate' an acting agent, say, an 'apple-drawing' artist, entails many factors — among them the real apple, the information specific to its character, the recalled 'apple' information, together with the involved perceptual (e.g., haptic and visual) systems, the brain and involved neuro-muscular system, and of course the intention to draw the apple — all of which contribute to situating the agent's action in question.

Furthermore, the action receives equal causal and informational support from the physics, biology, and psychology of the situation — a situation that might be descriptively called an 'apple-drawing agent' ecosystem. The action portrayed exemplifies what we have called 'intentional' dynamics — a dynamics in which the agent's intention plays an indispensable role of setting the final condition (goal) around which the unfolding initial conditions (of the information detected and the controlling forces applied) are continually and, when successful, felicitously tailored.

## III: Thesis and Illustrative Cases

Gibson's rationale for characterizing perception as direct rather than indirect, or immediate rather than mediated, was to avoid Locke's problem: If to be aware of the world we must first be aware of our own ideas, then how do we ever get past the ideas to be aware of the world? If we cannot tell the difference between our ideas about the world and our made-up ideas, then how can we ever check the validity of our beliefs about the world against what is actually true? And, finally, if the above ignorance is inevitable, then how do we avoid solipsism — the belief that we are the only reality, and that it is of our own making?

This is not the place to defend this thesis that if perception were direct, then knowledge of the world would be possible, otherwise not. Rather we introduce the issue primarily to clarify a chief characteristic of ecological psychology that tends to be misunderstood because of traditional cognitive psychology's bias in favour of representational, or indirect, realism. It would be helpful if examples might be cited where direct perception seemed plausible. Here are a few candidate cases.

### *Case 1: Probing a cavity*

Here is perhaps the simplest case of direct perception. I perceive the shape of the cavity in my back molar by probing its boundaries with a three inch metal pick. Clearly I am in contact with this dental tool, which is in contact with my molar's cavity, but I am also in contact with my tooth. How can this be? It can because the probe (tool) is informationally transparent to the object probed so that the probing action is guided by the geography of the cavity. To the extent that the probe is not transparent to this information, then the agent lacks the requisite informed awareness for success.

Let's generalize this case. Primary to direct perception is the demand that the medium (probe) be transparent to the flow of information specifying the target (cavity) to the agent. To be direct is an all-or-nothing proposition. For example, a ship whose signal gets weaker and weaker as it gets farther and farther from the shore remains in contact with its shore base so long as the signal can be detected. In general, it does not matter how remote the target is so long as the signal-to-noise ratio is favourable throughout the medium.

Specification fills the gap regardless of its breadth or the complication of the medium. It could include the central nervous system, tools, or other linkages, such as air or water in the case of optical information about a source.

*Case 2: Intercepting a Target*

Imagine that a pilot of a boat is given the task to intercept another boat. Is there a simple rule the pilot might follow that would guarantee a successful interception — even if the boat pursued carried out radically evasive manoeuvres? There is and it goes like this: Select a mark on the windshield of your boat to be the foot of an imaginary lead-vector which you adopt as a sightline intersecting the other boat. So long as you keep the other boat targeted by the sightline, and keep your boat's speed up, then regardless of what evasive actions taken, the other boat will eventually be intercepted. Minimally, the action rule to be followed is:

*Keep your sightline zeroed in on the target boat!.*

The concept of an *action rule* does not entail the rule to be a mediator of the action — either causally or psychologically. Rules, as the philosopher, Wittgenstein taught us, can either be involved in an action as when you follow a recipe in cooking or a map when travelling, or be entailed by the action in the sense that it describes the constraints that are always observed to be satisfied when the action succeeds. Construed in this latter way, a rule for action expresses the invariant information to which an agent's control acts should conform, that is, the rule is a *control law*. A theory of how such action rules accomplish their ends is called *intentional dynamics*. Here, information and control are shown to be mutual and reciprocal just in case the action succeeds (Shaw, 2003; Shaw & Kinsella-Shaw, 1988; Shaw *et al.*, 1992).

*Case 3: Controlled Descent*

Assume a helicopter flight instructor has the task of teaching novice pilots how to make a safe vertical landing. Is there a simple action rule that might help them succeed? Indeed there is one actually used by flight instructors:

> *As you descend keep the optic flow rate constant and expanding symmetrically around the target!*

To succeed, a pilot must have informed awareness of the craft, landing target and wind conditions. For the quick and subtle control responses called for, the information detected must be immediate and direct (Figure 3).

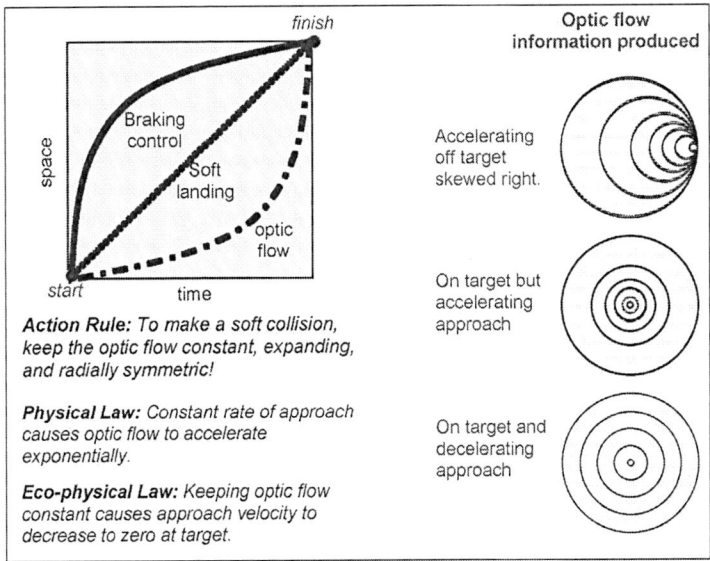

Figure 3: Illustrates how an Action Rule couples physical and ecological Laws. The figure on the left depicts the reciprocal variation of control (braking) and information (optical texture flow) responsible for realizing an intended successful 'soft' landing.

We can generalize the import of Figure 3 in a graphical summary that incorporates the main ingredients of ecological psychology as applied to goal-directed actions. Earlier we saw illustrated in Figure 2 the case of intending to draw an apple. Both figures illustrate how the dynamical process, a rule for action, functionally identifies the object of intention with the object of reference.

The main thesis of this paper can be revisited in an anecdote. A chronically colour-blind girl, Mary, undergoes a new treatment that allows her to see the colour red. Would this new-found perceptual ability make her more fit to survive? She lives on the coast and loves to swim in the ocean. One summer a dire warning is issued by the Center for Disease Control to avoid contact with a deadly red tide (mutant red algae) that causes a fatal infection. Clearly, Mary, who swims in the ocean daily, would be at greater risk before treatment than after treatment since then she could recognize the danger and avoid it.

This anecdote indicates how incredibly important awareness of information can be for survival — even a single invariant environmental property can matter. Here the colour red does. With enough individuals producing off-spring who can stave off a threat — such as the red tide — long enough to procreate, the doctrine of the survival of the fittest is satisfied and natural selection exploited. The psychological capacity of informed awareness seems as likely a heritable trait as any biological ones. (To see that this view of informed awareness eschews Chalmers' problems, ask whether a robot might not be designed to perform the same feat as Mary. But also ask if they perform it in the same way).

In addition to its survival value, agents capable of responding to imminent threat quickly have a clear advantage over those who cannot. Both blindness to threats and inefficiency in response to them can cost a species survival advantage; they both can reduce the number of progeny available to procreate and thus reduce the likelihood that the gene pool is biased in favour of the trait. Response efficiency also endows the agent with an edge in competing for scarce resources. In short, the cost of inefficiency is a relevant variable in calculating the likelihood estimates for an agent thriving or even surviving.

In summary: To survive, organisms must be both biologically fit and psychologically viable. They are biologically fit if they are self-sustaining and psychologically viable if they are competent to care for their needs and tend to their wants. In addition, they must live within a congenial environment — that is, one with appropriate resources, and which poses no insurmountable obstacles to the felicity of actions aimed at obtaining them.

More explicitly, satisfying these conditions, presupposes that agents must be aware of several kinds of information:

- information specifying their vital needs or they would not be motivated to satisfy them;
- information specifying goals that afford fulfilling such needs or they would have no opportunity to choose to act toward them;
- information specifying effective means at their disposal or they could not choose to act appropriately;
- information specifying how well they enact those means or they could not control them;
- information specifying their progress toward the goal or they would not know when to alter their course or stop.

Thus a system without awareness of these sources of information could be neither fit nor viable and would not survive.

One of the most intriguing arguments in favor of the survival value of informed awareness is the following: If consciousness contributed nothing to survival of the fittest, then there would be no reason for its natural selection; but conscious life forms did in fact evolve. Therefore, consciousness must have survival value. Or contrariwise, assuming consciousness had no survival value, shouldn't we expect nonconscious humanoid species equivalent in fitness to conscious humans to be equally abundant today. But since no scientific evidence suggests that such zombie humanoids have appeared then consciousness must have survival value. The philosophers' fanciful assumption that zombies might be indiscernible from humans *in all ways imaginable* can be reasonably rejected on grounds that trying to prove a null hypothesis (that discernibles do not exist) is ill conceived and hence its acceptance a violation of Occam's razor (the admonition that one should avoid assumptions that multiply entities beyond necessity).

Finally, the so-called 'weak' Anthropic Principle (as ably defended by Barrow and Tipler, 1988) argues from the properties of life-forms observed today, e.g., consciousness, that the laws of nature must have evolved just so. There is nothing mysterious about this principle for it follows from the same 'weak' (abductive) logic that allows a forensic expert to argue from current evidence to the earlier circumstances that produced it or that allows a doctor to infer from current symptoms the disease that must have produced them. Under this view, informed awareness is as natural an outcome of cosmological evolution as any other aspect of the physical universe.

## References

Armstrong, D. (1981), *A Materialist Theory of Mind* (London: Routledge and Kegan Paul).
Baars, B. (1988), *A Cognitive Theory of Consciousness* (Cambridge: Cambridge University Press).
Bain, A. (1873), *Mind and body: The Theories of Their Relation* (London: Henry King).
Barrow, J. D. and Tipler, F. J. (1988), *The Anthropic Cosmological Principle* (Oxford: Oxford University Press).
Chalmers, D.J. (1996), *The Conscious Mind* (New York: Oxford University Press).
Chalmers, D.J. (2002), 'Developing a Science of Consciousness,' (Transcript from September 25, 2002 2:00–3:15 PM Eastern. Copyright by International Society for Complexity, Information, and Design 2002).
Gibson (1966): *The Senses Considered as Perceptual Systems* (Boston, MA: Houghton Mifflin).
Henle, M. (1978), 'Gestalt psychology and Gestalt therapy,' *Journal of the History of Behavioral Science*, **14**, pp. 23–32.
Holt (1915), *The Freudian Wish and its Place in Ethics* (New York: Henry Holt).

Kadar, E. & Shaw, R. (2000), 'Toward an ecological field theory of perceptual control of information,' *Ecological Psychology*, **12** (2), pp. 141–80.

Lehar, S. (2003), 'Gestalt isomorphism and the primacy of subjective conscious experience: 'A Gestalt bubble model,' *Behavioral and Brain Sciences*, **26**, pp. 375–444.

Penfield, W. (1975), *The Mystery of Mind: A Critical Study of Consciousness and the Human Brain* (Princeton, NJ: Princeton University Press).

Reed, E. S. (1988), *James J. Gibson and the Psychology of Perception* (New haven, CT: Yale University Press)

Reed, E. S. & Jones R. (1982), *Reasons for Realism: Selected Essays of James J. Gibson* (Hillsdale, NJ: Lawrence Erlbaum Associates, Inc).

Russell, B. (1927), *The Analysis of Matter* (London: Kegan Paul).

Shaw, R. (2002). 'Theoretical Hubris and the Willingness to be Radical,' *Ecological Psychology,* **14** (4), pp. 235–47.

Shaw, R. & Kinsella-Shaw, J. (1988), Ecological Mechanics: A Physical Geometry for Intentional Constraints,' *Human. Movement Science*, 7, pp. 155–200.

Shaw, R., Kadar, E., Sim, M. & Repperger, D. (1992), 'The intentional spring: A strategy for modeling systems that learn to perform intentional acts,' *Journal of Motor Behavior,* **1** (24), pp. 3–28.

Shaw, R. (2003), 'The agent-environment interface: Simon's indirect or Gibson's direct coupling?,' *Ecological Psychology*, **15**, pp. 37–106.

Schneider, W. & Schiffrin, (1977), 'Controlled and automatic processing, detection, search and attention,' *Psychological Review*, **84**, pp. 1–64.

Van Gulick (2004), 'Consciousness,' in *Stanford Encyclopedia of Philosophy*, http://plato.stanford.edu/aerchives/fall/entries/consciousness/.

Bernhard Hommel

# Consciousness and Control
## Not Identical Twins

*Abstract: Human cognition and action are intentional and goal-directed, and explaining how they are controlled is one of the most important tasks of the cognitive sciences. After half a century of benign neglect this task is enjoying increased attention. Unfortunately, however, current theorizing about control in general, and the role of consciousness for/in control in particular, suffers from major conceptual flaws that lead to confusion regarding the following distinctions: (i) automatic and unintentional processes, (ii) exogenous control and disturbance (in a control-theoretical sense) of endogenous control, (iii) conscious control and conscious access to control, and (iv) personal and systems levels of analysis and explanation. Only if these flaws are overcome will a comprehensive understanding of the relationship between consciousness and control emerge.*

The topic of control is hot in the cognitive sciences, as witnessed by a dramatic increase of hits for the keywords 'executive functions', 'executive control', and 'cognitive control' in the Web of Science® database from zero in 1945–1954 to 3672 for 1995–2004. The feeling is that researchers were occupied for a long time with analysing the cognitive machinery but now the time is ripe to find out the way this machinery is used by intelligent agents to realize their intentions (Monsell, 1996). In other words, human will is back on stage. Given that control processes are often considered to be inevitably conscious (e.g., Atkinson & Shiffrin, 1968; Norman & Shallice, 1986; Umiltà,

1988), there is also a strong connection to another hot topic, which makes the study of control even more interesting.

In the following, I will briefly sketch the transition from will to executive control and present two examples of how the concept of executive control is used in contemporary research. Next, I will discuss the relationship between control and consciousness and point out major flaws in the theorizing about this relationship in the cognitive sciences. Only if these flaws are overcome, so I will conclude, can a less simplistic, systematic theory regarding the function of consciousness in the control of cognition and action emerge.

## From Will to Executive Control

The transition from 'will', the philosophical grandfather of control terms, to 'executive' was not smooth and continuous. In the beginnings of experimental psychology a chapter on the will was a must in every textbook and many authors presented their own views on this issue. Lotze (1852), for instance, was struck by the fact that we know so little about how we do the things we do — just think of how little you know about how you manage to tie your shoes. Lotze suggested that we monitor and store the contingencies between our body movements and the events in the external world or inside our body by which these movements are triggered, so that we can later mimic (i.e., imagine, simulate) the stimulus events and thereby trigger the associated body movement. In other words, the will need not impose anything on the body. Rather, it simply exploited the laws according to which the body works anyway. Later authors like Harless (1961) and James (1890) gave this approach a more intentional twist by assuming that agents also acquire contingencies between movements and their sensory consequences. Representations of movements and consequences were assumed to be associated bidirectionally, so that agents could imagine or simulate a consequence and thereby trigger the associated movement. This provided the theoretical basis for what we now know as *ideomotor theory* (see Hommel *et al.*, 2001; Stock & Stock, 2004).

The next step was to address the dynamical aspects of will and choice. The Würzburg school was much less afraid of considering unconscious contributions to the control of cognition and action than the introspectionists Lotze or James were. The ex-Würzburger Ach (1910; 1935) developed the first large-scale experimental research project on human will, which anticipated the architecture of later dual-process theories (e.g., Atkinson & Shiffrin, 1968; Posner & Snyder, 1975) in assuming that will can be measured most purely if it is put into competition with opposing, practice-induced tendencies (habits). Very similar to recent approaches of task switching performance (De Jong, 2000), Ach took the amount of (practice-induced) competition that an individual can overcome as a measure of will power.

Despite these early and rather substantial contributions, the impression one gets from contemporary textbooks of cognitive psychology is that the scientific treatment of executive control in general, and the interplay between so-called intentional and automatic processes in particular, set in no earlier than with the paper of Atkinson and Shiffrin (1968). These authors re-introduced the distinction between automatic processes, which are believed to be independent of attention and intention, and processes that are 'under the control of the subject'. Automatic processes are claimed to result from practice and to operate through relatively permanent sets of associative connections in long-term memory, which makes them 'difficult to suppress, to modify, or to ignore' (Schneider & Shiffrin, 1977, p. 2), whereas control(led) processes, such as retrieval, rehearsal, or coding, reflect a person's current attentional set, intentions, and the task requirements. Accordingly, cognitive operations emerge from a competition between automatic and control(led) processes, exactly as Ach (1910) suggested earlier. Since Atkinson and Shiffrin's article, the distinction between automatic and controlled (or willed, intentional, voluntary, conditional...) processes has enjoyed great popularity and been built into numerous processing models of all sorts of cognitive phenomena (Hommel, 2000; Neumann, 1984). The following two sections will focus on two, relatively representative and broadly discussed families of models addressing the control of visual attention and of response selection.

*Attention: The control of stimulus selection*

Following Atkinson and Shiffrin's lead, attentional research distinguishes between *endogenous* or *top-down* control and stimulus-induced *exogenous* or *bottom-up* control of attention (e.g., Posner, 1978). One widely used paradigm to investigate endogenous control and its interplay with exogenous factors is the singleton or popout task (e.g., Theeuwes, 1992). In this task, subjects detect or identify a visual target that appears randomly in one of several objects. Interestingly, performance is substantially better if the object in which the target appears has a unique feature (e.g., a single green square among red squares or among green circles), that is, if it is a singleton. This suggests that visual attention is attracted 'automatically' to singletons (Theeuwes, 1992) and sometimes the attraction is so strong, even the eyes cannot be prevented from moving to the location of the singleton (Theeuwes, Kramer, Hahn & Irwin, 1998). Singletons, so these authors argue, can capture attention and take over its control — an apparently clear case of exogenous control.

There is an extended discussion going on concerning how strongly such demonstrations of attentional capture depend on the task, the context, and the strategy of the subjects. As some authors have argued, it may be that asking subjects to respond to singletons or rewarding them for attending to singletons induces an endogenous bias towards singletons, with the side effect that any singleton now attracts attention — even the 'wrong ones' (e.g., Folk *et al.*, 1992). More important for present purposes, however, is the question of how the control concept is used in this context.

First, consider the *agent* of control. Who does the controlling? As it is common in experimental psychology, the theorizing on attentional capture is based on the implicitly shared assumption that instructing a voluntary subject in some way induces a goal state in this subject, which in some way biases attention towards the instructed target stimuli — for example by making the perceptual system more sensitive to the target-defining features (Müller *et al.*, 2003). The true controlling is thus done by the experimenter, which is remarkable inasmuch as researchers consider the impact of instructed task goals as particularly good examples of endogenous control (e.g., Monsell, 1996). But the idea is that instructions are somehow 'taken over' by subjects, who then make them goals of their own.

Second, consider the *target* of control, that is, the state, event, or parameter that is assumed to be controlled. Theeuwes and Godijn (2001, p. 121) open their recent review of attentional and oculomotor capture by claiming that 'in order to behave in a goal-directed manner, it is important that we select only the relevant information from the environment and ignore information that is irrelevant, particularly when this information disrupts our actions'. Selecting an object means prioritizing it in the competition for action control, so that a failure to exclude an irrelevant object from selection implies a *loss of endogenous control*. (As I will explain below, this characterization is based on a misconception of how control processes work.)

*Figure 1*. An overview of two popular conflict tasks. The upper row of the schematic stimulus displays shows examples of congruent or compatible conditions and the lower row shows examples of in congruent or incompatible conditions (which produce comparatively worse performance). In the flanker task, subjects respond to a stimulus in a particular location, such as the central letter of a string (here: left keypress for H and right keypress for S), and ignore the flankers. In the Simon task, subjects respond to a nonspatial stimulus feature (here: left keypress for H and right keypress for S, not shown), while stimulus location varies randomly.

## *Intention: The control of response selection*

In addition to inspiring theories of attention, the idea of a dynamic interplay between will and habit or, in more modern terms, between control and automatic processes has inspired theories of response selection. Particularly good examples for experimental tasks that capture the essence of this more dynamic view of response selection are so-called conflict or interference tasks, such as the flanker-compatibility task and the Simon task (see Figure 1). The observation that people show worse performance with response-incongruent flankers has been taken to imply that task-irrelevant stimuli can activate the response they are assigned to in this task. Indeed, flanker stimuli have been found to activate a lateralized readiness potential (LRP) corresponding to the response they signal (Coles *et al*., 1985) and even incorrect subthreshold responses (Eriksen *et al*., 1985). Theoretical accounts of the flanker-congruency effect have made ample use of Ach's and Atkinson and Shiffrin's controlled-automatic dichotomy. The idea is that the target is translated into the correct response in a controlled manner but automatic processes somehow make use of the implemented stimulus-response translation rules and translate the flankers into an activation of the corresponding responses (e.g., Eriksen & Schultz, 1979; Gratton *et al*., 1992).

Very similar observations have been made with the Simon task, where responses to nonspatial stimuli are faster and more accurate if the stimulus happens to spatially correspond with the response. Again, this leads one to suspect that stimulus location can somehow activate a spatially corresponding response, and this is indeed supported by the finding of location-induced LRPs (Sommer *et al.*, 1993) and subliminal response tendencies (Zachay, 1991). Almost all models of the Simon effect have made use of the controlled-automatic logic by assuming that the nonspatial target feature is translated into the response in a controlled manner, whereas an automatic process translates stimulus location into a response location (e.g., De Jong *et al.*, 1994; Kornblum *et al.*, 1990).

As with attention, the *agent* of intention(al) control is again Atkinson and Shiffrin's 'subject' and the task set he or she implements in response to the instructions. The issue of the *target* of control is also treated similarly but one can find a more explicit and clear-cut distinction between *on-line control* and *off-line control*. A comprehensive approach to off-line control is Logan and Gordon's (2001) ECTVA model. It holds that preparing efficiently for a task entails the translation of task instructions into four parameters, three configuring the perceptual system in such a way that the task-relevant stimulus information can be extracted and one controlling the speed and accuracy of response selection. Executive control consists in passing the necessary parameters to subordinate processes that are responsible for the on-line handling of stimulus information and response production. If time allows, this programming of subroutines takes place before the first task-relevant stimulus appears and thus represents off-line control.

It is assumed that on-line control solves the problems that cannot be entirely prevented by off-line control. For example, since off-line control settings are apparently unable to prevent the activation of incorrect responses brought about by irrelevant stimuli or stimulus attributes, it is assumed that on-line control processes resolve the response conflict. Kornblum and colleagues (1990) suggest that control processes are responsible for terminating ('aborting') incorrectly activated response programs before the correct program can be retrieved. A further on-line control process is necessary to detect whether an abortion is necessary; this is done by identifying the correct response and verifying whether responses that are already active are congruent or incongruent with it. Ridderinkhof (2002) claims that activated incorrect responses need to be suppressed before the correct response can be carried out. Other on-line control processes are assumed to operate after the response is carried out. As suggested by Carter *et al.* (1998), response monitoring processes may detect the presence of response conflict and adjust stimulus-response associations accordingly. For instance, strong conflict may result in strengthening the 'controlled' pathways and/or weakening or suppressing 'automatic' pathways (e.g., Gratton *et al.*, 1992).

## Control and Consciousness

The concept of consciousness is anything but well-defined (cf., Velmans, 1996). While some authors have equated consciousness with the human mind, others have restricted it to self-consciousness or the awareness of states of affairs. Recent approaches distinguish between one (Baars, 1988), two (Block, 2005a), or three (Pinker, 1997) types of consciousness, and there is little hope various authors will agree on one conceptual system, let alone locate their own research within it (e.g., Baars & Laureys, 2005; Block, 2005b). Researchers commonly try to circumvent this problem by resorting to an operational definition, such as verbal reportability (e.g., Chalmers, 1995). However, given that there is no reason to assume that conscious experience or access is restricted to states that can be communicated or even verbalized (e.g., take the Würzburgian concept of *imageless thought*), this practice seems to reflect a rather arbitrary choice that is mainly driven by methodological convenience.

With very few exceptions (e.g., Baars, 1988; Wegner, 2002) control-related models in cognitive science leave little space for a well-defined, functional role for consciousness. This does not prevent researchers from using the concept. Indeed, the way it is used points to an apparently strong belief that consciousness and (endogenous) control are at least highly correlated. Indeed, the belief is often so strong that authors speak of 'conscious control' as if there could be no alternative (i.e., no other type of control is ever mentioned; cf., Wegner & Bargh, 1998). For instance, Norman and Shallice (1986) contrast automatic, stimulus-driven actions with actions that are under 'deliberate conscious control', as if unconscious deliberate control would be inconceivable. In addition, the only control-related entries in the subject index of Johnson and Proctor's (2004) textbook on attention are 'controlled and automatic processing' and 'conscious control'.

Given the ill-defined status of consciousness and conscious processes, one can only speculate why there is such a strong tendency to identify endogenous control with conscious control. One reason is that researchers may find it difficult to ignore the introspective impression that it is their own conscious will that sets their body in motion(Wegner, 2002). Another possible reason is that Atkinson and Shiffrin (1968) suggested such a relationship between endogenous control and consciousness in their controlled-automatic distinction. Automatic processes are characterized, sometimes even defined by (see Neumann, 1984), the fading out of conscious awareness. Indeed, practice-induced automaticity (however defined) is commonly accompanied by a continuously decreasing awareness of the stimulus events and action components involved (Fitts, 1964). This fading of consciousness may lead some to theorists to the conclusion that since automatic processing is unconscious, control processing should obviously be conscious.

Yet another reason to believe that endogenous control must be conscious is probably the fact that the goals and intentions that are thought to trigger the control processes investigated in psychological experiments are commonly not the subject's own goals and intentions, at least not originally. Subjects need to be convinced through money and social skills to 'take over' the goals and intentions the experimenter wants them to have, and it is difficult to imagine that the communicative process achieving this interpersonal transfer should go unnoticed by the subject. Given that subjects are aware of the transfer and, thus, the goals and intentions imposed on them, researchers may be tempted to assume that the implementation of the goals must be correlated with, and perhaps even dependent upon conscious experience. Indeed, some authors have explicitly claimed that conscious experience is the only agent that is able to carry out control operations (e.g., Umiltà, 1988).

The assumption that control and consciousness must be coupled is particularly popular among attention researchers. How popular it is depends on the particular function attributed to attention. Schneider (1995) has pointed out that there are at least three families of attentional theories: some focus on 'selection for object recognition', some on 'selection for feature integration', and some on 'selection for action', a term introduced by Allport (1987). Theories belonging to the first two families assume that the major purpose of attention is to select stimulus events for conscious perception (e.g., Posner & Snyder, 1975; Treisman & Gelade, 1980). If one considers attention the means by which selection is controlled (e.g., Treisman, 1988; Umiltà, 1988) and conscious experience the ultimate purpose of selection, it seems to be very obvious indeed that control must have something to do with consciousness.

Theories belonging to the third family have a less natural connection with consciousness — and so do the authors defending them (Allport, 1987; van der Heijden, 1992; Neumann, 1987). These theories claim that input selection is not necessitated by limitations related to perception or conscious experience but, rather, by the fact that people can only perform one action at a time. In other words, the ultimate purpose of attention is action control, not perception. This latter view does not assume that consciousness must be involved in the control of attention.

There are also theories that explicitly connect consciousness to action control. Lotze (1852) was among the first to assume that creating a conscious image of an action's trigger stimulus or context is a necessary precondition (actually, the only cognitive precondition) for voluntary action to occur. James (1890) and later ideomotor theorists emphasized the intended consequences of the action, which were assumed to constitute the crucial retrieval cue that mediated the selection of an action (see also Baars, 1992). Norman and Shallice (1986) went one step further and claimed that consciousness is directly involved in regulating and solving conflicts among competing action tendencies. However, they fail to explain exactly why conscious experience is necessary in this process and exactly how it becomes functional. More recent approaches have revived Vygotsky's (1962) idea that inner speech — a commonly conscious activity — may play a major role in action control (Zelazo, 1999; 2004), and some evidence has been gathered in its support (Emerson & Miyake, 2003; Goschke, 2000).

Theories in which consciousness plays a defined, functional role in endogenous control are still the exception but they do exist. It is interesting to note, however, that they do not restrict the role of consciousness to input selection (or even identify consciousness with attention), as many attentional theories seem to imply, or to output selection, as action control theories suggest. Rather, they assign to consciousness some integrative role (for an overview, see Baars, 2002). Baars (1988), for instance, relates consciousness to what he calls a global workspace, a medium where information from different processing modules can be exchanged and related. Koch (2004) claims that consciousness-related states provide a summary of the present states of affairs in the world and one's own body, which informs and provides the basis for further planning and decision-making. This view fits well with that of Milner and Goodale (1995). They distinguish between a ventral processing pathway, which handles and integrates visual information with memory contents to create conscious awareness of the best possible interpretation of the visual world, and a dorsal pathway, which is responsible for the on-line processing of action-relevant information. Consciousness and integration are also connected in the approach of Zelazo (1999; 2004), who assumes that consciousness creates relations between mental representations, which provides the basis for higher cognitive functioning.

We can conclude that the concept of consciousness is much more often used in the context of endogenous control than it is defined, motivated, explained, or justified. Hence, there is some implicit association between consciousness and control that seems so self-evident to many researchers that they do not even bother to explain why they are using it. Researchers that do bother assume that consciousness reflects or is related to some sort of global integration.

*The concept of control*

If researchers theorize about the control of attention or action they commonly do not define what they mean by control (but see LaBerge, 2002, for an exception) and they do not justify their use of this term. So let us first consider when and in which sense the use of the term is appropriate.

Control is an operation mode of a control system (e.g., Powers, 1973). Minimally, a control system consists of a controller (C), the agent of control, and a controlled system or variable (T for target), the target of control (see Figure 2). To exert control, C must be able to accomplish the following: (i) act upon T, (ii) perceive the resulting impact on T, and (iii) compare this impact (i.e., the actual behaviour of T) with a reference or goal, that is, the intended behaviour of T. The

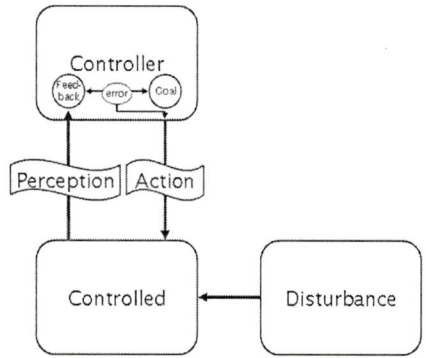

*Figure 2.* Basic design of a simple control system.
See text for further explanation.

difference between the intended behaviour of T and its actual behaviour is called *error*, and control is characterized by Cs attempt to minimize the magnitude of this error. That is, the controller can only be assumed to be in control if it can *compensate for disturbances*, that is, for the effects of other factors on T's behaviour. Indeed, control can be defined by 'consistency produced in the face of disturbance' (Marken, 1986, p. 268).

Probably the most popular example of such control is a central heating system. The goal of the control loop is defined by the user, who specifies a room temperature, say 20° Celsius. The intended temperature is be compared to the actual temperature (the perceptual branch of the control loop). In the case of a negative error (i.e., if the room is colder than 20°) a heat generator is switched on (the action branch of the control loop) and kept working until the error is no longer negative.

The main reason such a control system has perceptual input (i.e., feedback) is that T might be influenced by factors other than C (i.e., disturbances). If these disturbances are unpredictable there is no way to know whether control is effective other than to measure the combined effects of C and disturbances. However, if the disturbances can be assumed to be negligible, or if they can be fully predicted, *feedforward* control is possible. That is, C can take into account possible disturbances and adjust its action on T accordingly, so that the perception branch of the loop is no longer necessary. Obviously, such a control mode is only reasonable in a highly modularized processing system, otherwise C would easily loose control. To the degree that consciousness and control are connected through the need to integrate information, we need to assume that control is not feedforward but, rather, includes feedback.

## Conceptual flaws

We have seen that many researchers are tempted to draw a connection between consciousness and control, but it is not clear what this connection is. Determining the nature of this assumed connection is further complicated by the fact that both control and consciousness are not well-defined concepts, and both exist in everyday language. As a result, many authors do not bother to even attempt to define or explain the way they use these concepts. Accordingly, it is far from clear whether different authors using these terms refer to the same phenomena, systems, or functions. Given that we have no a-priori reason to believe that consciousness is a unitary thing (Allport, 1988), and strong reasons to believe that control is not (Duncan *et al.*, 1997;

Miyake *et al.*, 2000), it may be the case that apparent contradictions in the literature are due to different statements being made on different issues. Making progress therefore requires some agreement on the phenomena to be addressed and on the way control- and consciousness-related terms are used to theorize about these phenomena. As a first step in this direction I will try to point to some of the most impeding confusions in the discussion of control and conscious phenomena.

*(a) Confusing automatic and unintentional processing*

When authors refer to or compare automatic and control(led) processes they often refer to the work of Atkinson and Shiffrin (1968) and Schneider and Shiffrin (1977), or the equivalent distinction of Posner and Snyder (1975). The logical and empirical shortcomings of this distinction have been discussed in detail elsewhere (Jonides *et al.*, 1985; Neumann, 1984; Ryan, 1983), and I will not repeat the arguments here. What is important for our purposes, however, is that automatic processes are often, and perhaps always, contingent on the current intention and task goal (Bargh, 1989). As pointed out earlier, people's attention is captured by irrelevant events mainly if these events share some characteristic or feature with the target (Folk, Remington & Johnston, 1992). That is, automatic processes seem to reflect the current task set. The same is true for conflict tasks, where stimuli have been found to activate corresponding or associated responses only if subjects have prepared themselves for responding to these particular stimuli (Valle-Inclán & Redondo, 1998) with these particular responses (Hommel, 1993). These and other examples (Bargh & Ferguson, 2000; Bauer & Besner, 1997; Hommel, 2000; Neumann, 1984) suggest that automatic processes do not represent the opposite of controlled processes but, rather, are functional in realizing intended goals (Bargh, 1989) — even if they may be fooled by highly artificial experimental conditions. Indeed, it is extremely difficult to find cognitive processes that truly fulfill Schneider and Shiffrin's (1977, p. 2) automaticity criteria by being 'difficult to suppress, to modify, or to ignore'.

*(b) Confusing exogenous control and disturbance*

Imagine you are driving your car on the highway. Suddenly, a strong, unexpected squall emerges from the right. Your car moves to the left. You notice this and turn the steering wheel right. The car is now back on track. This is a perfect example of a control operation in a functioning feedback system. You are in control, which means you constantly compare the current state of affairs (i.e., the actual position of the car) to your goal (to keep the car in the middle) and compensate, if necessary, for unexpected disturbances.

Now compare this situation to attentional capture. You identify your target and plan the appropriate saccade to its location. But then a distractor attracts your attention, perhaps even your eyes, before you eventually home in at the target location. Again, so one would think, a typical demonstration of (endogenous) control: consistency in the face of disturbance. Surprisingly, however, these cases are discussed in the literature as evidence of a (temporary) loss of endogenous control and a takeover of exogenous control. The same argumentative pattern can be found with regard to response selection. Conflict tasks demonstrate that action control is challenged by irrelevant stimuli and the response conflicts they induce, but they also demonstrate that these challenges are commonly overcome: errors are commonly rare and the reaction times are only slightly elevated. This means that people are able to reach their instructed task goals in the face of disturbances: an excellent example of endogenous control but not, as suggested by most authors, a demonstration of exogenous control.

This confusion regarding the relationship between control and disturbance may be the result of utilizing a time-scale of analysis that is of too-fine a grain. A local piecemeal analysis can only measure and compare the relative impacts exogenous and endogenous sources have on a given process or state. But such a piecemeal analysis makes little sense because control takes place on a coarser time scale that involves processing feedback and reacting to it. Hence, the essence of control does not lie in the fact that disturbances can appear and control can be challenged but, rather, in the observation that such challenges are successfully met.

Is this more than a play on words, or might it be possible to replace 'exogenous control' with 'disturbance'? I think the answer strongly depends on one's research strategy. Until now, the strategy express in research on attentional capture and response-conflict conformed rather will with the traditional strategy of posing binary questions, as aptly portrayed by Newell (1973): We argue and design experiments to figure out how automatic or controlled particular processes are, whether pure exogenous control really exists, and so forth, but we have little idea about exactly where this may lead us. A more productive strategy may be to consider the whole interplay of disturbance and compensation as a single act of control, which needs and deserves theoretical explanation. Recent, more comprehensive accounts have demonstrated the fruitfulness of such an approach by investigating, among other things, what output the controller produces (see Logan &

Gordon, 2001) or how disturbances are registered and compensated (Blakemore *et al.*, 2002; Carter *et al.*, 1998).

In my view, the most interesting implication of treating the whole, temporally extended control loop as an important unit of analysis is that it emphasizes the need and function of global processing. Taking and maintaining control requires the integration of a lot of information: the goal needs to be related to the output of the controller, which needs to be related to the output of the controlled system (i.e., the input of the controller), which again needs to be related back to the goal. Functionally and anatomically speaking this involves quite a number of processing systems and, thus, must be a global operation (Allport, 1988). As pointed out earlier, global operations have been suspected to be more related to conscious experience than local, modular processes (Baars, 2002). In support of this hypothesis, recent studies have shown that conscious awareness of visual events is strongly correlated with global cortical communication (Gross *et al.*, 2004) and that the resolution of stimulus-induced response conflict is tied to conscious awareness (Dehaene *et al.*, 2003; Kunde, 2003; see Mayr, 2004). Hence, running through a whole control cycle may indeed be a consciousness-related global operation.

*(c) Confusing conscious control and conscious access to control states*

Another conceptual problem that emerges from the common, uncritical use of the term 'conscious control' is that it does not specify which causal relationship the term is meant to imply. First, it may mean that any control operation must be conscious and that operations can only control by virtue of being conscious — a view explicitly defended by Umiltà (1988) and implied by the popular model of Norman and Shallice (1986). Second, it may mean that control states or operations are consciously accessible — suggesting that if something is consciously accessible it is likely to be a control state, but not all control states need to be consciously represented. And, third, it may mean that conscious awareness and control are correlated for some, still to be determined reason.

The first option is extremely difficult to test — not only because its supporters commonly fail to describe exactly those aspects of a process that need to be experienced in order to control it, but also because any demonstration that unconscious processes can affect behaviour could be 'explained away' by claiming such processes to be 'automatic'. However, recent findings suggest that people may not only be unable to explain *how* they exert control over a particular event (which the control-through-consciousness account could accommodate) but they sometimes do not even know *whether* they do. For instance, people's feeling that they have caused an event is much more determined by whether they expected that event (even if this expectation is induced by subliminal primes: Aarts *et al.*, 2005) than by whether they actually produced it (Wegner & Wheatley, 1999).

These and similar observations (Wegner, 2002) do not confirm the assumption that consciousness and control are equivalent (the first option) and they also let one doubt whether human agents have a privileged conscious access to their own control processes (the second option). By exclusion, this leaves us with the possibility that conscious awareness and control are correlated but do not necessarily depend on each other. As claimed by Wegner (2002), true control may be taking place in an entirely unconscious fashion but the successful prediction of its outcome may trigger the illusion of 'conscious control'.

One may object that Wegner's theory throws out the baby with the bath water. Indeed, demonstrating that people can be made to think that they have caused an action which they didn't rules out the idea that the relationship between consciousness and control is particularly intimate, but it does not prove that conscious contents can never cause an action or that all control experiences are illusions. Moreover, Haggard (2005) has emphasized that some aspects of control, such as the integration of an action and its effects, may depend on the presence of an action intention. Even though this does not require that it is the intention that exerts the control, it would seem premature to close the book before further research has brought some more light into this matter. What seems clear, however, is that the correlation between conscious experience and (endogenous) control is less perfect than some approaches suggest or even presume.

*(d) Confusing personal and systems levels of analysis and explanation*

The popularity of the concept 'executive control' undoubtedly derives from the translational trick it provides: It exploits the technomorphic analogy to a central processing unit in a digital computer, and thereby signals the promise of a mechanistic account. And it does so without violating our introspective experience of ourselves as a deciding and controlling agent (Goschke, 2003). Given that the term is only a *translation* of a concept defined on a personal explanatory level (where agents control actions) to a concept defined on a systems level (where the executive sends control signals to subroutines), nothing is gained if the translation is all that is provided.[1] Although this seems obvious, a number of models and accounts of aspects of cognitive control have treated the translation as coming with some explanatory surplus. For instance, Posner and Snyder (1975) and Schneider and Shiffrin (1977) have identified 'the conscious control of the subject' as the origin of the control that is exerted on the 'controlled' processes and strategies that are doing the main jobs in their models, and Norman and Shallice (1986) explain the ability to suppress unwanted response tendencies through the intervention of a clever but unspecified 'supervisory attentional system', which they readily equate with the human will. These and other conceptual oddities have been discussed and criticized at length elsewhere (Allport, 1980; Neumann, 1984), so that I can restrict myself to emphasizing what I consider the most problematic consequence of mixing personal and systems levels: the creation, rather than the solution, of theoretical problems.

For instance, Monsell (1996, p. 95) describes 'the mystery of how cognitive processes are controlled' by asking '… what causes me to devote my processing resources, organized in a particular way, to this one task rather than another, and when, and how?' Apart from the fact that this question contains at least two Rylean category mistakes (Ryle, 1949), the need for an executive control mechanism is motivated by pointing out that humans can respond to the same stimulus in different, task-specific ways — an ability that we however share with rats, pigeons, and other animals (e.g., Mackintosh, 1974) that until now were not suspected to have particularly impressive executive functions at their disposal. Another example: In a description of 'the theoretical problem' of 'controlled processing', Shallice (1994, p. 395) takes the fact that people can attend to different stimuli to mean 'that the behavior of human subjects in information-processing experiments depended not only on the structural organization of the cognitive system but also on the strategy employed to carry out such tasks' (Shallice, 1994, p. 395). The concept of strategy also looms large in Logan's (1985) account of the 'executive control of thought and action'; he takes the observation that human subjects exploit contingencies between stimuli (e.g., Logan & Zbrodoff, 1979, p. 197) to

---

[1] Some authors have chosen to enrich their translation by the assumption that the executive controller resides in the frontal lobe (e.g., Baddeley, 1986; Shallice, 1994). On one hand, this seems to follow a straightforward logic, given that frontal cortical areas are crucially involved in everything that looks like a 'willful' process — be that preparation for actions and tasks, attentional selection, inhibition of reflexes, or the planning of action sequences (see Stuss & Knight, 2002, for an overview). On the other hand, though, this double translation from a personal to *two* systems levels as such does not bring in any more theoretical meat, it just offers two displacements of the problem for the price of one.

'demonstrate that subjects will adopt strategies that allow them to maximize the attainment of their goals'. Given the demonstrations of selective attention (Mackintosh, 1975) and associative stimulus-stimulus learning (Pavlov, 1927/1960) in all sorts of nonhuman animals, it is difficult to see why such observations motivate researchers to resort to a fancy but theoretically opaque mental system, which then is taken to 'explain' the experimental effect, instead of making use of available theoretical principles.

## Prospects for a Theory of Consciousness and Control

In view of the flaws and shortcomings in the theorizing about the role of consciousness in the control of cognition and action it seems clear that a lot needs to be done. Fortunately, some lessons are to be learned from the history of the concept of attention: Research started with the commonsense version of the concept, which was rather uncritically translated into a unitary scientific concept (e.g., James, 1890). Even though a unitary view on attention is still nurtured in some areas of the cognitive sciences, researchers increasingly acknowledge that different types of attention, different attentional functions exist, as well as different brain areas housing them and different neurotransmitter systems to make them work (e.g., Allport, 1987; Posner, 2004; Schneider, 1995). This history seems to be recapitulated by the concept of control. While theorizing was first dominated by the discussion of a 'central executive', 'operating system', or 'controller', more recent approaches increasingly favour distributed and specialized 'executive' or 'control functions' (e.g., for an overview, see Monsell & Driver, 2000). Another healthy development is the increasing tendency to break up the traditional dichotomy of automatic and control(led) processes and to consider more integrated conceptualizations in which automatic processes are functional in *achieving* control (Baars & Franklin, 2003; Bargh & Ferguson, 2000). Indeed, if a systems level analysis aims at explaining how cognition and action (as defined on the personal level) are controlled, it makes sense to assume that it is the organization of the processes that achieves the control, not the characteristics of isolated individual processes. Accordingly, there is little use in assigning the labels 'automatic' and 'controlled' to individual processes unless we understand how they interact with each other and how this interaction creates the phenomenon of control (objectively defined as persistence in the face of disturbance).

Important next steps to be taken are, first, to make stronger attempts to concretize the possible or likely roles of consciousness awareness in control. It seems inappropriate to treat consciousness and control almost as a synonym without explaining how the having of a phenomenal experience can cause (rather than reflect) the organization of cognitive processes in the service of a goal. Weaker claims, such as that control states are consciously accessible, must be specified and empirically tested, not simply taken for granted on the basis of personal introspection. Of special interest will be the further investigation of the causal (or only correlative) relationship between conscious intentions and actions (Aarts *et al.*, 2005; Wegner, 2002), as the outcome of such research will be particularly informative with respect to the relevance of introspective evidence. Finally, it seems important to avoid the mixing of analytical and, even more important, explanatory levels. Describing a simple process in fancy terms is unlikely to serve the progress of the scientific understanding of control, especially if it conceals the view on less imaginative but presumably more appropriate and already available explanations.[2]

## References

Aarts, H., Custers, R. & Wegner, D.M. (2005), 'On the inference of personal authorship: Enhancing experienced agency by priming effect information', *Consciousness and Cognition*, **14**, pp. 439–58.

Ach, N. (1910), *Über den Willensakt und das Temperament* (Leipzig: Quelle & Meyer).

Ach, N. (1935), *Analyse des Willens* (Berlin: Urban & Schwarzenberg).

Allport, D.A. (1980), 'Patterns and actions: Cognitive mechanisms are content-specific', in *Cognitive Psychology*, ed. G. Claxton (London: Routledge).

Allport, D.A. (1987), 'Selection for action: Some behavioral and neurophysiological considerations of attention and action', in *Perspectives on Perception and Action*, ed. H. Heuer & A.F. Sanders (Hillsdale, NJ: Erlbaum).

Allport, A. (1988), 'What concept of consciousness?' In *Consciousness in Contemporary Science*, ed. A.J. Marcel & E. Bisiach (Oxford: Clarendon).

Atkinson, R.C. & Shiffrin, R.M. (1968), 'Human memory: A proposed system and its control processes', in *The Psychology of Learning and Motivation, Vol 2*, ed. K.W. Spence & J.T. Spence (New York: Academic Press).

Baars, B.J. (1988), *A Cognitive Theory of Consciousness* (New York: Cambridge University Press).

Baars, B.J. (1992), 'A new ideomotor theory of voluntary control', in *Experimental Slips and Human Error*, ed. B.J. Baars (New York: Plenum).

Baars, B.J. (2002), 'The conscious access hypothesis: Origins and recent evidence', *Trends in Cognitive Science*, **6**, pp. 47–52.

Baars, B.J. & Franklin, S. (2003), 'How conscious experience and working memory interact', *Trends in Cognitive Sciences*, **7**, pp. 166–72.

Baars, B.J. & Laureys, S. (2005), 'One, not two, neural correlates of consciousness', *Trends in Cognitive Sciences*, **9**, p. 269.

---

[2] Support for this research by a grant of the Deutsche Forschungs- gemeinschaft (DFG, HO 1430/8-3) is gratefully acknowledged. Correspondence and requests for materials should be sent to the author.

Baddeley, A.D. (1986), *Working Memory* (Oxford: Clarendon Press).
Bargh, J.A. (1989), 'Conditional automaticity: Varieties of automatic influence in social perception and cognition', in *Unintended Thought*, ed. J.S. Uleman & J.A. Bargh (London: Guilford Press).
Bargh, J.A. & Ferguson, M.L. (2000), 'Beyond behaviorism: On the automaticity of higher mental processes', *Psychological Bulletin*, **126**, pp. 925–45.
Bauer, B. & Besner, D. (1997), 'Processing in the Stroop task: Mental set as a determinant of performance', *Canadian Journal of Experimental Psychology*, **51**, pp. 61–8.
Blakemore, S.J., Wolpert, D.M. & Frith, C.D. (2002), 'Abnormalities in the awareness of action', *Trends in Cognitive Sciences*, **6**, pp. 237–42.
Block, N. (2005a), 'Two neural correlates of consciousness', *Trends in Cognitive Sciences*, **9**, pp. 46–52.
Block, N. (2005b), 'The merely verbal problem of consciousness: Reply to Baars and Laureys', *Trends in Cognitive Sciences*, **9**, p. 270.
Carter, C.S., Braver, T.S., Barch, D.M., Botvinick, M.M., Noll, D.C. & Cohen, J.D. (1998), 'Anterior cingulate cortex, error detection, and the online monitoring of performance', *Science*, **280**, pp. 747–49.
Chalmers, D.J. (1995), 'Facing up to the problem of consciousness', *Journal of Consciousness Studies*, **2** (3), pp. 200–19.
Coles, M.G.H., Gratton, G., Bashore, T.R., Eriksen, C.W. & Donchin, E. (1985), 'A psychophysiological investigation of the continuous flow model of human information processing', *Journal of Experimental Psychology: Human Perception and Performance*, **11**, pp. 529–53.
Dehaene, S., Artiges, E., Naccache, L., Martelli, C., Viard, A., Schurhoff, F., Recasens, C., Martinot, M.L.P., Leboyer, M. & Martinot, J.-L. (2003), 'Conscious and subliminal conflicts in normal subjects and patients with schizophrenia: The role of the anterior cingulate', *Proceedings of the National Academy of Sciences USA*, **100**, pp. 13722–7.
De Jong, R. (2000), 'An intention-activation account of residual switch costs', in *Control of Cognitive Processes: Attention and Performance XVIII*, eds. S. Monsell & J.S. Driver (Cambridge, MA: MIT Press).
De Jong, R., Liang, C.C. & Lauber, E. (1994), 'Conditional and unconditional automaticity: A dual process model of effects of spatial stimulus response correspondence', *Journal of Experimental Psychology: Human Perception and Performance*, **20**, pp. 731–50.
Duncan, J., Johnson, R., Swales, M., Freer, C. (1997), 'Frontal lobe deficits after head injury: Unity and diversity of function', *Cognitive Neuropsychology*, **14**, pp. 713–41.
Emerson, M.J. & Miyake, A. (2003), 'The role of inner speech in task switching: A dual-task investigation', *Journal of Memory and Language*, **48**, pp. 148–68.
Eriksen, C.W., Coles, M.G.H., Morris, L.R. & O'Hara, W.P. (1985), 'An electromyographic examination of response competition', *Bulletin of the Psychonomic Society*, **23**, pp. 165–8.
Eriksen, B.A. & Schultz, D.W. (1979), 'Information processing in visual search: A continuous flow conception and experimental results', *Perception & Psychophysics*, **25**, pp. 249–63.
Fitts, P.M. (1964), 'Perceptual-motor skill learning', in *Categories of Human Learning*, ed. A.W. Melton (New York: Academic Press).
Folk, C.L., Remington, R.W. & Johnston, J.C. (1992), 'Involuntary covert orienting is contingent on attentional control settings', *Journal of Experimental Psychology: Human Perception & Performance*, **18**, pp. 1030–44.

Goschke, T. (2000), 'Involuntary persistence and intentional reconfiguration in task-set switching', in *Control of Cognitive Processes: Attention and Performance XVIII*, eds. S. Monsell & J.S. Driver (Cambridge, MA: MIT Press).

Goschke, T. (2003), 'Voluntary action and cognitive control from a cognitive neuroscience perspective', in *Voluntary Action: Brains, Minds, and Sociality*, eds. S. Maasen, W. Prinz & G. Roth (Oxford: Oxford University Press).

Gratton, G., Coles, M.G.H. & Donchin, E. (1992), 'Optimizing the use of information: strategic control of activation of responses', *Journal of Experimental Psychology: General*, **121**, pp. 480–506.

Gross, J., Schmitz, F., Schnitzler, I., Kessler, K., Shapiro, K., Hommel, B. & Schnitzler, A. (2004), 'Long-range neural synchrony predicts temporal limitations of visual attention in humans', *Proceedings of the National Academy of Sciences USA*, **101**, pp. 13050–5.

Haggard, P. (2005), 'Conscious intention and motor cognition', *Trends in Cognitive Sciences*, **9**, pp. 290–5.

Harless, E. (1861), 'Der Apparat des Willens', *Zeitschrift fuer Philosophie und philosophische Kritik*, **38**, pp. 50–73.

Hommel, B. (1993), 'Inverting the Simon effect by intention: Determinants of direction and extent of effects of irrelevant spatial information', *Psychological Research*, **55**, pp. 270–9.

Hommel, B. (1994), 'Spontaneous decay of response code activation', *Psychological Research*, **56**, pp. 261–8.

Hommel, B. (2000), 'The prepared reflex: Automaticity and control in stimulus-response translation', in *Control of Cognitive Processes: Attention and Performance XVIII*, eds. S. Monsell & J.S. Driver (Cambridge, MA: MIT Press).

Hommel, B., Müsseler, J., Aschersleben, G. & Prinz, W. (2001), 'The theory of event coding (TEC): A framework for perception and action planning', *Behavioral and Brain Sciences*, **24**, pp. 849–78.

James, W. (1890), *The Principles of Psychology* (New York: Dover Publications).

Johnson, A. & Proctor, R.W. (2004), *Attention: Theory and practice* (Thousand Oaks, CA: Sage).

Jonides, J., Naveh-Benjamin, M. & Palmer, J. (1985), 'Assessing automaticity', *Acta Psychologica*, **60**, pp. 157–71.

Koch, C. (2004), *The Quest for Consciousness: A Neurobiological Approach* (Englewood, CO: Roberts & Company).

Kornblum, S., Hasbroucq, T. & Osman, A. (1990), 'Dimensional overlap: Cognitive basis for stimulus response compatibility — a model and taxonomy', *Psychological Review*, **97**, pp. 253–70.

Kunde, W. (2003), 'Sequential modulations of stimulus-response correspondence effects depend on awareness of conflict', *Psychonomic Bulletin & Review*, **10**, pp. 198–205.

LaBerge, D. (2002), 'Attentional control: Brief and prolonged', *Psychological Research*, **66**, pp. 220–33.

Logan, G.D. (1985), 'Executive control of thought and action', *Acta Psychologica*, **60**, pp. 193–210.

Logan, G.D. & Gordon, R.D. (2001), 'Executive control of visual attention in dual-task situations', *Psychological Review*, **108**, pp. 393–434.

Logan, G.D. & Zbrodoff, N.J. (1979), 'When it helps to be misled: Facilitative effects of increasing the frequency of conflicting stimuli in a Stroop-like task', *Memory & Cognition*, **7**, pp. 166–74.

Lotze, R.H. (1852), *Medicinische Psychologie oder Physiologie der Seele* (Leipzig: Weidmann'sche Buchhandlung).

Mackintosh, N.J. (1974), *The Psychology of Animal Learning* (New York: Academic Press).
Mackintosh, N.J. (1975), 'A theory of attention: Variations in the associability with reinforcement', *Psychological Review*, **82**, pp. 276–98.
Marken, R.S. (1986), 'Perceptual organization of behavior: A hierarchical control model of coordinated action', *Journal of Experimental Psychology: Human Perception and Performance*, **12**, pp. 267–76.
Mayr, U. (2004), 'Conflict, consciousness, and control', *Trends in Cognitive Sciences*, **8**, pp. 145–8.
Milner, A.D. & Goodale, M.A. (1995), *The Visual Brain in Action* (Oxford: Oxford University Press).
Miyake, A., Friedman, N.P., Emerson, M.J., Witzki, A.H., Howerter, A. & Wager, T.D. (2000), 'The unity and diversity of executive functions and their contributions to complex frontal lobe tasks: A latent variable analysis', *Cognitive Psychology*, **41**, pp. 49–100.
Monsell, S. (1996), 'Control of mental processes', in *Unsolved Mysteries of the Mind*, ed. V. Bruce (Hove: Erlbaum).
Monsell, S. & Driver, J. (ed. 2000), *Control of Cognitive Processes: Attention and Performance XVIII* (Cambridge MA: MIT Press).
Müller, H.J., Reimann, B. & Krummenacher, J. (2003), 'Visual search for singleton feature targets across dimensions: Stimulus- and expectancy-driven effects in dimensional weighting', *Journal of Experimental Psychology: Human Perception and Performance*, **29**, pp. 1021–35.
Neumann, O. (1984), 'Automatic processing: A review of recent findings and a plea for an old theory', in *Cognition and Motor Processes*, ed. W. Prinz & A.F. Sanders (Berlin: Springer).
Neumann, O. (1987), 'Beyond capacity: A functional view of attention', in *Perspectives on Perception and Action*, ed. H. Heuer & A.F. Sanders (Hillsdale, NJ: Erlbaum).
Newell, A. (1973), 'You can't play 20 questions with nature and win: Projective comments on the papers of this symposium', in *Visual Information Processing*, ed. W.G. Chase (New York: Academic Press).
Norman, D.A. & Shallice, T. (1986), 'Attention to action: Willed and automatic control of behavior', in *Consciousness and Self-Regulation Vol. 4*, ed. R.J. Davidson, G.F. Schwartz & D. Shapiro (New York: Plenum Press).
Pavlov, I.P. (1927/1960), 'Conditioned Reflexes: An Investigation of the Physiological Activity of the Cerebral Cortex', ed. G.V. Anrep (New York: Boyer).
Pinker, S. (1997), *How the Mind Works* (New York: Norton).
Posner, M.I. (1978), *Chronometric Explorations of Mind* (Hillsdale, NJ: Erlbaum).
Posner, M.I. (ed. 2004)., *Cognitive Neuroscience of Attention* (New York: Guilford).
Posner, M.I. & Snyder, C.R.R. (1975), 'Attention and cognitive control', in *Information Processing and Cognition: The Loyola Symposium*, ed. R.L. Solso (Hillsdale, NJ: Erlbaum).
Powers, W.T. (1973), *Behavior: The Control of Perception* (Chicago: Aldine).
Ridderinkhof, K.R. (2002), 'Activation and suppression in conflict tasks: Empirical clarification through distributional analyses', in *Attention and Performance XIX: Common Mechanisms in Perception and Action*, eds. W. Prinz & B. Hommel (Oxford: Oxford University Press).
Ryan, C. (1983), 'Reassessing the automaticity-control distinction: Item recognition as a paradigm case', *Psychological Review*, **90**, pp. 171–8.
Ryle, G. (1949), *The Concept of Mind* (Chicago: The University of Chicago Press).

Schneider, W. & Shiffrin, R.M. (1977), 'Controlled and automatic human information processing: I. Detection, search, and attention', *Psychological Review*, **84**, pp. 1–57.

Schneider, W.X. (1995), 'A neuro-cognitive model for visual attention control of segmentation, object recognition, and space-based motor action', *Visual Cognition*, **2**, pp. 331–75.

Shallice, T. (1994), 'Multiple levels of control processes', in *Attention and Performance XV*, eds. C. Umilta & M. Moscovitch (Cambridge, MA: MIT Press).

Sommer, W., Leuthold, H. & Hermanutz, M. (1993), 'Covert effects of alcohol revealed by event-related potentials', *Perception & Psychophysics*, **54**, pp. 127–35.

Stock, A. & Stock, C. (2004), 'A short history of ideo-motor action', *Psychological Research,* **68**, pp. 176–88.

Stuss, D.T. & Knight, R.T. (ed. 2002), *Principles of Frontal Lobe Function* (New York: Oxford University Press).

Theeuwes, J. (1992), 'Perceptual selectivity for color and form', *Perception & Psychophysics*, **51**, pp. 599–606.

Theeuwes, J. & Godijn, R. (2001), 'Attention and oculomotor capture', in *Attraction, Distraction, and Action: Multiple Perspectives on Attentional Capture*, ed. C. Folk & B. Gibson (Amsterdam: Elsevier Science).

Theeuwes, J., Kramer, A.F, Hahn, S. & Irwin, D.E. (1998), 'Our eyes do not always go where we want them to go: capture of the eyes by new objects', *Psychological Science*, **9**, pp. 379–85.

Treisman, A. (1988), 'Features and objects: The fourteenth Bartlett memorial lecture', *Quarterly Journal of Experimental Psychology*, **40A**, pp. 201–37.

Treisman, A. & Gelade, G. (1980), 'A feature integration theory of attention', *Cognitive Psychology*, **12**, pp. 97–136.

Umiltà, C. (1988), 'The control operations of consciousness', in *Consciousness in Contemporary Science*, ed. A.J. Marcel & E. Bisiach (Oxford: Oxford University Press).

Valle-Inclán, F. & Redondo, M. (1998), 'On the automaticity of ipsilateral response activation in the Simon effect', *Psychophysiology*, **35**, pp. 366–71.

Van der Heijden, A.H.C. (1992), *Selective Attention in Vision* (London: Routledge).

Velmans, M. (1996), 'An introduction to the science of consciousness', in *The Science of Consciousness: Psychological, Neuropsychological and Clinical Reviews*, ed. M. Velmans (London: Routledge).

Vygotsky, L. (1962), *Thinking and Speaking* (Cambridge, MA: The M.I.T. Press).

Wegner, D.M. (2002), *The Illusion of Conscious Will* (Cambridge, MA: MIT Press).

Wegner, D.M. & Bargh, J.A. (1998), 'Control and automaticity in social life', in *Handbook of Social Psychology, Vol. 1*, ed. D. Gilbert, S.T. Fiske & G. Lindzey (New York: McGraw-Hill).

Wegner, D.M. & Wheatley, T. (1999), 'Apparent mental causation: Sources of the experience of will', *American Psychologist*, **54**, pp. 480–92.

Zachay, A. (1991), *Diskrete und kontinuierliche Informationsverarbeitungsmodelle zur Erklärung von Reiz-Reaktions-Inkompatibilitäten: Evidenz für einen Antwortkonflikt beim Simon-Effekt* (Unpublished master's thesis, Tübingen, Germany).

Zelazo, P.D. (1999), 'Language, levels of consciousness, and the development of intentional action', in *Developing Theories of Intention: Social Understanding and Self-Control,* ed. P.D. Zelazo, J.W. Astington, D.R. Olson (Mahwah: Erlbaum).

Zelazo, P.D. (2004), 'The development of conscious control in childhood', *Trends in Cognitive Sciences*, **8**, pp. 12–17.

J. Scott Jordan and Marcello Ghin

# *The Role of Control in a Science of Consciousness*
## *Causality, Regulation and Self-sustainment*

*Abstract: There is quite a bit of disagreement in cognitive science regarding the role that consciousness and control play in explanations of how people do what they do. The purpose of the present paper is to do the following: (1) examine the theoretical choice points that have lead theorists to conflicting positions, (2) examine the philosophical and empirical problems different theories encounter as they address the issue of conscious agency, and (3) provide an integrative framework (Wild Systems Theory) that addresses these problems and potentially naturalizes conscious agency. It does so by grounding conscious and control in the notion of self-sustaining energy-transformation systems (i.e., living systems), versus computational or self-organizing systems, as is the case in information processing theory and dynamical systems theory, respectively. Given its assertion that content (and consciousness) emerges in self-sustaining systems, Wild Systems Theory may also provide a sound theoretical basis for a science of consciousness in general.*

There is quite a bit of disagreement in cognitive science regarding the role that consciousness and control play in explanations of how people do what they do. Some deny the need for consciousness altogether and assume behaviour to be under the control of environmental stimuli. Some model people as conscious agents capable of controlling their own behaviour. And some argue that the conscious experience of controlling behaviour is actually an illusion. Given these disagreements, the purpose of the present paper is to do the following: (1) examine the theoretical choice points that seem to have lead theorists in these different directions, (2) examine the problems each approach poses for a science of conscious agency, and (3) present an alternative approach to consciousness and control (*Wild Systems Theory*) that integrates current approaches in a way that provides a theoretical grounding for a science of conscious agency.

## Consciousness, Control and Choice Points

One of the main reasons there are different approaches to consciousness and control is because different theorists use the term *control* in different ways. Some use it to refer to simple *causality*—event A *controls* event B because event A *causes* event B, as is the case when a particular stimulus event *causes* a particular behaviour. In contrast, some theorists use the concept *control* to refer to *regulation*—system A *controls* event B because system A works to keep event B in a particular state, as is the case when one drives a car and produces actions such as braking and steering in order to keep the car on the road. In what follows, we argue both approaches are at work in cognitive science and have implications for how one models the relationship between consciousness, control and conscious agency.

### *Control as causality*

Scientific psychology began in the mid 1800s as a science of consciousness (Ash, 1995; Boring, 1950). Since then most scientists interested in 'how people do what they do' have conceptualized *control* in terms of *regulation*, and assumed an individual's conscious states play some role in regulating behaviour. A *causality* approach to *control* became popular however, when behaviourists such as Watson, Weiss and Holt decided psychology should be a science of behaviour, not a science of consciousness. In order to describe psychological phenomena solely in terms of third-person observables, these researchers ignored consciousness and focused on lawful relationships between environmental events (i.e., stimuli) and observable body events (i.e., behaviour). This is illustrated in Figure 1. Later behaviourists such as Skinner committed themselves to not only avoiding consciousness, but avoiding references to internal states as well (Boring, 1950).

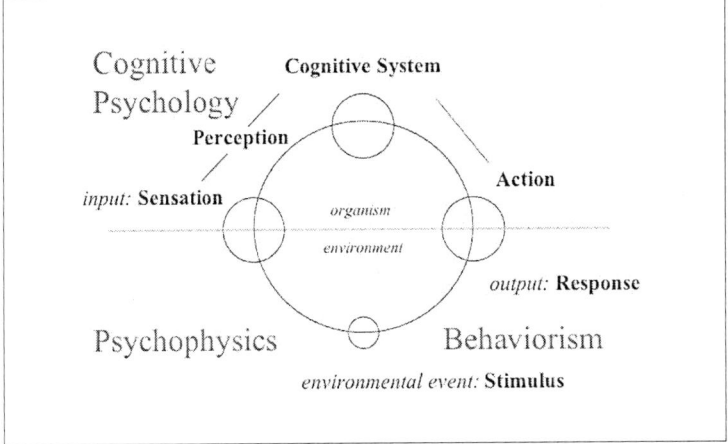

*Figure 1.* With the advent of behaviourism, psychologists ignored consciousness and, instead, measured lawful relationship between environmental events (i.e., stimuli) and behavioural output (i.e., response). Psychophysics investigated the lawful relationships between environmental events (i.e., stimuli) and perception (i.e., consciousness). Cognitive scientists re-introduced internal states.

Having removed consciousness and internal states from the list of possible explanations of how people do what they do, researchers such as Skinner utilized a *causality* model of control that asserts behaviour is *controlled* by environmental contingencies in the sense that *control* means *cause*. As Skinner (1976) himself famously declared,

> A scientific analysis of behavior must, I believe, assume that a person's behavior is *controlled* [italics added] by his genetic and environmental histories rather than by the person himself as an initiating, creative agent. (p. 208)

In this *causality* approach to control, environmental stimuli *control* behaviour in much the same way a billiard ball *controls* the movements of another billiard ball when the former strikes the latter and *causes* it to move. There is no reference to either the organism or the environment *regulating* the relationship between the two (i.e., working to keep the relationship in a particular state). Rather, the environment *controls* behaviour because its efficacy is greater than that of the organism.

*Causality* approaches to *control* are still in use today. For example, many researchers investigate a phenomenon known as *stimulus control* (Dube & McIlvane, 1997; Ghirlanda & Enquist, 1999; Touchette

& Howard, 1984) which is defined in the following way, '...a stimulus comes to *control* [italics added] behavior when it predicts something about positive or negative reinforcement' (Staddon, 2003, p. 10.5). Again, in these more recent behavioural models, a stimulus *controls* behaviour because it *causes* it.

Once control is defined in terms of environmental causality, there is no room for a meaning of *control* associated with conscious agency. Rather, it is assumed people do what they do because environmental stimuli *cause* them to do so. And the fact that researchers who make such assumptions tend to either argue against or ignore the notion of conscious agency is no coincidence. Once a theory refuses to allow conscious states into explanations of the patterns we see in what people do, *control* — forced to mean *causality* instead of *regulation* — belongs to the world.

## Control as regulation

Control as *regulation* refers to the idea that system A works to keep event B in a particular state, as is the case when a person (system A) produces actions in order to keep a car on the road (event B). The important difference between *regulation*- and *causality*-based approaches is that in *regulation* approaches, the system doing the controlling (e.g., an auto driver) actively re-organizes itself (i.e., produces actions) in order to keep an event (i.e., the car-road relationship) in a state specified by the system doing the controlling (i.e., the driver). In *causality* approaches, the system doing the controlling (i.e., the environment) *does not* actively reorganize itself *in order to* keep an organism's behaviour in a particular state, and the system doing the controlling (i.e., the environment) *does not* pre-specify specific states an organism should produce.

At present most cognitive scientists utilize a *regulation*-based notion of control. In what follows we describe how the regulation-based approach is utilized in the two major approaches to cognitive systems; information processing theory and dynamical systems theory.

*Information-processing theory and regulation.* A *regulation*-based approach to *control* gained popularity in the midst of behaviourism's reign as researchers began to report behavioural phenomena that seemed to justify an appeal to internal states. Tolman (1948) for example, discovered rats could make behavioural choices that strongly indicated the use of internal cognitive maps. And Cherry (1953) discovered people could selectively attend to one of two simultaneously presented auditory messages, as long as the two were sent to different ears.

In order to theoretically address the role of internal states, cognitive scientists utilized Shannon's (1948) information processing theory (IPT). This made it theoretically possible for internal states to play a causal role in explanations of how people do what they do. Weiner (1948) for example, utilized IPT and the cybernetic notion of *regulatory* control to distinguish purposive from non-purposive systems. In his framework, non-purposive systems such as a rock are unable to sustain on-going relationships with the environment. Instead, their relationship with the environment is *determined* by the environment. Purposive systems on the other hand, are able to sustain on-going relationships with the environment and they do so by offsetting environmental disturbances to internal states that pre-specify the system-environment relationship to be sustained.

This servo-mechanistic regulation-based conceptualization of control, the entire closed-loop of which is depicted in Figure 1, once again allowed consciousness into explanations of how people do what they do. Shiffrin and Schneider's (1977) classic distinction between controlled and automatic processing is defined in terms of processes that 'feel' as though they require conscious effort (i.e., controlled processing) versus those that don't 'feel' controlled (i.e., automatic processing). And while this regulation-based conceptualization of control seems to provide a means of re-establishing conscious agency as a viable topic of scientific investigation, the IPT that underlies it has recently come under both philosophical and empirical attack.

Philosophically, IPT encounters difficulties explaining how an internal state comes to 'represent' something external to the brain. That is, how do internal states gain their content? To be sure, there are many competing answers to this question. Given the present paper's focus on conscious agency, we focus on *teleological* theories (Neander, 2004), which assume that internal states entail content because they provide a *function* for the organism that is shaped by its individual history as well as the evolutionary history of its species. Bickhard (2001) claims that a problem with such accounts is that they potentially render internal content epiphenomenal because they leave open the logical possibility of an organism spontaneously emerging from a convergence of atoms in the air (Millikan, 1984). Such an organism would have internal states, but given its lack of either personal or evolutionary history, the internal states would lack function and content.

Regardless if teleological theories of content ultimately overcome the issue of epiphenomenal function, the IPT approach to content still faces the problem (as do physicalist theories in general) of accounting for why certain contents are conscious. Thus, while it makes scientific sense to model the causal properties of internal states in terms of IPT, it is not logically necessary that the internal states entail any sort of conscious content. Rather, it is logically possible there could be an identical physical copy of me whose brain entails all the causal relations of mine, yet does not have consciousness. This is known as the zombie argument (Chalmers, 1996). And it has been posed as a major challenge to any physical account of consciousness.

Collectively, the above philosophical attacks indicate that while the regulation approach to control espoused by IPT provides a solid grounding for the causality of internal states and their role in agency, it does not provide solid grounding for any consciousness that might be associated with internal states, because it has yet to posit a necessary role for consciousness.

A somewhat similar conclusion has recently been reached via empirical, as opposed to philosophical means. Specifically, social psychologists have made use of Shiffrin and Schneider's (1977) distinction between 'automatic' and 'controlled' processing and have argued that while conscious controlled processing does exist, the vast majority of our behaviours are under the control of environmentally-triggered automatic processes (Bargh & Chartrand, 1999; Wegner & Wheatley, 1999). In these dual-process theories, both meanings of control are being used at the same time. The *causality* approach is used in regards to the environment's ability to *control* (i.e., cause) automatic behaviour, while the *regulation* approach is used in relation to conscious states that are used in the agentic control of behaviour. Given the data indicate a minimal contribution of conscious processing to the behaviours people actually produce, these researchers tend to conclude that conscious will, although present, might actually be an illusion (Wegner, 2002). As a result, IPT once again seems incapable of providing a successful framework for a science of conscious agency.

*Dynamical systems theory and regulation.* In light of the above-mentioned problems with IPT, some researchers have begun to model 'how people do what they do' in terms of dynamical systems theory (DST). While there are many different interpretations as to how to apply DST to cognitive science, common to most is the assertion that the work of cognition is to be found in the synergetic, circular causality of continuous interactions between brain, body and world (Clark, 1997; Jordan, 2003a; Kelso, 1995; O'Regan & Noë, 2001; Tschacher & Dauwalder, 2003; Thelen & Smith, 1994; van Rooij, Bongers & Haselager, 2002; Varela *et al.*, 1991; van Gelder, 1998). As regards the role of consciousness and control, there are again many competing alternatives. A common starting point however, is the notion of *self-organization*. A classic example of a self-organizing system is a convection roll. If one applies heat to a pan of cool oil, a rather complex system of convection rolls will emerge as the heated oil rises to the top and the cooler oil sinks to the bottom.

> The resulting convection rolls are what physicists call a collective or cooperative effect, which arises without any external instructions ... Such spontaneous pattern formation is exactly what we mean by self-organization: the system organized itself, but there is no 'self', no agent inside the system doing the organizing (Kelso, 1995, pp. 7–8).

Such an application of the concept *self-organization* implies a *causality* approach to control that is entailed in the concept *control parameter*. Briefly stated, a control parameter is a variable which, when varied, *forces* a system through phase transitions (Vetter & Stadler, 1998). In the convection roll example, heat is the control parameter. When it is increased, it *controls* (i.e., causes) the system's progression through a phase transition (i.e., a change to a qualitatively distinct state of the system) from stillness to convection rolls. This constitutes a *causality*-based use of the concept *control* because there is no system actively working to keep the convection roll in the convection roll state. Heat, the 'control' parameter, *causes* a change in the collective arrangement of the oil molecules, but the heat does not 'work' to regulate the convection roll state.

Though the notion of self-organization might imply that DST theorists advocate a *causality* approach to control, the notion of regulation is still apparent in many DST accounts of how people do what they do. Different theorists however, acknowledge regulation in different ways. Van Gelder (1998) for example, strongly rejects the IPT notion that behaviour is controlled (i.e., regulated) by internal structures such as codes and plans. Instead, he proposes it is possible for a system to give rise to regulatory behaviour solely on the basis of self-organizing dynamics. He presents the Watt Governor as an example. A Watt Governor is a mechanism that keeps the velocity of a flywheel constant. It does so because the velocity of the flywheel influences itself recursively. That is, the faster the flywheel moves, the more it slows itself down. This is because the movements of the flywheel cause two weighted arms, attached to the flywheel via a spindle, to rise as the flywheel moves faster. These movements cause a valve, connected to a steam-engine driving the flywheel movement, to close, thereby reducing the amount of steam released which, in turn, slows the flywheel and allows the weighted arms to lower. Because of the constant, mutual influence all the components have on one another, flywheel velocity can be held fairly constant. Van Gelder proposes the Watt Governor as a prime example of regulated behaviour emerging out of purely self-organizing processes. At no point in the Watt Governor system is there a 'code', a 'representation', or information being processed. As a result, he argues it should be possible to model cognitive systems solely in terms of self-organizing dynamics.

While van Gelder accounts for regulatory control solely in terms of self-organization, others believe his model of regulation is not sufficient to account for human cognition. Clark and Toribio (1994) for example, argue that the Watt governor is not a good model for cognition because cognitive agents can predict outcomes and take counterfactual events into account when planning actions. Thus, the problem with using the Watt governor as a model for cognition is that the kinds of problem-domains invoked are just not sufficiently 'representation-hungry'. To address this issue and attempt to account for the 'representation-hungry' types of regulatory control humans seem to be able to accomplish, DST theorists often combine DST and IPT concepts. Thelen (1995, 2003) for example, argues that most behaviour is self-organizing, yet admits the need for regulatory mechanisms by claiming that some behaviour is *goal-directed* and *intentional*. These terms are not re-stated or re-defined within the language of dynamical systems theory. Rather, DST and IPT concepts are used simultaneously. Kelso (1995; 2003), as another example, attempts to reconcile intentionality and behavioural control (i.e., regulation) with dynamical systems theory by claiming that certain dynamics are *informational*:

> Formally, an intention is conceived as specific information acting on the dynamics, attracting the system toward the intended pattern. This means that intentions are an intrinsic aspect of the pattern dynamics, stabilizing or destabilizing the organization that is already there (Kelso, 2003, p. 140).

Collectively, all of these hybrid theories seem dissatisfied with the *causality*-based notion of control implied by self-organization and the notion of control parameters. And in their attempt to instantiate a regulation-based approach to control, they utilize the concepts of IPT.

While on the one hand it seems these hybrid approaches successfully integrate IPT and DST approaches to regulatory control, their utilization of IPT concepts leaves them vulnerable to all the attacks IPT encounters as it attempts to account for conscious agency (i.e., how do internal representations gain their content, why are some of them conscious, and why does conscious will seem so unnecessary).

Given this problem, some DST theorists address the issue of consciousness directly (Myin & O'Regan, 2002; O'Regan & Noë, 2001; Varela, Thompson & Rosch, 1991). These theorists take issue with IPT's assertion that consciousness is a property of isolable internal representations. Instead, they argue that the content of consciousness is grounded in dynamic, on-going interactions between brain, body and world. While this manoeuvre seems to resolve the issues faced by theories espousing internal conscious states, it still has the problem of explaining why a nesting of brain, body, and world is accompanied by consciousness. Rather, conscious content is defined in terms of our bodily abilities to do things in the world. In enactive theory (O'Regan & Noë, 2001) content is grounded in our knowledge of sensorimotor contingencies. In skill theory (Clark, 2000) content is constituted by the behavioural skills available to the perceiver by virtue of perception. In both cases, there is no qualification of what a body is or why it is necessary (cf. Varela *et al.*, 1991). Thus, until these theories can explain why a brain nested in a body, nested in the world is accompanied by consciousness, there still seems to be the logical possibility of such dynamic interactions existing without conscious content.

*Summary*

Though the above analysis may seem complex, it is actually reducible to a fairly simple issue. Specifically, scientists have found it difficult to provide an account of 'how people do what they do' without utilizing an internally based model of *regulatory* control. At the same time, it has proven very difficult, and seems impossible to some, to account for why regulatory control is often accompanied by a sense of conscious agency. In light of these issues, we now present an approach to control and consciousness (i.e., *Wild Systems Theory*) that integrates IPT's commitment to internal regulatory control with DST's commitment to localizing the content of consciousness in dynamic, on-going interactions between brain, body and world, all in the hope of providing a philosophical-theoretical grounding for a science of conscious agency.

## Consciousness and Self-sustaining Systems: Wild Systems Theory

In what follows, we describe *Wild Systems Theory* (WST) by addressing the following issues: (1) what is an organism, (2) what do organisms control, and (3) why is control accompanied by content and ultimately consciousness? We then examine the possibility of utilizing WST as a framework for a science of conscious agency.

### *Wild Systems Theory*

*What is an organism?* As stated above, both IPT and DST acknowledge the need to use *regulation*-based versus *causality*-based models of control in explanations of how organisms do what they do. But what are organisms? And what exactly do they control? Though certain answers might seem immediately obvious, we believe there is something to be gained by understanding that any scientific description of what organisms *do* is always based on the conceptual tools one chooses to describe what organisms *are*. IPT chose the computer. DST chose self-organizing systems. And neither choice has yet to provide a sound foundation for a science of conscious agency.

As an alternative, some have modelled organisms as far-from equilibrium energy-transformation systems (Bickhard, 2001; Boltzmann, 1905, Jordan, 2000a, 2000b, 2003a; Kauffman, 1995; Lotka, 1945, Odum, 1988; Ruiz-Mirazo & Moreno, 2004; Schrödinger, 1945; Vandervert, 1995; Varela *et al.*, 1991; Weiner, 1948). Different researchers use this approach for different reasons. For the present purpose (i.e., accounting for conscious agency) we focus on Kauffman (1995) and his assertion that self-sustaining energy-transformers (i.e., organisms) emerged spontaneously out of the pre-biotic soup as a phase transition from non-self-sustaining chemical systems to self-sustaining chemical systems. Chemical systems can be said to be self-sustaining (i.e., *autocatalytic*) when they produce their own catalysts. That is, the work they do (i.e., their chemical reactions) produces a product that serves as a catalyst, either for the reaction that produced the catalyst or for some other reaction in the system. Such systems, according to Kauffman, are autocatalytically closed. Autocatalytic closure however, does not mean thermodynamic closure. On the contrary, such systems are nested within an energy-transformation hierarchy (e.g., the pre-biotic soup) and are thermodynamically open — the maintenance of their self-sustaining dynamics requires the continuous intake, transformation and dissipation of energy.

*What do organisms control?* IPT models organisms after computers. As a result, 'what organisms do' is conceptualized in terms of input-computation-output (Clark, 2001). Within this framework, perception constitutes the input side of the system, behaviour constitutes the output side, and cognition, the 'software' housed between the input and output. What the system is 'doing' in this model is selecting and producing appropriate behaviours based on perceptually acquired information about the environment. What is being 'controlled' (i.e., regulated or kept in a particular state) therefore, is the system's behaviour. Or, said another way, the system controls its output.

The majority of DST theorists on the other hand, chose self-organizing systems such as convection-rolls and Watt Governors as their metaphor. According to this model, regulated behaviour emerges continuously out of the on-going, dynamic interactions between brain, body and world. Behaviour, in this model, still refers to 'output' in the sense it is what we observe an organism doing (i.e., its behaviour) — it's what comes 'out' of the system as a result of all the on-going dynamics forces acting upon it as well as within it (Turvey & Shaw, 1999). Regulatory control, according to both IPT and DST therefore, refers to the system's control over its *output* — specifically, its *behaviour.*

Despite a long-standing commitment to the notion of controlled behaviour, there are those who argue such control is not possible. William Powers (1989) for example, stated the following:

> Natural systems cannot be organized around objective effects of their behavior in an external world; their behavior is not a show put on for the benefit of an observer or to fulfill an observer's purposes. A natural control system can be organized only around the *effects* [italics added] that its actions (or independent events) have on its inputs (broadly defined), for its inputs contain all consequences of its actions that can conceivably matter to the control system. (p. 132)

Thus, while Powers agrees that accounts of how organisms 'do what they do' need to utilize *regulation*-based (versus *causality*-based) models of control, he disagrees with the notion that what they regulate (i.e., control) is their observable behaviour.

Kauffman's (1995) conceptualization of organisms as self-sustaining (i.e., autocatalytic) energy-transformation systems is consistent with Powers' assertion that organisms control their input. Take, for example, a bacterium making its way through a concentration gradient of food molecules. From a 'control-of-output' perspective, the bacterium is controlling (i.e., regulating — keeping in a constant state) the 'spin', 'tumble' or 'swim' it manifests in response to changes in the concentration gradient. From a 'control-of-input' perspective, the bacterium is controlling (i.e., again, regulating — keeping in a constant state) the passage of food particles across its membrane (i.e., through certain of its cell-wall proteins). If one were to measure the two variables over time one would find that the output (i.e., spinning, tumbling, or swimming) varies inversely with changes in the concentration gradient (i.e., less food is correlated with more swimming), while the amount of food crossing through the cell wall proteins (i.e., the inputs) remains fairly constant. This is because the bacterium is regulating (i.e., controlling — working to keep in a particular state) its inputs (i.e., the food particles crossing its membrane), not its outputs (i.e., the 'spinning', 'tumbling' or 'swimming' we observe from the third-person perspective).

As an example at the human scale, a person driving a car does not control arm movements in the sense they specify certain arm positions and work to produce them. Rather, the driver specifies car-road relationships — that is, inputs to be achieved (e.g., continue moving forward, avoid an on-coming car, stop at the stop-light) — and uses behaviour (i.e., arm movements) — to produce the specified car-road relationship. If one were to record arm position over time, the changes in position would vary with external disturbances to the car-road relationship (e.g., a bump in the road, a strong wind, or a curve), while the car-road relationship would remain fairly constant. It is the car-road relationship (i.e., the driver's input) that is being specified and regulated, not the arm movements (i.e., output). Regulatory control therefore, according to WST, refers to the control of input, not the control of output (Hershberger, 1976; 1998; Jordan, 1999; 2003a).

*Why is control accompanied by content (and ultimately consciousness)?* Jordan and Ghin (2006) have recently described autocatalytic systems as self-sustaining *micro-macro synergies* in which the nested micro-level work produces and sustains the macro-level context in which the micro-level work can continue. This notion of self-sustaining micro-macro synergies provides an account of content (i.e., proto-consciousness) because within such synergies the micro-level transformations are *necessarily* 'for' the macro-level whole they sustain (Bickhard, 2001). As an example, the micro-level autocatalytic processes nested within a bacterium give rise to and sustain the bacterium as a macro-level whole, while the sustained macro-level whole (i.e., bacterium) constitutes the context in which the micro-level work can continue. It is in this sense of being 'for' something that micro-level work attains the status of being *content*.

To be sure, there is a potential problem with defining content in terms of functional necessity (i.e., the internal processes of a self-sustaining system constitute content because they are necessarily 'for' the macro-level whole they generate and sustain). Specifically, the notion of functional necessity might seem to imply that any functionally necessary relationship between parts and wholes constitutes content (e.g., the legs of a table or the tires on a car). Instead of taking a 'yes' or 'no' stance on this issue, we simply accept the idea there might be many different types of content, and then focus on the necessary functionality embodied in self-sustaining systems because it constitutes a type of content that was capable of evolving into consciousness. This is because self-sustaining systems *naturally* and *necessarily* constitute self-sustaining *embodiments* of the context in which they phylogenetically and ontogenetically emerged (Jordan, 2003a; Jordan & Ghin, 2006). That is, the internal states of such systems are naturally and necessarily *about* the external context in which they must work to sustain themselves. In this sense, the *inside* is naturally and necessarily *about* the outside.

This natural and necessary *aboutness* phylogenetically bootstrapped itself into consciousness because it existed as a self-sustaining energy-transformation system and, as a result, constituted a potential fuel source. Thus, while the self-sustaining work of plants rendered them a fuel source for herbivores, the self-sustaining work of herbivores rendered them a fuel source for carnivores. An important constraint for both herbivores and carnivores was the *distality* of their fuel source. That is, while single cell organisms were able to sustain themselves by controlling inputs at a very proximal scale (i.e., the intake of food particles at their membrane), herbivores and carnivores had to sustain themselves by controlling inputs regarding the relationship between their body as a whole, and events taking place on a larger, more distal scale (i.e., the location of their fuel source). Jordan (2003a) argues this distal constraint on control lead to the embodiment of body-world regularities in the dynamics of neuromuscular architectures. Said another way, bones constitute an embodiment of gravity. Muscles constitute an embodiment of the forces necessary to propelling a mass through a gravity field. And brains, an embodiment of the need to coordinate all these embodiments in a way that affords sustainment of body-world relations. Given these body-world embodiments are naturally and necessarily *about* body-world distality, the content they constitute is inherently *about* the control of body-world distality. Seen in this light, conscious perception, what we also call distal consciousness, is framed as a subset of body-environment control events (Jordan, 1998; 2003b). (For an account of how this inherently distal, perceptual consciousness evolved into phenomenal self-consciousness, see Jordan & Ghin, 2006).

## *WST, IPT and DST*

In what follows we clarify how WST's approach to consciousness and control provides a framework for a science of conscious agency that addresses the problems encountered by IPT (i.e., how do internal states garner their content, why is some content conscious, and why does conscious will seem so unnecessary) and DST (how to talk about regulatory control without utilizing IPT concepts, and why are brain-body-world interactions accompanied by consciousness).

*Addressing problems faced by IPT.* As pointed out by Bickhard (2001), conceptualizing content in terms of self-sustaining systems, as opposed to developmental and evolutionary histories (Millikan, 1984) avoids the logical possibility of a spontaneously generated organism whose lack of history renders its internal states void of content. Given this approach to *content*, WST also provides a means of addressing why some contents are conscious (the zombie problem — Chalmers, 1996). This is because understanding content in terms of micro-macro synergies leaves no space for an exact physical copy of a self-sustaining system to lack content, because content is entirely captured by the processes going on in the micro-macro synergies. The 'work' going on within the micro-macro synergy *constitutes* the content. Given that the neuromuscular architectures of self-sustaining systems such as herbivores and carnivores *necessarily* constitute embodiments of body-environment regularities (i.e., controlling the trajectory of a 'body' as a whole toward a *distal* fuel source) these embodied body-environment regularities are naturally and necessarily *about* body-environment distality. It is this embodied distal *aboutness* that we define as distal consciousness (i.e., perception). According to this framework, it is logically impossible for an exact copy of such a self-sustaining system to lack its self-sustaining distal *aboutness*.

In addition to the issues of content and consciousness, WST provides a response to recent empirical challenges regarding the efficacy of conscious will (Bargh & Chartrand, 1999; Wegner, 2002; Wegner & Wheatley, 1999). Researchers challenge such efficacy because their experiments indicate people can be systematically fooled into believing they consciously willed an action they in fact did not, while they can also falsely believe they did not consciously will an action they in fact did. This apparent lack of a necessary causal connection between consciousness and action is interpreted to mean that the former does not cause the latter. As a result, the idea of conscious will is taken to be illusory.

While WST would agree that conscious thoughts do not cause actions, WST would also argue that conscious thoughts were never supposed to do so. The idea that they should derives from dual-process theory's commitment to IPT's input-computation-output description of what organisms do, and its implicit assumption that conscious thoughts cause actions (Jordan, 2003c). WST on the other hand, asserts that thoughts do not cause actions as much as they constrain them. This is because, in the framework of WST, thoughts and actions constitute separate yet coupled scales of sustainment (i.e., scales of control). A person can dance in the dark (i.e., generate and sustain relationships among body parts — *action*), dance across a well-lit room (i.e., sustain body-environment relationships — *perception*), and think about doing so with another (i.e., sustain virtual body-environment relationships — *cognition*). While each level of scale constitutes an act of sustainment (i.e., control), no level of

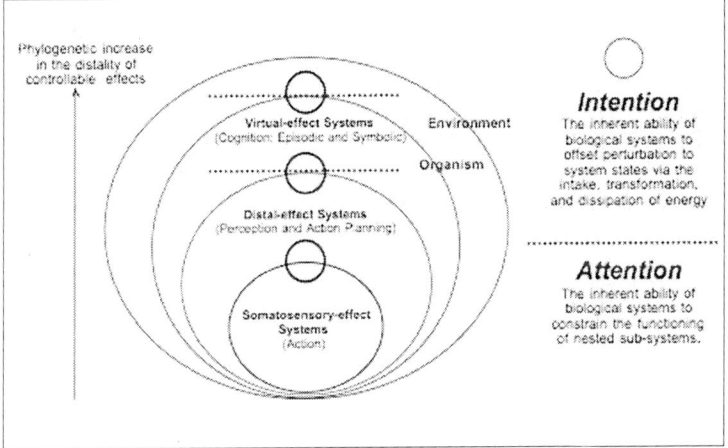

*Figure 2.* According to WST, action, perception, and cognition all constitute autocatalytic input-control systems that allow organisms to sustain relationships with events taking place at increasingly larger spatio-temporal scales. Action is referred to as the control of somatosensory inputs (i.e., effects), perception as the control of distal-effects, and cognition as the control of virtual-effects. Within this model, consciousness (i.e., content) derives its quality from the synergistic, dynamic interplay among (1) the phylogenetic and ontogenetic constraints a self-sustaining system embodies, (2) the nested ends such systems work to sustain, and (3) the energy-transformation context (i.e., world) in which the system is embedded.

sustainment constitutes the cause of another. Rather, all three levels synergistically constrain one another. Thus, if one generates and sustains the thought of leaving on a trip tomorrow, the thought will constrain the body-world relations one sustains (e.g., packing a suitcase), which, in turn, constrains the body configurations one sustains (e.g., the body movements necessary to successfully packing the suitcase).

The relationships between these nested scales of sustainment (i.e., control) are illustrated in Figure 2. Within the context of this framework, the fact that conscious thoughts do not cause actions does not render conscious will illusory. Conscious will is not about controlling actions. Rather, conscious will is about generating and sustaining *possible* body-environment relationships that constrain action systems toward producing specified body-environment relationships. Given these systems share a constraining versus directly causal relationship one should expect to find conditions under which the two appear to be non-causally related. These are the conditions that have recently been tapped into by those claiming conscious will to be an illusion.

*Addressing problems faced by DST.* WST's assertion of synergistically nested scales of sustainment (i.e., control) allows one to conceptualize *regulatory* control within the framework of DST without combining the concept *self-organization* with IPT concepts such as *representation*, *intentionality* and *information* in ways that engender the content issues faced by IPT. This is because the *regulatory* control expressed by self-sustaining systems (i.e., organisms) *is* self-sustaining. That is, the regulatory control serves to sustain the functional architecture that makes the regulatory control possible. In a sense, regulatory control and sustainment are synonymous in self-sustaining systems. In servomechanisms such as thermostats and guided missiles, regulatory control is *not* self-sustaining. The functional architecture of a thermostat is *not* sustained by the energy transformations that allow it to control its inputs.

Given this synonymous relationship between self-sustainment and control within WST, IPT concepts such as *representation*, *information* and *intention* find themselves conceptualized as natural properties of what self-sustaining systems do. Since they are naturally and necessarily embodiments of the contexts in which they must sustain themselves, every aspect of a self-sustaining system constitutes a *representation* of the context it has embodied (e.g., bones constitute a *representation* of gravity, muscles, a *representation* of the forces necessary to propel a mass through a gravity field, and brains, a *representation* of the constraints that need to be addressed to coordinate body-environment control). Given self-sustaining systems are naturally and necessarily 'about' the contexts they have embodied, they need not be 'informed' by the environment in order to be 'about' it. Rather, what they need do is sustain body-environment configurations that allow their natural 'aboutness' to be *modulated* by environmental regularities in ways that afford self-sustainment. Thus self-sustaining embodiments are *intentional* in the sense that they are directed towards the events they are about (i.e., embody).

To be sure, WST is not the only DST-based theory of 'how organisms do what they do' that conceptualizes regulatory control in terms of synergistically-nested scales of control, and does so without retreating to concepts from IPT. Van Orden, Moreno and Holden (2003) for example, conceptualize organisms in terms of *Control Hierarchy Theory*, which asserts that the vertically separated levels within an organism's structural hierarchy (e.g., neurons, neural networks and the brain as a whole) synergistically constrain one other's intrinsic dynamics which, ultimately, gives rise to self-organizing regulatory control.

While the notion of synergistic constraint is common to both WST and *Control Hierarchy Theory*, WST's emphasis on *self-sustaining embodiment* allows it to address content issues. *Control Hierarchy Theory*, at least as it is currently presented, does not conceptualize organisms as self-sustaining embodiments and, as a result, still allows the logical possibility that all the self-organizing regulatory control can occur without any accompanying consciousness.

A final contribution of WST to DST accounts of consciousness and control is that it provides grounding for DST's commitment to localizing content and consciousness in on-going, dynamic interactions between brain, body and world. It does so because it conceptualizes these different levels of scale (i.e., brain, body and world) in the same framework; specifically, energy transformation. This common framework clarifies how organisms are embedded in their world as self-sustaining energy transformers, as well as how and why such transformers constitute embodiments of that world and are therefore naturally and necessarily 'about' the constraints they embody.

## Conclusions

The purpose of the present paper was to examine the theoretical choice points that led to conflicting views regarding the role consciousness and control play in accounts of how people do what they do. Theorists who either downplay or ignore consciousness and internal processes tend to conceptualize *control* in terms of environmental *causality*. As a result, their accounts of how people do what they do are stated in terms of agent-free environmental contingencies. Theorists who conceptualize control in terms of *regulation* often appeal to conscious internal states and the role they play in regulating behaviour. IPT accounts of regulatory control rely on the computer metaphor and, as a result find it difficult to account for how internal states entail content, why some contents are conscious, and why conscious will seems so unnecessary. DST on the other hand, accounts for *regulatory* control by combining the notion of 'control' parameters with IPT meanings of concepts such as *representation*, *intentionality* and *information*. This manoeuvre renders them vulnerable to all the attacks made on IPTs approach to content. When DST theorists attempt to overcome IPTs problems with internal content by localizing it in on-going dynamic interactions between brain, body and world however, they find it difficult to explain why such dynamic interactions entail content.

In light of these issues we proposed *Wild Systems Theory* (WST) as a potentially integrative framework for a science of conscious agency. WST conceptualizes organisms as self-sustaining energy transformation systems that emerged out of the pre-biotic soup. Such systems are self-sustaining regulatory control systems because (1) they are autocatalytic — the internal transformations produce their own catalysts, and (2) the internal transformations and the global whole they sustain are synergistically enmeshed in such a way that the system can sustain (i.e., control) a flow of energy (e.g., food particles) into itself. Given such systems are naturally and necessarily about the contexts they have embodied, WST conceptualizes *control* as the self-sustaining autocatalytic control of input, and *distal consciousness* (i.e., perception) as the sustained 'aboutness' inherent to self-sustaining systems that have embodied the constraints necessary to regulating their relationship with distal events.

Given WST's ability to account for consciousness and control in a way that integrates IPT's commitment to internally based regulatory control with DST's commitment to self-organization and dynamic interactive couplings, yet avoids the pitfalls these theories encounter, it seems well suited to serve as a theoretical grounding for a science of conscious agency. In addition, given that it grounds content and ultimately consciousness in self-sustaining systems, WST may provide a theoretical framework for a science of consciousness in general. The main conceptual tool for this framework however, is neither a computational system nor a self-organizing system. Rather, it is a naturally evolved self-sustaining system. In short, it is a wild living system.

*Acknowledgement*

We would like to thank Erik Myin, Andrew Bailey and Dawn McBride for comments on an earlier version of this manuscript.

## References

Ash, M.G. (1995), *German psychology in German culture 1890-1967: Holism and the quest for objectivity* (New York: Cambridge University Press).
Bargh, J. & Chartrand, T. (1999), 'The unbearable automaticity of being', *American Psychologist*, **54** (7), pp. 462–79.
Bickhard, M.H. (2001), 'The emergence of contentful experience', in *What should be computed to understand and model brain function?* ed. T. Kitamura (Singapore: World Scientific).
Boltzmann, L. (1905), *The Second Law of Thermodynamics* (Dordecht: Reidel).
Boring, E.G. (1950), *A History of Experimental Psychology* (New York: Appelton-Century-Crofts).
Chalmers, D.J. (1996), *The Conscious Mind: In Search of a Fundamental Theory* (New York: Oxford University Press).
Cherry, E.C. (1953), 'Some experiments on the recognition of speech, with one and with two ears', *The Journal of the Acoustical Society of America*, **25**, pp. 975–9.
Clark, A. (1997), *Being There: Putting Brain, Body, and World Together Again* (London: MIT Press).
Clark, A. (2000), 'Phenomenal immediacy and the doors of sensation', *Journal of Consciousness Studies*, **7** (4), pp. 21–4.
Clark, A. (2001), *Mindware: An Introduction to the Philosophy of Cognitive Science,* (New York: Oxford University Press).
Clark, A. & Toribio, J. (1994), 'Doing without representing?' *Synthese*, **101**, pp. 401–31.
Dube, W. V. & McIlvane, W. (1997), 'Reinforcer frequency and restricted stimulus control', *Journal of the Experimental Analysis of Behavior*, **68**, pp. 303–16.
Ghirlanda, S. & Enquist, M. (1999), 'The geometry of stimulus control', *Animal Behaviour*, **58**, pp. 695–706.
Hershberger, W.A. (1976), 'Afference copy, the closed-loop analogue of von Holst's efference copy', *Cybernetics Forum*, **8**, pp. 97–102.
Hershberger, W.A. (1998), 'Control systems with a priori intentions register environmental disturbances a posteriori'. In *Systems Theories and a Priori Aspects of Perception*, ed. J.S. Jordan (Amsterdam: Elsevier).
Jordan, J.S. (1998), 'Recasting Dewey's critique of the reflex-arc concept via a theory of anticipatory consciousness: Implications for theories of perception', *New Ideas in Psychology*, **16** (3), pp. 165–87.
Jordan, J.S. (1999), 'Cognition and spatial perception: Production of output or control of input?' in *Cognitive Contributions to the Perception of Spatial and Temporal Events*, ed. G. Aschersleben, J. Müsseler & T. Bachmann (North Holland: Elsevier).
Jordan, J.S. (2000a), 'The role of "control" in an embodied cognition', *Philosophical Psychology*, **13**, pp. 233–7.

Jordan, J.S. (2000b), 'The world in the organism: Living systems are knowledge', *Psycoloquy*, **11**.

Jordan, J.S. (2003a), 'The embodiment of intentionality', in *Dynamical Systems Approaches to Embodied Cognition,* eds. W. Tschacher & J. Dauwalder (Berlin: Springer Verlag).

Jordan, J.S. (2003b), 'Consciousness on the edge: The intentional nature of experience', *Science and Consciousness Review* (December, No.1). Online serial, URL: *http://www.sci-con.org/news/articles/20040101.html*

Jordan, J.S. (2003c), 'Emergence of self and other in perception and action', *Consciousness and Cognition*, **12**, pp. 633–46.

Jordan, J.S. & Ghin, M. (2006), 'Proto- (Consciousness) as a contextually emergent property of self-sustaining systems', *Mind & Matter*, **4**, pp. 45–68

Kauffman, S. (1995), *At Home in the Universe* (New York: Oxford University Press).

Kelso, S.A. (1995), *Dynamic Patterns: The Self-organization of Brain and Behavior* (Cambridge MA: MIT Press).

Kelso, S.A. (2003), Cognitive coordination dynamics, in *Dynamical Systems Approaches to Embodied Cognition,* eds. W. Tschacher & J. Dauwalder (Berlin: Springer Verlag).

Lotka, A. J. (1945), 'The law of evolution as a maximal principle', *Human Biology*, **17**, pp. 167–94.

Millikan, R.G. (1984), *Language, Thought, and Other Biological Categories* (Cambridge, MA: MIT Press).

Myin, E. & O'Regan, J. K. (2002), 'Perceptual consciousness, access to modality and skill theories: A way to naturalise phenomenology?' *Journal of Consciousness Studies*, **9** (1), pp. 27–45.

Neander, K. (2004), 'Teleological theories of mental content', in *The Stanford Encyclopedia of Philosophy (Summer 2004 Edition)*, ed. E.N. Zalta, URL = <http://plato.stanford.edu/archives/sum2004/entries/content-teleological/>.

Odum, H.T. (1988), 'Self-organization, transformity, and information', *Science*, **242**, pp. 1132–9.

O'Regan, J.K. & Noë, A. (2001), 'A sensorimotor account of vision and visual consciousness', *Behavioral and Brain Sciences,* **24** (5), pp. 939–1011.

Powers, W.T. (1989), *Living Control Systems: Selected Papers of William T. Powers* (Gravel Switch, KY: Control Systems Group).

Ruiz-Mirazo, K. & Moreno, A. (2004), 'Basic autonomy as a fundamental step in the synthesis of life', *Artificial Life*, **10** (3), pp. 235–60.

Schrödinger, E. (1945), *What is Life?* (Cambridge: The University Press; New York: The Macmillan Company).

Shannon, C.E. (1948), 'A mathematical theory of communication', *Bell Systems Technical Journal*, **27**, pp. 279–423. [Reprinted in C.E. Schannon & W. Weaver, *The Mathematical Theory of Communication*. Urbana: University of Illinois Press, 1949]

Shiffrin, R.M. & Schneider, W. (1977), 'Controlled and automatic human information processing: II. Perceptual learning, automatic attending, and a general theory', *Psychological Review*, **84**, pp. 127–90.

Skinner, B.F. (1976), *About Behaviorism* (New York: Vintage Books).

Thelen, E. (1995), 'Motor development: A new synthesis', *American Psychologist*, **50**, pp. 79–95.

Thelen, E. (2003), 'Grounded in the world: Developmental origins of the embodied mind', in *Dynamical Systems Approaches to Embodied Cognition*, eds. W. Tschacher & J. Dauwalder (Berlin: Springer Verlag).

Thelen, E. & Smith, L. (1994), *A Dynamic Systems Approach to the Development of Cognition and Action* (Cambridge, MA: MIT Press).
Tolman, E. C. (1948), 'Cognitive maps in rats and men', *Psychological Review*, **55**, pp. 189–208.
Touchette, P.E. & Howard, J.S. (1984), 'Errorless learning: Reinforcement contingencies and stimulus control transfer in delayed prompting', *Journal of Applied Behavior Analysis*, **17**, pp. 175–88.
Tschacher, W. & Dauwalder, J.P. (ed. 2003), *The Dynamical Systems Approach to Cognition* (New York: World Scientific).
Turvey, M.T. & Shaw, R.E. (1999), 'Ecological foundations of cognition. I. Symmetry and specificity of animal-environment systems', *Journal of Consciousness Studies*, **6** (11–12), pp. 95–110.
Vandervert, L. (1995), 'Chaos theory and the evolution of consciousness and mind: A thermodynamic-holographic resolution to the mind-body problem', *New Ideas in Psychology*, **13** (2), pp. 107–27.
van Gelder, T.J. (1998), 'The dynamical hypothesis in cognitive science', *Behavioral and Brain Sciences*, **21**, pp. 1–14.
Van Orden, G.C., Moreno, M.A. & Holden, J.G. (2003), 'A proper metaphysics for cognitive performance', *Nonlinear Dynamics in Psychology and the Life Sciences*, **17** (1), pp. 49–60.
Van Rooij, I., Bongers, R.M. & Haselager, W.F.G. (2002), 'A non-representational approach to imagined action', *Cognitive Science*, **26**, pp. 345–75.
Varela, F., Thompson, E. & Rosch, E. (1991), *The Embodied Mind: Cognitive Science and Human Experience* (Cambridge, MA: MIT Press).
Vetter, G. & Stadler, M. (1998), 'Phase transitions in cognition', in *Systems Theories and a Priori Aspects of Perception*, ed., J.S. Jordan (Amsterdam: Elsevier).
Wegner, D.M. (2002), *The Illusion of Conscious Will* (London: MIT Press).
Wegner, D.M. & Wheatley, T. (1999), 'Apparent mental causation: Sources of the experience of will', *American Psychologist*, **54**, pp. 480–91.
Weiner, N. (1948), *Cybernetics: Control and Communication in the Animal and the Machine* (New York: Wiley).

Dawn M. McBride

# Methods for Measuring Conscious and Automatic Memory
## A Brief Review

*Abstract*: *Memory researchers have discussed the relationship between consciousness and memory frequently in the last few decades. Beginning with research by Warrington and Weiskrantz (1968; 1970), memory has been shown to influence task performance even without awareness of retrieval. Data from amnesic patients show that a study episode influences task performance despite their lack of conscious memory for the study session. More recently, issues of intentionality, awareness, and the relationship between conscious and unconscious forms of memory have come to the forefront. Conscious memory has sometimes been defined by intention to retrieve and sometimes by awareness of retrieval. This distinction has been debated as measurement methodologies have developed. In addition, the functional relationship between conscious and automatic forms of memory has implications for measurement of memory processes and the development of models of memory task performance. Several measurement techniques for conscious and automatic memory are reviewed. The current state of these issues is also discussed.*

The study of consciousness is often discussed in terms of intention and awareness (e.g., Freeman, 1999; Frith, 2002; Lethin, 2002). Memory researchers have also used these concepts to distinguish conscious and automatic memory forms of memory. Specifically, conscious memory processes are proposed to involve either intentional retrieval of a previous episode (Schacter, 1992), awareness of the retrieval of a previous episode (Jacoby & Witherspoon, 1982; Warrington & Weiskrantz, 1968; 1970), or both (Richardson-Klavehn & Gardiner, 1996; Richardson-Klavehn *et al.*, 1994). An important goal of research on conscious and automatic memory in the past few decades has been the measurement of these processes in the retrieval of information. The distinction between intention and awareness has been important in the development of these measurement techniques. In some methods, subjects are asked to complete a task by intentionally retrieving a study episode (measuring conscious memory) or are asked to complete a task without intentional retrieval of a study episode (measuring automatic memory). In other methods, awareness that a study episode was previously experienced distinguishes conscious from automatic memory processes.

The goal of this paper is to describe the ways that memory researchers have treated the concept of consciousness as they have attempted to measure both conscious and automatic processing in retrieval tasks. To this end, I will review the development of a subset of experimental measurement methods and how these methods were designed to overcome the limitations of previous methods. Three issues relating to these methods will also be discussed: (1) the implications of measuring task performance or estimating processes on the accuracy of the measurements, (2) the implications of definitions of conscious memory on measurement of this process, and (3) the implications of the functional relationship between conscious and automatic memory on the measurement of these processes. The review will not be comprehensive with regard to the methods, but instead will briefly describe a few popular methods researchers have developed in the past several decades and review some of the important findings that have been reported using these methods (for a more thorough review of results reported for automatic memory, see Roediger & McDermott, 1993).

Each method defines conscious and automatic memory in a slightly different way. As each method is reviewed, the definitions of conscious and automatic memory and their implications for measurement will be discussed. I will use the terms conscious and automatic memory throughout the paper to distinguish types of memory that researchers have attempted to measure. Variations in definitions will be discussed in the context of each method.

## Implicit and Explicit Tests

For the last few decades memory researchers have measured and compared conscious and automatic memory using sets of tests called *implicit* and *explicit* memory tests. In most cases, the tests are identical except for the instruction given to the subjects in the test. In studies using implicit and explicit tests, a study episode precedes the tests. In explicit tests, subjects are instructed to *intentionally* retrieve items from the study episode to complete the test. Examples of explicit tests include free recall (free-form recall of all study items), cued recall (retrieval cues are presented and subjects are asked to recall study items using the cues), and recognition (items are presented and the subjects are to judge which items were presented in the study episode and which were not). In implicit tests, subjects are asked to complete the tests with no reference made to the study episode. They may be asked to complete cues with the first word they think of or to identify words as quickly or as accurately as they can. Generally, studied items show a performance advantage over unstudied items suggesting that *unintentional* retrieval is influencing subjects' responses. Examples of implicit tasks include word stem completion (three-letter word stems are presented and subjects are asked to complete the stems with the first word that comes to mind, e.g., *app-* for *apple*), word fragment completion (words with deleted letters are presented and subjects are asked to complete the fragments with the first word that comes to mind, e.g., *a_p_l_* for *apple*), and perceptual identification (items are presented at very rapid rates and subjects are asked to identify the items as quickly or as accurately as they can). For explicit tasks, conscious memory is measured by performance in the task. For implicit tasks, automatic memory is measured by the performance advantage for studied items over unstudied items.

Modern comparisons of conscious and automatic memory were spurred by early findings reported for amnesic patients. Warrington and Weiskrantz (1970) showed that although amnesics displayed decremented performance in explicit tasks like recognition, they displayed equivalent performance to controls in implicit tasks like word stem completion. These results provided evidence that some forms of amnesia result from retrieval deficits (not encoding deficits during the study episode) and that certain retrieval tasks allow amnesics access to episodic memories. Results like these motivated researchers to broaden their investigations of automatic forms of memory.

Memory researchers have also focused on the comparison of implicit and explicit task performance with non-amnesic subjects.

Several experimental manipulations have been tested to examine possible dissociations between conscious and automatic memory. For example, level of processing effects (better memory for items studied with a meaning-based task than for items studied with a surface-feature task) are not reliably found in implicit tests (see Brown & Mitchell, 1994; Challis & Brodbeck, 1992, for some exceptions), but are found in comparable explicit forms of the tasks (Jacoby & Dallas, 1981). Divided attention at encoding is another variable that typically affects explicit but not implicit task performance (Mulligan, 1998). Implicit and explicit tasks typically show a double dissociation for read/generate manipulations. Words generated from contextual cues (i.e., subjects respond with a word associated in meaning to a cue word or fill in a missing word in a cue sentence) at encoding show a memory advantage over words read without cues in explicit tests, while words read at encoding have an advantage over generated words in implicit tests (Jacoby, 1983).

The implicit tests described above (e.g., word stem completion, word fragment completion, perceptual identification) have been classified as *perceptual* implicit tests due to the perceptual nature of the test cues (Roediger, 1990). Alternatively, implicit tasks that present cues related to the meaning of studied items have been classified as *conceptual* implicit tests. Examples of these tests include word association, category production, and general knowledge questions. While performance in perceptual implicit tests is driven by the perceptual relation between the test cues and the studied items (e.g., *app-* for *apple* in stem completion), performance in conceptual implicit tests is driven by the semantic association between the test cues and the studied items (e.g., *What type of fruit is red?* for *apple* in general knowledge tests). For example, in a category production test, subjects are presented with category names (e.g., *Fruit*) and asked to generate the first items they can think of that belong to that category (e.g., *apple*). If category items have been studied, they are typically produced more often than when they have not been studied, illustrating use of automatic memory in completion of the task.

Conceptual implicit tests do not always show the same effects that are shown with perceptual implicit tests. For example, conceptual implicit tests (i.e., involve processing of meaning) typically show level of processing effects similar to those found for explicit tasks (Weldon & Coyote, 1996). Dividing attention at encoding can also affect conceptual implicit task performance (Mulligan, 1997). A generation effect (better memory for generated study items than read study items) has also been found for conceptual implicit tests

(Blaxton, 1989). These results are different from those typically found for perceptual implicit tests (as described above). The results from perceptual and conceptual forms of implicit tests show that automatic memory may operate in different ways, depending on the type of retrieval cue given in the test (primarily perceptual or primarily conceptual).

Regardless of the type of implicit test used to measure automatic memory, researchers who use these tests generally make the assumption that a single memory process (conscious or automatic) can be measured by performance within one test (Jacoby et al., 1993). In the case of implicit and explicit tests, the assumption is that implicit test performance is indicative of the use of automatic memory and that explicit test performance is indicative of the use of conscious memory, with intention to retrieve as the only difference between the tests. This definition of conscious memory is based on the instructional difference between the tests. Subjects are asked to intentionally retrieve studied items in the explicit tests, but will not intentionally retrieve studied items in the implicit tests if they are following the instructions to use the first word that comes to mind. Therefore, explicit test performance is assumed to measure conscious memory as *intentional* retrieval and implicit test performance is assumed to measure *unintentional* retrieval. It is also assumed that during retrieval in explicit tests, subjects are *aware* that they are retrieving studied items. However, even if subjects are following instructions in the implicit test, they may still become *aware* that the items that come to mind are studied items. In this way, *intention* may differ between implicit and explicit tests, but *awareness* may not (Richardson-Klavehn et al., 1994).

The possibility that subjects become aware of using studied items in the implicit test may create difficulties in measuring conscious and automatic memory with explicit and implicit test performance, respectively. If subjects do become aware of the connection between the study episode and the retrieval task, they may engage in intentional retrieval in the implicit test, making the measurement of automatic memory invalid. Likewise, in the explicit test subjects may respond with items they do not actually remember from the study episode (i.e., they 'guess') and in some cases automatic memory may influence their responses. In other words, the implicit and explicit tasks may not be 'process pure' measures of automatic and conscious memory (Jacoby et al., 1993). Therefore, there are two primary issues in using implicit and explicit tests to measure conscious and automatic memory: (1) test performance may be indicative of more than one process (i.e., it is not 'process pure') and (2) intention may be distinguished in the measures of conscious and automatic memory, but awareness may not be.

## On-line Recognition Measure

Richardson-Klavehn et al. (1994) addressed the issue of distinguishing *awareness* of studied items and *intention* to retrieve studied items in implicit and explicit tests (i.e., the second issue described above). They claimed that even if subjects follow instructions for implicit memory tests (i.e., they do not intentionally retrieve studied items), this does not prevent them from becoming *aware* that items they generate were studied earlier in the experiment. In other words, implicit responses might reflect *involuntary conscious memory*. By using the term involuntary conscious memory, they are equating *conscious* memory (voluntary or involuntary forms) with *awareness* that the item was previously studied. They proposed use of an on-line recognition measure with completion of the implicit test to ask subjects to identify specific items they recognized as studied items. In this way, voluntary conscious memory is measured by performance on the explicit test, involuntary conscious memory is measured by performance on the implicit test (above unstudied performance) for items subjects recognize as studied items, and automatic memory (unintentional, unaware) is measured by performance on the implicit test (above unstudied performance) for items subjects do not recognize as studied.

On-line recognition measures have been used less frequently to measure conscious and automatic memory than the other methods reviewed here. However, it is the only method reviewed here that measures all three possible processes related to conscious and automatic memory: voluntary conscious (intention), involuntary conscious (unintentional, awareness), and automatic (unintentional, unaware) memory.

In one study employing this method, Richardson-Klavehn et al. (1994) included an on-line recognition measure to distinguish involuntary conscious memory from both voluntary conscious memory (i.e., intentional retrieval) and automatic memory (i.e., lack of both intention and awareness). They asked subjects to study words with either a semantic or a graphemic encoding task (i.e., level of processing manipulation). Subjects completed one of three memory tests with word stem completion cues for the items. They were given an explicit test (intentionally retrieve studied items), an implicit test (complete the cues with the first item that comes to mind), or an opposition test (complete the cues with the first item that comes to mind, but if you recognize that item as one you studied, use a different item to complete the cue). In their opposition test, involuntary conscious memory (i.e., recognition of an item as studied) would prevent the subject using that item. If a subject generates a studied item in the opposition test with automatic memory, awareness that it was studied (with the on-line recognition instructions) will prevent the subject from using the studied item as a response. If awareness of a study episode for the item does not occur, the studied item will be used as a response.

Richardson-Klavehn et al. (1994) compared level of processing effects across the three tests. Semantic study resulted in more studied item responses than graphemic study in the explicit test (intentional retrieval) only. In the implicit test (unintentional retrieval, but could reflect awareness of study episode), no level of processing effect was found, and in the opposition test (unintentional retrieval and no awareness of the study episode), graphemic study resulted in more studied item responses than semantic study (i.e., reverse level of processing effect). In other words, the three memory processes were dissociated by the level of processing manipulation using the three tests that were presumed to reflect these processes (explicit – intentional memory, implicit — unintentional memory with awareness, and opposition — unintentional and unaware memory).

Richardson-Klavehn and Gardiner (1996) also included an on-line recognition measure in their study with a modality manipulation and implicit and explicit stem completion tests. The modality manipulation compared the effects of using the same modality presentation at study and test (i.e., visually presented study words, test stem cues presented visually) and using different modalities at study and test (i.e., auditory study presentation, visual test cue presentation). Above chance memory performance for items in the different modality conditions represents a cross-modal effect. Cross-modal effects have been found in past studies for both explicit and implicit tests (see Roediger & McDermott, 1993, for a review of these effects). Richardson-Klavehn and Gardiner tested whether cross-modal effects in implicit tests were due to voluntary conscious memory (i.e., intentional retrieval), involuntary conscious memory (i.e., awareness of retrieval), or automatic memory (i.e., unintentional, unaware). They also included a level of processing manipulation to confirm the results reported in their previous study described above (Richardson-Klavehn et al., 1994). Their results supported their previous findings. In the explicit test, a level of processing effect was found. In the implicit test, no level of processing effect was found; however, when memory for items not recognized as studied in the implicit test was examined (i.e., unintentional, unaware), a reverse level of processing effect was found. Cross-modal effects were found in both the explicit and implicit tests. However, when memory for items not recognized as studied in the implicit test was examined, no cross-modal effect was evident, supporting their proposal that cross-modal effects found in previous studies with implicit tests may have been due to involuntary conscious memory (awareness of the study episode).

While the use of on-line recognition measures is the only measurement method to distinguish voluntary and involuntary forms of conscious memory (where conscious memory is equated with awareness of a study episode for an item), this method still relies on an assumption that processes can be measured directly with task performance. The process purity issue (the first issue with implicit and explicit tests described above) plaguing implicit and explicit test measures without on-line recognition is still present when using on-line recognition measures to measure conscious and automatic forms of memory. This issue was addressed in the measurement methods described below.

## Process Dissociation Procedure

The process dissociation procedure (PDP; Jacoby, 1991) was developed to address the issue with implicit and explicit tasks described above: process purity. This procedure was originally designed to estimate memory processes within recognition tasks (Jacoby, 1991), but was quickly adopted to measure conscious and automatic memory within the explicit and implicit tests discussed in this paper (e.g., Jacoby *et al.*, 1993; Toth *et al.*, 1994).

Instead of relying on test performance from one test to measure conscious or automatic memory (explicit and implicit tests, respectively), the PDP directly estimates conscious and automatic memory processes from performance across two tasks given with retrieval cues typically used in implicit and explicit tasks. In the PDP, subjects receive a study episode and then are asked to complete two tasks in which conscious and automatic memory processes are used in different ways. In the *inclusion* task, subjects are asked to respond to the retrieval cues (e.g., three-letter word stems for stem completion or category names for category production) with items they remember studying. If they cannot remember a studied item for the cue, they are asked to complete the cue with the first item they can think of. In this way, both conscious (C) and automatic (A) memory processes may contribute to the production of studied items as responses. Automatic memory may influence responses when conscious memory for an item is absent. The probability of producing a studied item in the inclusion task can be stated as

$$p(\text{Studied item Inclusion}) = C + A(1-C).$$

In the *exclusion* task, subjects are asked to respond with items they did not study earlier in the experiment. They are to exclude studied items and use alternate items as responses. In this task, conscious and automatic memory processes are in opposition with regard to producing studied items. If a subject consciously recalls an item as studied, they are instructed not to respond with that item. In the absence of conscious recollection, however, automatic memory may influence a subject to respond with studied items. The probability of producing a studied item in the exclusion task can be stated as

$$p(\text{Studied item Exclusion}) = A(1-C).$$

These equations can be algebraically combined to produce equations that solve for $C$ and $A$ processes used in the tasks:

$$C = p(\text{Studied item Inclusion}) - p(\text{Studied item Exclusion})$$
$$A = p(\text{Studied item Exclusion}) / (1-C).$$

The PDP has been used in several studies to verify effects found for perceptual explicit and implicit memory tasks and to measure $C$ and $A$ memory processes within these tasks. For example, when the PDP was applied to a word stem completion test, a level of processing study manipulation affected $C$ estimates, but not $A$ estimates (Toth et al., 1994). In other PDP experiments with word stem completion, Jacoby et al. (1993) reported that dividing attention at encoding also affected $C$ estimates, but not $A$ estimates. Jacoby *et al.* and Toth *et al.* both included generate/read manipulations (i.e., study items are generated from contextual cues or are read during the study episode) in their experiments. In these studies, higher $C$ estimates were found for words generated at study than for words read at study, while higher $A$ estimates were found for words read at study than for words generated at study. These results reported for the PDP are consistent with results found for perceptual implicit tests, as described above. They confirmed that effects found in implicit and explicit test comparisons indicated dissociations between automatic and conscious memory processes and not just test performances.

Results for conceptual implicit tests have also been confirmed with the PDP. For example, higher $C$ and $A$ estimates have been found for semantic study tasks than graphemic study tasks (i.e., level of processing effect) in a word association task with the PDP (Bergerbest &

Goshen-Gottstein, 2002). Schmitter-Edgecombe (1999) has also shown that both $C$ and $A$ estimates are reduced with divided attention at study when the PDP was applied to a category production task.

While the PDP has confirmed many findings reported for implicit and explicit tests, there have been some differences in results reported for these tests and $C$ and $A$ estimates from the PDP, indicating that the implicit and explicit tests may not be process pure. As described above for on-line recognition measures, this is especially evident in studies examining cross-modality effects (i.e., memory evident for items studied in a different modality than the modality of the retrieval test). Studies with implicit and explicit tests typically report a cross-modality effect for both tests (Roediger & McDermott, 1993). For example, Graf *et al.* (1985) presented words both visually and auditorily at study and found implicit memory for both types of items in a visual word stem completion test. In other words, cross-modality priming was evident in the stem completion task. Rajaram and Roediger (1993) reported similar results for four different implicit tests. However, when Jacoby *et al.* (1993) included a modality manipulation in PDP experiments with word stem completion, they found that $A$ estimates were almost nonexistent for the items studied in a different modality from the test. These results support the results reported by Richardson-Klavehn and Gardiner (1996) and suggest that cross-modality effects reported in implicit tests may be due to conscious retrieval in these tests.

One reason for the consistency in results (i.e., no cross-modal effect on automatic memory processes) across Jacoby *et al.*'s (1993) and Richardson-Klavehn and Gardiner's (1996) studies is that automatic memory is defined in the same way in both studies. Both sets of researchers defined automatic memory as retrieval that is unintentional with no awareness of a study experience for the item retrieved. With the on-line recognition measures used by Richardson-Klavehn and Gardiner (1996; Richardson-Klavehn *et al.*, 1994), automatic memory is measured with implicit performance for items not recognized as previously studied. In the PDP, automatic memory is distinguished from conscious memory in the exclusion task by awareness of a study episode for the item. Subjects are asked to exclude any item they remember studying. Therefore, in the PDP, conscious memory is defined as awareness of the study experience, while automatic memory is defined as a lack of awareness of the study experience. Therefore, both the PDP and the on-line recognition methods define automatic memory through both awareness and intention. These methods require that subjects intentionally retrieve the study episode in order to respond to the test cues, while asking them to respond differently for items they are aware of having studied earlier. It is possible for subjects to become aware of having studied an item at any point in the retrieval process, a situation that is not present in the implicit task performance measurement method. Therefore, automatic memory estimates with the PDP and on-line recognition methods should generally be lower than estimates of automatic memory made from implicit task performance (see Horton, Wilson, Vonk, Kirby & Nielsen, 2005, for a similar argument).

There are two primary differences between the PDP method and the on-line recognition method: (1) involuntary conscious memory is not distinguished from voluntary conscious memory in the PDP; the PDP only measures memory with awareness ($C$) and memory without awareness ($A$), and (2) the PDP does not rely on test performance to measure memory processes; instead, the memory processes are estimated by a model of the operation of these processes in the inclusion and exclusion tasks. Therefore, the PDP has a more limited definition of conscious memory than the on-line recognition method by only measuring memory with and without awareness, but it also allows researchers to measure conscious and automatic memory more directly than can be done with implicit and explicit test performance. In other words, whereas implicit and explicit task performance each contain contributions of conscious and automatic processes, the tasks used in the PDP allow researchers to measure the conscious and automatic processes themselves that contribute to task performance.

The PDP equations for estimating $C$ and $A$ described above rely on an assumption of independence between conscious and automatic memory. This assumption has been the main criticism of the PDP in the literature. For example, Curran and Hintzman (1995) reported correlations between $C$ and $A$ estimates and suggested that an independence assumption may not always be appropriate for conscious and automatic memory (for further discussion of this issue see Hintzman & Curran, 1997; Jacoby *et al.*, 1997; Jacoby & Shrout, 1997; Joordens & Merikle, 1993; Wilson & Horton, 2002). Jacoby (1998) also reported that different strategies of retrieval can affect the relationship between conscious and automatic memory in the PDP. He asked subjects to use either a direct-retrieval strategy (attempt to generate studied items for both tasks) or a generate-recognize strategy (generate any item for each task and then evaluate if the item was studied) to complete the inclusion and exclusion tasks in the PDP. Results indicated that the independence equations were only appropriate when subjects used a direct-retrieval strategy to complete the inclusion and exclusion tasks. The results reported by Curran and Hintzman and by Jacoby suggest that the independence assumption may be inappropriate under certain conditions, placing limits on when the PDP can be used to measure conscious and automatic memory processes.

## Multinomial Models

Multinomial models (see Batchelder & Riefer, 1999) offer a measurement method for conscious and automatic memory that is related to the PDP method, but these models are more flexible with regard to the functional relationship that may exist between the memory processes. Correctly defining the relationship between conscious and automatic memory can be important for the accuracy with which these processes are measured (see discussion above regarding the independence assumption of the PDP). The models estimate latent processes (e.g., conscious and automatic memory) by fitting models describing response production in the inclusion and exclusion tasks from the PDP to response frequency data from these tasks. The models follow a tree structure, where branches represent the processes (e.g., conscious memory) in the model. Each process is assumed to either occur or not occur for a particular trial of the tasks. The branches end in a response category (e.g., target item, alternate item), such that each type of response in the inclusion and exclusion tasks is described by a branch or across several branches in the tree. These models can be fit to the response frequency data from the inclusion and exclusion tasks, with a fit statistic indicating the goodness of fit. Fits of the models result in parameter estimates for C and A, similar to estimates generated in the PDP with the equations reviewed above.

Figure 1 displays a multinomial model based on the PDP equations that assume independence between conscious and automatic memory. Conscious memory (conscious retrieval of a study item) is represented by the $C$ parameter in the model; automatic memory (automatic retrieval of a study item) is represented by the $A$ parameter in the model. Independence is represented such that $A$ and $1-A$ follow both $C$ and $1-C$ branches in the tree.

Multinomial models have also been developed to represent other possible relations between processes that occur in the inclusion and exclusion tasks. For example, Jacoby (1998) fit a version of the model that reflects dependence (rather than independence) between conscious and automatic memory. In his study, he asked some of his subjects to complete the inclusion and exclusion tasks by first generating an item and then evaluating if it was studied or not

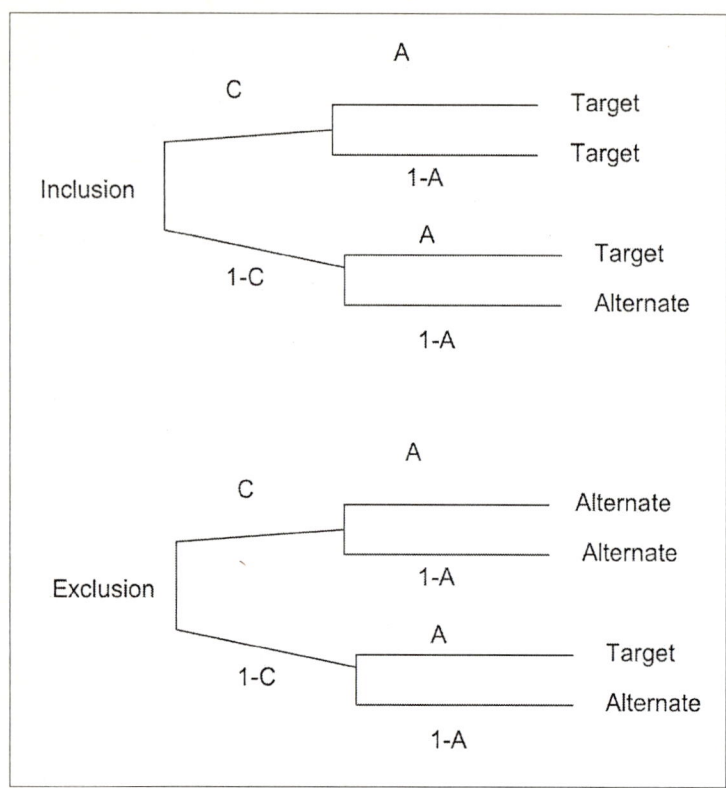

*Figure 1.* Independence multinomial model that estimates conscious and automatic memory for PDP (Jacoby, 1991) inclusion and exclusion tasks. *C* represents conscious recollection of studied items and *A* represents automatic memory of studied items. Targets are responses that match studied items. Alternates are responses with non-studied items.

(generate-recognize strategy). The independence model was found to be inappropriate for data following this strategy. He suggested that a generate-source model was more appropriate in this case.[1] Because subjects cannot recover a source (studied or unstudied) if they do not generate a target item, the conscious and automatic processes have a dependence relationship.

Figure 2 displays a dependence model. The *A* parameter represents the automatic generation of a studied item; the *C* parameter represents correct source identification of the generated item as studied.

---

[1] Horton *et al.* (2005) have argued, however, that Jacoby's (1998) inclusion task instructions in his generate/recognize group do not qualify as an appropriate comparison condition, as instructions were equivalent to typical implicit task instructions.

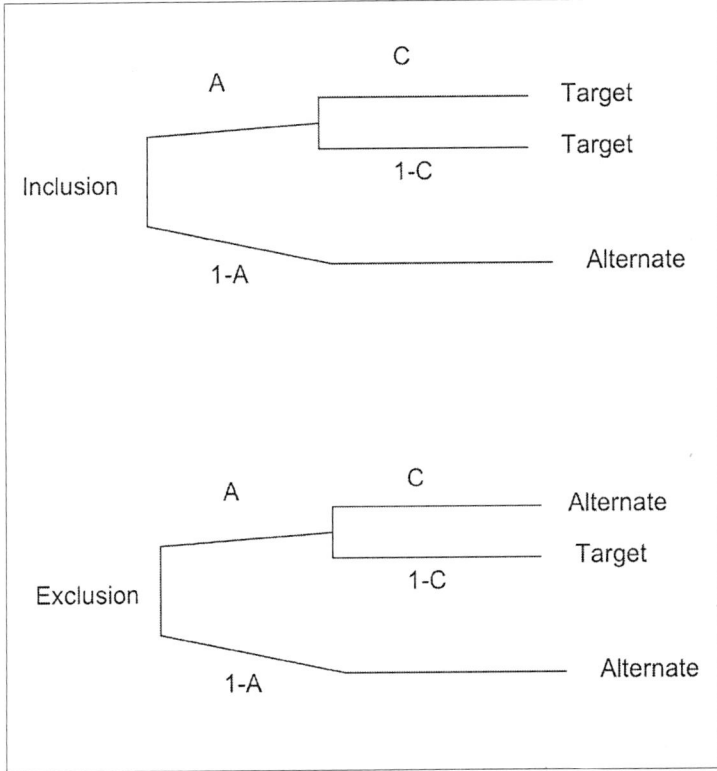

*Figure 2.* Dependence multinomial model that estimates conscious and automatic memory for PDP (Jacoby, 1991) inclusion and exclusion tasks. *A* represents automatic generation of studied items and *C* represents conscious recollection of the source (studied or unstudied) for studied items. Targets and alternates are defined as in Figure 1.

Independence is not assumed in this model, as the target source identification process ($C$) only occurs if a studied item has been generated with the automatic process.

Several sets of researchers have begun to apply multinomial modelling techniques to the implicit and explicit tasks described above as a method of measuring conscious and automatic memory processes. An important finding from these studies is that the independence models do not always provide good fits to data from the inclusion and exclusion tasks. For example, McBride and Dosher (1999; 2002; McBride *et al.*, 2001) found that a dependence model fit data from word stem and word fragment completion tasks very well and provided good fits to the data in some cases where the independence model did not fit the data. Bodner, Masson and Caldwell (2000) further reported that the dependence model fits inclusion and exclusion stem completion data (but the independence model does not) even when subjects are asked to consciously retrieve studied items in the tasks. Taken with results from the Jacoby (1998) study and the studies by McBride and Dosher, Bodner et al.'s results seem to indicate that an assumption of independence may not always be appropriate for PDP data. In cases where it is not, multinomial models offer researchers a more flexible method of estimating conscious and automatic memory process.

## Summary

I have reviewed four primary techniques currently used to measure conscious and automatic memory. The most commonly used method is to compare performance on implicit and explicit memory tests. However, this method is subject to criticism because performance on the tests may not be process pure; thus, measurements of conscious and automatic memory may not be accurate (Jacoby, 1991). In addition, this method does not address the distinction between intention and awareness as definitions of conscious memory. With explicit tests, performance is driven by intentional retrieval of studied items, but with implicit tests performance is driven by unintentional retrieval. However, subjects may still become aware in the implicit test that items were studied, and this awareness may influence performance in the test (Richardson-Klavehn et al., 1994). On-line recognition measures and the PDP were designed to control for these issues (respectively) in the measurement of conscious and automatic memory. In particular, on-line recognition measures allow intention and awareness to be separately measured and the PDP assumes conscious memory is defined by awareness. The PDP has been used more frequently, but assumes independence between the memory processes. This assumption may not always be appropriate (see Bodner *et al.*, 2000; Curran & Hintzman, 1995; Jacoby, 1998; McBride & Dosher, 1999; 2002). Multinomial modelling techniques have been applied to tasks from the PDP to allow measurement of conscious and automatic memory with flexibility in the relational assumptions between the processes. Use of these models continues to expand in the measurement of conscious and automatic memory (see Bellezza, 2003, for a recent expansion of the use of these models).

While definitions have varied across studies, conscious memory has been defined primarily by either intention to retrieve or awareness of retrieval. These definitions reflect definitions of consciousness used outside of memory research (e.g., Freeman, 1999; Frith, 2002; Lethin, 2002) and seem to indicate that memory researchers are exploring the concept of consciousness as it relates to memory in a similar manner to explorations of consciousness in other areas. Although there may not be a common definition of consciousness that researchers settle on across fields of study, such commonalities are important to reflect on as we progress in the scientific study of consciousness.[2]

## References

Batchelder, W.H. & Riefer, D.M. (1999), 'Theoretical and empirical review of multinomial process tree modeling', *Psychonomic Bulletin & Review*, **6**, pp. 57–86.

Bellezza, F.S. (2003), 'Evaluation of six multinomial models of conscious and unconscious processes with the recall-recognition paradigm', *Journal of Experimental Psychology: Learning, Memory, and Cognition*, **29**, pp. 779–96.

Bergerbest, D. & Goshen-Gottstein, Y. (2002), 'The origins of level-of-processing effects in a conceptual test: Evidence for automatic influences of memory from the process-dissociation procedure', *Memory & Cognition*, **30**, pp. 1252–62.

Blaxton, T.A. (1989), 'Investigating dissociations among memory measures: Support for a transfer appropriate processing framework', *Journal of Experimental Psychology: Learning, Memory, and Cognition*, **15**, pp. 657–68.

Bodner, G.E., Masson, M.E.J. & Caldwell, J.I. (2000), 'Evidence for a generate-recognize model of episodic influences on word-stem completion', *Journal of Experimental Psychology: Learning, Memory, and Cognition*, **26**, pp. 267–93.

Brown, A.S. & Mitchell, D.B. (1994), 'A reevaluation of semantic versus non-semantic processing in implicit memory', *Memory & Cognition*, **22**, pp. 533–41.

Challis, B.H. & Brodbeck, D.R. (1992), 'Level of processing affects priming in word fragment completion', *Journal of Experimental Psychology: Learning, Memory, and Cognition*, **18**, pp. 595–607.

Curran, T. & Hintzman, D.L. (1995), 'Violations of the independence assumption in process dissociation', *Journal of Experimental Psychology: Learning, Memory, and Cognition*, **21**, pp. 531–47.

Freeman, W.J. (1999), 'Consciousness, intentionality, and causality', *Journal of Consciousness Studies*, **6** (11–12), pp. 143–72.

Frith, C. (2002), 'Attention to action and awareness of other minds', *Consciousness & Cognition*, **11**, pp. 481–7.

Graf, P. Shimamura, A.P. & Squire, L.R. (1985), 'Priming across modalities and priming across category levels: Extending the domain of preserved function in amnesia', *Journal of Experimental Psychology: Learning, Memory, and Cognition*, **2**, pp. 386–96.

Hintzman, D.L. & Curran, T. (1997), 'More than one way to violate independence: Reply to Jacoby & Shrout (1997)', *Journal of Experimental Psychology: Learning, Memory, and Cognition*, **23**, pp. 511–13.

Horton, K.D., Wilson, D.E., Vonk, J., Kirby, S.L. & Nielsen, T. (2005), 'Measuring automatic retrieval: A comparison of implicit memory, process dissociation, and speeded response procedures', *Acta Psychologica*, **119**, pp. 235–63.

---

[2] The author thanks Jeff Wagman, Scott Jordan, and two anonymous reviewers for helpful comments on earlier versions of this manuscript.

Jacoby, L.L. (1983), 'Remembering the data: Analyzing interactive processes in reading', *Journal of Verbal Learning and Verbal Behavior*, **22**, pp. 485–508.

Jacoby, L.L. (1991), 'A process dissociation framework: Separating automatic from intentional uses of memory', *Journal of Memory & Language*, **30**, pp. 513–41.

Jacoby, L.L. (1998), 'Invariance in automatic influences of memory: Toward a user's guide for the process-dissociation procedure', *Journal of Experimental Psychology: Learning, Memory, and Cognition*, **24**, pp. 3–26.

Jacoby, L.L., Begg, I. M. & Toth, J.P. (1997), 'In defense of functional independence: Violations of assumptions underlying the process-dissociation procedure?', *Journal of Experimental Psychology: Learning, Memory, and Cognition*, **23**, pp. 484–95.

Jacoby, L L. & Dallas, M. (1981), 'On the relationship between autobiographical memory and perceptual learning', *Journal of Experimental Psychology: General*. **110**, pp. 306–40.

Jacoby, L.L. & Shrout, P.E. (1997), 'Toward a psychometric analysis of violations of the independence assumption in process dissociation', *Journal of Experimental Psychology: Learning, Memory, and Cognition*, **23**, pp. 505–10.

Jacoby, L.L., Toth, J.P. & Yonelinas, A.P. (1993), 'Separating conscious and unconscious influences of memory: Measuring recollection', *Journal of Experimental Psychology: General*, **122**, pp. 139–54.

Jacoby, L.L. & Witherspoon, D. (1982), 'Remembering without awareness', *Canadian Journal of Psychology*, **36**, pp. 300–24.

Joordens, S. & Merikle, P.M. (1993), 'Independence or redundancy? Two models of conscious and unconscious influences', *Journal of Experimental Psychology: General,* **122**, pp. 462–67.

Lethin, A. (2002), 'How do we embody intentionality?', *Journal of Consciousness Studies*, **9** (8), pp. 36–44.

McBride, D.M. & Dosher, B.A. (1999), 'Forgetting rates are comparable in conscious and automatic memory: A process-dissociation study', *Journal of Experimental Psychology: Learning, Memory, and Cognition*, **25**, pp. 583–607.

McBride, D.M. & Dosher, B.A. (2002), 'A comparison of conscious and automatic memory processes for picture and word stimuli: A process dissociation analysis', *Consciousness & Cognition*, **11**, pp. 423–60.

McBride, D.M., Dosher, B.A. & Gage, N.M. (2001), 'A comparison of forgetting for conscious and automatic memory processes in word fragment completion tasks', *Journal of Memory & Language*, **45**, pp. 585–615.

Mulligan, N.W. (1997), 'Attention and implicit memory tests: The effects of varying attentional load on conceptual memory', *Memory & Cognition*, **25**, pp. 11–17.

Mulligan, N.W. (1998), 'The role of attention during encoding in implicit and explicit memory', *Journal of Experimental Psychology: Learning, Memory, and Cognition*, **24**, pp. 27–47.

Rajaram, S. & Roediger, H.L. III (1993), 'Direct comparison of four implicit memory tests', *Journal of Experimental Psychology: Learning, Memory, and Cognition*, **19**, pp. 765–76.

Richardson-Klavehn, A. & Gardiner, J.M. (1996), 'Cross-modality priming in stem completion reflects conscious memory, but not voluntary memory', *Psychonomic Bulletin & Review*, **3**, pp. 238–44.

Richardson-Klavehn, A., Gardiner, J.M. & Java, R.I. (1994), 'Involuntary conscious memory and the method of opposition', *Memory*, **2**, pp. 1–29.

Roediger, H.L. III (1990), 'Implicit memory: Retention without remembering', *American Psychologist*, **45**, pp. 1043–56.

Roediger, H.L. III, & McDermott, K.B. (1993), 'Implicit memory in normal human subjects', in *Handbook of Neuropsychology*, eds. F. Boller & J. Grafman (Amsterdam: Elsevier).

Schacter, D.L. (1992), 'Priming and multiple memory systems: Perceptual mechanisms of implicit memory', *Journal of Cognitive Neuroscience*, **4**, pp. 244–56.

Schmitter-Edgecombe, M. (1999), 'Effects of divided attention on perceptual and conceptual memory tests: An analysis using a process-dissociation approach', *Memory & Cognition*, **27**, pp. 512–25.

Toth, J. P., Reingold, E. M. & Jacoby, L. L. (1994), 'Toward a redefinition of implicit memory: Process dissociations following elaborative processing and self generation', *Journal of Experimental Psychology: Learning, Memory, and Cognition*, **20**, pp. 290–303.

Warrington, E.K. & Weiskrantz, L. (1968), 'New method of testing long-term retention with special reference to amnesic patients', *Nature*, 217, pp. 972-974.

Warrington, E. K. & Weiskrantz, L. (1970), 'Amnesic syndrome: Consolidation or retrieval?', *Nature*, **228**, pp. 629–30.

Weldon, M.S. & Coyote, K.C. (1996), 'Failure to find the picture superiority effect in implicit conceptual memory tests', *Journal of Experimental Psychology: Learning, Memory, and Cognition*, **22**, pp. 670–86.

Wilson, D. E, & Horton, K. D. (2002), 'Comparing techniques for estimating automatic retrieval: Effects of retention interval', *Psychonomic Bulletin & Review*, **9**, pp. 566–74.

# Michael Spivey and Sarah Cargill

# *Toward a Continuity of Consciousness*

***Abstract:*** *Real-time cognition is continuous in time and contiguous in mental state space. This temporal continuity implies that the majority of mental life is spent in states that are partially consistent with multiple representations. The state-space contiguity implies that different cognitive processes interact in ways that make them quite non-modular. As the evidence for such information-permeability expands to include not just neural subsystems but also the entire brain and even the entire organism, this radical interactionism leads one to hypothesize that mental activity, and perhaps consciousness itself, is something that emerges amid the interface between one's body and one's environment. We portray mental activity as a continuous trajectory through a brain-body-environment state space, where close visitations with labelled attractors may constitute reportable self-consciousness and traversals through unlabeled regions may constitute unutterable immediate conscious awareness.*

## A Universal Medium of Mental Activity

Intuition seems to tell us that, when we think, we usually have one complete thought followed by another complete thought. Imagine a sequence of stitches on the hem of a skirt: you see one quarter-inch line of thread, followed by a quarter-inch gap, followed by another quarter-inch line of thread. This series of non-overlapping, individuated elements corresponds nicely with the theoretical construct of a series of logical symbols on the tape of a Turing machine, imported from computing theory to motivate the information-processing approach in cognitive psychology (e.g., Dietrich & Markman, 2003; Neisser, 1967; Newell et al., 1958; Pylyshyn, 1980). In this brief article, we hope to make progress toward dispelling this illusion of sequential discrete thoughts, or symbol strings, and to reveal the continuous thread of thought that weaves its way through the skirt's fabric. We offer an attractor-landscape description of mental contents, with a continuous trajectory through that state space being the process of mental activity, visiting word-recognition attractors, object-recognition attractors, internal-monologue attractors, and everywhere in between.

The crucial step for exploring the utility of this attractor-based framework is defining the dimensions of the state space that contains the attractor landscape. During the past few decades, cognitive psychology has dedicated much of its effort to dividing the mind into separate mental modules, thus devoting a small number of dimensions to each module's independent state space. Although this method has resulted in some important advances in our understanding of the brain's functions, such advances are now fewer and farther between (cf. Uttal, 2001). Mounting evidence suggests that a new approach, aimed at uniting the mind by redefining how its many subsystems interact, will be necessary for further progress. Much of current cognitive research provides evidence to reject a modular view of the mind altogether and to support a view of cognitive processing as a continuously dynamic, interactive process occurring in real-time (e.g., Kelso, 1995; Port & Van Gelder, 1995; Shimojo & Shams, 2001; Spivey, 2007).

Such a revision to our theories about the brain would necessitate it being conceived of as an open system. By the very definition of an open system, this revision requires us to look outside of each supposed module to examine the larger system within which it operates. Evidence that cognitive processing is interactive, rather than divided into discrete modules, serves to blur boundaries between processes that were previously clearly delineated. These fuzzy boundaries thereby require us to zoom out the lens of our inquiry, and envision a universal state space in which the variety of mental faculties are interwoven, rather then partitioned.

In this article, we will investigate several implications of viewing the mind as an open system. First, we will review evidence that cognitive processes flow in a continuously dynamic manner, rather than through a sequence of discrete stages (cf. Spivey & Dale, 2004). Following that, we will examine how feedback loops exist not only between subsystems in the brain but also between the brain and the environment, thus encouraging one to envision the brain-*cum*-environment as a system itself (cf. Turvey & Shaw, 1999). Finally, we will explore the consequences that this radically interactive view of the mind has for notions of consciousness and self-consciousness.

## Temporal Continuity in Cognition

One phenomenon that presents a particularly compelling example of the temporal continuity of cognition is spoken word recognition. A great many behavioural experiments have documented the observation that partway through hearing a word, multiple lexical representations become partially active (cf. Cutler, 1995; Marslen-Wilson, 1987). For example, during the first 150 milliseconds of the word 'dualism,' the initial phonemes, /d/ and /u/, are also consistent with the onset of the words 'dubious' and 'doomed' (as well as a host of other words, such as 'duel' and 'dual-purpose'). Semantic priming experiments have demonstrated that, at this point in hearing the word, a person is slightly faster in responding to words like 'incorrect' and 'ruined' (due to their semantic similarity to the partially active lexical representations, 'dubious' and 'doomed') than to neutral control words. However, another 150 milliseconds into the word, the /a/ and /l/ phonemes have been heard, and the lexical representations for 'dubious' and 'doomed' are no longer substantially active. What *would* still exhibit semantic priming at that point are the words 'duel' and 'dual-purpose,' as they are still consistent with the acoustic-phonetic input up to that point in time. But by the time the /i/ in 'ism' is heard, 50 milliseconds later, the speech stream has become more or less unique to the word 'dualism' (except perhaps for the phrase, 'do a little trick'). Thus, due to the continuous uptake of acoustic input during spoken word recognition, the mind gives simultaneous partial consideration to multiple possible lexical alternatives over time. In a number of computational models of spoken word recognition, this process is treated as a collection of individual word representations that rise in activation, then some fall in activation as finally only one remains active (e.g., Gaskell & Marslen-Wilson, 2002; Luce *et al.*, 2000; Magnuson *et al.*, 2003; McClelland & Elman, 1986).

A similar kind of process is also observed in visual object recognition. Even though the visual stimulus is presented all at once (not incrementally like speech), the population of neurons that coordinate to enable the recognition of a banana or a tree or a face, achieve this coordination in a time-dependent manner (e.g., Perrett *et al.*, 1998; Rolls & Tovee, 1995). For example, when Rolls and Tovee (1995) calculated the amount of information encoded in fourteen inferotemporal neurons for discriminating among 68 objects and faces, they observed that the bits-per-neuron rises sharply from zero to 0.35 over a mere 150 milliseconds following stimulus onset. The rise of this curve then tapers off, reaching an asymptote of 0.6 pits-per-neuron at about 500 milliseconds. Thus, very quickly, the pattern of neural activation organizes about half of the information necessary for discriminating a given object from the other 67 objects. However, the remaining half of the information required for full recognition accrues slowly over the course of another 350 milliseconds. If we treat a population of neurons that together cooperate to achieve the recognition of a particular object as though they were a functional unit, then we can describe the temporal dynamics of object recognition in a fashion remarkably similar to that used to describe spoken word recognition. Several potential object representations initially rise in activation, but as they compete with one another over time (e.g., Desimone & Duncan, 1995), eventually one representation continues rising in activation and the others fade away.

Rolls and Tovee (1995) also performed multidimensional scaling on their data to show the distribution of their 68 object and face representations in a two-dimensional layout. As expected, inanimate objects, faces, and body parts each formed distinctly separate clusters. This multidimensional scaling approach is an extremely useful framework for conceptualizing the recognition process. If each neuron in your brain is treated as a dimension in space, then all your population codes (i.e., representations) correspond to locations scattered throughout the volume of that billion-dimensional space. And the gradual fulfilment of a particular population code (i.e., the gradual recognition of an isolated stimulus) involves starting in some neutral location in that space and continuously gravitating toward several attractors (population codes), away from others, and then eventually settling on a unique point attractor.

However, this description so far really only works if you hear a single word in isolation and think about nothing else, or if you fixate solely on a single object for several seconds. That is the only way the trajectory might actually start in a neutral location and settle motionlessly on one particular point attractor. However, as J.J. Gibson (1950) noted, it is extremely unusual for a human to be exposed to an isolated stimulus. Rather, humans typically encounter flowing arrays of continuous stimulation. Natural everyday circumstances do not just involve hearing one word and settling into its point attractor to recognize it, or seeing one object and settling into its point attractor to recognize it. Speakers follow almost every word with a new one (often with no acoustic pause whatsoever between them), usually before the comprehension process of the previous word has had a chance to settle into a unique attractor. Moreover, observers move their eyes 3-4 times per second, which does not allow enough time for the recognition process of the previously fixated object to perfectly settle into a unique attractor. As a result, a series of heard words, or a series of fixated objects, elicits a continuous trajectory through state space that 'flirts with' attractors but never quite settles into them (e.g., Botvinick & Plaut, 2004; Elman, 2004; Spivey, 2007; Spivey & Dale, 2004).

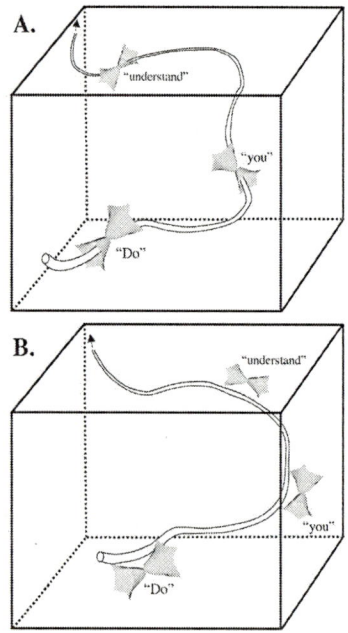

*Figure 1.* Panel A depicts an idealized version of a state-space trajectory that passes directly through a series of point attractors (which become repellers once visited) in order to elicit speech. Panel B depicts an idealized version of a state-space trajectory that only has time to 'flirt with' those attractors as a listener is comprehending speech in real-time. (The actual state space would be very high-dimensional.)

For example, imagine someone asking you, 'Do you understand what I'm trying to convey?' Figure 1A depicts a cartoon version of what the speaker's mind is doing. The state of the system must activate the population code that causes the speech apparatus to produce the word 'do,' then activate the population code for 'you,' then the population code for 'understand,' etc. However, transitioning from one specific pattern of neural activation to another is not instantaneous. Intermediate unlabeled patterns are necessarily instantiated along the way. In a state space, these population codes can be envisioned as 'spatiotemporal hourglasses' that attract the state of the system from various regions and then propel the system in various potential directions. The trajectory must visit these labelled locations in space reasonably accurately in order to cause the speech apparatus to correctly utter the associated word, but it also cannot help but spend much of its time in the regions in between those labelled locations.

Figure 1B depicts a cartoon version of what the listener's mind is doing. (Note that the spatiotemporal hourglasses are in roughly isomorphic, but not identical, locations in the two people's mental state spaces.) The labelled locations are not perfectly visited because the normal rate of speech often does not allow enough time for the listener to settle into an attractor point — nor is there really a need to do so, unless the listener is shadowing the speech. The listener's continuous trajectory through state space, which describes his/her mental activity, merely flirts with the attractors and spends most of its time in the 'outer space of the mind,' as it were. And thus, one of the consequences of this temporal continuity in cognition is that the majority of our conscious daily lives involves traversing regions of mental space that are far from discrete, far from expressible, and far from symbolic.

## Spatial Continuity in Cognition

Not only do cognitive events blend into one another in time, but different cognitive processes blend into one another in mental state space as well. Recent evidence suggests that vision and language may be better conceived as sharing a single state space. For example, visual object recognition has an immediate real-time influence on spoken word recognition (Allopenna *et al.*, 1998; Spivey *et al.*, 2005), and spoken language input has an immediate real-time influence on visual search processes (Spivey *et al.*, 2001; Reali *et al.*, in press).

Using goal-directed hand movements to explore the continuous-time influence of visual context on spoken language comprehension, Spivey *et al.* (2005) tracked the streaming x,y coordinates of computer-mouse movements in a spoken word recognition task. Since arm movements are relatively continuous and can smoothly change direction mid-flight, competition between partially activated lexical representations was revealed in the shape and curvature of the computer-mouse trajectories. When viewing a scene consisting of a candle and a piece of candy, and instructed to 'Click the candy,' participants' mouse trajectories were initially curved toward the midpoint between the two similar-sounding objects — much like a mental trajectory in neural state space would initially travel toward two strong attractors before curving into the correct one. However, when the scene consisted of a flower and a piece of candy, the same instruction elicited trajectories that were more directly aimed at the candy. Therefore, the real-time continuous uptake of acoustic-phonetic input appears to be processed in a fashion that immediately takes into account the alternatives available in the visual context.

Not only can visual context affect language processing, but linguistic input can affect visual processing as well. In a series of reaction-time studies, Spivey *et al.* (2001) manipulated the efficiency of visual search functions via on-line spoken language processing. In *single-feature* search experiments, where the target is distinguished from the distractors by a single feature (e.g., a red bar amid green bars), response time to find the target stays constant as the number of distractors increases. By contrast, in *conjunction* search experiments, where the target object is defined by having two features (e.g., a red vertical bar amid red horizontal bars and green vertical bars), response time to find the target increases linearly with the number of distractors (typically in the range of about 20 milliseconds per distractor). However, Spivey et al. found that when the target identity is delivered via recorded speech while the display is visible (e.g., 'Is there a red vertical?'), a conjunction search behaves more like a single-feature search. Essentially, the continuous-time processing of the spoken input allowed participants to begin an efficient single-feature search upon just hearing the first adjective (e.g., 'red'). By the time the second adjective was being heard (e.g., 'vertical'), it could be used to instantaneously identify the single vertical bar amidst the red bars. As a result, incremental spoken delivery of the target identity, concurrent with viewing the display, produced set-size slopes of about 5-7 milliseconds per distractor, instead of 20. And a localist attractor network simulates these results across a variety of conditions (Reali *et al.*, in press).

These results, and many like them (cf. Shimojo & Shams, 2001), suggest that perceptual systems specialized for language and for vision interact more fluidly than was previously thought. They serve to blur distinctions between brain systems that were once thought of as dedicated to a single cognitive task. Although there are regions of the brain that do appear to be roughly devoted to word recognition and to visual attention, experiments that show the continuous interaction behind such processes suggest a more open system of interacting cognitive processes. This also suggests that such systems cannot be fully understood without reference to the other subsystems to which they are open. After all, the very nature of an open system requires not only an examination of the smaller system, but an examination of the larger system within which that smaller system operates (cf. Rosen, 2000).

Now that the distinction between mental subsystems has been sufficiently blurred, making pointing out a single autonomous cognitive faculty difficult, the blurring of the line between smaller and larger systems may continue even beyond an organism's brain. That is, just as information continuously streams between neural subsystems, so does it also stream between the person and the environment. Therefore, perhaps the brain itself should not be considered a module that is independent from its body and surrounding environment. For example, Hurley (1998, p.3) notes that '...if internal relations can qualify as [representational] vehicles, why not external relations? Given a continuous complex dynamic system of reciprocal causal relations between organism and environment, what in principle stops the spread? The idea that vehicles might go external takes the notion of distributed processing to its logical extreme.' Such a radical interactionism leads one naturally to a brand of psychology called *ecological psychology* and a perspective in philosophy called *externalism*.

Ecological psychology and philosophical externalism treat aspects of an organism's environment as part and parcel to the definition of that organism's mental activity. Interestingly, change blindness studies provide a unique opportunity to demonstrate that the environment does indeed act as a repository for some of a person's knowledge. If the external environment were in fact fully internalized, as suggested by philosophical internalism (Segal, 2000), then significant changes made to the visual environment (that take place during saccades or brief visual interruptions) would be noticed almost at once. If we are indeed completely aware of the contents of the visual scene before our eyes, as we often feel we are, then we should notice changes in that visual scene almost immediately.

However, this is not the case. A variety of change blindness experiments have demonstrated that people typically detect changes to a scene less than half of the time (e.g., Grimes, 1996; Rensink et al., 1997; Simons & Ambinder, 2005). For example, Simons and Levin (1998) developed an experiment in which a fellow experimenter stopped someone to ask for directions on the Cornell University campus. Half-way through the conversation, two men carrying a door walked between the direction-giver (the participant) and the direction-receiver (the experimenter), and replaced the latter with one of the individuals carrying the door (a second experimenter). Even though this change created significant alterations in both the visual and auditory environment, only about half of the participants realized that the direction-receiver had been switched! That the participants were oblivious to such large changes in parts of their environment they had been attending suggests that humans do not internalize all aspects of their external environment. This experiment demonstrates that change blindness does occur in dynamic real-world situations, and serves as a dramatic mantelpiece to this body of literature which has been interpreted as support for the claim that little is stored in the way of internal mental representations and that the locus of perception may be as much in the environment itself as it is in the organism (cf. O'Regan & Noë, 2001).

However, it could alternatively be the case that pre-change visual properties are still represented internally, they just tend not to be spontaneously *compared* to the current afferent input (Simons et al., 2002). Under such circumstances, one may ask: Is it this stored and *non-updated* internal representation of the visual environment that is somehow being used for perceptual guidance of motor movement? Or is it the visual environment itself that is being used? If an internal representation of the visual scene is the means by which we perceive and act on our visual environment, then it would seem that frequent *updates*, *comparisons*, and cross-indexing of the images received during eye fixations would actually be necessary to produce our pervasive sense of space constancy (i.e., a stable visual world). In fact, such updating and comparing is exactly what the spatiotopic fusion hypothesis originally proposed for how we patch together the partially-overlapping snapshots that we gather in between saccades to produce a full 3-D spatiotopic model of the world in our brains (Jonides et al., 1982; Niemeier et al., 2003). And it is the resounding empirical rejection of the strong form of this hypothesis (Bridgeman et al., 1994; Irwin, 1991; O'Regan & Noë, 2001) that led many to form the suggestion that the 'stable visual world' is an illusion brought about by the fact that 'if we so much as faintly ask ourselves some question about the environment, an answer is immediately provided by the sensory information on the retina, possibly rendered available by an eye movement.' (O'Regan, 1992, p.487).

Not only is information from the external environment not always actively internalized, but also internal information can also be actively *externalized* — via the use of deictic pointers in the environment (e.g., Ballard *et al.*, 1997; Pylyshyn, 1999; Richardson & Kirkham, 2004). Deictic pointers are a type of spatial index that conserves working memory by storing the spatial 'address' of an object or event but little of the 'content' of that object or event. Much of that content is offloaded onto the environment as a kind of external memory. For example, rather than store in your neural memory what colour, orientation, and fullness your coffee mug has, you can simply store its location on your desk, and access those properties from the environment by making an eye movement to that location. Deictic pointers provide an opportunity to explore how properties in the external environment and properties of neural processing coordinate to produce a form of cognitive processing that is not enclosed in the brain (Spivey *et al.*, 2004; see also Kirsh, 1995).

Richardson and Spivey (2000) presented participants with four talking heads, one in each of the four quadrants of the computer screen, and each delivered a tidbit of information auditorily before disappearing. Later the computer presented statements to the participant about the facts they had heard from the four talking heads, and participants were asked to determine the veracity of each statement. While participants considered their answer, they were twice as likely to spontaneously fixate the empty quadrant where the talking head that had delivered that fact had originally appeared.

Why did participants afford one quadrant more overt attention when the information had been presented auditorily and therefore could not be accessed visually? Richardson and Spivey (2000) suggested that participants allocated spatial indices to the four quadrants of the computer screen in an effort to assist in sorting and separating the events they had seen. Even though working memory ultimately had to be the only determinant of accuracy in this task, because the information was no longer present at the pointer's external location, the eye-movement subsystem was nonetheless accustomed to treating its environment as an external memory that will often contain the content being sought.

A natural next step in this kind of experimental design would be to convert eye position into an independent variable instead of a dependent variable. When participants are allowed to look at the original location (compared to being explicitly instructed to fixate a neutral location), memory performance improves by about 20% (Laeng & Teodorescu, 2002; see also Sacks & Hollingworth, 2005). Thus, the linking of the eyes to particular locations in the environment not only *provides a measure* of how we use external space to sort our visual memories, it can even *influence* our visual memories.

The findings of radical interactionism, change blindness, and external memory use are consistent with ecological psychology's approach to treating mental activity as something that takes place not merely inside a neural module, and not even inside the whole brain, but in the encompassing interface between an organism and its environment (Gibson, 1979; Turvey & Shaw, 1999; see also O'Regan & Noë, 2001). As a result, the dimensions that define the state space in which this mental activity occurs may be a combination of neural parameters, biomechanical parameters, and environmental constraint parameters (which often includes other organisms with their own neural and biomechanical parameters) — a 'shared manifold of intersubjectivity' (Gallese, 2003), if you will. And the mind is a trajectory through this space that recounts the continuous changes in state over time, visiting some attractors closely, and merely 'flirting' with others.

## The Soluble and Insoluble Problems of Consciousness

This is all well and good, one might say, for normal cognitive processes and even for self-consciousness, but those are the 'easy problems' of consciousness (cf. Chalmers, 1996). What about the 'hard problem' of consciousness? Does *a continuous trajectory through a state space, that occasionally visits labelled attractors closely enough to elicit speech or internal monologue,* tell the scientific community anything at all about 'what it is like' to undergo the immediate experience of perceiving a colour or of feeling pain? The honest answer to that question is 'no.' This is not because the theoretical framework of an attractor landscape is in any way deficient, but because the question, as posed, is worse than 'hard;' it is insoluble. No matter what theory you put in place of the italicized portion of the above question, the honest answer will always be 'no.' This is because even what we, ourselves, *think* is our immediate conscious experience cannot help but actually be a short-term memory of that experience, once-removed from the original instance (cf. Dennett, 1991). That is, even our own phenomenological experience of perceiving a colour or feeling pain over the course of just a few seconds is unavoidably filtered through working memory and linguistic processes, making it a form of self-consciousness. Thus, the pure form of immediate conscious awareness is not really even *subjectively observable* by oneself. The moment one begins this phenomenological self-interpretation, one is engaging in self-consciousness, not 'pure consciousness.'

It naturally follows, then, that the immediate conscious experience of perceiving a colour or feeling pain will never be *intersubjectively observable* by the scientific community either. By the time a conscious experience is being linguistically related to other people, it has been profoundly altered by a host of cognitive, social, and cultural variables. Curiously, some proponents of pure-consciousness would actually go even farther and suggest that immediate conscious experience will also not be detectable in measures of neural activation or cerebral blood flow. According to this perspective, neuronal processes do not contribute to the instantiation of conscious awareness. Following Kant, such a proponent might suggest that, although the tangible world of *perception and action* (Sinnenwelt) belongs to physics, chemistry and biology, the ineffable world of *thought* (Verstandeswelt) functions via 'laws that, being independent of nature, are not empirical but have their ground in reason alone' (Kant, in Seidler, 1986).

This ineffable quality inherent to the notion of pure-consciousness is particularly apparent in musings about a hypothetical entity called the 'zombie.' To philosophers of mind, this fantasy construct is not the flesh-eating slow-moving undead human from B-movies, but instead a person who has all the normal cognitive processes and behaviours of a conscious human, except that they lack any immediate experience of conscious awareness (e.g., Block, 1978; Chalmers, 1996; Güzeldere, 1995; Kirk, 1974; Polger, 2004). The theoretical possibility of a zombie is thus argued as evidence for pure-consciousness being something that cannot be explained by the neuronal processes that explain normal cognition and action. Since zombies and conscious humans are indistinguishable to observers, this pure-consciousness would be entirely epiphenomenal from an intersubjective point of view (cf. Huxley, 1902), but would nonetheless be a very real constituent of the personal phenomenology of the individual experiencing it.

However, this juxtaposition of zombies and conscious humans can be used, just as easily, to argue the opposite. Note that the only bits of evidence that the scientific community has regarding the existence of this precious non-neuron-based immediate conscious experience are people's *verbal reports* that they have them. And, according to the definition of a zombie, if every single one of those persons was actually a zombie, they would still be making those subjective claims — because that's what zombies do: they behave in ways that make them indistinguishable from conscious humans. This leaves us with two alternatives. These people claiming to experience immediate conscious awareness are either: a) zombies whose mental activity consists of all the cognitive processes associated with the 'easy problems' of consciousness and nothing else, or b) conscious beings whose mental activity consists of all the cognitive processes associated with the 'easy problems' of consciousness, plus an additional phenomenon of immediate conscious experience, which does not adhere to known physical laws and does not alter their behaviour in any way. We suspect that Occam's razor was forged exactly for situations like this. As alternative (a) can explain all of our scientifically observable data with fewer parameters, it is the natural choice. Hence, perhaps we are all zombies, and the hypothetical entity of a 'conscious being' is the fantasy construct that we are musing about.

What we suggest that everyone *does have*, whether they are a zombie or a conscious being, is the continuous trajectory in mental state space that constitutes mental activity. And perhaps it is the portions of the trajectory that sidle up very close to labelled point attractors that form the contents of linguistically expressible self-consciousness. Is it possible, then, that the remaining portions of the trajectory, those stretches of mental time and space that do not have cognitive labels associated with them, are what comprise the precious ineffable immediate experience of awareness that is just too delicate and ephemeral to make its way into language and memory? If that is what pure-consciousness is, the 'spaces in between,' then perhaps it can be treated as a soluble puzzle after all, along with the 'easy problems' of consciousness such as memory, language, and visual perception.

## The Describable and the Indescribable in Mental Activity

Mental activity is continuous in time and contiguous in state space, and it is not limited solely to neural parameters. When we think in terms of an organism smoothly interacting with its environment, the bi-directional flow of information between its various neural subsystems is not qualitatively different from the bi-directional flow of information between that brain and the environmental constraints on its biomechanical interfaces. According to this radical interactionism, looking for where to draw the line that artificially severs the causal chain between the brain and the body, or between the body and the environment, quickly becomes a woefully arbitrary enterprise (cf. Spivey *et al.*, 2004). As sketched in Figure 2, the bi-directional influences between the Language, Vision, and Memory subsystems

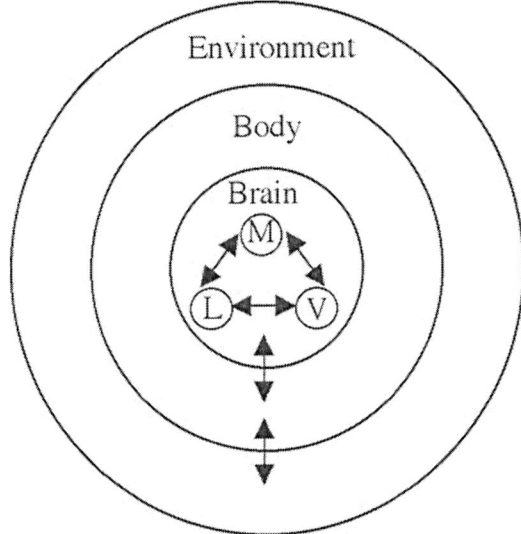

*Figure 2.* A schematic illustration of radical interactionism, where memory, language and vision are 'open systems' in the brain, sharing their mutual influences with one another continuously. Although the brain encompasses these neural subsystems, it too is an open system with respect to the body, which in turn is an open system with respect to the environment. Crucially, when a system is open, it cannot be fully characterized without reference to the larger system in which it is embedded.

(among others not depicted) are of the same basic kind as the bi-directional influences between brain and body and between body and environment. Thus, rather than there being some internal neural module from which a causal chain can be spontaneously initiated (with no preceding causes of its own), the state of affairs is perhaps best described as 'mutual influences all the way down.'

Such a framework encourages us to conceive of personal identity, personal responsibility, and personal phenomenology in some new and interesting ways. If part of *who you are* includes the interactions between your body and its environmental constraints, what does that say about circumstances where your body is cooperating with another body in a joint activity (e.g., Knoblich & Jordan, 2003; Sebanz *et al.*, 2003)? Moreover, if the chain of causal influences for anti-social behaviour is always traceable (at least, in principle) to forces outside of an individual's body, then greater effort should obviously be made toward identifying and remedying those external causal forces when possible, so that they do not cause other organisms to conduct similar anti-social behaviour (Haney, 2002; Pereboom, 2001). And finally, in this framework, our conscious experience of sensory impressions, emotions, and intentions is no longer seen as something that happens privately in your brain, but instead emerges in the interplay between (and in the shared medium of) brains, bodies and environment (e.g., Clark & Chalmers, 1997; O'Regan & Noë, 2001; Spivey *et al.*, 2004; Van Orden & Holden, 2002; see also Barsalou *et al.*, 2003).

This shared medium of neural, biomechanical, and environmental parameters forms a volumetric state space, in which a continuous trajectory is a way to visualize what the mind is doing both when it is self-conscious (e.g., visiting sufficiently close to linguistic and visual-object point attractors to instigate an internal picturesque monologue) and when it is not engaging in any form of self-report at all (e.g., traversing regions of state space that contain shallow attractor basins that do not have linguistic or categorical labels, yet nonetheless involve fluid motoric interaction with the environment). In this way, the 'easy problems' of consciousness (which are hard enough, thank you very much) can begin to come together in a universal medium that promises to explain the continuous temporal dynamics of the describable and the indescribable: language processing, visual perception, memory, self-consciousness and everywhere in between.

## References

Allopenna, P.D., Magnuson, J.S. & Tanenhaus, M.K. (1998), 'Tracking the time course of spoken word recognition using eye movements: Evidence for continuous mapping models', *Journal of Memory and Language*, **38**, pp. 419–39.

Ballard, D., Hayhoe, M., Pook, P. & Rao, R. (1997), 'Deictic codes for the embodiment of cognition', *Behavioral and Brain Sciences*, **20**, pp. 723–67.

Barsalou, L.W., Niedenthal, P.M., Barbey, A. & Ruppert, J. (2003). In B. Ross (Ed.), *The Psychology of Learning and Motivation*, Vol. 43 (pp. 43–92). San Diego: Academic Press.

Block, N. (1978), 'Troubles with functionalism', in *Perception and Cognition, Minnesota Studies in the Philosophy of Science*, Vol. 9, ed. W. Savage (Minneapolis: University of Minnesota Press).

Botvinick, M. & Plaut, D. (2004), 'Doing without schema hierarchies: A recurrent connectionist approach to normal and impaired routine sequential action', *Psychological Review*, **111**, pp. 395–429.

Bridgeman, B., van der Hejiden, A., Velichkovsky, B. (1994), 'A theory of visual stability across saccadic eye movements', *Behavioral and Brain Sciences*, **17**, pp. 247–92.

Chalmers, D. (1996), *The Conscious Mind: In Search of a Fundamental Theory* (New York: Oxford University Press).

Clark, A. & Chalmers, D. (1998), 'The extended mind', *Analysis*, **58**, pp. 7–19.

Cutler, A. (1995), 'Spoken word recognition', in *Handbook of Cognition and Perception*, eds. J. Miller & P. Eimas (Academic Press).

Dennett, D. (1991), *Consciousness Explained* (Boston, MA: Little, Brown & Company).
Desimone, R. & Duncan, J. (1995), 'Neural mechanisms of selective visual attention', *Annual Review of Neuroscience*, **18**, pp. 193–222.
Dietrich, E. & Markman, A. (2003), 'Discrete thoughts: Why cognition must use discrete representations', *Mind and Language*, **18**, pp. 95–119.
Elman, J. (2004), 'An alternative view of the mental lexicon', *Trends in Cognitive Sciences,* **8**, pp. 301–6.
Gallese, V. (2003), 'The manifold nature of interpersonal relations: The quest for a common mechanism', *Philosophical Transactions of the Royal Society of London B: Biological Sciences*, **358**, pp. 517–28.
Gaskell, M. & Marslen-Wilson, W. (2002), 'Representation and competition in the perception of spoken words', *Cognitive Psychology*, **45**, pp. 220–66.
Gibson, J. (1950), *The Perception of the Visual World* (Oxford: Houghton Mifflin).
Gibson, J. (1979), *The Ecological Approach to Visual Perception*, (Boston, MA: Houghton Mifflin).
Grimes, J. (1996), 'On the failure to detect changes in scenes across saccades', in *Perception: Vancouver Studies in Cognitive Science,* ed. K. Akins (Oxford: Oxford University Press).
Güzeldere, G. (1995), 'Varieties of zombiehood', *Journal of Consciousness Studies,* **2**, pp. 326–33.
Haney, C. (2002), 'Making law modern: Toward a contextual model of justice', *Psychology, Public Policy, and Law, pp.* **8**, pp. 3–63.
Hurley, S. (1998), 'Vehicles, contents, conceptual structures, and externalism', *Analysis*, **58**, pp. 1–6.
Huxley, T. (1902), *Methods and Results* (New York: Appleton Co).
Irwin, D. (1991), 'Information integration across saccadic eye movements', *Cognitive Psychology,* **23**, pp. 420–56.
Kelso, J. (1995), *Dynamic Patterns: The Self-Organization of Brain and Behavior* (Cambridge, MA: MIT Press).
Jonides, J., Irwin, D. & Yantis, S. (1982), 'Integrating visual information from successive fixations', *Science*, **215** (4529), pp. 192–4.
Kirk, R. (1974), 'Zombies v. materialists', *Proceedings of the Aristotelian Society,* **48**, pp. 135–52.
Kirsh, D. (1995), 'The intelligent use of space', *Artificial Intelligence*, **73**, pp. 31–68.
Knoblich, G. & Jordan, J. (2003), 'Action coordination in groups and individuals: Learning anticipatory control', *Journal of Experimental Psychology: Learning, Memory, and Cognition*, **29**, pp. 1006–16.
Laeng, B. & Teodorescu, D. (2002), 'Eye scanpaths during visual imagery reenact those of perception of the same visual scene', *Cognitive Science*, **26**, pp. 207–31.
Luce, P., Goldinger, S., Auer, E. & Vitevitch, M. (2000), 'Phonetic priming, neighborhood activation, and PARSYN', *Perception and Psychophysics*, **62**, pp. 615–25.
Magnuson, J., Tanenhaus, M., Aslin, R. & Dahan, D. (2003), 'The time course of spoken word learning and recognition: Studies with artificial lexicons', *Journal of Experimental Psychology: General*, **132**, pp. 202–27.
Marslen-Wilson, W. (1987), 'Functional parallelism in spoken word recognition', *Cognition*, **25**, pp. 71–102.
McClelland, J. & Elman, J. (1986), 'The TRACE model of speech perception', *Cognitive Psychology*, pp. **18**, 1–86.
Neisser, U. (1967), *Cognitive Psychology* (East Norwalk, CT: Appleton-Century-Crofts).

Newell, A., Shaw, J.C. & Simon, H.A. (1958), 'Elements of a theory of human problem solving', *Psychological Review*, **65**, pp. 151–66.
Niemeier, M., Crawford, J. & Tweed. D. (2003), 'Optimal transsaccadic integration explains distorted spatial perception', *Nature, 422(6927)*, pp. 76-80.
O'Regan, J.K. (1992), 'Solving the "real" mysteries of visual perception: The world as an outside memory', *Canadian Journal of Psychology*, **46**, pp. 461–88.
O'Regan, J. K. & Noë, A. (2001), 'A sensorimotor account of vision and visual consciousness', *Behavioral and Brain Sciences*, **24**, pp. 939–1031.
Pereboom, D. (2001), *Living Without Free Will* (New York: Cambridge University Press).
Perrett, D., Oram, M. & Ashbridge, E. (1998), 'Evidence accumulation in cell populations responsive to faces: An account of generalization of recognition without mental transformations', *Cognition*, **67**, pp. 111–45.
Polger, T. (2004), *Natural Minds* (Cambridge, MA: MIT Press).
Port, R. & van Gelder, T. (ed. 1995), *Mind as Motion: Explorations in the Dynamics of Cognition* (Cambridge, MA: MIT Press).
Pylyshyn, Z. (1980), 'Computation and cognition: Issues in the foundations of cognitive science', *Behavioral and Brain Sciences*, **3**, pp. 111–69.
Pylyshyn, Z. (1989), 'The role of location indexes in spatial perception: A sketch of the FINST spatial index model', *Cognition*, **32**, pp. 65–97.
Reali, F., Spivey, M., Tyler, M. & Terranova, T. (in press), 'Inefficient conjunction search made efficient by concurrent spoken delivery of target identity', *Perception and Psychophysics*.
Rensink, R., O'Regan, J. & Clark, J. (1997), 'To see or not to see: The need for attention to perceive changes in scenes', *Psychological Science*, **8**, pp. 368–73.
Richardson, D. & Kirkham, N. (2004), 'Multi-modal events and moving locations: Eye movements of adults and 6-month-olds reveal dynamic spatial indexing', *Journal of Experimental Psychology: General*, **133**, pp. 46–62.
Richardson, D. & Spivey, M. (2000), 'Representation, space and Hollywood Squares: Looking at things that aren't there anymore', *Cognition*, **76**, pp. 269–95.
Rolls, E. & Tovee, M. (1995), 'Sparseness of the neuronal representation of stimuli in the primate temporal visual cortex', *Journal of Neurophysiology*, **73**, pp. 713–26.
Rosen, R. (2000), *Essays on Life Itself* (New York: Columbia University Press).
Sacks, D. & Hollingworth, A. (2005), 'Attending to original object location facilitates visual memory retrieval', *Journal of Vision*, **5** (8), p. 443a.
Sebanz, N., Knoblich, G. & Prinz, W. (2003), 'Representing others' actions: Just like one's own?', *Cognition*, **88**, pp. B11–B21.
Segal, G. (2000), *A Slim Book About Narrow Content* (Cambridge, MA: MIT Press).
Seidler, V. (1986), *Kant, Respect and Injustice: The Limits of Liberal Moral Theory* (London: Routledge & Kegan Paul).
Shimojo, S. & Shams, L. (2001), 'Sensory modalities are not separate modalities: Plasticity and interactions', *Current Opinion in Neurobiology*, **11**, pp. 505–9.
Simons, D. & Ambinder, M. (2005), 'Change blindness: Theory and consequences', *Current Directions in Psychological Science*, **14**, pp. 44–8.
Simons, D.J., Chabris, C.F., Schnur, T.T. & Levin, D.T. (2002), 'Evidence for preserved representations in change blindness', *Consciousness and Cognition*, **11**, pp. 78–97.
Simons, D. & Levin, D. (1998), 'Failure to detect changes to people during a real world interaction', *Psychonomic Bulletin and Review*, **5**, pp. 644–9.

Spivey, M. & Dale, R. (2004), 'On the continuity of mind: Toward a dynamical account of cognition', in *The Psychology of Learning and Motivation*, Vol. 45, ed. B. Ross (Elsevier).

Spivey, M. (2007), *The Continuity of Mind* (New York: Oxford University Press).

Spivey, M., Grosjean, M. & Knoblich, G. (2005), 'Continuous attraction toward phonological competitors', *Proceedings of the National Academy of Sciences of the USA*, **102**, pp. 10393–8.

Spivey, M., Richardson, D. & Fitneva, S. (2004), 'Thinking outside the brain: Spatial indices to linguistic and visual information', in *The Interface of Vision, Language and Action*, eds. J. Henderson & F. Ferreira (New York: Psychology Press).

Spivey, M., Tyler, M., Eberhard, K. & Tanenhaus, M. (2001), 'Linguistically mediated visual search', *Psychological Science*, **12**, pp. 282–6.

Turvey, M. & Shaw, R. (1999), 'Ecological foundations of cognition: I. symmetry and specificity of animal-environment systems', *Journal of Consciousness Studies*, **6** (11–12), pp. 111–23.

Uttal, W. (2001), *The New Phrenology: The Limits of Localizing Cognitive Processes in the Brain* (Cambridge, MA: MIT Press).

Van Orden, G. & Holden, J. (2002), 'Intentional contents and self-control', *Ecological Psychology*, **14**, pp. 87–109.

Natalie Sebanz

# *The Emergence of Self*
## *Sensing Agency through Joint Action*

**Abstract**: *This article explores the role of social factors in the emergence of self and other. It is suggested that the experience of causing actions contributes to a basic sense of self in which awareness of mental states and the experience of a mental self are grounded. According to the proposed evolutionary scenario, the experience of agency emerged as individuals acting in social context learned to differentiate between effects caused by their own actions and effects resulting from joint action. Through joint action, individuals also developed an understanding of others' actions as goal-directed, paving the way for imitation. The ability to distinguish between action capabilities of self and other and the understanding that action-effect principles apply equally to self and other may have provided important advantages in circumstances where cooperative action and social learning were critical. The current proposal adds to previous evolutionary scenarios in that it identifies social conditions that may have shaped a basic sense of self. This, in turn, could have given rise to theory of mind and the cultural construction of mental selves.*

### Introduction

One of the most puzzling and yet most intriguing characteristics of the human mind is our awareness of our own mental states. We experience ourselves thinking thoughts, recalling memories, having intentions, and making decisions. In other words, we experience a mental self. But what is a mental self good for? And how did it evolve? While we are a long way from definite answers, some progress might be made by considering the role of social forces in the evolution of consciousness. This idea is by no means new (cf. e.g., Burns & Engdahl, 1998a,b; Mead, 1956). However, while previous work has focused on the role of language and collective representations, I here explore how very basic forms of social interaction may contribute to the emergence of a mental self.

It is becoming increasingly evident that a deeper understanding of many cognitive processes, ranging from visual perception (Wilson & Knoblich, 2005) to executive functions (Roepstorff & Frith, 2004), can be achieved by investigating their role in social context, and by exploring how they may have been shaped by demands of social interaction (Sebanz et al., 2006). This perspective can also be applied to the cognitive processes that give rise to awareness of one's mental states and to the experience of a mental self. It has been suggested that conscious awareness of mental states evolved because it increased individuals' ability to predict others' actions (Frith, 2002), and because it allowed individuals to distinguish between self- and other-generated thoughts (Prinz, 2003).

While clearly acknowledging the role of social and cultural forces in the emergence of consciousness, these proposals have not spelled out in detail how the transition from self-less beings to individuals aware of their own mental states may have actually occurred. I propose that the experience of agency, defined here as the experience of oneself as being the cause of actions, might have constituted a crucial first step in the emergence of mental selves. So far, the experience of agency has been treated more or less on a par with awareness of other mental states (Frith, 2002) or has been left out of the picture all together (Prinz, 2003). Yet, recent studies suggest that experiencing oneself causing actions may be a fundamental building block of the self (Knoblich et al., 2003; Knoblich & Sebanz, 2005) and forms part of a 'minimal self' (Gallagher, 2000). I will argue that a sense of agency developed because crucial forms of social interaction, including joint action and imitation, relied on the ability to distinguish between action effects produced by oneself and action effects caused by others.

In the first part of this paper, I will review some arguments for looking for a role of conscious awareness of mental states beyond individual action. Secondly, I will argue that existing proposals in cognitive science do not specify the origins of self-awareness, but rather describe how an existing sense of self could have been further shaped by social interactions. Thirdly, I will propose that the experience of agency solved basic problems related to the attribution of action effects in social context, enabling individuals to coordinate their actions and learn from each other through imitation. Finally, I will discuss how one could empirically investigate certain assumptions about the socio-cultural emergence of mental selves.

## Acting In Isolation

One may wonder whether there are good reasons at all for searching for a role of conscious awareness of mental states outside the context of individual action. Obviously, seeking the roots of consciousness in the social realm rests on the assumption that the experience of a mental self cannot be explained by the workings of a mind in isolation (cf. Burns & Engdahl, 1989a,b). But don't we simply need to be aware of mental contents so that we can decide what to do and to monitor our actions? A review of findings related to action selection and action control shows a limited role of conscious awareness for individual action (see also Frith, 2002).

### Action control

Several findings suggest that the performance of goal-directed actions does not necessarily depend on conscious awareness. It has been demonstrated that people can make fast and accurate grasping and reaching movements without being aware of the information they rely on to control these movements (e.g., Goodale *et al.*, 1986; Pisella *et al.*, 2000). For example, participants can hit a target that changed its location after they initiated their movement, even when they are not aware of the change (cf. Bridgeman *et al.*, 1979). Related to this, many studies have shown that actions are planned at the level of goals, whereas the exact implementation is left under-specified. Once an action goal has been selected, control is delegated to lower-level sensorimotor systems (for an overview, see Hommel, 2006). Finally, an impressive demonstration that action control can occur despite a lack of awareness of central aspects of the action comes from extensive study of a patient with form agnosia (Milner & Goodale, 1995). Due to damage in the inferior temporal lobe, this patient cannot perceive the shape of things. However, although this patient has no conscious awareness of an object's shape, she is still able to grasp objects appropriately.

### Action selection

What about the role of conscious awareness in action selection? Two kinds of findings (also highlighted in Frith, 2002) have been regarded by some as a serious challenge to the view that conscious awareness of intentions plays a causal role in the selection of actions. Experiments by Libet (Libet *et al.*, 1983), and, more recently, Haggard and colleagues showed that the intention to act is experienced only after changes in brain activation reflecting the selection of an action have occurred (Haggard *et al.*, 1999; Haggard & Eimer, 1999; for an overview, see Haggard, 2006). The time at which participants reported an intention to perform a hand movement was correlated with the onset time of the lateralized readiness potential. The lateralized readiness potential reflects a shift of central brain activity to the hemisphere that supports action performance, which is always contra-lateral to the hand that will move. This suggests that an intention to act is only experienced once the action has been specified. However, Pacherie (2006) recently pointed out that these findings do not necessarily warrant the conclusion that conscious intention is not causally involved in action selection. She argued that 'there is no good reason to think that only the initial element in a causal chain may genuinely qualify as a cause' (p. 19). Accordingly, given that the intention to act typically precedes an action, it may still play a causal role, even though it does not trigger the whole causal process.

A further set of findings calling into question the causal role of conscious intention in action selection comes from studies that have investigated illusions of conscious will. These studies showed that we sometimes experience agency for consequences we have not actually caused, or do not experience agency for consequences we have caused. Wegner and colleagues devised experiments where it was ambiguous whether participants themselves or a confederate caused a certain action effect to happen. In one study, participants experienced causing effects that were actually produced by another person when action-consistent thoughts were induced before the action effect occurred (Wegner & Wheatley, 1999). Another experiment showed that the opposite can also occur: Participants perceived themselves as influenced by another's action, although there was no such influence. They were asked to answer knowledge questions with 'yes/no', by 'reading' the intention of another person from their finger movements. Although the person was a confederate who did not know the questions, participants had a strong tendency to attribute their answers to the other person, and did not feel that they had selected the responses (Wegner et al., 2003).

These studies provide evidence that the experience of a conscious intention causing an action is sometimes illusory. According to Wegner (2002), we are most likely to infer that we have caused an action when the action was preceded by a thought (priority) that was consistent with the consequences of the action (consistency), and no alternative cause of the consequences is evident (exclusivity). Wegner and others have argued that if the experience of agency is susceptible to cognitive biases, it remains questionable to what extent conscious intention plays a causal role in action selection. However, several philosophers have pointed out that from the fact that people's experience of conscious will is sometimes non-veridical, one cannot conclude that for all of our actions, intentions are not causally involved in action selection (e.g., Bayne & Levy, 2006; Pacherie, 2006).

Taken together, there is evidence supporting the claim that action control does not critically depend on conscious awareness of actions. It is less clear to what extent action selection would be possible without conscious awareness of intentions. While one should certainly not dismiss the role of conscious awareness of intentions for action selection all together, it can be concluded that the search for a functional role of consciousness outside the context of action selection and action control has some empirical grounding.

## Thinking About Others

Could demands of social interactions have fostered the emergence of mental selves? Frith proposed that the need to predict others' actions by representing their mental states may have constituted a powerful driving force behind the evolution of consciousness (Frith, 2002). In particular, the conscious experience of our intentions causing our actions might be critical for taking an intentional stance towards others, assuming that the same mechanisms underlie the mental representation of our own and others' mental states (Frith & Frith, 1999; Frith, 2002). Thus, according to this proposal, demands of social life shaped a property of human minds (namely awareness of mental states) that initially surfaced for unspecified reasons. Humans proceeded from awareness of their own mental states to awareness of others' mental states.

The opposite birth order has been advocated by Prinz (2003). Following his proposal, our experience of a mental self emerges from perceiving mental selves in others (see also Happé, 2003). In a nutshell, Prinz suggested that interacting with others created problems of source attribution. If a thought[1] is being communicated by somebody else, it can be ascribed to the other because one can observe the other speaking. However, a thought arising in the absence of another

---

[1] Following Prinz (2003), by 'thought' I here refer to all forms of mental representations that are internally generated. I also include action goals, which are treated separately in Prinz's account.

individual must be attributed to a source. To modern, healthy human beings it seems strange that a thought arising in the absence of communication would not be attributed to oneself. However, as Prinz points out, thoughts may have been ascribed to the voices of gods, priests, kings and the like, in other words, to authorities believed to exert an influence on one's actions through their invisible presence (see also Prinz et al., 2006). Thus, Prinz's account stresses the role of cultural processes that allegedly set in once a cognitive architecture had evolved that allowed for a separation between internally generated thoughts and actions, and events perceived in the world.

*A mental self only for higher-level social cognition?*
The two proposals sketched above are important for the endeavour of understanding consciousness because they suggest that rather than looking at individuals in isolation it may be more fruitful to consider the challenges individuals meet in social context. However, both proposals focus on quite complex social interactions, where individuals need to infer the intentions of others (Frith), or communicate by use of symbolic language (Prinz). This seems to suggest that there is no need for a mental self in more simple social interactions, such as imitating what others do, or acting in synchrony.

Furthermore, while reasons are given for *why* awareness of mental states could have emerged, it remains underspecified *how* it could have developed: Following Frith's proposal, it seems that some individuals just happened to be more aware of their own mental states than others, which gave them evolutionary advantages. But why would some individuals have become aware of their own mental states? Was this the result of random mutation? Or were there more basic forms of self-awareness that supported the emergence of a mental self? Prinz's proposal implies that self-awareness is born anew in each person socialized in a context that attributes individuals with a self-morphic organization of their mental structures. The transfer from attributing thoughts to oneself rather than to supernatural beings may have occurred only during historical times (cf. Jaynes, 1976). Again, one may ask whether the emergence of a mental self through cultural processes was linked to a more basic sense of self. While humans may have blamed gods for actions they performed, these humans certainly felt themselves acting, thus experiencing a sense of self in action (Gallagher, 1995).

It seems likely that the cognitive processes underlying awareness of mental states emerged out of more simple forms of self-awareness, such as the experience of causing action effects. I suggest that no matter whether one regards the experience of a mental self as nothing but a cultural construct, as suggested by Prinz, or also as a faculty of the mind shaped by evolutionary pressures, it is important to consider the possibility that more simple forms of social interaction may have contributed to the growing awareness of self and other. By identifying conditions that require a basic sense of self, we may gain clues as to how awareness of mental states could have gradually developed.

## Acting With Others

Most likely, early in human history, individuals engaged in basic forms of social interaction that did not depend on the use of symbolic communication and required little or no ability to infer others' mental states. For example, individuals could have performed the same action at the same time to bring about changes in the environment without relying on symbolic communication, and without sharing an understanding of each other's intentions, let alone having a shared 'we-intention' (Sebanz et al., 2006; Tollefsen, 2005). I propose that by engaging in very simple forms of joint action, individuals gained a sense of self in action. Those who were able to distinguish between their own action capabilities and the combination of their own and others' capabilities — or 'self' and 'self-plus-other' — may have had important advantages.

### *Joint action: Performing the same actions*

I suggest that in the beginning, individuals acted together not intentionally, but incidentally. Individuals did not experience a sense of self, and hence did not distinguish between self and other. There was no such concept as 'acting alone' or 'acting together'. By chance, two or more individuals sometimes pursued the same action goal at the same time. To give an example, two individuals might have encountered an obstacle, say, a heavy rock, on their way to a food source. Each individual would have tried to push the heavy rock out of the way without being aware of the fact that another individual was attempting to do the same at the same time. However, over time, individuals would have encountered the same kinds of situations as they were alone and together. They may have started to notice certain contingencies: some effects are achieved more easily in one condition (joint) than in the other (alone), and some effects can even only be achieved in one condition (joint) and not in the other (individual). Through repeated experiences of this kind, individuals may have developed an understanding of what they could do and could not do by themselves. Thus, they may have started to distinguish between 'acting alone' and 'not acting alone'.

Making this distinction can be regarded as the start of a basic sense of self. Knowledge about one's own action capabilities would have constituted the essence of this rudimentary sense of self. Once individuals had some knowledge about their action capabilities, they could use this in two ways. First, when encountering a situation where their own efforts did not produce the desired results, they could actively seek the 'not acting alone' condition. This implies understanding that 'not acting alone' entails other actors. At this early stage, individuals may not have regarded others as beings like themselves, but as useful 'tools' for achieving desired effects. Second, once individuals had access to stored knowledge about what they could do, they could predict whether their efforts would be successful in a given situation, rather than wasting precious energy through trial and error. Clearly, those who grasped the powers of joint action and actively sought others' help may have had many advantages, suggesting that individuals with the ability to distinguish between self and self-plus-other might have been favoured by evolution.

*Joint action: Performing complementary actions*

Once a rudimentary sense of self based on individual action capabilities had emerged, the understanding of others could also be refined, allowing for more complex forms of joint action to emerge. By observing others, individuals would have come to understand that others had similar action capabilities as they themselves. They would have noticed that the same contingencies hold for themselves and others, e.g., that a small rock can be pushed by a single individual (self or other) while a large rock cannot. This would have allowed them to combine their own and others' actions more flexibly. In many situations, desired changes in the environment can only be achieved if individuals perform complementary actions and are not achieved if individuals perform the same actions at the same time (Jordan & Knoblich, 2004; Knoblich & Jordan, 2003). For example, imagine a rock blocking the way that needs to be pushed and turned at the same time. Individuals might have realized that two different actions must be performed at the same time, but could only perform one at a time. Knowing that they could push and turn, they would have been able to infer that another being could also push and turn, and so the two tasks could be distributed. It is important to keep in mind that this did not require inferring the others' mental states or having a shared intention. Rather, the other could still be regarded as a 'tool' whose capabilities were known.

*Joint attention*

Of course, getting the other to do what one wanted would have been far from easy. Individuals would have come to realize that joint action only takes place in certain circumstances, and that their efforts to get others' action capabilities to work for them were only successful when certain conditions were fulfilled. For example, they would have noticed that others only perform actions that help reach a desired object if the object is visible to these others. Thus, in addition to learning about action capabilities of others, individuals also learned about perceptual regularities. Importantly, they would have come to understand that others cannot always perceive what they themselves perceive (cf. Hare *et al.*, 2000). Once they understood that others needed to see what they saw to engage in joint action, they could have learned to draw others' attention to certain objects and locations (Bayliss *et al.*, 2004; Tomasello, 2000). It is tempting to speculate that joint attention, the ability to direct one's attention to where someone else is attending (Emery, 2000; Moore & Dunham, 1995), developed in close connection with joint action (see also Tollefsen, 2005). Individuals who were able to manipulate others' attention and to share perceptual information were at an advantage because they could engage in joint action more easily.

*Imitation*

Furthermore, individuals would have noticed that engaging in joint action usually meant that if they got what they wanted, a piece of it (or more!) would soon be gone because it was taken away by the other. For example, once the rock was successfully pushed out of the way together, the food would not have been one's own alone. Through experiences of this kind, individuals would have come to understand the similarity between self and other not only in terms of action and perception, but also in terms of action goals (Bekkering *et al.*, 2000). They would have understood that when others perform actions, this results in desirable effects for others, just as when oneself performs actions. The understanding that actions of others result in desirable effects provides a basis for imitation. To imitate goal-directed actions, one needs to understand that what one observes in others can be mapped onto one's own body (Barresi & Moore, 1996; Decety &

Chaminade, 2003; Mitchell, 1993). For this reason, imitation is often considered as evidence of self-awareness (Lewis, 1994; Hart & Fegley, 1994).

Once individuals had understood that actions of self and other lead to effects in similar ways, it was possible to create a mapping between actions and effects at a more general level, and then use observed action-effect principles for oneself. Understanding about the similarities between self and other allowed individuals to exchange useful sequences of goal-directed actions. Once again, individuals who were better able to understand relations between self and other were at an advantage.

It is tempting to think that early forms of imitation may have been similar to the imitation observed in non-human primates (Parker & Milbrath, 1994). However, there are some crucial differences that should be noted. First, the present account assumes full imitation, whereby individuals learn not only about new action effects that can be achieved, but also imitate the means whereby these effects are achieved (Call, 2001). In contrast, it is assumed that imitation in non-human primates is mostly restricted to the reproduction of action outcomes (Tomasello, 1996; for a more recent review, see Call, 2005). Furthermore, the account of imitation proposed here includes delayed imitation. Individuals may well have observed a new action-effect principle, and only later used this for their purposes. In non-human primates, imitation is usually immediate and suggests more a learning of desirable effects than one of a general link between an action and its outcome (Call, 2005).

*Beginning awareness of mental states*

While in the beginning, the sense of self was probably nothing but a momentary and fleeting experience occurring in response to specific interactions (such as the change from pushing the rock on one's own to pushing it with another being), with repeated experiences, a more stable sense of self emerged. Individuals memorized contingencies that defined themselves as an acting entity (Jordan, 2003) and separated them from others on a more constant basis. Such knowledge could be used implicitly in joint action and reciprocal imitation, but might have also taken more explicit forms. In particular, it might have become important to remember who is able to do what and who accomplished what, independent of the present circumstances. To achieve particular action effects, one could take into account one's own capabilities (e.g., remembering how one did in a similar situation) and then choose a suitable co-actor based on what one remembers about other individuals.

For example, if an object can only be reached through strength and dexterity, and one remembers that last time, one could do the part of the action requiring dexterity, but not the part requiring strength, one may try to recruit the help of an individual whom one has seen achieving actions that require strength. This does not involve ascribing a mental state to the other, it just involves attributing action capabilities to the other. If memories for actions and their consequences are tagged for agency (Daprati *et al.*, 2005), individuals can explicitly draw upon episodic memories, which ultimately, may lead to the experience of oneself as a person with a coherent biography (Neisser, 1988; Prinz, 2003)[2]. Importantly, the idea that how others see oneself is critical for the emergence of self may be echoed here in a rudimentary way. One's self-concept may have entailed knowledge about what one can do with respect to the goals and values of a social group (Burns & Engdahl, 1998b; Mead, 1956). However, in the present framework, this kind of positioning in the social environment does not rely on language.

In addition to what oneself and others could do, individuals might have started to memorize who liked what. After all, if one needs a co-actor, they must be interested in achieving the same action effects as oneself, so it is important to know about others' preferences. As individuals became aware of the fact that others' preferences sometimes differed from their own, the concept of subjectivity was born. Individuals no longer assumed that others would always want what they themselves wanted, but would try to find out what others desired. This implies they attributed others with — however basic — mental states like desires or intentions. Intentions may thus have been the first kind of mental states individuals became aware of.

I suggest that the scenario proposed by Frith really only sets in at this stage. The present proposal is quite compatible with Frith's account, if one assumes that there was increasing pressure to predict others' actions based on mental states because individuals engaged in more and more complex social interactions. The foundation for the awareness of mental states, I argue, was the understanding of self and other that emerged through more simple forms of social interaction like joint action and imitation. While Frith suggested that awareness

---

[2] This goes together with the notion of a 'projectable' mind (Metcalfe & Kober, 2005). While initially, awareness of mental states may have been limited to the here and now (metacognition), it could have gradually extended to the past (episodic memory), the future (action planning), and others (theory of mind).

of one's own mental states came first, I could imagine awareness for self and other developing in parallel.

Prinz's account sets in at an even later stage, where individuals engaged in symbolic communication. Crucially for the present discussion, this account makes it clear that being aware of mental states might not be the same as experiencing a mental self the way we do today. Mental states can be treated as an independent variable that helps to predict behaviour. Using mental states this way is different from attributing them to a person as the source and owner of mental contents. The attribution of mental states to mental selves may indeed have emerged only in historical times, and the experience of a mental self may well be a cultural construct (Burns & Engdahl, 1998a,b). Nevertheless, I would argue that in order to emerge at all, this construct needed a foundation that was provided by the experience of agency shaped through joint action.

## From Just-So Stories to Experiments

Unfortunately, there is no way to directly test the speculative claims of our hypothetical evolutionary scenarios. However, empirical studies may provide findings that help to evaluate specific claims and constrain further theorizing. In the final part of this paper, I will discuss how certain claims of the present proposal could be tested in developmental studies as well as in 'pseudo-evolutionary' experiments.

### Developmental Predictions

A central claim of the present proposal is that individuals engaged in joint action long before they attributed mental states to others. This implies that at least simple forms of joint action do not rely on theory of mind. If this assumption is correct, one should observe joint action in very young children whose theory of mind is not yet fully developed (cf. Tollefsen, 2005). Research on cognitive development shows that at 12 months, children play together with others, e.g., building a tower or pretending to bake a cake together, but do not pass theory of mind tests that rely on the understanding that people can have different beliefs about the same situation (Gopnik & Astington, 1988; Flavell *et al.*, 1995). While such findings clearly support the idea that a full-blown theory of mind, which is probably not in place until age four, is not required to engage in joint action, it remains to be investigated whether one needs to think about others in terms of mental states at all to engage in joint action. The present account predicts that joint action is possible even if actors do not take an intentional stance, because unlike other accounts (e.g., Clark, 1996; Tuomela, 1995) it does not assume that shared intention is a necessary pre-condition for joint action to take place. A way to address this issue is to investigate joint action in individuals with autism, who have difficulties representing others' mental states. First evidence suggests that individuals with autism integrate others' actions in their own action planning just like healthy controls (Sebanz et al., 2005), but again, whether joint action occurs in the absence of mental state attribution remains to be investigated.

A further claim of the present proposal is that joint action emerged before goal-directed imitation.[3] Accordingly, one should also see simple forms of joint action very early in ontogenetic development. Children should be able to engage in joint action before they start to imitate others' actions. As described above, engagement in joint action would be based on the understanding that one can reach desirable effects jointly, but not alone. A more refined understanding of self and other would not be required. In contrast, imitation is based on the understanding that mappings between actions and effects derived from observing others can be employed by oneself. Thus, imitation implies that one attributes action goals to others. Research indicates that from 14 months of age, children only imitate a specific action when they consider it to be the most rational alternative to achieve a particular goal (Gergely et al., 2002). At around 12 months, they already show evidence of understanding others' actions in terms of goals (Gergely & Csibra, 2003). The present account predicts that joint action should occur even before others' actions are interpreted as goal-directed.

## *Pseudo-evolutionary Predictions*

Besides developmental studies, a way to investigate ideas about the evolution of cognitive abilities is to re-model conditions in 'pseudo-evolutionary' experiments. This kind of approach has been used, for example, to study the emergence of symbolic communication systems (see Galantucci, 2005, for a recent study). As a way to test the present account, one could create experimental situations that allow one to examine how individuals acting together in ambiguous situations learn to attribute action effects to their source. This would help to capture presumed characteristics of the beginnings of joint action, where through repeated experiences individuals learned that

---

[3] Imitation is here conceptualized as a selective, goal-directed process, and not just a simple re-enactment of observed actions (cf. Bekkering et al., 2000; Wohlschlaeger et al., 2003).

acting alone is different from acting with others. Imagine two participants acting together, neither of them knowing whether (s)he her-/himself, the other, both of them together, or none of them caused a particular action effect. Over time, contingencies between actions and effects could be learned. The present account predicts that individuals would first learn to distinguish between effects resulting from their own actions and effects resulting from joint (simultaneous) action. The action-effect mappings relevant for the other should only be learned at a later stage.

*Cultural predictions*

Finally, if we agree with the idea that the mental self we experience is a cultural construct, it follows that cultural differences in self-awareness should be observed. If the mental self is grounded in a sense of self in action, cultural differences should not only be reflected in different discourses about the self (Prinz, 2003), but should also affect the immediate experience of the self in action. It seems possible that individuals in different cultures would show differences in the experience of mental causation (Wegner, 2003), the perceived timing of actions and effects (Haggard, 2006), and the attribution of action effects to self and other (Georgieff & Jeannerod, 1998; Jeannerod, 2006).

## Conclusions

The study of human cognition used to focus on single individuals responding to stimuli. While this remains a useful approach, there is growing optimism that a more comprehensive understanding of cognition can be achieved by investigating how certain cognitive processes are shaped by social context (Knoblich & Sebanz, 2006; Sebanz et al., 2006).[4] This approach also extends to theorizing about the origins and evolution of certain characteristics of the human mind, including that which seems perhaps most puzzling of all: the awareness of our own and others' mental states. While many just-so stories about the emergence of consciousness could be told based on hypothesized demands of social interactions, the present proposal aimed at identifying conditions that could have provided the origin of a sense of self in action. It was suggested that joint action played a crucial role in the emergence of the experience of agency and the understanding of

---

[4] It should be noted that this approach differs from the current trend of studying the cognitive and neural basis of social phenomena (e.g., Ochsner & Lieberman, 2001) in that it assumes that *any* cognitive process can be shaped by social context.

others' actions as goal-directed. Needless to say, both further theorizing and empirical studies are needed to improve our understanding of the emergence of mental selves. While we are a long way from definite answers, considering social and cultural forces in the phylo- and ontogenetic evolution of the human mind may help us ask the right questions.[5]

## References

Barresi, J. & Moore, C. (1996), 'Intentional relations and social understanding', *Behavioral & Brain Sciences,* **19**, pp. 107–54.

Bayliss, A.P., di Pellegrino, G. & Tipper, S.P. (2004), 'Orienting of attention via observed eye gaze is head-centered', *Cognition,* **94**, pp. B1–B10.

Bayne, T. & Levy, N. (2006), 'The feeling of doing: Deconstructing the phenomenology of agency', in *Disorders of Volition,* ed. N. Sebanz & W. Prinz (Cambridge, MA: MIT Press).

Bekkering, H., *et al.* (2000), 'Imitation is goal-directed', *Quarterly Journal of Experimental Psychology,* **53A**, pp. 153–64.

Bridgeman, B., Lewis, S., Heit, G. & Nagle, M. (1979), 'Relation between cognitive and motor-oriented systems of visual position perception', *Journal of Experimental Psychology: Human Perception and Performance,* **5**, pp. 692–700.

Burns, T. & Engdahl, E. (1998a), 'The social construction of consciousness. Part 1: Collective consciousness and its socio-cultural foundations', *Journal of Consciousness Studies,* **5** (1), pp. 67–85.

Burns, T. & Engdahl, E. (1998b), 'The social construction of consciousness. Part 2: Individual selves, self-awareness, and reflectivity', *Journal of Consciousness Studies,* **5** (2), pp. 166–84.

Call, J. (2001), 'Body imitation in an encultured orangutan', *Cybernetics and Systems,* **32**, pp. 97–119.

Call, J. (2005), 'The self and other: a missing link in comparative social cognition', In *The Missing Link In Cognition. Origins of self-reflective consciousness,* ed. H.S. Terrace & J. Metcalfe (Oxford: Oxford University Press).

Clark, H. (1996), *Using Language* (Cambridge: Cambridge University Press).

Daprati, E., Nico, D., Saimpont, A., Franck, N. & Sirigu, A. (2005), 'Memory and action: an experimental study on normal subjects and schizophrenic patients', *Neuropsychologia,* **43**, pp. 281–93.

Decety, J. & Chaminade, T. (2003), 'When the self represents the other: A new cognitive neuroscience view on psychological identification', *Consciousness and Cognition,* **12**, pp. 577–96.

Emery, N.J. (2000), 'The eyes have it: The neuroethnology, function, and evolution of social gaze', *Neuroscience and Biobehavioral Reviews,* **24**, pp. 581–604.

Flavell, J., Flavell, E. & Green, F. (1995), 'Young children's knowledge about thinking', *Monographs of the Society for Research in Child Development,* **60**.

Frith, C.D. (2002), 'Attention to action and awareness of other minds', *Consciousness and Cognition,* **11**, pp. 481–7.

Frith, C.D. & Frith, U. (1999), 'Interacting minds: a biological basis', *Science,* **286**, pp. 1692–5.

---

[5] I would like to thank Guenther Knoblich for helpful discussions and encouragement. Thanks are also due to Dawn McBride, Sabine Maasen, and one anonymous reviewer for their comments on an earlier draft.

Galantucci, B. (2005), 'An experimental study of the emergence of human communication systems', *Cognitive Science,* **29**, pp. 737–67.
Gallagher, S. (1995), 'Body schema and intentionality', in *The Body and the Self,* ed. J.L. Bermudez & A.J. Anthony (Cambridge, MA: MIT Press).
Gallagher, S. (2000), 'Philosophical conceptions of the self: Implications for cognitive science', *Trends in Cognitive Sciences,* **4**, pp. 14–21.
Georgieff, N. & Jeannerod, M. (1998), 'Beyond consciousness of external reality: A "who" system for consciousness of action and self-consciousness', *Conciousness and Cognition,* **7**, pp. 465–77.
Gopnik, A. & Astington, J. (1988), 'Children's understanding of representational change and its relation to the understanding of false belief and the appearance-relaity distinction', *Child Devleopment,* **59**, pp. 26–57.
Gergely, G., Bekkering, H. & Kiraly, I. (2002), 'Rational imitation of goal-directed actions in 14-month-olds', *Nature,* **415**, p. 755.
Gergely, G. & Csibra, G. (2003), 'Teleological reasoning in infancy: The naive theory of rational action', *Trends in Cognitive Sciences,* **7**, pp. 287–92.
Goodale, M.A., Pélisson, D. & Prablanc, C. (1986), 'Large adjustments in visually guided reaching do not depend on vision of the hand or perception of target displacement', *Nature,* **320**, pp. 748–50.
Haggard, P. (2006), 'Conscious intention and the sense of agency', in *Disorders of Volition,* ed. N. Sebanz & W. Prinz (Cambridge, MA: MIT Press).
Haggard, P. & Eimer, M. (1999), 'On the relation between brain potentials and the awareness of voluntary movements', *Experimental Brain Research,* **126**, pp. 128–33.
Haggard, P., Newman, C. & Magno, E. (1999), 'On the perceived time of voluntary actions', *British Journal of Psychology,* **90**, pp. 291–303.
Happé, F. (2003), 'Theory of mind and the self', *Annals of the New York Academy of Sciences,* **1001**, pp. 134–44.
Hare, B., et al. (2000), 'Chimpanzees know what conspecifics do and do not see', *Animal Behavior,* **59**, pp. 771–85.
Hart, D. & Fegley, S. (1994), 'Social imitation and the emergence of a mental model of self', In *Self-awareness in animals and humans: Developmental perspectives,* ed. S.T. Parker, R.W. Mitchell, & M.L. Boccia (Cambridge: Cambridge University Press).
Hommel, B. (2006), 'How we do what we want: A neuro-cognitive perspective on human action planning', in *Planning In Intelligent Systems: Aspects, motivations and methods,* ed. R.J. Jorna, W. van Wezel & A. Meystel (New York: John Wiley & Sons).
Jaynes, J. (1976), *The Origin of Consciousness In the Breakdown of the Bicameral Mind.* (Boston, MA: Houghton Mifflin).
Jeannerod, M. (2006), 'From volition to agency: The mechanism of action recognition and its failures', in *Disorders of Volition, ed.* N. Sebanz & W. Prinz (Cambridge, MA: MIT Press).
Jordan, S. (2003), 'Emergence of self and other in perception and action: An event-control approach', *Consciousness and Cognition,* **12**, pp. 633–46.
Jordan, J. S. & Knoblich, G. (2004), 'Spatial perception and control', *Psychonomic Bulletin & Review,* **11**, pp. 54–9.
Knoblich, G., Elsner, B., Aschersleben, G. & Metzinger, T. (2003), 'Grounding the self in action', *Consciousness and Cognition,* **12**, pp. 487–94.
Knoblich, G. & Jordan, S. (2003), 'Action coordination in groups and individuals: Learning anticipatory control', *Journal of Experimental Psychology: Learnning, Memory, and Cognition,* **29**, pp. 1006–16.

Knoblich, G. & Sebanz, N. (2005), 'Agency in the face of error', *Trends in Cognitive Sciences,* **9**, pp. 259–60.

Knoblich, G. & Sebanz, N. (2006), 'The social nature of perception and action', *Current Directions in Psychological Science*, **15**, pp. 99–104.

Lewis, M. (1994), 'Myself and me', in *Self-awareness in Animals and Humans: Developmental perspectives*, ed. S.T. Parker, R.W. Mitchell, & M.L. Boccia (Cambridge: Cambridge University Press).

Libet, B., Gleason, C.A., Writh, E.W. & Pearl, D.K. (1983), 'Time of conscious intention to act in relation to onset of cerebral activity (readiness potential): The unconscious initiation of a freely voluntary act', *Brain,* **106**, pp. 623–42.

Mead, G.H. (1956), *George Herbert Mead on Social Psychology.* Edited by Anselm Strauss. (Chicago: University of Chicago Press).

Metcalfe, J. & Kober, H. (2005), 'Self-reflective consciousness and the projectable self', in *The Missing Link In Cognition: Origins of self-reflective consciousness*, ed. H.S. Terrace & J. Metcalfe (Oxford University Press).

Milner, A.D. & Goodale, M.A. (1995), *The Visual Brain In Action* (Oxford University Press).

Mitchell, R.W. (1993), 'Mental models of mirror self-recognition: Two theories', *New Ideas in Psychology,* **11**, pp. 295–325.

Moore, C. & Dunham, P. J. (ed. 1995), *Joint Attention: its origin and role in development*. (Hove: Lawrence Erlbaum).

Neisser, U. (1988), 'Five-kinds of self-knowledge', *Philosophical Psychology*, **1**, pp. 35–59.

Ochsner, K.N. & Lieberman, M.D. (2001), 'The emergence of social cognitive neuroscience', *American Psychologist,* **56**, pp. 717–34.

Pacherie, E. (2006), 'Towards a dynamic theory of intentions', in *Does Consciousness Cause Behavior? An Investigation of the Nature of Volition*, ed. S.Pockett, W. P. Banks & S. Gallagher (Cambridge, MA: MIT Press).

Parker, S.T. & Milbrath, C. (1994), 'Contributions of imitation and role-playing games to the construction of self in primates', in *Self-awareness in Animals and Humans: Developmental perspectives*, ed. S. T. Parker, R. W. Mitchell & M. L. Boccia (Cambridge: Cambridge University Press).

Pisella, L. *et al.* (2000), 'An "automatic pilot" for the hand in human posterior parietal cortex: Toward reinterpreting optic ataxia', *Nature Neuroscience,* **3**, pp. 729–36.

Prinz, W. (2003), 'Emerging selves: Representational foundations for subjectivity', *Consciousness and Cognition,* **12**, pp. 515–28.

Prinz, W., Dennett, D. & Sebanz, N. (2006), 'Towards a science of volition', in *Disorders of Volition,* ed. N. Sebanz & W. Prinz (Cambridge, MA: MIT Press).

Roepstorff, A. & Frith, C. (2004), 'What's at the top in the top-down control of action? Script-sharing and "top-top" control of action in cognitive experiments', *Psychological Research,* **68**, pp. 189–98.

Sebanz, N., Bekkering, H. & Knoblich, G. (2006), 'Joint action: Bodies and minds moving together', *Trends in Cognitive Sciences,* **10**, pp. 70–6.

Sebanz, N., Knoblich, G., Stumpf, L. & Prinz, W. (2005), 'Far from action blind: Representation of others' actions in individuals with autism', *Cognitive Neuropsychology,* **22**, pp. 433–54.

Tollefsen, D. (2005), 'Let's pretend! Children and joint action', *Philosophy of the Social Sciences,* **35**, pp. 75–97.

Tomasello, M. (2000), 'Culture and cognitive development', *Current Directions in Psychological Science,* **9**, pp. 37–40.

Tuomela, R. (1995), *The Importance of Us: A philosophical study of basic social notions* (Stanford, CA: Stanford University Press).

Wegner, D.M. (2002), *The Illusion of Conscious Will* (Cambridge, MA: MIT Press).
Wegner, D.M., Fuller, V.A. & Sparrow, B. (2003), 'Clever hands: Uncontrolled intelligence in facilitated communication', *Journal of Personality and Social Psychology*, **85**, pp. 5–19.
Wegner D.M. & Wheatley, T. (1999), 'Apparent mental causation: Sources of the experience of will', *American Psychologist,* **54**, pp. 480–92.
Wilson, M. & Knoblich, G. (2005), 'The case for motor involvement in perceiving conspecifics', *Psychological Bulletin,* **131**, pp. 460–73.
Wohlschläger, A. *et al.* (2003), 'Action generation and action perception in imitation: An instance of the ideomotor principle', *Philosophical Transactions of the Royal Society London,* **358**, pp. 501–16.

Sabine Maasen

# *Selves in Turmoil*
## Neurocognitive and Societal Challenges of the Self

*Abstract*: As the cognitive neurosciences set out to challenge our understanding of consciousness, the existing conceptual panoply of meanings attached to the term remains largely unaccounted for. By way of bibliometric analysis, the following study first reveals the breadth and shift of meanings over the last decades, the main tendency being a more 'brainy' concept of consciousness. On this basis, the emergence of consciousness studies is regarded as a 'trading zone' (Galison) in which experimental, philosophical and experiential accounts are dialectically engaged. Outside of academic discourse, a neurocognitive concept of consciousness is embraced by popular self-help literature that sweepingly adopts this new discourse and the novel neuropharmacological tools in the self-help toolbox. Consciousness studies are hence not only the product of epistemological and methodological struggles (scientific dimension) but also part of the current re-alignments regarding the notion of consciously acting selves in society (societal dimension).

The self, the conscious, volitional individual and its agency have come under attack — and not for the first time. About twenty years ago, postmodernists had already declared the death of the subject. In their view, the self is a fiction invented *post hoc*. Rather than acting on the basis of 'own' intentions, motives or habits, the subject came to be thought of as driven by relations of power and knowledge. To postmodernists, these intentions, motives or habits are not the source of a pure and self-conscious individuality but result from subconscious desires and discourses external to the self.

Although this debate has not been resolved, other issues such as agency and empowerment (or lack thereof) have become more prevalent concerns. These deliberations rest on the assumption that the self, the acting and reflecting self, *needs* to be more than just a crossing of desires and discourses. At least, the self is said to have, and indeed, cultivate, a capacity to reflect upon inner and outer conditions for his or her actions, rather than being fully determined by these conditions. To this end, all kinds of educational, therapeutic and self-instructing practices emerged, indicating the belief that the self can be *advised* to determine his or her own actions, albeit within the limits of, e.g., physical or social constraints.

However, as social practice arrives at this kind of position, another challenge occurs: This time, the self, the conscious, volitional individual and its agency are being attacked by the neuro-cognitive 'front'. In its view, the self is a fiction invented by the brain. Consciousness and volitional decision-making are but recollections of something already accomplished by the brain. Accordingly, neuroscientific findings claim the concepts of self, consciousness, and will to be scientifically untenable, specifying that it is our brain rather than our 'self' who decides what we want, what we do, and who it is who says 'I'.

On this basis, consciousness has become the focus of a concerted *scientific* effort. Inspired by the 'cognitive turn' in psychology, the 'decade of the brain', and the institutionalization of the 'cognitive sciences', neurobiologists, cognitive psychologists and cognitively-inclined philosophers counter our intuitions about what consciousness is, challenging this 'inner feel' accompanying perception, reflection, and action. They insist on consciousness being nothing but the name for the interplay of various regions in the brain upon which cognitive functions operate. Talking about experiential aspects of consciousness is relegated to folk psychological wisdom. Now that heuristics, techniques, and instruments are available, the 'issues proper,' that is, the neural correlates of consciousness can and should be addressed. The self is fully determined by the brain.

Yet, the skeptics are not convinced. Are we indeed, and do we simply act upon, an assembly of neurons and cognitive functions? Most philosophers keep reminding the neuroscientists that we are still discussing the 'mind-body problem', hence, an age-old paradox: While we believe ourselves to be physical beings, we also believe that we are conscious beings whose awareness of physical beings cannot be physical. It thus appears that we are both physical and non-physical. The problem is, how do the physical and non-physical relate?

In view of all these tensions regarding the relation of consciousness and selves, efforts emerge that try to assemble the different factions. Most prominently, the *Journal of Consciousness Studies* (JCS) set out to convene the heterogeneous community of scholars studying consciousness and, hence, to establish a field called consciousness studies. It calls for both *ontological rapprochement* between physicalists and phenomenalists, as well as for *epistemological reconsiderations* in order to overcome the fruitless opposition between reductionist and dualist accounts. Only then, thus the JCS, may we hope to solve what has been termed the 'hard problem' of consciousness.[1] As yet, the effort has resulted in a lively and multifaceted, yet not particularly interactive discourse (Maasen, 2003).

From a sociology-of-science point of view, however, the current moves, although partly ignorant of, partly antagonistic to each other, testify to the emergence of a field of consciousness studies. Indeed, the heterogeneity of epistemologies, methodologies, theories, and questions are not detrimental to but rather constitutive of any science discipline. Moreover, such heterogeneity is not only restricted to early stages of field formation (Kuhn, 1962) but characterizes most fields at most stages. In the words of Peter Galison, 'science is disunified, and — against our first intuitions — it is precisely the *dis*unification of science that underpins its strength and stability' (Galison, 1997, p. 137). Far more important than unity is *discursiveness*: Occasions and platforms for debating controversial issues constitute so-called trading zones.

> Indeed, far from melting into a homogeneous entity, different groups often maintain their distinctness, whether they are ... theorists and engineers, or theorists and experimenters. The point is that these distinct groups, with their different approaches to instruments and their characteristic forms or argumentation, can nonetheless coordinate their approaches (Galison, 1997, pp 805f.).

The issue of consciousness, thus my argument, already has become such a trading zone — a heterogeneous field of e.g., experimental, genetic, neurobiological study as well as of philosophical, historical, political or literary deliberation. Moreover, the field of consciousness

---

[1] This refers to a distinction of 'hard' and 'easy' problems in the study of consciousness introduced by David Chalmers in 1996: The easy problems refer to the empirical concerns of the cognitive neurosciences and their investigation of the cognitive and behavioural functions of consciousness. The hard problem is about the question of how any physical system could give rise to experience, to first-person perspective. While easy problems (such as reportability of mental states, the focus of attention, the control of behaviour) can be approached scientifically, the hard problem, namely the problem of subjective experience, resists scientific explanation.

studies ultimately concerns itself with *selves*: While we already knew ourselves as being determined by many factors, be they, e.g., genetic, political, psychic or historical, today we come to see ourselves as neurological beings as well whose consciousness cannot be based on experiential factors alone — if at all.

Yet, this lesson does not hit us unprepared as will be demonstrated with a seemingly unrelated phenomenon, the recent fad for self-help: Other than humanistic approaches that encouraged us to search for our 'true self' by 'raising our consciousness', self-help today is all about 'managing oneself,' and consciousness is seen as either a vehicle of self-monitoring or as a target of psychological or pharmacological treatment. This pragmatic view of our consciousness is not so much about liberation from social or other constraints but rather about rendering them conscious, thus amenable to rational transformation. Recently, enlightened by the neuroscience of consciousness, the self-managing individual operates not only upon psychic and social but also upon an enriched concept of somatic factors that can and should be taken into account – consciously, that is. In the course of this happening, individuals are becoming more 'brainy' selves. Yet, contrary to neuroscientists' assumptions, the general discourse is hardly shocked by this development but responds in a mixed way: There is evidence for *both* a pragmatic approach to self-shaping by 'neuroceutics' (Novas & Rose, 2000) as well as for a rebirth of (neurobiological) essentialism and reductionism in everyday discourse.

Before detailing this issue, I will first look at the scientific landscape of knowledge about consciousness. This view from within will briefly look at some bibliometric data, at how the challenges for the main disciplines involved are reflected in reviews and at the state of the discourse as evidenced by the JCS. The view will then be confronted with recent societal practices (self-help, neuroceutics), the tentative conclusion being that the making of consciousness studies occurs not only in the midst of ongoing scientific, philosophical and experiential controversy but also in the midst of current societal practice and ethical deliberation of (consciously) shaping one's consciousness. Consciousness has become an object of 'trading' meanings – scientific and social ones. In the course of this happening, *both* academic controversies and societal practices have paved the way for a more neurocognitively inclined understanding of consciousness.

## On Method(ology): Metaphors of Consciousness / Consciousness as Metaphor

From a sociology-of-knowledge point of view, 'consciousness' is but a piece of knowledge circulating in society. Consciousness does not 'belong' to any special discourse, neither to philosophy, to psychology, nor to the forefront of brain research. Rather, it occurs in various contexts, thereby assuming various meanings, partly ignoring each other, partly interacting, and partly competing. A sociology-of-knowledge approach seeks to reveal these multi-discursive constructions of terms or concepts.

Yet, how should those selective processes and largely incremental turns in the re-making of consciousness be shown? To this end, the following study employs a method called metaphor analysis, the idea being that, by way of interacting with novel contexts, consciousness assumes ever-new meanings. Seen this way, consciousness acts *like* a metaphor: A metaphor is a term or phrase that is somewhat unfamiliar with respect to its poetic context. Both unfamiliar phrase and poetic context need to interact, thereby producing an innovative reading in order to 'make sense' (Black, 1962). Likewise, consciousness, formerly to be found in non-scientific contexts only, comes to be applied in various scientific fields: Interacting with them, it undergoes shifts in meaning and use.[2]

It has frequently been noted that theories of consciousness abound with metaphors in order to gain access to an ever-elusive concept. Among many other things, consciousness has been likened to a spotlight, a recursive loop, a stage; the specific quality of consciousness has been described as a state, an act, input or output, as a unity, a diversity, or a *unitas multiplex* (Bruner & Fleisher Feldman, 1990, p. 230). Regarding the neurosciences, it has been suggested that 'theatres' exist in the brain to allow numerous convergent influences to shape a coherent performance on stage (Damasio, 1989). However, the theatre metaphor — as any metaphor — has met with criticism as well: Dennett and Kinsbourne, for instance, deem it Cartesian and thus misleading (Dennett & Kinsbourne, 1992).

---

[2] Since antiquity, the term metaphor has denoted the transfer of a concept endowed with a meaning derived from a specific context to another context, where it unfolds its 'transferred' meaning. The assumption is that the transferred familiar concept interacts with a new, unfamiliar context and produces shifts of meaning that cannot be sufficiently controlled. This conception follows the 'interaction view of metaphor' introduced by Max Black and elaborated by Mary Hesse (Black, 1962; Hesse, 1972; 1974). This model underscores both the *pragmatic* and the *semantic* aspects of metaphorization: the unusual usage of a construct (cf. Davidson 1981) produces a creative tension that may result in a *cognitive surplus* (cf. Hesse, 1974).

Indeed, by confronting consciousness with various metaphors, some of its aspects, functions, and modes of operation have been highlighted, whereas others have been shaded, or have turned out to be neutral (Hesse, 1972; 1974). Every new metaphor provokes new ideas as well as criticism. Whatever consciousness is supposed to mean at a given point in time is the result of an interaction of the discourses involved in explaining the concept with their preferred set of vocabulary, methods, and theories. And this means change: True to its Greek origin, a metaphor is about transferring and shifting meanings.

Seen this way, metaphors function as sites and media of knowledge transfer (Bono, 1990). In the following, instead of analysing *metaphors of consciousness* I suggest to treat *consciousness itself as a metaphor*. Rather than going into the details of this approach called metaphor analysis,[3] I will pinpoint its basic methodical procedure: first, one follows the term consciousness to those discourses in which it happens to occur, looks for the ways in which it interacts with these discourses, thereby trying to trace the meanings resulting from these interactions. One example: If an already established discourse (cognitive psychology) selects for a certain metaphor ('consciousness'), it necessarily varies the meaning of consciousness by interpreting it discourse-specifically (e.g., in terms of information processing), and perhaps it retains this new meaning.

As to the analytical procedure, these are steps to take:

- Step one: 'Pick one!' — I pick 'conscious/ness'.

- Step two: 'Draw a discursive map!' and: 'Reconstruct a discursive calendar!' With the aid of bibliometric methods I follow the term or concept chosen through all scientific and philosophical discourses in which it appears. The results of this step provide a fair approximation as to the when and where of the metaphor in question.

- Step three: 'Discourse analysis!' Here I select a set of publications that seems most productive and enlightening with regard to the dynamics of consciousness. Discourse-by-discourse, I look for specific interaction with the term and try to confront it with literature commenting on the history and/or systematics of any discursive developments (e.g., reviews).

- Step four: 'Local specificity — global significance?' Do the specific shades of meaning converge on a heterogeneous topic (be it an issue, a paradigm, a world view, ...)? Can we see a

[3] Cf. Maasen & Weingart (2000).

challenge or a factual change in the dominant perception of consciousness and the meaning of 'self' attached to it?

## On Method: A bibliometric sketch

Stating that consciousness is not a single phenomenon today borders on a truism (Chalmers 1996, p. 7). On a very general level, one can isolate a social aspect of the term, that is, joint knowledge shared by a community of people (e.g., Marxist, feminist consciousness) and a mental sense.[4] The latter can be subdivided into the notion of a state concomitant of all thought, feeling, and volition (transitive: conscious of), or as the normal condition of a healthy waking life (intransitive). However, a look at the most comprehensive data-bases (the ISI: Science Citation Index/SCI and Social Science Citation Index/SSCI) reveals a far more detailed picture, as it lists journal articles encompassing a broad range of disciplines over some 50 years:

- How often do the terms 'conscious' and 'consciousness' appear in titles of articles?
- What is the range of disciplines covered by these articles? Does the attention shift from one set of disciplines to another?
- What are the themes associated with consciousness?

At this stage of analysis, the occurrences indicate when, how often, and in which disciplines authors deal with the subject. By way of illustration, I will focus on a few results only.

***Absolute and relative occurrences.*** In a first step, I investigate the absolute and relative occurrence of the terms 'conscious/ness' during a 50 years period (1955/6–2004). Looking at the publications in absolute numbers, the SCI reveals an increase by a factor of two (1956: 206 → 2004: 423) and the SSCI an increase by a factor of 1.5, although on a lower level (1974: 156 → 2004: 221).

The relative frequency of publications paints a different picture: In the natural sciences it remains at about 0.5‰, after a peak of about 0.9‰ in the mid-1980s. In the social sciences index, the data show an increase (1974: 1.30‰ → 2004: 1.67‰), after a peak in 1992 (2.11‰).

---

[4] Note also that '... an expression initially metaphoric may become literal (a 'dead' metaphor), and what is at one time literal may become metaphoric' (Hesse, 1972, p. 253) — this dynamic also accounts for homonyms that may occur over time (e.g., 'feminist consciousness'): On the approach favoured in this paper, one *first* has to acknowledge the variety of meanings attached to the term under analysis over a given period of time, and *only then* try to make sense of the landscape of knowledge emanating from it, a homonym being an element of that landscape.

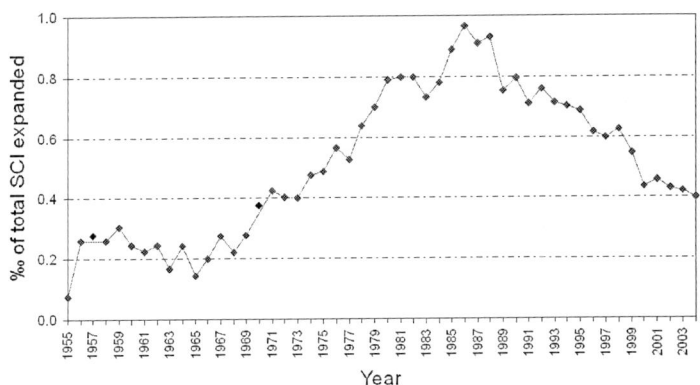

*Figure 1.* Relative frequency of 'consciousness' publications 1955–2004 (SCI)

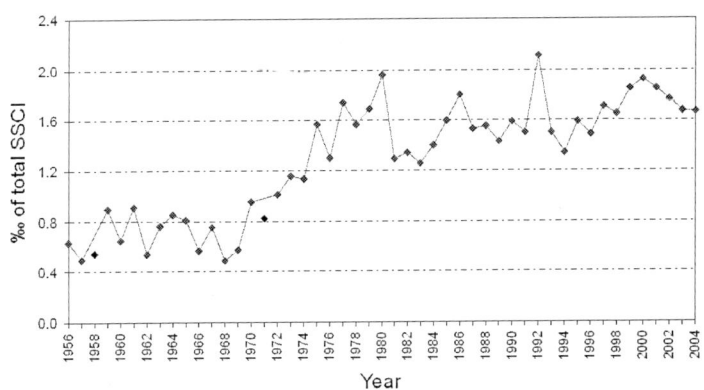

*Figure 2.* Relative frequency of 'consciousness' publications 1956–2004 (SCCI)

*Fields.* Focusing on three selected periods of time (1982–1984, 1992–1994, 2002–2004), the question is which *disciplines* or *fields* participate in research activities on conscious/ness?

In the SCI, the neurosciences, which had been of minor importance in the early eighties, have become the most important field dealing with conscious/ness, followed by pharmacology & pharmacy and physiology. Biology, including cell biology, covers middle ground. In the SSCI, the leading field throughout the years is psychology, ranging from 14.3% (1982–84) to 63.8% (1992–94) and 76.8% in 2002–04: While this includes sub-fields such as clinical, developmental, and social psychology, there is a noticeable increase in experimental psychology dealing with conscious/ness (1982-84: none; 1992-94: 12.5%; 2002-04: 19.9%).

Complementarily, philosophy and the social sciences show a decrease in articles on consciousness (SSCI). To sum up: Throughout these years, the academic occupation with consciousness becomes more experimental, more cognitive, more 'neuro', and, most of all, more pharmacological.

**Journals.** These findings mentioned above are corroborated by the journals containing pertinent articles. The leading journals deal with physiology and pharmacology (*British Journal of Pharmacology*, *Circulation*), followed by the neurosciences (*Brain Research*, *Neurophysiology*).

As for social scientific articles on conscious/ness, they are scattered over a broad spectrum of different journals that publish one or two articles at most. Since 1990, a few journals have been founded which bring together philosophical and psychological concerns with conscious/ness (*Journal of Mind and Behavior*) or which try to establish even broader interdisciplinary perspectives, most explicitly, the *Journal of Consciousness Studies*.

**Titles/themes.** Based on the lists of full-length titles for the three periods of time, the analysis yields the following general results:

- In *anthropology, sociology*, and *law,* the term 'consciousness' is regularly connected to certain groups or strata, such as class, ethnic group, or gender. It is a political, historical, or moral/religious concept: e.g., national consciousness, or Jewish consciousness. Finally, the term refers to specific practices and technologies: For example, sorcery as a practice of consciousness, or the technocratic consciousness.

- In *philosophy* we find the accounts of metaphors on consciousness used by various philosophers throughout the centuries (Descartes, Hobbes, Kant, Husserl, Heidegger, Hegel, ...). Moreover, a number of articles, published in 1978, deal with political topics, such as social structure and consciousness, predominantly Marxist accounts, that is. Alongside some esoteric listings, one also finds a slightly increasing number of articles dealing with 'machine consciousness' as well as with neuro/evolutionary topics, such as 'consciousness & the brain.'

- In *psychology* the titles can be attributed to various fields of studies, too. One group is concerned with social science/psychology and deals with questions of identity formation, self-constitution, self-perception, and self-regulation. Another group addresses various states of consciousness, such as multiple/divided/altered states (sometimes discussing therapeutic interventions), as well as consciousness while sleeping, in coma, or under hypnosis.

- In the *neurosciences*, the situation seems less diverse. A notable group of titles refers to studies on patients in coma, that is, in non-conscious states. Another group discusses altered states of consciousness (pathologies, drugs, etc.). Various titles focus on the issue of attention, awareness, and alertness. In rare instances, we also find the question whether conscious experience (qualia!) can affect brain activity.

All indicators considered signal the prevalence of pharmacological studies and the beginning of a trend toward a more *scientific*, especially more *cognitive* and more *neuro-scientific* approach to consciousness. While political, moral, philosophical, educational notions are present as well, they are concerned with different issues, mostly pertaining to collective representations. Consciousness studies are thus characterized by a clear division between scientific accounts and 'other approaches.'

This result is also reflected in reports from within, that is, from those who now form the inner circle of consciousness studies, i.e., the neurosciences, cognitive psychology, and philosophy. As I will show, their answers differ: While neuroscientists have simply conquered novel territory without further ado, cognitive psychologists have had to re-acknowledge consciousness as an object of scientific inquiry, and philosophers have had to face the risk of being used on a case-by-case basis, rather than systematically informing the experimental results or research.

## On Scientific Approaches to Consciousness: Views From Within

*Making claims on 'consciousness': Neuroscience*

Already in the year 2001, a review in the realm of the neurosciences is plainly entitled 'consciousness' (Zeman, 2001). This title is a statement: The review tells us what does reside within the confines of consciousness research today according to a neuroscientist. The answer is: Consciousness is investigated by the *science of wakefulness* and the *science of awareness*. While the science of wakefulness inquires into the associated neural, behavioural, and psychological functions and their control systems, the science of awareness predominantly rests on the study of the visual system in animals and man and searches for increasingly fine-grained correlations between cerebral activity and experience, namely in the areas of (visual) perception, memory, and action.

The dominant approaches include neurobiological theories dealing with the neural correlates of consciousness and information processing theories dealing with mechanisms directing our waking behaviour. When it comes to the relationship between conscious and neural events that each single theory postulates, Zeman refers to three different ones:

- *Identity theories* hold that neural events are identical to the corresponding conscious events. They offer a reductionist and materialist, or physicalist solution to the mind-body problem.

- *Functionalist theories* conceive of our experience as a series of judgements made in response to sensory information. This approach, too, does not take qualitative properties of consciousness into consideration.

- *Dualist theories* concede a close relationship between neural and conscious events, yet consider them to be fundamentally distinct classes of phenomena that require a set of psychophysical laws describing *the relationship between* conscious and neural events.

Zeman concludes: 'Future work in philosophy and science may change the ways in which we think about consciousness so radically that its reduction to physical processes begins to look plausible. For the time being we have no alternative but to use all three vocabularies of biology, behavior and experience to understand the mind' (Zeman, 2001, p. 1284). These 'vocabularies' assume the role of a heuristics eventually leading to a brain-based explanation of consciousness.

This view from within confirms the view from outside: There is a marked shift in reasoning about consciousness, that merely grants philosophy a commenting role and largely excludes the social sciences.

*Rediscovering/reclaiming consciousness:*
*Psychology and philosophy*

Psychology and philosophy are well prepared to meet the neuroscientific challenge. To begin with, psychology has a notable history concerning the question whether or not to study consciousness at all. While at the beginning of the century 'introspectionism' looked for the atomic table of the human mind, albeit in vain, behaviourism relegated consciousness into the black box. Only with the advent of cognitive psychology in the seventies, consciousness became a kind of component or aspect of information processing models, thereby regaining scientific status. The idea 'was that the basic phenomenological concept — consciousness — can be mapped onto the information-processing concept' (Shallice, 1972, p. 383).

Another aspect of reframing consciousness was connected to psychology's rediscovery of the *un*conscious- the *cognitive* unconscious. Its existence is due to the way our perceptual/cognitive system is constituted and is, in principle, inaccessible. On these grounds, various dichotomies have been proposed: '...unconscious vs. conscious, ... automatic vs. controlled, reflexive vs. reflective, and many others' (Holyoak & Spellman, 1993, p. 265). Thus, as far as cognitive psychology is concerned, consciousness has regained the status of a scientific object and is currently being investigated by various strands of study: It finds itself re-framed by an impressive number of dual conceptions, leaving the self as something largely ruled by automatic and unconscious processes. Only in the case of corrective behaviour do we find control and reflexivity.

Today, neuroscientific findings alert cognitive psychologists to the fact that their long-standing history of producing knowledge about consciousness contributes a rich inventory of theories and experimental designs that complements and, indeed, informs neuroscientific data. On these grounds, some authors call for closer cooperation between both fields (e.g., Prinz & Singer, 2005).

Philosophy is also characterized by a long-standing occupation with consciousness. The positions vary widely. Rather than repeating the main stances above-mentioned, I will refer to but one, most provocative, comment on the current situation. According to Yanina Shapiro, both psychologists and philosophers are guilty of producing eclectic forms of interdisciplinarity. Shapiro's basic critique is that scientists, as yet, have only bits and pieces of scientific facts pertaining to the brain. They glue them together with just the kind of philosophy that seems right to them, whereas the philosophers, in turn, select neurobiological and cognitive facts as they need them. Embracing the scientific study of consciousness, she accuses the field as a whole of a 'quilt-a-theory' approach (Shapiro, 1997). In this perspective, controversy and disunity within consciousness studies is bound to continue not only due to differences among the disciplines involved but also, given the premature state of neuroscientific knowledge, due to the different types of interdisciplinarity advanced by both philosophy and psychology.

Summarizing: Given the views from within, consciousness studies seems to be in a pre-paradigmatic state, notably due to the ongoing struggle among and between the accredited disciplines (neuroscience, cognitive psychology, philosophy) about the right questions to ask and to determine whether or not to be a science (Kuhn, 1962). It 'trades' highly controversial notions about consciousness.

## *JCS*: An exercise in Extending & Integrating the Debate on Consciousness

The *Journal of Consciousness Studies*, introduced in 1994, explicitly calls for *ontological rapprochement* between physicalists and phenomenalists. A brief sketch of themes and approaches covered in JCS will show that it thus provides what Galison has termed a trading zone.

### Themes and approaches in JCS

Looking at the first 4 volumes of the JCS, the big issues are the 'hard problem', 'Zombies', neuroscience of consciousness, quantum theories of consciousness, the self. Another bias is toward the basic cognitive functions on which consciousness operates, such as perception, memory, and awareness. Moreover, various articles and issues draw connections between cognitive processes and mysticism. Special issues address empathy, morality, and art. Numerous single articles concern themselves with the epistemological foundations of consciousness research, with social, emotional, and corporeal aspects of consciousness and a variety of specific problems (e.g., consciousness in plants, poetry, politics and psychoanalysis).

Not surprisingly, the concept of the self is a prominent one. The variety of responses to the problem of self includes assertions that there is no self; that the idea is a logical, psychological, or grammatical fiction; that the sense of self is properly understood and defined in terms of brain processes, that it is the centre of personal and public narratives, or that it is an ineffable category all of its own. Approaches involve philosophy, psychology, neuroscience, theories of embodiment, and artificial intelligence, trying to explore, and, at times, relate various ideas: Is the self enduring or not, a computer model, a neural or linguistic entity, a social phenomenon? (Gallagher & Shear, 1997).

Two things are lacking, however: First, with one exception (Güzeldere, 1995 a,b), there is no paper that gives a general overview of consciousness studies. Second, the *social* foundation of consciousness is only explicitly addressed on two occasions (Burns & Engdahl, 1998 a,b). That is to say, neither consciousness nor the self are the subject of *one all-encompassing account*. Rather, they are the subject matter of various *specific interdisciplinarities*. The most active interdisciplinary level is delineated by those discourses that engage themselves with the neuro, cognitive, and experimental. On a less active level, the experiential account talks back (uniting phenomenologists, mystics, art theorists, and deconstructivists).

## Consciousnesses: The Novel Landscape

The general picture thus is one of consciousness comprising a variety of phenomena and consciousness studies being a disunited enterprise, albeit consisting of discernable clusters:

- The cognitive and neurosciences have mainly approached consciousness in two ways; first, by denying its experiential aspect, and second, by exploring higher levels of complex electrophysiological and bioelectrical phenomena in the brain that would exhaustively explain the brainy bases of consciousness (i.e., including its experiential aspects).

- Philosophy has responded in a split fashion, too. While a considerable number of philosophers have continued to work on standard issues (e.g., reconstructions of classical accounts), others have responded to the cognitive and neuroscientific challenge, either affirmatively or critically with regard to the different claims offered.

- Transpersonalists of various branches (religious, meditative, psychedelic) have insisted on the experiential aspect of consciousness. In some instances, they have even denied that experiences of 'Pure Consciousness' can be studied scientifically. Others, however, have pleaded in favour of the integration of the 'experiential experts' (e.g., long-term meditators) within the scientific study of consciousness, so as to grasp the neural correlates of such states.

- Social scientists have not denied the experiential aspect of consciousness, yet have emphasized that both contents and feelings associated with consciousness are socially co-constituted. While consciousness operates on brains, cognition, and individuals, it is a fundamental social phenomenon.

The many 'consciousnesses' thus emerging do not leave our (everyday-) concepts of selves unaffected. They become increasingly more 'brainy'. In the course of this happening, a more neuroscientific approach to self, consciousness and free will gain plausibility.

## Managing Consciousness in Neurosociety

This development, however, does not take place in the ivory tower of academic discourse alone but rather in the midst of (post-) modern societies in which the consciously acting self is taking centre stage. Current Western societies are not only highly individualistic, they are also regarded as highly differentiated, thus demanding and risky. Accordingly, modern selves need to sort out desires and demands, representing internal and external constraints for shaping decisions on what to do. More often than not, these constraints are manifold, if not contradictory, and have to be balanced. The flip-side of the coin named reasoned choice is continuous monitoring of oneself and others. In fact, neoliberal societies increasingly rely on this capacity of conscious self-regulation that, as I will briefly elaborate, recently has become more 'brainy' as well.

As the call for pervasive self-regulation is not easy to follow, we get help from a host of more or less rationalized programs that teach us how to govern ourselves. One such program is called self-management. Countless books, brochures, seminars, and coaching-letters are at our disposal. They address individuals (e.g., housewives, students) and institutions (e.g., firms, administrations). We are surrounded by a culture of efficiency and efficiency-enhancing procedures, all of which are more or less visibly connected to the conscious effort of working on oneself.

Most interestingly, one observes a split usage regarding the concept of consciousness in current self-management practices: On the one hand, 'becoming conscious of something' is treated as prime vehicle of self-monitoring. In order to enhance individual efficiency, the manuals make use of all techniques known in psychology and other domains of thought to monitor and educate oneself, hence to become conscious of one's behavioural patterns and options for changing them: questionnaires, tests, check lists and exercises to relax. Here, consciousness is treated and used in its *experiential dimension*. On the other hand, consciousness is treated in its *material, neurocognitive dimension* as there is a strong tendency to perform another type of self-shaping: The best selling drugs these days are not those that treat acute illnesses, but those that are prescribed chronically — Premarin, Prozac, Viagra. The power to reshape life, including one's states of consciousness, seems to extend way beyond what we previously understood as illness. Drugs for 'panic disorder', for instance (e.g., Alazopram) are, in fact, rewriting the norms of what it should feel to be a normal self, capable of effective social interaction. Thus, pharmacological intervention redefines what is amenable to correction or modification, i.e., amenable to shaping one's self by conscious use of drugs altering one's state of consciousness. In these practices, experiential and neurocognitive dimensions coalesce. As Rose maintains, these practices are not so much about widening the net of pathology. Instead, 'we are seeing an enhancement in our capacities to adjust and readjust our somatic existence according to the exigencies of the life we wish to aspire' — and the self we wish (others) to be (Rose, 2004). Indeed, people begin to call for a human brainome project and take an interest in the idea of neuroenhancement, or cosmetic neurology (Chatterjee, 2004).

Accordingly, the scientific *and* the general discourse converge on a more brainy concept of the self. While one could have suspected a deep-seated distrust concerning drug intervention into one's states of consciousness, this is not the case. Rather, pharmacological intervention, in particular, aligns with a neoliberal regime of individuals who *have* to govern themselves and who do this via self-management practices of various kinds. Neuroceutics are a new 'tool in the tool-box.' Supported by broad media coverage (Maasen, 2006) and extended marketing campaigns, the neuroscientific image of a neurochemical self gains acceptability.

Acceptability, however, comes in various fashions and degrees. A recent study on how the media shape the social understanding of the 'neuronal aspects' of our reality revealed three rather uncritical variants: neuro-realism, neuro-essentialism and neuro-policy (Racine *et al.*, 2005, pp. 159ff.) Based on the press coverage of the fMRI technology, the authors found proof for neuro-realism in that fMRI investigations were uncritically presented as validation or invalidation of our ordinary view of the world. Neuro-essentialism could be detected in the ways in which fMRI research is depicted as equating subjectivity and personal identity to the brain, implicitly, using the brain simply as a shortcut for 'person', 'individual', 'self'. Finally, there are attempts to use fMRI results to promote neuro-politics: In this vein, some neuroscience is extending to new areas of social concern (e.g., education) and, accordingly, neuroscientists are being tapped for advice in policy development. Given these types of reaction, among others, professionals become wary of possible risks and call for a 'neuroethics' in order to grasp the (alleged) specific problems of neuroscientific findings for individuals as well as for society at large (cf. *American Journal of Bioethics*, 5, 2005).

As the field of neurocognitively-inclined consciousness studies is emerging, the society, already prepared by way of consciousness-shaping practices of various kinds, readily adapts to its findings, promises and horrors — this happens pro-actively by looking and longing for help *and* by way of deliberating its risks. Yet again, ambivalent responses to a brainy concept of consciousness are not detrimental to but promote (a conscious!) societal discourse about risks and chances entailed in these new strands of research. Recently, citizens' juries deliberating on this matter indicate a heightened social awareness of the impact that brain research, in particular, may have for all of us (see 'Meeting of Minds,' 2005). Consciousness studies are hence not only the product of epistemological and methodological struggles (*scientific dimension*) but also part of the current realignments regarding the notion of consciously acting selves in society (*societal dimension*). Both dimensions are likely to stabilize an ever-evolving new field named consciousness studies for quite a while.[5]

## References

Black, M. (1962), *Models and Metaphors: Studies in Language and Philosophy* (Ithaca, NY: Cornell University Press).

Bono, J.J. (1990), 'Science, discourse, and literature: The role/rule of metaphor in science', Stuart Peterfreund, ed., *Literature and science: Theory and practice* (Boston, MA: Northeastern University Press), pp. 59–89.

Bruner, J.S. & Fleisher Feldmann, C. (1990), 'Metaphor of consciousness and cognition in the history of psychology', David E. Leary (ed.), *Metaphors in the History of Psychology* (Cambridge: Cambridge University Press), pp. 230–8.

---

[5] I am grateful for helpful comments by J. Scott Jordan, Dawn McBride, and two unknown reviewers.

Burns, T. & Engdahl, E. (1998a), 'The social construction of consciousness. Part 1: Collective consciousness and its socio-cultural foundations', *Journal of Consciousness Studies,* **5** (1), pp. 67–85.
Burns, T. & Engdahl, E. (1998b), 'The social construction of consciousness. Part 2: Individual selves, self-awareness and reflectivity', *Journal of Consciousness Studies,* **5** (2), pp. 166–84.
Chalmers, D.J. (1996), *The Conscious Mind: In Search of a Fundamental Theory* (New York: Oxford University Press.)
Chatterjee, A. (2004), 'Cosmetic neurology: The controversy over enhancing movement, mentation, and mood.' *Neurology,* **63**, pp. 968–74.
Damasio, A.R. (1989), 'Time-locked multiregional retroactivation: A systems-level proposal for the neural substrates of recall and recognition', *Cognition,* **33**, pp. 25–62.
Davidson, D. (1981), 'What metaphors mean', in *Philosophical Perspectives on Metaphor,* ed. M. Johnson (Minneapolis: University of Minnesota Press), pp. 199–220.
Dennett, D. & Kinsbourne, M. (1992), 'Time and the observer', *Behavioral and Brain Sciences,* **15**, pp. 183–247.
Foucault, M. (1974), *Die Ordnung des Diskurses* (Frankfurt/Main, Berlin and Wien: Ullstein).
Gallagher, S. & Shear, J. (1997), 'Editor's Introduction (to "Models of the Self")', *Journal of Consciousness Studies,* **4** (5–6), pp. 399–404.
Galison, P. (1997), *Image and Logic: a Material Culture of Microphysics* (Chicago: University of Chicago Press).
Güzeldere, G. (1995a), 'Consciousness: What it is, how to study it, what to learn from its history', *Journal of Consciousness Studies,* **2** (1), pp. 30–51.
Güzeldere, G. (1995b), 'Problems of consciousness: A perspective on contemporary issues, current debates', *Journal of Consciousness Studies,* **2** (2), pp. 112–43.
Hesse, M. (1972, 7th edition), 'The explanatory function of metaphor', in *Logic, Methodology, and Philosophy of Science,* ed. Y. Bar-Hillel (Amsterdam: Elsevier), pp. 249–59.
Hesse, M. (1974), *The Structure of Scientific Interference* (London: Macmillan).
Holyoak, K. & Spellman, B. (1993), 'Thinking', *Annual Review of Psychology,* **44** (51), pp. 265–315.
Kuhn, T.S. (1962), *The Structure of Scientific Revolutions* (Chicago: University of Chicago Press).
Maasen, S. (2003), 'A view from elsewhere: The Emergence of consciousness in multidisciplinary discourse', in *Voluntary Action: Brains, minds, and sociality,* ed. W. Prinz, G. Roth and S. Maasen (Oxford: Oxford Universtiy Press), pp. 323–59.
Maasen, S. (2006), 'Neurosociety ahead? Debating free will in the media', in *Does Consciousness Cause Behavior? An Investigation of the Nature of Volition,* ed. S. Pockett, W.P. Banks and S. Gallagher (Cambridge/MA: MIT Press).
Maasen, S. & Weingart, P. (2000), *Metaphors and the Dynamics of Knowledge* (New York and London: Routledge).
'Meeting of Minds' (2005), *European citizen jury on brain research,* Deutsches Hygiene-Museum, Dresden, November 25–27, 2005.
Novas, C. & Rose, N. (2000), 'Genetic risk and the birth of the somatic individual', *Economy and Society,* **29** (4), p. 485–513.
Prinz, W. & Singer, W. (2005), 'Wer deutet das Denken? *Die Zeit,* 31.
Racine, E., Bar-Ilan, O. & Illes, J. (2005), 'fMRI in the public eye', *Nature Reviews /Neuroscience,* **6** (2), pp. 159–64.

Rose, N. (2004), 'Becoming neurochemical selves', in *Biotechnology. Between Commerce and Civil Society*, ed. N. Stehr (New Brunswick and London: transaction publishers ), pp. 89–126.
Shallice, T. (1972), 'Dual functions of consciousness', *The Psychological Review,* **79** (5), pp. 383–93.
Shapiro, Y. (1997), 'The consciousness hype: What do we want explained?', *Theory & Psychology*, **7** (6), pp. 837–56.
The Editors (1997), *Journal of Consciousness Studies,* **4** (5–6), pp. 385–8.
*The American Journal of Bioethics* (2005), **5** (2).
Zeman, A. (2001), 'Consciousness', *Brain,* **124**, pp. 1263–89.

# *Index*

affordance, 97, 105, 146
agency, 89, 172, 177-8, 180-2, 185-6, 190, 194, 234-5, 237-8, 244, 245, 248-9, 252-3
attractor, 124-5, 217, 219-22, 226, 230
autism, 91, 246, 250

blindsight, 4, 37, 53-4, 74
bottom-up, 55, 157

causality, 178-80, 182-3, 194, 213
change blindness, 51, 61, 223-4, 226, 232
colour, 94, 100, 102-11, 113-14
compatibility, 29, 32, 174
complementarity, 32
computational model, 79, 218
connectionism, 37, 46, 50, 61
content
    conceptual, 62, 66
    mental, 49, 69, 71-2, 74, 139, 196, 217, 236
    non-conceptual, 65, 67
control
    endogenous, 157-8, 161-4, 167
    exogenous, 158, 166-7
cultural processes, 239

decade of the brain, 253
disturbance, 155, 165-7, 171
dynamical systems, 34, 124, 130, 132, 135, 177, 180, 182, 184
dynamics
    neuro, 18, 31, 34
    nonlinear, 28
    symbolic, 30-1

'easy problems', 120, 140-1, 143, 226, 228, 254
ecological psychology, 137-8, 144, 146-7, 149, 151, 223, 226
embodied, 19, 77-9, 82-4, 88-91, 189-190, 192-6
energy transformation, 14, 186, 192-4
evolution, 13, 18, 115-18, 123-4, 130, 147, 153, 196-7, 235, 238, 241, 246-8
externalism, 8, 10, 15, 71, 73, 223, 231

eye movements, 230-1

first-person, 14, 77, 79, 81, 84-9, 140, 254
functional connectivity, 118

gestalt
    phenomena, 120-1
    phenomenology, 103
    psychology, 80, 100, 153
    theory, 97, 105

'hard problem', 50, 130, 138, 140-1, 143, 254

identity theory, 133
ideomotor theory, 156, 172
imitation, 85, 234-6, 242-3, 245-6, 248-251
informed awareness, 137-8, 147, 149-150, 152-3
inner speech, 163, 173
intention, 53, 77, 87, 89, 99, 123, 134, 136, 148, 151, 157, 160, 166, 169, 174, 184, 192, 198-9, 202-3, 207, 212, 237-8, 242, 246, 249-50
intentional
    object, 80, 94, 106-7
    reference, 94, 99-100, 112
    relation, 77, 79-83, 85-6, 88, 90-1
    retrieval, 199, 203, 212
    schema, 84-5
    subject, 80
intentionality
    derived, 63-4
    intrinsic, 63

joint action, 234-5, 240-3, 245-6, 248, 250
joint attention, 242

landscape of knowledge, 258
levels of reality, 20, 96-7, 114
memory
    automatic, 198-212, 214
    conscious, 198-9, 202-8, 212, 214
    explicit, 37, 51-2, 200, 212, 214
    implicit, 37, 51-2, 206-7, 213-15

(cont.)

memory (cont.)
  involuntary conscious, 203-4, 208
  visual, 232
mental chronometry, 127
mental imagery, 37, 44, 49, 59
metaphor, 55, 121, 186-7, 194-5, 256-8, 268-9
  analysis, 256-7
methodological solipsism, 79
microgenesis, 108
mirror neuron, 87
modularity, 117, 131

neglect, 37, 53-4, 57-8, 60
neuroceutics, 255
neuroethics, 268

oscillations, 48, 95, 124

partitions, 18, 31, 32, 34
perceptual organization, 120-1, 132, 135
phenomenology, 79, 82, 91, 96-8, 114-16, 138, 196, 227, 229, 248
process dissociation procedure, 205-212
processing
  automatic, 52-3, 144, 154, 157, 159-162, 166, 171, 181-2, 199, 208, 210-1
  controlled, 37, 51, 52-3, 166, 170, 181-2
production system, 37, 45-6, 49, 53

qualia, 10, 48, 59, 65, 73, 96, 131, 261

representation
  digital, 41-2, 46, 48-9, 67
  linguistic, 41-2
  mathematical, 42
  spatial, 41-2, 57
representationalism, 63, 72-4

self, 59, 77, 80-1, 85-6, 189, 193, 247, 248, 249, 252-53, 263-7
  and other, 81-4, 86-90, 196, 234, 240, 242-3, 245-7, 249
  -awareness, 235, 239-240, 243, 247-8, 269
  -concept, 244
  -consciousness, 79, 89, 91, 161, 190, 216, 218, 226-8, 230, 249
  -help, 252, 255
  -help literature, 252
  (cont.)

self (cont.)
  in action, 247-9
  management, 255, 266-7
  mental, 89, 91, 234-5, 238-40, 245, 247
  minimal, 235
  -monitoring, 255, 266
  -organizing, 177, 183-4, 186-7, 193, 195
  -recognition, 87, 89, 250
  -regulation, 261, 266
  sense of, 88, 234-5, 239-41, 243, 265
  -sustaining, 133, 152, 177, 186-96
Simon effect, 160, 174, 176
small worlds, 118
social cognition, 92, 239, 248
social understanding, 86, 88, 91, 248, 267
sociology-of-knowledge, 256
statistical mechanics, 18, 24-7
steriokinesis, 106, 111
subjective experience, 7, 37, 50-1, 55, 254
supervenience, 22-3, 28, 32-4
survival value, 137-8, 152-3
symbolic communication, 240, 245-6

theory of mind, 89, 91-2, 234, 244-5
thermodynamics, 19, 24-5, 27
third-person, 14, 77, 81, 84-90, 178, 188
top-down, 54, 135, 157, 250
transcendental subject, 80
triadic interaction, 83, 86-7, 92
'Twin Earth', 69-70

veridicality, 13, 106-7, 113

word recognition, 218-19, 221-3, 230-1

zombies, 60-1, 119, 153, 227-8